Anticlimax Leviathan
by Ryan Bartek

*"There are only 3 things you can do with a woman –
you can love her, you can suffer for her, or you can
turn her into literature."*

– L. Durrell
(or something to that effect)

~ In Dedication ~

Lady Shiva, Destroyer of Worlds

(Eternal, Amorphous, Omnipresent)

Acropolis Now

anticlimax leviathan // volume one

YEAR ZERO

My past now holds the distinction of another man passing by in traffic, face blurred by the whirl of rampant automobiles. Swimming through ludicrous tides of struggle, the mask is disingenuous – *the smooth skin before the scars' indentation…*

I glimpse an era of 7 years long passed, grease-streaked in navy blue, red-rimmed eyes choked by monoxide, that name-tag "Ryan"– smeared in oil & scrubbing public buses in sub-zero winter; gaseous, misty diesel stinging the lungs. The transports would pour in all night, having lugged the dregs of Metro Detroit – *a quarter mile of them, parked like 50 foot tombs in subsequent rows…*

The g-thugs avoiding the foreman, huddled by soda machines & sports replays. No sign of life, lest the slam-dunk of orange rubber. These men, able to move the world had they the imagination, all willingly, flaccidly entrapped by a life sentence of drudgery. Some barely 23, trumpeting retirement at 55 & 7 days paid vacation per year. Scrubbing, gassing, wiping: *"We're 'Made Men,' don't you know?"* In 25 years, I will make $3 more dollars an hour…

America berates its civilian to accept "The Grid." As a child I questioned everything; as a teenager I yearned incineration. I wanted to destroy every last trace of the joke which created me. And so as an adult, I still refuted everything. I'd no allegiance to The Grid & was its sworn enemy. What I wanted was to slip through the cracks as forgotten Lazarus, wholly annihilating myself from the face of the earth. I wanted full evacuation from the human race.

Everything told me to flee Michigan – I was never meant to rot there. But back then, I never thought I could do it alone – just book a flight to Europe or Seattle, or show up to SF or Hollywood.

With all my street smarts, I'd never really been homeless; I never relied on a travel-pack or ate from a trash can, never hitchhiked or rode rails. I knew paycheck to paycheck, but never savage rock bottom. I grasped the ruthlessness of death, but at 21, with adults reiterating a ripe old age, *that if you just go to college…*

So there you have me, in a nutshell, on a Saturday night like all Saturday night of 2002, reserved & ghost-like, retinas glued to the floor, soft eyes morphing gray by association, scribbling away in a composition book – the soft-belly news flickering & touch-screen games bleeping gaudy casino sounds. In the break room it's cold, always cold, and reeking like stale, withered gasoline…

Saturdays I am alone here, maintaining the shift completely devoid of management. To prove its impotent nature, I simply upped & left without clocking out. I hit the diner, the comic store – actually went to the movie theatre & sat through a 2 hour film – *then afterwards my sweet ass time at the video rental store...*

4 hours later & 8 buses were waiting to be cleaned. A mechanic gave a funny eye: *"Hey man, where'd you go – been lookin' forever!"* Then, lying to him in the coldest, most bullshitting way possible: *"Ah man, I've had the shits all night!!"*

Just like that, my domination was complete – even if lacking victory. See, whatever poor sap adopted this shift was only because random "lotto" selection. For many, it was a blessing to an overworked brother – *a black man could clock a 9 hour day & get paid for 2 hours of work.* Classic Deee-troit luck. And with zero Union oversight, Saturdays became a quiet party. The mechanics hit the grill out back & charred poultry drifted the halls; the Spaulding dribbled endless, twisting atmosphere from grim UAW to YMCA.

However, it does little to include the shy, quiet white kid reading *Naked Lunch* & jamming viking metal on his headphones. Sleeping in my car during 9pm lunch-break, I was often requested to shoot hoops; I was needled by jovial fists to yuck up the beating of homosexuals or nuking of the Middle East...

There was nothing I had in common with them aside from food & shelter, nothing I supported in which they believed so dispassionately, and to open my mouth would be a cataclysmic shift of alienation. Money bound me to them, and it disgusted me…

It was only a matter of strength before I hit the road. Detroit was cursed. It was a miserable, violent ghost town that could not be rehabilitated. To wage war against it was futile; to plant seeds for a faraway future one would never gaze was all a sane person could do. Look to one another, we find our greater power – if anything, my wrap-it-up psychological/artistic drive here was hammer this central message home to any who'd listen before I split for good.

I had a vendetta with Detroit's inherent grimness, and it is from battling this beast where I calculated my methods of creation. While I'd little awareness of my capabilities to manifest another world counter to it, I was well-read on all manner of occultic manifestation, propaganda, psychology…

I was a shadow worker, and I'd my designs. Something of a loner, I was regardless a zealot of hardline D.I.Y. Punk/Metal ethos. I stood for community and aggressively promoted it, even if I generally preferred solitude. I was full of quasi-anarchist ideas without ever quite realizing it or understanding it – I scoffed at the term, and would never label myself so.

I was working class, even if I hated the wild, unhinged capitalism of my countrymen & refused to participate. I wanted to build structures; the anarchism I "knew" was a fountainhead of ill-informed, flakey arguments – the gibberish of teenage punk rock kids or uptight college students, and only fashionably so.

My vantage point was practical, ever-unfolding and consistently blossoming – fanatically, I honed in on the most obvious doctrine for effecting change – the continual fusion of all subcultures as a united mass, bolstered to recognize themselves as a wide-ranging community against the machine we mutually fought. It was an Us vs Them logic, which is a logic doomed to fail because it rests entirely upon a concept of a "Them" – and to determine a "Them" you must create an "Other," and in creating an "Other" you risk a slippery-slope descent into unintended totalitarianism.

Still, you have to take a stand somewhere – and in building community, you have to decide what you are for and against. The "smart thing" to do – the "right thing" – is to keep your opinions to yourself and let things naturally blossom. Punk Rock, Heavy Metal, Goth/Industrial, etc – these began as organic things which just kind of happened for different reasons. They were never designed or intended for the cultish magnitude they eventually developed.

In the year 2002, our music scene subcultures are like tribes – minor civilizations with their own growing mythologies. The beauty is when you participate, you both feed on and continually create the unfolding mythology. The connections between various subcultures are there, but exceedingly loose. I wanted to see the American Underground function how I later learned the Celtic people did – one big patch-work tribe glued together on similar mythology.

I was a self-appointed ambassador between tribes, like some blueprint Druid ignorant of what he was or what that meant, drifting through endless scenes, creating networks & synergy. Detroit was not my home but a tough-as-nails training ground of manifestation techniques before exporting them abroad.

So, anyway... Instead of driving me out, my fellow crew broke all Union rules & dropped the "random Saturday shift" on me permanently, mercilessly. It's not "reverse racism," see, rather blue collar terrorism –

and truth be told, I don't mind, because if I was in their position, I'd do the same thing.

I can see the dialogue hidden in their eyes, writhing like snakes: *"We are lifers in this pyramid scheme, Mr. Suburbanite, and we want to party. We can just smell the future which is in store for you, the studious freak doing whatever it is you are doing back there. Whatever you are annotating & researching, we know it's your ticket far, far away from this terrible place. It is a future which unnerves us, because we do not have the insight to grasp it, nor the imagination to make it our own."*

I see them gaze, that flash of arcane coil: *"Whatever Ryan's up to back there,"* they say, *"is frightening and mystifying. His eyes flash to a plane alien to the earth we know. He isn't 'right' but he certainly is at one with something illegible, vague, deceptively obscene. What happens when he snaps out of that funk? What happens when he takes for certain – as he certainly will – the reigns of The Union? How will this looming Hoffa implode, and what shall be the consequences for us all?"*

"First," they think aloud, obvious as the prismatic light, *"we must annihilate his will to fight. We need not drive him out directly, only wind him down in slow castration. The slow motion drawl of economic manhood will do its bidding – same as us, same to him. So long as we keep him feeling no personal investment in anything this place is, we have nothing to fear. The python is ours & ours alone, and no one – let alone this paltry, over-fed white-boy – will thieve our hard-earned, fang-bared 7 days paid vacation..."*

The only saving grace is a man named Wendell, the *"loon"* of the crew & brunt of their jokes. Wendell, confused Wendell, the skinny mulatto with his manly man's mustache & powder blue earmuffs. The guy who wears moon-boots to work and those earmuffs in the summer, who talks to himself in the lunchroom and takes his vacations at Kingswood Asylum. It's only a matter of time until he disappears for good, and that's when I'll be singled out. Wendell, sad Wendell, who's looming departure was my great dilemma, my grand crux of uncertainty 7 years long passed...

"Ryan," again & again – that Clark Kent-like front. Of all the tags I've inherited, *"Ryan"* is the one for co-workers and my mom. That bus-scrubbing, UAW shit-hole was his world – never mine.

"Ryan." – just some corny mask saying whatever they wanted to hear insomuch as Mr. Bartek could excuse himself to a dimly lit corridor to scribble volumes of notations somehow leading light-years from the grasp of draining, monetary monotony...

I see myself murdering myself in my prime, a ragged teeth-skin existence in which perhaps a $100 dollars will be left by the end of the month. 5pm-2:30am, Tuesday-Saturday, cleaning used condoms & blood puddles from the floors of transit bison. With every waking moment I plot my escape; with every turned head of the foreman I lunge for my notebook stashed beneath moldy washcloths putrefied by orange cleanser.

Alone I log my thoughts and desires, evading this mechanical horror. At every op I scribe another extreme metal album review, jot questions for underground bands – men I will never meet – encased by the same vile curse of work, food, water, housing. Some rocking the basements of Minneapolis, Tampa, Redding, Buffalo, Cleveland – *some exotic as Denmark, Brazil, Gothenburg, Tel Aviv.*

Somehow, as a freelance journalist – my hopeless unemployable fascination – I can find the key to change it all. Through propaganda, Pan-Tribalism, gypsy clans, moon mono-maniacs and fleeting ghost-people… Somehow all of us bohemian rat-maze shit-stains will unite. The light of a new world is dawning; it rages the facade of a sarcophagus. The gears of Moloch sputter in the audacity of cessation…

That is, to say: *The Revolution.* At the switchboard, I tend the fires – PIT Magazine, 30,000 quarterly in every niche market worldwide. Real Detroit Weekly – 75k print run in my hometown, my bastard agenda free in 1500+ locations, columns churning out bad ideas with volcanic power: *Yellow Journalism, Groucho Marxism, NSK, CrimthInc, Scandinavian Black Metal, Grey Magick, Anti-Theism, all the BDSM joys of the Marquis de Sade.* If an idea was dangerous, you could count on me to make it public…

70 hours a week of rat-maze convulsions to fund a one-bedroom $525 apartment crawling with ants & water-bugs springing from drains like black gold/Texas tea; $140 a month for the cheapest auto insurance, $150 in gas to get absolutely nowhere but an ever-expanding, hopeless radius; $60 for land-line phone; $20 internet, $20 for CDR's, $30 for flyers, $200 on food, $100 towards some music equipment, $30 towards mail-outs of promos or writings like cannonballs of astray inertia intending to gestate the portal out of this dead stretch of earth like a blind man swinging at a piñata...

And maybe, just maybe, I'll have $15 for a few comics, a book I've no time to read; a vinyl, a concert ticket, a six-pack. Drug tests for that evil job and never a shred of green. One slip up & cornered with State-backed legal prosecution – since the bus job was technically a State/Federal conjunction, you had the choice of jail time or lock-away bed-bunk rehab packed with the lowliest Detroit crack-heads, dope addicts, tweekers & ulcer drunks…

From dusk till dawn typing, editing, compacting my book *The Silent Burning*. Countless hours & pots of black coffee on this unpublishable tome of disjointed hatred, this gargantuan attack on all that stands… From the rise of the moon to the birth of the sun, twiddling away on guitar writing songs for a band I can never get off the ground & musical style which is unmarketable, unclassifiable, unplayable to any musician I snaggle into my half-ass, incomplete web of destruction. *FILTHPIMP, the destroyer. FILTHPIMP, the beast. FILTHPIMP, the unanswered classified…*

Yet there was a gooey Oreo filling, a home amidst the cubicle – Lana, sweet Lana. This world of grim auto-worker plague & clock-watching cancer-causing hoopla – it is impossible to register any of it without addressing her.

She was at the core, day after day, a fixture as immovable as the furniture itself. *Her curly mop of hair, those golden natural streaks, striking curves precise as silhouette; those round vacant eyes, mahogany pupils like pin-prick black holes – flesh a lightly tanned strain of mixed Latino heritage & striking Italian features…*

Two months after meeting her – after 60 days of vague, phantasmal existence – she simply moved in. She never asked, and we never even addressed it. One day, from whatever obscurity she existed, she just showed up and never left…

She told me that I was Howard The Duck, that she had a crush on me since age 5, and now that she found me – after eons of fruitless search – the adventure would never end. There would be sequels forever, multitudes of them – some direct to video, some re-released on the big screen by Japanese admirers of the Tokyo public – all these outcries of film artistry, all of them centered around her getting plugged by myself, the feathery hero Howard J. Duck…

Everyday the same nucleus, this floating nebula of abstraction – this doll-like beauty with the characteristics of an alien youth. For hours on end re-watching the same films – RepoMan, *Body Rock, Warriors of the Lost World*. Dancing around making pancakes and singing the Garbage Pail Kids song, trumpeting that yes – *yes* – we really <u>can</u> do anything by working with each other…

Lana, who I'd met at the 3rd annual Detroit Electronic Music Festival in pinstripe slacks, wandering with a clipboard of signatures towards the legalization of pot; white dress shirt seductively opened, full figured breasts catching Hancock after Hancock...

Lana, who I never assumed would actually call, who I never remotely thought in my league, who I assumed preppy and of the house/jungle enamored, who I flatly assumed would never worship at the altar of the Marshall stack...

Lana, who showed up the next weekend in her green corvette after a long shift at Kentucky Fried Chicken, who wandered the streets beside me all night – through parks, alley turns; beneath dull-prism lamp-posts and purple sky. Lana, playing the first-date role of interview courting & cautiously relating snippets of her life ...

I'd no belief of this going anywhere, assuming this one-night parody would end as she vacated a few hours later. To kill time, to make a final judgment, I put her to the *"video rental"* test...

"Miss Lana," I said to her as Christ would in a parable, *"Wander the aisles, determine the full range this Blockbuster has to offer – but only pick one film, any you so desire. And do not choose something to placate me. Pick only the one that's been burning images inside your cranium for months, the one you need to view tonight lest it drive you mad."*

I expected something weak – something Barrymore, Cusack or Chris Tucker... After 15 minutes of gallivanting through the aisles scanning intently, she came bopping towards me gripping her prize, joy-filled & smile-laden – *Henry: Portrait of a Serial Killer*, the X rated directors cut... And then we went & fucked for hours...

Later, scratching my head that this actually occurred – that this bombshell was wandering my apartment naked & draped in a blanket while cricket chirps outside the body-fogged window... Her sweat-drenched brow resting on my chest, twirling her golden strands as she slept... *I was a grown man, and I was home.*

Her existence, tight-lipped and fleeting, showing up in the dead of night to screw & disappear – never calling, never demanding anything of me, no burning gut-romance of frenetic encircling. Just this floating ghost-person coming & going as she pleased, this frantic two-month ovary plunging, escalating rapidly as manic schools of trout upstream...

Back then, that rocky transition from The Old World, the culmination of my views towards inter-human value were relegated by the aftermath of One Big Fall – one endless, bottomless plunge that began at 13...

The cold spirals which transformed me also launched this period of upstart manhood. For it was my first solo apartment, a Herculean effort of independence. In this incubation, all had reset...

The Old World, a world I've written about so lengthy in the past – it died on September 11th 2001. It was that defining moment when all that had come before simply mounted a grim stallion and galloped into twilight, leaving a trail of maggots & dead flesh...

The malicious irony composing that event was quite personal. I grew up in East Dearborn, "*Little Lebanon*" as it's called – the largest Arab population per-square-mile outside the Middle East. After 9/11, the FBI raided 30 terror cells in my hood. I spent my teen existence in predominantly Arabic schools where many students supported jihadi extremism, parroting the ugliest of views from the Islamic world.

The tension was heavy – even if many Muslims were friendly & respectful, "Infidel" was in their eyes, their behavior, their language – something to be exploited, if not exterminated. Race riots erupted, usually sparked by football jocks confronting larger "tough guy" Arabic crowds – the idiot white male meathead jocks would gang-fight the moronic, Jihad-promoting ruthlessly womanizing & religious-shaming types. There were shootings, stabbings, rumbles...

Thus, I had an early education about bin Laden and al Qaeda. What if, in 1999, during the Y2K scare, I actually went to Northern Michigan as a precautionary measure? That with a rag-tag group, we waited out the looming national panic of power grid melt-down and the much-chattered, highly possible suit-case nuke attacks al Qaeda had been busted trying to rig in NYC for the 1999 ball drop?

That on the same occasion – unable to accept this was paranoid head-play – that I nearly shot myself at rock bottom? That I'd went mad to large degree from visions in dreams so seemingly real, and the nightmare of a girlfriend's rape still fresh in my mind.

That after years of reassuring myself I was the victim of an amplified paranoia and these nightmare visions shall never come to pass, I instead woke up to find jumbo jets crashing into the World Trade Center with a surge of extreme Déjà vu? The same Déjà Vu jigsaw puzzle that had sent me to Northern Michigan on Y2K?

That within an hour of 911's blatant inside job, I found the entire world engulfed by my paranoid delusion? And furthermore, how quickly & easily they were lulled into the idea that gasoline fires make enormous steel structures simply explode into dust. That I now was the "crazy one" for a whole new reason – *scientific fact!*

First they called me "conspiracy nut" for explaining an attack like this might happen in the future; now I'm the madman for pointing out airplane crashes do not make concrete explode long after the impact already happened...

Lana & I were lying on my bed when my tolerance for interview politeness sheered with a surge of frankness. I shot to my feet, standing naked & gazing down at this likewise nude specimen. Her eyes aloof & vaguely dazed – hair flowing like a mane: *"Ok, this is ridiculous. Everything I've told you makes no sense – cause I make no sense. I've never gotten this far with any girl, and I'm totally unable to understand what happens beyond the chase. When we bang, I can only think of lions fucking on the Discovery Channel…"*

"This ain't me – this has been some lingering job application, like you're a boss I have to wow for a job I have no skills to operate. I'm totally out of my gourd; I've done [this & this & this & etc] & you should run screaming immediately. I am the Antarctic, I am Greenland, I am the fog of Transylvania…"

And then Lana, never blinking, repeated the same variegated combo of nothingness from an unbreakable, immovable position of distant hypnosis consumed by bastard wood patterns, upholstery stains & plywood shambles that's static existence screamed defects of mortality, the terror of age, the frenetic strife against the clicking of the clock & the black suture of death's totalitarian embrace…

We were locked in an eternal question mark embrace – a coronation of absurd hierarchy. Forever locked in non-embrace, colliding in acid-headed isolationism and incapable of proceeding in any given direction. Just a whirlwind, indissoluble; a genetic symbiosis of North/South freezing to Negative 14 degrees Calvin…

Had I any sense I would've married her on the spot. Had I any inclination of what would become of her, had I the courage to been real, I would have thrown myself at the altar of her needs. I would have made her into the goddess she was that I was unable to see – glass slippers, champagne rooftops & crystalline souls.

I would've rendered portraits of her stretched fertile across the davenport, listened to everything, dramatized everything for joyful escalation. I would have bought her steak dinners, zoo passes, frilly lingerie, black licorice & scorpion tanks…

But I was young, lustful & anticipating a lifetime of partners. And I was still horribly in love with Zelda – and before Zelda was Natasha, and before Natasha was Daisy, and before Daisy was Lisa, and before Lisa was Kaitlin, sweet Kaitlin of the dark golden age…

Kaitlin, the crux of all, the closest thing to a high school sweetheart I could ever claim... I lost her to a maelstrom of LSD, solitude, asylum internment & self-mutilation – and my own cursed inability to overcome the age of my environment…

Lisa, sweet Lisa, whom designated me Big Brother & regarded as guardian. Lisa, whom I promised never to fail, who at 18 hung herself in the closet of a Detroit crack-house…

Jezzi, that trash-punk, big-breasted, loud-mouthed drunk-ass. After 4 years of hoops we'd become an item. At least for a week or two, I'd say, before she was abducted, bound and raped. A scummy band rehearsal complex, a dark empty room, drunk, snagged & gagged with duct tape, Cannibal Corpse blasting on the PA to drown her screams, thrown back into the hallway after as nothing happened. She could never deal with it & left me for Jesus Christ…

Natasha, the beauty of Mexican town – cute skater girl, backpack of spray paint, fave film *Hackers*. So adorable & fragile. Her father tried to kill her because I was white. He strangled her, leaving purple fingerprints on her neck. Taken into custody, mother attempts suicide, the children threatened with foster home…

She tells them it's all one big lie, one big misunderstanding, that no charges are to be filed. He'd molested her for years and she chose family over trauma, sent away on an airplane for Texas, taken from me, 5 days before Y2K. 5 days before I nearly put a bullet through my skull….

She came back years later and we sloppily reunited. To my disbelief she was again living with her father. Still saying grace at the dinner table, still dancing to salsa at the cantata. Tells me, "*Family is family.*" Tells me, "*I'm his little princess, and he buys me whatever I want.*" She had no idea why I stopped calling her… Showed back up engaged not long after…

And Zelda, who demands a constitution of her own making, a republic in her service, a tarot deck firmly aligned & magnificently tailored… It was Zelda, above all, who made impossible for me to give myself wholly to Lana. Whereas Lana was the eternal question mark, Zelda was the real Harley to my Joker, the Bill to my Ted, the Eva Braun of my fascist imperium… Yet never quite mine.

The Lana of yore, the Lana of 2002, unable to admit her bisexuality save for displaced hints, save for a kind-of-sort-of-but-not-really crush on Linnea Quiggly dancing nude & crimson punk atop the age-worn tombstone…

Sex she always wanted, sex she was always prepared for. I never had to ask, only to take. Any moment, any time, just wander in my room and there she was. Walking around the apartment in panties, naked under the covers, fully clothed on my bed for 9 long months lest hypnotized by the image whirlpool of *Dawn of the Dead, Terrorvision,* Heavens Gate training videos...

But in sex, just laying there, discarded like a toy, always staring off into the corner from the vortex of those eyes, those periscopes rising above the water from another galaxy... Lana, who would haunt comic book conventions, forcing the Zombie Illuminati to swoon. Lana, escorting John Russo to luncheons; Lana, ignoring the drooling Tom Savini; Lana, singled out by the bespeckled Ted Raimi, always showered in the cell number of horny key grips...

Lana, taking comic con refuge with The Ghoul, that horror-flick, late-night air-wave champ of 70's Detroit. Together they plotted the return of his show with Lana as the new side-kick of Froggie the puppet...

Lana, 15 times committed to the asylum; Lana, the ex-mob tied rave scene princess, reborn after 3 years of MDMA & K incubation... Lana, jealous of every girl, jealous of everything, anchoring me to that couch, chain-smoking American spirit foof cigarettes tube-shot from the can... Lana, the slug, complaining of rigor mortis... Lana, whose father was rendered weak-willed Jello in the hands of a domineering ultra-Christian stepmother....

Lana, whose real mother is dying of Aids, strung out, living nomadically from crack-house to junk-pad. She saw the needle, knew it was infected with HIV, and shot it up anyway because she couldn't handle the junk sickness. Used to shoot up in front of Lana as a kid. leave at crack houses while she worked or hustled...

Lana, with her half-ass omelets masquerading as reuben-scrambles with 50 cent packs of pastrami. Dead cow flesh brunt crusty; half-melted cheese in clumps beneath viscous, snotty egg-whites; strands of hair like thin dental floss in lumps of yolk... Lana, digging through my phone book & calling people at random... *Glistening in moonlight, animalistic mumbles of "Howard"*...

Away from Lana – back to communications with the mysterious "other people" who arranged my magazine articles on computers I'd never see, in offices I couldn't fathom. Among them were PR wizards who hit buttons and would have Metal Gods call my house. I can get almost anyone on the horn, if I so will it.

It's all part of The Revolution, you see. To control the media is to control the flow of information, and once controlled shit-rock will be decimated by the Euro metal blitzkrieg – Darkthrone shall replace Nickelback.

The underground will understand its worldwide force – Pan-Tribalism in the interest of a world beyond the scars. We shall be as Roman Gods upon the earth, forging our own civilization, our own Anti-Empire. We will take into account the gross injustices bestowed upon our ancestors and no matter how imperiled our mission, we will at every cost avenge them... *through metal.*

I might as well have been a skinhead, for I resembled one completely – an anti-fascist blackshirt. Head cleanly shaved, shit-kickers polished, nails trimmed, clothing black black black. Always SWAT pants, a mechanic work-coat insulated by Carhart hoodie, steel chain connected to my wallet, extreme metal or punk t-shirt.

I'd always go back to 13, the slim desires of that sad child. In Middle School, reality was painful – its teachers were impotent, the adults terrifying; my friends nonexistent (*save for the bands I listened to*). I always imagined these musicians went off to some glorious land & lived in an empire of freaks. Was this the thing called The Northwest? Was it a fortification in remote Outlands, seething with maniacs living like a metal army in barracks?

I had no real dream other then I could one day be paid to listen to heavy metal and write about it. That somehow, every label would send me everything they released for free because they knew I was a true believer, that I was their shining propagandic star in a galaxy of dull lights. *The dream to never again pay for a concert...*

At 20 years of age, I was there full bloom. Whilst all others intrigued by journalism killed themselves with the bottomless debt college, I just snuck in the back door. I spotted an ad for internship & blew up Real Detroit's phone lines. 2 months later I had my own column metal/punk column – the first a major Detroit paper had ever seen. Then freelance at PIT Magazine – 30,000 copies quarterly, an ever-lethal dose to 100+ countries.

Once I name dropped PIT & RDW to labels, Ali Baba grappled his impending doom – the prison cell made entirely of circular plastic. I became a man held hostage by his CD collection, a mailbox of infinite bubble-wrapped packages. At Real Detroit I'd be let loose on the vaults of promo discs collecting dust. I took everything I could carry – if not to jam, then for used record shops' credit swap. 8 such stores within a mile of my apartment, all smiling as I snaked in. On & on it went, 30 to 60+ albums a week – DVD's, t-shirts, stickers, posters, concert tickets...

All I ever wanted out of life is before me – showered by albums & propaganda turrets blasting away in every record store, movie theatre, restaurant & venue (*so why am I not happy?*). Everyone who doubted me – well now I'm The Man, The King, the snake of sundry, the swindler of the swine, the enigma of anatomy, the blaster to bits of all aristocracies (*so what's missing?*).

No matter, no matter just keep moving no sleep never sleep keep pushing building creating a better world for your people (*lest another Lisa*) no no no time to think no halt one slip up & bus world forever they got you in their grip boy they got that chain tight 'round that neck boy keep moving keep hustling keep grinding it to the bone keep trackin' it like a hound don't give up don't give up don't–

That's why things went horribly awry when Lana found out she was pregnant. I sent her away before Xmas. The address book was too much – she was calling people at random, *then Zelda*…

Zelda had been MIA. She'd had me come by at night, weeping the guilt of abortion. The visit before last, I had brought her happy socks, with tiny little smiley faces on them. Lana freaked. She chased me around shaking her finger & I made her leave. She could go back to her parents crib. She wasn't a throwaway…

Despite the depths to which Lana followed me, nothing she ever was compared to Zelda. With Lana we were just two dead things staring at each other in a vacuum; Zelda was an animated little fiend, made me feel alive & joyful. Even if she was a no-go, it was still the truth. Lana wasn't the only woman, and I was 21.

I have the ultimate woman in mind, the dream girl of 7 years long passed. She rides a black stallion in the name of Satan, decapitating Christians in the name of punk rock. She will fuck as no woman fucks, cremating men as phantasmal larvae...

She will bop-dance to Iron Maiden & devastate society with her abnormality. Her crotch will be tattooed in slogans of filth & her buttocks shall bear the mark of The Beast. Casually snorting miles of cocaine, her dialogue will sputter the fluency of kilometers & her raging lesbianism will lick their pelvic bones clean. I will fill her belly with mutant sperm & she will shit cathedrals of pythons... *Lana is the Hubble telescope, beaming its last transmissions...*

"*Ryan... I'm late.*" Dead pan. Blink. "*Over a month.*" Flashes of mechanical intestines sputtering black oil...

***Lana moves back in, says she wants to have the kid. Abortion never, adoption ludicrous. Admits she's whacked on Vicadin all the time –

xanax, perkasets, etc – the cause of her *"rigor mortis."* Tells me casually she's going over her pals house to smoke DXM 'cause they found out how to separate the chemical from Robitussin. Care free, with my kid in her stomach. Viscous fight ensues…

It's a week later & she's bleeding. *Labyrinth* is on television. It is Saturday afternoon, and our child is dead… More fights over Zelda's mention; Lana insane with jealousy. We shout, we curse, I make her leave – tell her it's over. She doesn't believe me... Keeps calling, I don't answer. Week goes by, shows back up at my front door & barges in. She goes directly to my bedroom & plops on my bed. Starts reading *Solipsist*.

"Just what the fuck do you think you're doing?" She doesn't answer. She thinks she's come home. She can't get it through her head – it's over, it's finished. *Kaput…* I grab all of her things & toss them in a trash bag as she cries in the other room. I'm tossing everything she owns onto the snow out front. She won't leave. *"But I'm your girlfriend."* I reach to grab her, but she pushes me away. Back to the corner, like a scared kitten that won't come out from beneath a front porch…

I drag Lana towards the door; she drags her feet sobbing. *"But I love you, Ryan I love you."* I push her out the door, like Darth Vader chucking the emperor down the energy shaft. But there is no blue lightning, just curly hair. She beats on the door sobbing, wanting to come home. On and on it goes, seemingly forever. Eventually she hobbles away crying with the rustle of a trash bag…

I drive around 8 mile for vodka, get home & dead quiet. No *Garbage Pail* kids, no Chilly D. Only thing left of hers is a single mitten stranded on the floor. Feel it creeping up...

You just lean against that wall boy, slam that gut-rot… You'll find someone else, won't take long. Zelda will be there, and you're only 21. You're still young & so is Lana. Do our own things & maybe hook back up when bad craziness has settled. If not, you can handle it – got Bigger Fish to fry. Everything'll pan out…

Oh the terrible thing you've done…

Oh Ryan, how you know it…

The Curse of GhostNomad

What is never related on Sesame Street, and takes the workhorse aesthetic to discover, is that writing is never the same thing. Its form is essentially baseless, morphing with every guise of utilization.

The first line of projectile text ejaculation becomes Point A of an empty crossword puzzle that is not a rectangle of imprisoned cubes but a crooked, illogical arch leading to obscurity.

The writer may begin with definitive ideas of expression, perhaps a glorious finale, all of which constitute the roof and bedrock of a fortress housing characters real or imagined, nouns & verbs building brick by brick the foundations of the whole – yet the joy of the writer, apart from the coagulation of experience which flows beneath the surface like a river of magma – is the eruption.

Every man is volatile. Some erupt in violence, some justice. Some frantically explode as painters, architects, while others, unable to grasp this gestation, feel perhaps this magma is really hot load, a spinning center of earth filled with jizzom & screaming expulsion.

The writer, much as the sex addict, much as the composer, erupts just as violently. What spills out is text, organic. If it is not organic it is contrived, and the organic strain which breeds like kudzu & envelops the landscape with text becomes in itself a jungle.

The writer thus becomes a voyager of this Amazon, hacking through vast inner foliage of sweltering heat and danger, colossal jungle kilometers to hitch Point B.

That which is revealed amidst the voyage is malleable, the antennae receiving what it may, the shape and form of the impulse a kaleidoscope. It's initial structure, no matter how sloppy, unedited and raw, is always the most marvelous.

The passion of the writer is the struggle to refine, to manage, to build upon the foundations a vast megalopolis of text. Of colonies, of workers toiling ceaselessly in one's subconscious - in dreams, in free association reveries the subways erected, the buildings painted, the copper polished, bridges extended, sewers vacated, main street compacted, with the steam whistle of the lunch clock all bellies filled... *amidst the waking world the gestation expands with all you inhale; in slumber the concentrations sort naturally as exhalation...*

Somewhere between worlds, in twilight hours, between fact and fiction, blurring them in an agoraphobic delirium – losing the self to become the self, tuning out the world and embracing the currents of isolation that constitute neither a loner impulse but one that is at one with oneself and therefore never alone in conjunction to the supreme, idiosyncratic wavelength of creation - these are the brutal impulses of artistic expression.

Art is truly mans best friend and that blaze of creation your eternal companion, for line, paper and form will never chew your shoes as you sleep.

Whatever is revealed along this campaign of hacking and marching, bogging through swamps and struggling through quick sand, Congo mosquitoes and territorial enraged gorillas, is essentially the analysis of the self.

The Point B arrival, almost always, lacks the potency which rang true upon the revolver fire of the race. One rushes blindly to cross the finish line, having leapt through detours and unseen curves to outmaneuver the pack.

Yet in that glorious return the bleachers are emptied, the stopwatch shattered, the balloons sagging as vacant rubber, the other participants a stomping phantasm never arriving, airy and unmade by whomever willed them to be (*i.e. yourself*).

The marathon had been a farce, the fruits of victory satirical. The great prize of attainment is not the object of competition. For even upon completion of the voyage, one doesn't turn around. Instead the writer pulls back into the waking world to stare deep into that vast megalopolis; skyscrapers smeared in symbols of blank ink.

Like a green-gown surgeon he slips on the latex, slices the cadaver, plunges into the intestines of his creation. An architect building, building, building. The race has begun anew, the exposition incomprehensible – more sewers, more taxis, more garbage dumps & opera houses; more ulcer-ridden stomachs and pancreatic cancers, transit stations, airports, hookah tents & bazaars.

And once complete, drawing backwards to meditate upon the shining marvel, the writer – despite his hubris – realizes it is but a speck on the sidewalk of a another great castle in the center of a another great world in the epicenter of another universe…

It can go forever. Stylists lose out, amateurs whither as plagued thin herd, prosaic professors postulate prosperity…

In my case, it's mutation until publication – like sweeping the room, trimming the hair. Always one last face-lift, one final overdub – a singular line orphaned and vetting for a foster home, anxious to correlate in a myriad of vacuity. With every "last" self-propagated editorial campaign the manuscript itself becomes more colossal, bizarre, utterly alien to the originating concept yet eons surpassing its crude formations…

It is Thursday, September 17th 2009, just past 11am in Metro Detroit. As soon as this book is done, I'm running away to Europe and never, ever coming back. Henry Miller made it there on ten bucks, which means I'll find a way, somehow. I have to. I am Ryan Bartek – I am the first GhostNomad.

I think there's a few more now, but that all depends on Dr. Jeremy Sullivan. He's somewhere in Portland, I think, but he isn't returning any of my phone calls.

I'm in Michigan; the room is cold and the walls are light blue. Stoner Joe says I'm typing on MC Hammer's desk. It is shiny and absurd, this art deco piece of interlocking Tetris blocks. You just kind of have to see it…

Stoner Joe's buddy found it trash-picking, and he's been sitting on it for a year now, just waiting for me to show back up. Somehow I always do. This is technically the third book I've written at Joe's house, even though this is his first *real* house. Before my life on the road, he & I were roommates in a trailer park…

We're not hicks, by the way. Stoner Joe lives as cheaply as possible with no possessions, because his life revolves around retreating to the wilderness for months on end.

Our existences are similar – bust your ass, snipe every cent, hit the road for a soul searching odyssey until raggedly broke. The difference is that he goes forest hiking, whereas I urban camp.

I have been homeless for 9 of the past 11 months. I own next to nothing and live out of a duffel bag. My only possessions are some thrift clothes, a half-broken acoustic guitar & decrepit laptop buckling under from viruses…

It took a lot of effort on my behalf to take anarchism seriously, and at some point I simply sacrificed the ghost with flesh intact. I now peer through spectral vision – *inhuman, elemental*…

The problem with Zen is once you attain it, that's all you have left. It makes dating tough, because you might as well be some hermit monk in an Appalachian enclave. See, it's this Dr. Manhattan kick I'm on – Paris is equivalent to Mars…

The sheer weight of my madness has infected countless scores along the way. There are hundreds of *living books* now being written, the characters of which populate an organic tapestry germinating gospels & tomes, united in spacial intolerance. In the vacuum of our distance we brace the coming polarization predicted to be the coldest winter in modern history, spliced ever so humbly with The Great Neo-Depression – and the apocalyptic *"economic recession"* which will strangle the rest of our adult primes…

Stoner Joe & I, we are living in a haunted house. In the walls are dolls – Romanian immigrant play dolls likely discarded by gypsy children. They are demonic and number in the half-dozen. During the homes ongoing renovation, they continued multiplying.

Sledge a wall, out pops another; tear up a floor, there lay a nest like Jews beneath the floorboards of Occupied France. Their eyes are red dots like blood splotched paint, their clothing ever ragged. At night I type in MC Hammer's desk, distracted by tiny footsteps & odd noises. In the morning we find the dolls in strange spots without pattern, without reason…

The escapist life is what Claudia feeds off, even though she's committed to Med School. She still speaks as if one day she'll dive into the vortex I've created, but no matter how gorgeous she may be, I cannot commit. In Detroit even the most enticing harpy is no more then a dung beetle singing a discordant Motown tune…

Claudia wandered Africa & South America for years on end, becoming a DIY nurse independent of Peace Corps. She has not been back long, having lived in pure tribalism with the natives of Coastal Africa. She fought malaria, typhoid, syphilis. Now she fights the paranormal…

Claudia has this Constantine thing going on – she speaks of demonic possession, poltergeist attacks, channeling. Claudia is a medium of omnipotent centrality amidst a world of shadow people ever active. She is like a human ghost. Her eyes are eerily calm – light blue ovals raging, the jungle perpetually surrounding her the way skyscrapers & concrete ensnare me...

In the mythology which I am entrapped she is *The Oracle,* but in reality she's more a transient romance, I guess. Claudia claims we've been doing this for a long time now, like this life keeps repeating itself on end. She keeps waiting for me to get stuck here, in Detroit – says it's already happened. Says she knew it the second we met – about how we'd eventually end up in Portland, in Oregon, in the distant future. Whenever Claudia finishes her nursing degree – and whenever I get rid of *"that stupid girl,"* the one I still don't even know yet...

This week in D.C. 2 million Americans marched against free health care. They held poster boards of Obama with that little Hitler 'stache scrawled in Sharpie, because he wants to give them free dental. They rage as a vanguard phalanx against the defunct Soviet empire. *They actually think socialism & communism are the same thing.*

I actually kind of wish Obama was a socialist. Not that this would in any way alter, you know, the New World Order and all their little schemes – but maybe, from a daily life standpoint, it would actually fix things just like they are fixed in Paris, where I'm currently trying to escape. France is where all my problems will just vanish, where I'll just marry the first fool that wants to move to America. Paris is where I will have free health care, and I will spend my days eating Croissants with a funny red beret...

President Obama – I met him in a bathroom a few years ago. I asked God, whom I don't even believe in, to grant a second miracle. I requested a sign of the future, and there he was – taking a giant shit at Seattle Central Library. The first miracle, consequently, was that God bring on the apocalypse. When I woke up the next day, planes were flying into the World Trade Center...

Again, I don't even believe in God, at least not in any Islamo-Judaeo-Hindu-Buddhist-Xtian sense. I got some thunder for Zeus & a grinding jaw for Loki, but those boys are in league with Odysseus, Sinbad & Nebuchadnezzar...

It all ties into what's happening now – it's all part of the dream. That's why I'm here right now, doing this, as if I'm the ilk of a St. Benedict. I know the dream is going to happen. I think it might be this Sunday, even though I always think it's a Sunday and it never happens. I've waited & waited to no avail, ever since 2003...

I have no desire to convince anyone of anything *and if anything* I wish to convince myself otherwise as well. I want out of my own mind because I have this nasty habit of dreaming jigsaw pieces of everything before it happens in Déjà Vu chunks, often years in advance. Whether or not I follow the signs, I always seem to end up exactly where I'm supposed to no matter how hard I squirm against the tide.

This specific Sunday premonition I speak of marks the beginning of my life. It means I can finally wake up, just like Tom Cruise in *Vanilla Sky*. It's scrambled though. I think its two nights together, or its one night and I have all of this going on in the back of my head, like a host of memories...

In the dream I'm standing on the porch of a home which resembles home but is not home at all. It has the semblance of what once was, and I'm ready to move on. There are three girls on my mind – one pregnant, one far away, the other in prison.

I'm confident, looking into the sky; the moon is full & bright. I think I've finished a new book, or I've inked a deal for a new book, or something to that effect...

In the background of my head (*or what might be going on that night*) I've been listening to a new president on TV who is definitely not George Bush. It's a black guy, a dark horse no one saw coming. There is a crisis in America, an escalation in the Middle East – his message is hope amid clamor.

Iraq has been at war for some time, but now it's spilled into Iran, or Iran has done something crazy, or its some massive regional conflagration, like an all out revolution gone haywire...

Someone calls & tells me something. They call me and I think they are crying. I'm fairly certain I'm waiting on one of those three girls to do so, but it's none of them at all. It's someone that I never saw coming. They tell me something & whatever it is makes me extremely happy, or so shell-shocked in its awfulness that I can't stop laughing...

The dream flashes forward a bit. I'm outside like before, somewhere else. A car pulls up, blasting music, or the music is in my head & I'm just thinking about it. I'm not sure who is in the car, but I keep thinking it's my band (*my old band*) A.K.A. MABUS. I somehow pulled it off – a record deal or something of substance, some tour, some momentous thing – or maybe it's just someone jamming our album, pulling up to whisk me off to the New World. *I'm not exactly sure...*

Then I woke up, grabbed a guitar, and wrote that song. I formed my band in response to that vision and made sure they learned the tune note for note. It was never one of our best, but it had that monster riff. The song itself was A.K.A. MABUS, it was like our theme song...

The band is long gone, but what I do know is that I am sitting here at a home that's not exactly home, waiting on a phone call, and this Sunday is the Obama media blitz. He's doing an unprecedented 5 television interviews in a row, grasping at straws to get his agenda across. It won't work though – I'm pretty sure they are going to kill him over free health care. He won't be sniped over anything real, but over free prostate exams. Assassinated over gibberish...

The dream in question might've already happened though, and I just didn't pick up the phone – October '07, waiting on my ride to the promised land, ready for Seattle forever...

Somehow I missed the call. Someone flicked the anonymous *67 & while it was ringing I couldn't detect it cause Stoner Joe barged in shit-drunk with his raucous laugh & curly Italian 'fro. He threw a pipe in my face, got me stoned as fuck 'n I fumbled...

I'm pretty sure it was Clownbaby, but I didn't have the guts to call back. I was scared she'd lasso me & I'd be stuck in Michigan forever, just like I apparently am now. Clownbaby & I were together then, but I didn't know who she was. It just kind of happened, and you never fall batshit crazy in love with someone until you're away from them...

Clownbaby is the ultimate woman, and thus being so is utterly impossible. She is an elusive human Frankenstein whom still has absolutely no idea who I am. And I, the mad-sick buffoon, ripped out my entrails to The Gods to regain her affection...

Back then, I was presented with a choice. I asked myself, as an old man on his deathbed, what would he really have wanted his younger incarnation to have done? Stick around Detroit for a girl he just met, or plunder the gold of Freak City Seattle? It wasn't a question of what I wanted, but what GhostNomad would do...

When you think you've reached the point where no savage burn of love can remotely touch the previous scorching – when you've been so beaten to pulp that you've rebounded across the galaxy for what seems decades – along comes another. But it's always for a different reason, something you hadn't processed...

Clownbaby was the Omega – the end-all-be-all, biggest, bloodiest crusher of all. I have written her tomes of text; I've moved mountains, thrown myself bleeding at her altar. handed her paradise on a golden platelet & enslaved the world for her disposal...

In the end, it had all the military power of a limp, wet noodle. And what am I to her? Some vague, tortured figure consumed in absence, just like all the other feeble men to whom she closed her heart. I am hardly alone in the mighty garbage pile of those slain in the void of her negated affection...

For this book she will defecate my corpse – yet for art I will horde the abuse. She has a special spot for me in her Dante-esque levels of domination. She takes great fancy in mutilating Slavic men.   But that side, among the endless panels of contorting selves, is but one fraction of an infinite intricacy. She is the craziest, most horrible Femme Fatale of all, and I worship the ground she walks on. *She is The Queen, The President, The Ruler, The Best...*

**6:17 pm, September 17th, 2009... *Stoner Joe shoots squirrels with an air-gun and steam dries apricots...* I pace around smoking cigarettes, parlaying the conviction to quit... Down to my last 2 & no papers to tray dive or snipe... *Oxymoronic hustles; tortoise paced speeds of extremity...*

Like Claudia, Henry Miller is always right. He did the same thing in Paris, but I make it pimp – this urban camping of ebb and flow. Seattle is my Paris, even if it's filled with Americans.

In the Labyrinth I am a hobo, 'though the best dressed vagrant of all. I got into the habit earlier this year – a far cry from the stitched up dental-floss jigsaw of my quasi-punk wardrobe. I only wear suits and the slap-dash tailoring is ever self-custom. I am the Armani of Value World, the Dolce/Gabanna of thrift – the cobbled stone back-alleys my unpopulated global runways.

Imagine a gaggle of clubbers drunk in high-heels, zinging of Canali. It's dark, arid, 'round 1am. Amidst their bar-hopping they stumble past an enclave of shadows. Nestled in the darkness of a store-front is a figure beneath a deflated pyramid of quilts.

In a trick of self-gratification the clubber male halts the pack to showcase his saintly empathy, that do-gooder leverage aiming to stuff clam. He slings a wad of bills tacked by golden clip, dramatically counting off ten singles. With a crooked smile his foot nudges the bum. *"Hey buddy,"* says he, intoxicated females swooning. *"Why don'tcha buy yourself a hot meal?"*

From beneath the fabric the derelict grumbles: *"Piss off you limey fuck! I gotta work in the morning!!"* The clubbers hover, unable to process. Annoyed by their cash distribution, the homeless wreck swings off the blankets like erupting volcano. He shoots upright as lightning, revealing himself to be surrounded by a fortress of Knut Hamsun paperbacks...

The bum is better dressed then the clubber himself, neatly groomed and in a $500 pin-stripe suit. He resembles a prohibition-era gangster or corporate hot-shot, despite the bright blue mohawk and shaved-skin sides. The vagrant snags the cash from the cement and tosses the wad right back at him: *"Some Grey Goose for the ladies, compliments of the house."*

He dives right back into his pile of quilts & moat of plastic trash bags as Scrooge McDuck would his vault of gold coins, immediately falling asleep with capital ZZZZZZZZ's... *Junkpile Jabba; Hobo Solo...*

When I was 20 years old, I read *Tropic of Cancer*.

Liar.

Okay, chunks of it.

Fraud.

Ok, the first chapter. And then I read a good chunk of *Capricorn*, and most of *The Air Conditioned Nightmare*. 9/11 happened shortly thereafter, then my little sister hung herself shortly thereafter, and then all of America was totally engulfed in my paranoid delusion of Islamo-Fascist revolution.

That short-lived Miller period in my 20th year was the last I remember feeling young, feeling independent. I was a landscaper for Ford Motor Company driving huge dump trucks, working with a crew of Arabs & g-thugs & South African immigrants digging trenches & swinging sledgehammers like a prison chain gang.

Every word Miller had scribed forced me to consider the panoramic essence of the world in which I operated. As in this is the world of the young man, these are the characters surrounding him – that life itself was a Broadway production and any show-tune was possible. I saw all the dynamics; I read all the signs. Once the planes hit, I put the *Tropics* down. I started my own book which only 8 people have ever read…

There is a difference between inspiration and plagiarism. Henry Miller is less some idol to me then he is a mystic Grandpa. Miller's great contribution to my stream was supplanting a host of terrible ideas in my head. Mainly, presenting *"the whole man"*– to fearlessly recreate oneself as the prophetic clown of anti-dilution.

There is nothing worth saying that he hasn't already said better and been translated in a dozen alternate languages. In Miller, the entire American desperation unravels with biblical grandeur…

I don't have influences, only kindred spirits. I found Hunter Thompson when I was 17, and that was already the sort of stuff I was writing. Then Kerouac at 18, Burroughs, Ginsberg. And know what? They were all ripping off Miller anyway. Old Hank is the craw-daddy of outlaw Americana...

For Miller Paris was China and France the Asiatic continent & all of its borders the Great Wall. For me Seattle is Paris and Paris is the labyrinth and Washington State is the jungle. Everything fits in the borders of Downtown, which is Alex Proyas' *Dark City*.

The U-District is Amsterdam and Shoreline is Moscow and Capitol Hill is East Village and Tukwilla is Georgia and Georgetown is Detroit, but I generally stay eons the fuck way from there since I'll probably run into Sadique, the meanest bartender in Seattle…

Sadique is Clownbaby's Satanic punk rock clone. Like Clownbaby, she cut off my head too, but I still love her. How can you not? She is Clownzeus... Both of them combined would spark the Clownocalypse, the Clownulation, Clownageddon. Sadique doesn't know anything about Henry Miller either, and neither of those Clowns have any inclination about Billy Jack. If I have an idol, it's Billy Jack. And even if

Billy Jack isn't real, Tom Laughlin is…

Athena gets Billy Jack because she lives in the Freedom School, basically, in Oklahoma, except its called Fortress Andromeda. It is my home away from home – this massive three level quasi-mansion with 15 rooms, large info-shop, music venue, art arena, basement kung fu training facility…

Fortress Andromeda was an abandoned mental institution until Kip the LSD Shaman decided to squat in it. After reworking the electrical grid 20 people now roost in its belly, all of them upstanding freaks. It is the dandiest anarchist commune I've ever stumbled into, and I hope to soon run there despite no chance of a job or food stamps…

Athena is the only female that lives there; she is the Queen Bee. Like Claudia, Athena is essentially a transient romance. She is my non-physical German Jew anarchist lover, 19 years old with the soul of an ancient. Her body is fused to her spirit, and it wiggles like a fish devoid of H2O.

She and I duel each other on acoustic guitars, song after song. I am her personal Charles Manson, since Uncle Charlie never replies to her letters. He never writes me back either…

Athena has Hepatitis C, a rare blood-fungus condition which is devouring her skin & radiation poisoning as a result of playing with glowing rocks as a child. Her father is a para-legal for redskin tribes and she discovered these Kryptonian nuggets outside an Apache grotto in the New Mexico desert. The US government had knowingly slid them an atomic test site…

Athena probably won't hold out long, despite being so young and beautiful. Even if she does make it to her late 30's, she will definitely need a liver transplant. This is why I want to drag her to Paris, to give her the world – but she doesn't want France, she wants Moscow. She has some reverse mail-order bride scheme going on, says it's a favor to a friend dislocated by Russian tundra…

Athena gets Henry Miller; she acted in a *Tropic of Capricorn* play in high school, although I do not know if she played June. Her room is covered in hand-written notes tacked to the wall, stacks of books in piles. White gloves & pearl necklaces, circus paraphernalia & big band vinyl…

Rogue is in Oklahoma but Catwoman is in Detroit and Tank Girl is in Arizona. To Catwoman I am the Joker and to Athena I am Gambit and to Tank Girl I am… *the cute punk guy with the blue mohawk she wants to rape with a strap-on…*

But I'm not going to Arizona, no matter how ginormous her boobs are. I'll just get stuck there with Tank Girl & her daughter Pantera, and that *"Mayor of Prescott"* is a very bad man. I don't know what that guy is up to, but he wears silk Hawaiian shirts and looks like The Rock with a jerry-curl...

Catwoman is of the tribe infesting the Theatre Bizarre, a self-quarantined carnival grotto wedged in a section of Detroit we call *"Nam."* It is The Last Stand – all the forces of old have gravitated in a vaudevillian collective, with a fresh crop of fire-breathers, snake charmers, burlesque dancers, ren-faire people, clowns, jugglers, wrestlers... Theatre Bizarre began in 2000 when two guys upstarted a haunted house venture. Now it a living, breathing city – an entire city block fenced in & running the length of a football field...

In addition to pro-wrestling & cabaret, quasi-rave parties, stolen media festivals & weirdo band showcases, they throw the definitive Halloween party every year in which hundreds fly in from all over the world just to oogle at it's spastic grandeur. The complex is a renegade combo of Paper Street, Rufio's abode from *Hook* & the *House of 1000 Corpses.* It is the visceral reincarnated Siamese twin of Ken Kesey & PT Barnum. I am eternally its clown, for their mascot Zombo is my new personal God, especially after that Amazonian shroom freak-out only two months ago...

The screeching whirl of power tools is ever constant as the mob of volunteer workers endlessly toil. Always building, molding, shaping – stages, gimmicks, fire-cages. You enter through the driveway of two humongous houses and encounter the pirate-like stage complete with the gigantic, looming clown-skull of Zombo, our panoramic Odin.

The stage is surrounded by a banner complex of sideshow paintings – entrances of wood corridors that lead to bonfire pits, severed rubber limbs, lizard mutants & cryptozoological curiosities. Hanging imprisonment cages, execution gallows, abnormality exhibitions, rusted lobotomy & electro-shock equipment...

Catwoman is in Detroit as is Hugo Strange, The Mime & Mad Hatter, but Firebug is in Seattle and Riddler is somewhere in Santa Rosa. Mr Zsasz is in Texas; Scarface, Clayface & Ra's Al Ghul are still in San Diego, but Anarky is totally anonymous in Ohio.

I'm still not sure who Killer Croc is, but I can privy to you that The Scarecrow has been deported to Norway and The Penguin is still running from the FBI.

I thought Clownbaby was my Harley but in reality she's Poison Ivy, and the real Harley is probably working a street corner in Detroit prostituting herself for heroin.

Harley II is dating a 34 year old Mexican guy with kids and the original Harley is now fairly domesticated and more into Prince & *Golden Girls* then causing any sort of mayhem. But they always think I'm The joker which is the biggest joke of all.

Back up a bit, to December 2006. I was a wasted husk of my former self, just drowning in whiskey, chain-smoking, stoned or hopped up on pain pills. Years of chiropractic adjustments had failed to remedy the feeling of constantly being kicked in the spine. I was a walking box of Rice Crispies – with every twist a snap, crackle & pop…

In the Detroit scene I'd went from media Golden Boy to object of detestation – from main event Face to the lowest card Jobber. Everyone from the early period were settling down, choosing careers, shitting out kids.

My band A.K.A. MABUS didn't respect me as they once had, for I was the puppet of my own wretched miasma. I had become Pink from *The Wall*, a slip-shod from shaving my eyebrows...

But I still wrote for some major magazines – my last refuge of escape. And one then one night, when all those phantoms hit the lowest fathoms, I simply popped.

Instead of putting a gun to my head, I creatively self-rendered. I comprised a mad press release, hit send, then launched it like 10,000 torpedoes to the worldwide underground media. I declared a new book entitled "*The Big Shiny Prison*" & explained from that moment onward I was now a character in my own living novel, a road book masquerading as an epic of music journalism.

For a year straight, I proclaimed, I would travel the United States penetrating every fringe abroad. I would vomit a word salad to rival the absurd lengths of Kerouac and splat it front & center on the shoes of the ringmaster.

In one week I quit my band, quit my job, quit my life. I gave everything away & just hit the road. That campaign began December 21st 2006 & ended October 13th, 2007 – 293 consecutive days & rampaging through 35 states.

When it was complete I barreled out the van, climaxing a 6 week spoken word tour. I collapsed on the soil with the velocity of an anvil. I had traversed every nook and cranny, subjected myself to the tirades of every lunatic. I started out a journalist, and in the end became GhostNomad. It was finally over, and I was finally free…

Laying there, I stared up into the Michigan night with the limbs of dead trees spiraling like veins through the blackness. I was exhausted, trying to catch my breath. My cell phone rang – Linda was down the street, at some weird bar I'd never heard of.

Everything said *"Don't do it."* Screamed: *"After all this bullshit you put yourself through, you can finally move on. Seattle is waiting for you like a whore with spread legs. All you need is two weeks here – just cut your album & flee. If you hang around Detroit you know exactly what's going to happen – you're gonna fall horribly in love with some terrible woman, and it's just going to ruin everything. If you're dumb enough to let it happen, then you deserve every last splinter of apocalypse freight-training your way..."*

But I went to that bar, yes I did. Despite all the screaming intuition, I swallowed my harangue & sauntered that cold mile. And when I arrived, Linda wasn't there but someone else was, eyeballing me from across the bar, swinging her head around the post, watching my every move, just laughing to herself as I pace around consciously trying to avoid her beady little clown eyes pulling me in like a tractor beam. She knows I can't talk to her, she knows I must escape. She doesn't care. She sees another Slavic man primed for mutilation. For she is Clownbaby, the Ultimate Woman...

Poor Kid don't like who he is, Poor Kid goes crazy, Poor Kid blacksmiths iron-mask. Volatile flight becomes reality, appended persona sustains insoluble life. Years go by. At the edge of the world, Poor Kid finds himself surrounded by ironic victims reconstructing themselves after his negligent Hyde... 6,000 miles away Poor Girl sits alone, isolated in darkness. Poor Girl don't like who she is, Poor Girl not one of them; Poor Girl belittled, told ugly & boyish. Poor Girl goes inward, reshaping the soul. In flight of escape Poor Girl turns supra-female, a concentrated powerhouse of Venus. Powerhouse, in blind terror of death, turns black heart conqueror... Poor Kid washes ashore, having clashed as Odysseus. Collapsing, he stares into the sky & meditates deeply. Poor Kid arises, dusts himself off & hobbles to the nearby tavern. Each step resounds the ticking of Poor Girl's watch. Sipping a rum & coke alone, she watches the time click by. Waiting, waiting, waiting... Poor Kid wanders inside, Poor Girl is across the way. Both at the peak of their powers, they lock eyes for the first time. Poor Girl is dynamite, Poor Kid the shrapnel. Somewhere astral the deities of both of clash valiantly. One last night & tragi-comedy abounds...

***Dr. Jeremy Sullivan is the key to everything. He is my ticket out of here   an impenetrable rock of confidence, a herald of destiny, the liberator of Hollow Earth, a mastermind of the Vegan Revolution, Dean of the Free Therapy institute of higher vibrational learning...

Dr. Jeremy Sullivan is the second GhostNomad, of which I am the first. He is hexed to sustain the curse until a suitable candidate arrives. It has to be passed down like the mask of Zorro, or the whip of Indy Jones. It's a pretty basic formula, and a sad commentary on our times – I had to perpetuate & embody my own myth, 'cause I couldn't interpret life under any other circumstance...

I met Dr. Jeremy Sullivan on my way back to Seattle over a year later, when I was escaping Michigan for the last time, in January 2009. It was the undisputed end of everything – or so it seemed – and I was left again with the Greyhound, headed through the familiar 2½ day route back home. Detroit to Chicago, Chicago to Minneapolis. Then Fargo, Bozeman, Butte & Billings...

20 hours of sparse Montana wasteland until Quarterlain Idaho, then another 12 to Spokane. 6 hours later, decimated by fatigue, one reaches downtown Seattle as the rising nova hits the Space Needle, casting the monolith shadow of a 70 foot sundial...

Or so it was supposed to go, in theory. The reality is that it took us a whopping 6 and ½ days to reach our destination. That set a new record for me, even having spent 600+ hours on Greyhounds in 2007 and completing an upwards of 40 cross-country trips on those killers. It was brutal beyond description...

The worst I'd ever sustained previously was Detroit to San Diego, which was normally a 3½ day ride bestial in its own right. I made that voyage 8 times back and forth – Detroit to St Louis, through Iowa into Denver.

Then ten hours south to Amarillo before another 8 to Albuquerque, spearheading Vegas all the way into LA. By the time we hit LA we missed the bus to San Diego by 5 minutes, and it tacked on another 5 hours of waiting before the Mexican bus to Tijuana – packed with stereotypes that actually had caged chickens as their carry on luggage – dumped us off in SoCal.

After all that, my ride had forgotten to pick me up. I made the last public bus by the skin of my teeth, chasing it for half a mile lugging a computer tower, guitar head, backpack & duffelbag filled with hardcover books...

This Seattle return was a different beast altogether though. I had already attempted to flee the prior week. I spent 2 days on the Greyhound before reaching Billings, Montana, where we were informed that due to the freak

Northwest snowstorm, all roads into Idaho/Washington had been closed for 11 days.

The officials knew this back in Detroit, but central authority kept pumping us through like greed-crazed vultures…

In Billings there were 60 people trapped inside the terminal, having been living there like Katrina refugees. It was -20 degrees outside and snowing heavy. The bulk of displaced were blue-tear ex-cons or Iraq vets on leave for holidays forced to spend Xmas inside the terminal. Everyone was broke, living on donuts & black coffee…

The ticket counter said I would be stuck there for at least 3 days – if I was lucky. Seattle gets 9 inches of snow a year, and most of it on the tip of Mount Rainier. They were now being bombarded with 34 inches, this freak blizzard that had crawled from Alaska. Half the city was without heat or power, and no one had the faintest idea what to do since the city has no salt trucks or contingency plans.

I was offered a reprint ticket back to Detroit for no charge – but not another one out. Which meant I'd be trapped in Michigan all over again, dumped off on Christmas morning lacking the fare to get back home. It was so ugly I took the offer …

This final escape where I met Dr. Jeremy Sullivan started a week later, on 1.3.09. Despite paying rent in advance, my former Seattle roommates left me homeless.

I'd called to let them know I was off and they cowardly admitted giving my room to someone else. They spent all my money on weed, promising to pay me back (*which they never did*). They said *"Well, you have friends here. You can make it happen."*

I already had my ticket and couldn't turn it off. As a last resort I contacted a friendly couple that lived in the boonies. I had a place for a month at least, but it was an hour bus ride from downtown Seattle & my old kitchen job that theoretically promised some part-time sympathy hours (*the management, of course, would flake out as well*).

The ride began at noon, Saturday the 3rd. We were only 30 minutes outside Detroit when the brake lines went out; derailed for two hours until a replacement coach could arrive. We made Chicago 6 hours later by the skin of our teeth, with 5 minutes to load.

A service announcement boomed through the loudspeaker: *"Due to road conditions, the midnight service to Fargo has been postponed until noon tomorrow."* Everyone grumbles, that long snake wraparound of beleaguered poverty.

I use this as an opportunity to visit a high school chum. To preserve my place in line, I stick a pillow and white bag filled with crumbled McDonalds wrappers in the column. So long as it sits there, that is my just claim. Generally no thieves tamper with the luggage clumps because they always suspect the owner is watching.

Thus, no one will complain when I nonchalantly stroll back in line the next morning, since the terminal is always so packed the people assume you're napping somewhere off in the corner.

By the time we make it to Minneapolis the following night, I've long been eavesdropping on this blow-hard schmuck who keeps having the "*I'm a hardcore Vegan, dontcha know?*" conversation to any who will listen. He's been sitting next to a huge black guy the entire ride. They bonded in Chicago and have both been on since Friday. He's headed to Portland, the black guy to Seattle...

An hour outside Minneapolis en route to Fargo, I wake up to the bus rattling like a 747 with a dying engine. The driver forgot to fuel up, and we run out of gas in arctic conditions – no heat, no salvage freight for an hour, metal casing pounded by raging blizzard.

Since the tanker is empty there is no air compression. No air compression means all underhand luggage is now trapped beneath the bus. Which means if I don't stay with this dead caravan until the bitter end, everything I own will be lost in transport. It's just what happens; I've seen it dozens of times...

We make it to Fargo by midnight, able to hop on the next bus by the skin of our teeth. I'm waiting it out another 12 hours though. In theory, the tow truck will arrive with the carcass in a few hours.

Vegan Guy asks why I'm not coming. "*If you ever want to see your shit again, just sit here. Trust me. I live on these things.*" He and the black guy eyeball each other.

I tell Vegan Guy: "*Just take the opportunity and sleep while you can. We'll all get a full rest and be back on the road by noon. You'll want this if you're going all the way Northwest. I know this route like the back of my palm.*"

Vegan Guy deadpans, words rattling. Says: "*Don't you mean the back of your hand?*" I say: "*No, that's why it was funny.*" I start digging through my notes and ignore him for 20 minutes. He's unsure how to interpret me, just as I like. I jet-snap from my pensive streak: "*So what are you all about? What's you whole schtick?*"

Vegan Guy immediately starts ranting about propaganda, skull & bones, Freemasons, the Illuminati. That our leaders were a bizarre, sadistic, inhuman cult worshiping Moloch the Owl God in the redwoods of

Northern California.

About Hitler as mad genius & how Adolf knew about Hollow Earth and was trying to stop the lizard people from taking over the planet. Vegan Guy explains that there are four races of aliens vying for control of the human race…

He going to Portland to find one of the 4 mythical openings in Hollow Earth, where the inner-sun is located. His goal is to follow the cavernous realm all the way to the other American portal, which is behind Niagara Falls. He already attempted to make it through the waterfall, but the Coast Guard was encircling it with gunner boats…

Next morning, I wake up Vegan Guy. Drag him into the -20 climate to wake & bake as we head to the local diner. I play the part of GhostNomad, marching along, telling him what he needs to know to survive this trip – all the ins-n-outs & the general blueprint one must be abide at all times…

We drink black coffee. His name is Jeremy Sullivan. He is not yet a doctor of Free Therapy, nor is he remotely capable of assuming the reigns of GhostNomad. He is still a wobbly bowl of jello, and this is his alpha run.

He's a skinny white guy with the word Vegan tattooed on the back of his neck. He has a shaved head and black goatee. His eyes are crazy; he is a human sponge. Every word you utter he soaks up like a computer, never blinking…

He says the Atlanteans & Plutonians must be stopped at all costs. He is convinced Hollow Earth is real because his grandfather was a Nazi Scientist who defected & worked on the Manhattan Project. Guy worked with Einstein & Oppenheimer.

On his deathbed he told Jeremy all his dark secrets, the combination to his hidden safe. Somewhere Jeremy has top secret classified documents stolen from both the National Socialist and US governments. He has photographs of his grandfather standing beside the trans-dimensional beings who helped work on the Philadelphia Experiment…

Jeremy was a battle rapper from The Bronx; a street hustler and choirboy for Baptist churches. He calls everyone "*brutha*" or "*sistuh*" in that heavy NYC accent. He is the blackest white man I know, apart from myself. There is no trace of the forced whigger thing – he is a legit product of the urban landscape.

His parents thought he was bat-shit crazy and had him committed a half-dozen times, moved him to Albuquerque as a teen to curb his behavior.

He soon ended right back in the Bronx putting together a hip hop collective. He is brilliantly talented in this respect – he flows across the galaxy on any impromptu subject, whether or not it rhymes at all. His style is more free-from rant.

Until New Years Eve, Jeremy had been living in Buffalo. He spent 4 turgid years attempting to finish his business degree, dating some girl that had relatives in the local police, the FBI. When he ditched her she struck down hard and made all sorts of trouble. They were denying his paychecks, breaking in his house, tapping his phone; sifting through his emails, following him…

I started laughing. He kept saying, *"No man I'm not fucking crazy – you don't understand, you don't understand."* His eyeballs were like lampposts ablaze. He was totally sincere, totally convinced he was being harassed by the FBI. New Years was the big moment for him. That's when he decided everything needed to change…

The ghost girl had done him in. He was dating a girl from some obscure rural town outside Buffalo no one else had heard of either. She would see him on the weekends, or strange intervals. She would just show up, randomly, knowing where he'd be. She would come to his work at odd times and never had friends with her. She'd just kind of come & go with shifty excuses. It had been going on for months.

He took concern when she disappeared abnormally long. Her cell number was out & the diner where she was a waitress – that number was dead. When he called information the listing was correct but the business had collapsed a decade ago. The phone had been disconnected 12 years.

Jeremy and a friend went to the diner and it was long closed – dusty tables, 2X4's strewn about, cobwebs in the windows. The town had a total *Innsmouth* vibe; a veritable ghost town. They went to the address information had given, the listing for the phone number she called home. It had also been abandoned for years. Jeremy's friend (*the only other person to have met her*) was totally spooked and refused to speak with him, at least for awhile…

It wasn't long after – with the cops having rummaged his apartment and stolen $1,000 – that Jeremy decided he was either going to shoot himself or simply ghost himself, gunning it for Portland to kick-start the Vegan Revolution.

He threw everything into a bag and told no one he was leaving, embarking on his first Greyhound mission with $300 to his name. *"Portland or death"* was his vocation. He didn't know anyone in Oregon, had never been homeless – didn't have the slightest knowledge of crusties, train-hoppers, squats or street culture. He had done the responsible adult thing until 30 where I now caught him midst of a suicidal breakdown…

I began training him as a Greyhound warrior – the education of the underground, Seattle contra Portland, adventures & calamities endured. I convinced him that Seattle was the way to go, if only for a week expedition. I drew him maps, diagrams; revealed bus schedules and hustler nests – pinpointed anarchist cells and vegan abodes...

It was noon in Fargo, the next bus to Billings had arrived – but none of the staff had bothered to call a tow-truck. The freight with our luggage was still aside the freeway. We were told we had to wait yet another 12 hours if we still had the crazy notion of milling around for our belongings. We decided to camp out.

We got social with the other stragglers. One was a kid from DC headed to Denver for college, and the big black guy was a restaurant mercenary of sorts named Tyreese. He was in his mid 30's and grew up in Chicago. He spent time in Detroit where he'd apparently met me in the music scene briefly.

He spent a stretch in Buffalo too, because he traveled the country with his kitchen organizer/media liaison scheme. He had a gig in Detroit but it soon fell through. His car died and he just kind of got stuck in the vortex of Michigan, just like everyone. He fought like a champ for the past 6 months to make an exit – "*Seattle or death*," no looking back…

By 7pm I'd developed a fever and was incapacitated by one too many painkillers, in no shape to move around. Despite their posted schedule, Greyhound decided to close down for 5 hours until the midnight bus arrived. Bastards kicked us out onto the street to walk around in -25 windshield factor. We were doomed.

As Jeremy, Tyreese, DC kid & I tried to comprehend our misfortune, the middle-aged Fargo chicks we met last night came to our rescue. They took us to a home in the suburbs, feeding as pizza and vodka. They were obnoxious, but we were grateful.

The doting one with the mom hair exploded over Obama – how anyone who supports the man is a fool, is insane. About how he is a communist, scum, the Antichrist. On her wall was a framed picture of George W. Bush praying with cusped hands, heavenly glow permeating his forehead, eagle soaring boldly over the luminescent cross in the sun.

I excused myself to the restroom and discovered a multi-task sauna – hot tub, bubble jets, faucet extensions; a pill-headed nirvana of ameliorate equilibrium…

We left the following afternoon; the 3 day mark and still a day & a ½ from Seattle. We made Billings without so much as a hiccup. All the people from the faulty Minneapolis bus are still there, as no bus has gone further west in 3 days.

It was perhaps the most joyous misery I'd witnessed, this uplifting reunion akin to prisoners catching up from Gulag to Gulag. When I asked the clerk how long I would have had to stay to make Seattle during my Christmas run: *5 days…*

The next bus departed 2 hours later, and all was well until we neared Spokane. Only 6 hours from home we'd gotten stuck in an ice bank. After an hour of revving forward into reverse to cradle us from peril, we broke free and drove into the mountains, air thick with fog. Tyreese started freaking out after checking the barometer. There were over 60 inches of fresh snow on those mountaintops, and ice happens to melt at 38 degrees. Tyreese has us clocked at 36…

The driver chances it when he obviously should not. No other cars on the road; none batty enough to attempt it. An echo too loud could disrupt the snow, sending it pummeling down instantaneously through reverberation…

We make it to Spokane 10 minutes before the final switch-over – the final ascent to the promised land. As Tyreese is rubbing his hands, bouncing in joy, we get the announcement: "*Due to five simultaneous avalanches, every mountain pass is now closed until further notice. We apologize for any disruption of service.*" Which means we literally bested the reaper by 20 minutes – and we are now trapped here for 2 more days. Which is why Tyreese, the devout Christian, repeatedly vents: "*FUCK——!!*"

A group of us decide to pitch in on a motel; en route Jeremy speaks Jedi destiny – that there is a force, a larger purpose, and all you have to do is follow the signs.

Everyday he says the signs are there. Doesn't matter if it's a receipt on the ground or a street corner chat with a pedestrian – he labors to pull the providential message. That's why he knew, for whatever reason, that Portland was his calling…

But maybe it was all just to meet me. Maybe I am the one he's supposed to get entangled with and that Seattle really is the answer, since I am the eerie clone of his first real traveling companion. Says I am the replica of a fire-breathing circus performer he'd embarked on a 3 week trip with a long, long time ago in a NYC far, far away. Said he thought I was the guy at first...

Originally I wanted to throw Sullivan through a window for his abhorrent vegan bullshit. He was pushing it hard, letting everyone know I was his sense of identity. But he grew on me.

It was as if his entire life was one obscure comedy act, a metaphysical stress comedy coalescing *Zardoz & What About Bob*. His steel-faith in destiny wormed its way into my perception. Maybe I'd found a successor. Since Sullivan's life was already dominated by ghosts, it only fit the myth that he become one himself...

Noon in Spokane, avalanches still isolating Washington State from the union. Defying corporate, the staff arranges us a reroute through the eastern edge of Oregon into the Northern tip of California, where we will then swing through the dry-lands crawling the I-5 into Portland. From thereon all that will stand in our way is a straight-shot of highway, a 3 hour burst into the Emerald City...

The only issue is that this will take 12 hours. In Spokane we are only 5 hours away from Seattle, and there is a slim chance the roads might clear by evening. I know its poppy-cock though – those people are doomed to sit there for 3 more days at least, no matter the cheery estimates...

Jeremy looks to me for the answer, says he's going wherever I am going There are a handful of others, mainly g-thug black guys looking to my council as well. The majority of the Minneapolis crew are staying put.

All eyes on me. "*Well*," I tell Jeremy, "*You always wanted to see California right?*" Tyreese starts doing that exasperated, over-the-top stressed out bit: "*Y'all are fucking crazy, y'all are... fuck it.*"

Cali is a sparse whizzing range of yellow flat land, distant mountains puncturing the air. We climb Southern Oregon, zagging through monolith canopies of redwoods that blot out the night sky in severe Plutonian blackness...

Portland; 5 days in. 10pm, Wednesday night – just a hop, skip & jump from Freak City. Ten minutes to load. As Tyreese is rubbing his hands, bouncing in joy, we get the announcement: "*Due to flooding, every road into Washington is now closed until further notice. We apologize for any disruption of service.*"

Which means we are now trapped here for at least 2 more days, just like the people we left behind in Spokane. Which is why Tyreese, the devout Christian, repeatedly vents the word "*FUCK!!*"

Jeremy, Tyreese and I sit there dumbfounded just like the 60 other people now trapped in Portland. There are about 20 of us still on from Chicago. One lady has been on for 9 days, having left Alabama. She smells like a wet dog.

CNN broadcasts live from Washington where a national emergency has been declared. Chunks of the state are submerged in water, and pockets of Seattle remain without heat or electricity. The I-5 is sunk beneath a half-mile stretch of water, and the state is losing 11 million a day in revenue. Even with FEMA pulling out the stops, we still have a day in limbo.

Tyreese grumbles himself to sleep while Jeremy and I hit the streets. It's pouring rain, the night mystical in rich ambiance; dark purple copulates with gray clouds hovering low like aerial fog. The bell tower above the terminal gives the appearance of city epicenter – the surrounding streets and corridors decorated as China Town with statues of golden dragons, twirling antique lampposts…

Jeremy is brain-storm ablaze. He's hatched a plan where instead of traveling the US interviewing musicians, as GhostNomad II he will hit every vegan restaurant, collective, venue, author & fanatic – he will worm his way into the back door of every meat-denouncing visionary through the sheer power of a tape recorder.

His grand vision is a multi-faceted website, a sprawling collective of traveling Greyhound journalists. With the mighty lungs of a propagandist and a PHD in bullshit, he will sail with the fluidity of the Argonaut.

He tells me that *"Ryan Bartek is my Tyler Durden,"* to which I respond: *"Don't start with that shit – I'm just some dumb asshole, get it through your skull."*

We drink $1 PBR drafts at the local crust dive as I explain in even greater detail the numerous facsimiles distinguishing subcultures. He keeps pointing to people in the bar: *"Well what are they?"* His knowledge thirst is voracious.

Things turn comical when on the street we pass a rather flamboyant gaggle. He asks: *"Well what do you call them?"* I look over at the limber, ballet movements of the fellow in spandex pants with the green & blue eyebrows. I chuckle and tell him: *"Umm… you call that flamingly gay."*

Jeremy isn't used to that world. I have to explain that San Fran is the big queer Disney land where everyone flocks in their spastic 20's – Portland & Seattle are where they settle afterwards. Portland is the lezzie capitol of the United States, and Seattle is socially & politically gay-male dominated…

Jeremy spazzes when he discovers Mighty-O donuts, the vegan pastry chain. He buys a half dozen tofu-chocolate delicacies and catches something on the overhead stereo: *"What is that playing right now? What you call that?"* I crank a big ole' smile. *"That, my friend, is power metal – & that, buddy boy, is Dragonforce."*

Jeremy stands frozen, ear cocked upwards. *"I've never heard anything like this. This is amazing… I want to know everything…"* I crack an even wider grin: *"Son, that's all I listen to when I travel. It is the soundtrack of the Greyhound limbo. I live for Dragonforce, and Dragonforce lives in me…"*

Next morning; 11am. Tyreese jumps up like a soldier. He flips the laminated Salvation Army badge around his neck and says, *"let's go."* Whatever humane services can be pulled from Downtown he is determined to bring to the forefront…

Tyreese spent months on the post-Katrina effort; he is a wool-dyed organizer. Like Jeremy, he has convinced himself that fate has put him here. It is God that set him on this path, and these poor souls of the Greyhound netherworld are his flock in need. Tyreese continues to quote the lines he's discovered, having been studying the bible this entire ride…

Jeremy and I follow him shelter to shelter, of which there are five in proximity. Salvation Army itself hoes us out despite Tyreese's connections. It is through the church-bred organization that we get 30 hygiene kits (*soap/comb/toothbrushes*) and several boxes of those lint-crushed bum blankets. We acquire boxes of donuts & five dozen snack-packs of pretzels and combos…

Back at the terminal we distribute 60 blankets, feed the hungry, and begin signing people up for the homeless shower nearby. The management want to throw us out – we have a verbal scuffle with security but Tyreese chews them out.

They don't want to fuck with us – there are too many starving, angry folks here. As is why the staff buckles under, handing out free food vouchers. Everyone gets sandwiches & burritos. Tyreese calls the local news to try and get coverage, food donations, but despite their interest no camera crew ever rolls up.

Jeremy is sitting alone, looking empty-eyed at the g-thug guys who symbolize his past. They never said thank you, they just took – and swiped more then anyone else. They lied trying to horde extra blankets. Out for themselves, gabbing bitches & money, how real men act in jail – fights they've won, scams hustled…

Jeremy had been consorting with them since Chicago. He lend them money he didn't have for sodas & snacks. He smoked them down with the little pot he had, when unbeknownst to us they were smuggling an ounce. They wouldn't let any of us hit on it either. When Jeremy threw them $10 for a dime, they shiested him with a nickel bag then asked for more vending money…

Despite our worker-ant accommodations, 6 of the Chicago people decide that enough is enough. Like a scene out of a zombie film, like the Titanic, the leader of their brilliant plan starts hollering *"Anyone wants out we're pitching in on a U-Haul! We're making it to Seattle even if we gotta drive through a mile flood! There's a way in!"*

Greyhound staff eyeball each other because they know better – every road in is tourniquet by flood. If there are rural back-roads, the gravel is packed for miles by knowledgeable hicks or tardy semi-trucks. Still they grasp at straws. The leader pulls up in the rental and a dozen refugees jump in the back, darting off with 400 horsepower.

Jeremy and I wander waterfront park smoking grass with a displaced Navy crewman. The river stretching through Portland is 17 inches higher then normal – 4 inches from spilling over & flooding the town with cholera & dysentery rising from the sewer mains. If this continues we'll be stranded atop the Greyhound roof until hazmat arrives or a helicopter lands to fly us out.

Back at the depot, live on CNN, everyone watches the fate of the U-Haul refugees. They pull up to the I-5 lake behind the reporter on air – plan foiled, for all to see. They back up and drove off, no one knowing what ever happened to them…

It's drawing night and I'm down to the last of my painkillers; my spine has been on fire this whole ride. That I haven't had REM sleep in 6 days, that I've kept waking up every two hours since Detroit from a radio announcement, changeover or cigarette break has not helped. I have the shakes, my eyes are red. The pills are raging, the pot we smoked so dank & green…

Jeremy asks that I step outside. Says he's been talking to a local on acid offering to take him somewhere – some weird hippie tripping balls in a tie-dye. Jeremy asks my opinion and I retort: *"What would GhostNomad do?"* Jeremy grins and waves goodbye. He is already 5 pages into the book he is now living, leaving his freshest notes in my care…

Awake in a surge with blurry recollections atop a pile of damp coats….

Sunny morning, 10am... Jeremy? Arrested, dead? Freaking on acid & grazing like a cow?

I go outside to the terminal to smoke and he slinks around the corner. Says he trailed the hippie who made no sense but found a pack of crusties outside a liquor store. The lead female made him pop a squat. They were in the progress of *"taxing their asses"* – squeezing cash out of the squares for polluting *"their streets"* with banality. To *"tax them"* is to get money from them, because they must pay thoroughfare of passage since they are not of the street universe, the only world which is real...

The unknown thing about crust culture is that for every dime taxed, they in turn give right back to the streets. While they sit outside an establishment panhandling or just going about their day, they are perpetually cleaning the area.

Since they are homeless, its part of the crust-Zen to tidy the outdoors as if they are cleaning their own room or managing a dinky bonsai. They give back much more then they take, and for every cent panhandled they sustain karma...

When the crust-lady asked Jeremy how he'd ended up there, he name dropped me. She said *"Oh, him. Ha! I know him. The scumfuck journalist right? How's Bartek been doing?"*

'Twas a Scumfuck making that Snake Plissken quip, one of the hardest-line of the Frisco tribe I'd rolled with April 2007. Jeremy hung with them all night at the train yard, cleaning the tracks. They were making a game of it – how many empty Pabst's they could fit in a trashcan. They worked like pigeons sniping every crumb...

The announcement bursts from the loudspeaker: *"We regret to inform you that the I-5 freeway is still submerged beneath water..."* Everyone grumbles and stares at the floor defeated.

"HOWEVER, the secondary freeway pass has now been opened... To all passengers headed to Seattle & beyond, we will be rerouting your tickets to go through the Western edge of the state as to head North into Seattle!! Congratulations, you're going home!!"

The terminal explodes in laughter & merriment. We are given another round of lunch tickets, and I opt for charred burritos...

20 minutes to departure I call Jeremy over: *"Look... This trip has really put everything into perspective. When I left Michigan, my faith in destiny was shattered. Like you, I followed the signs and it led to a standstill..."*

"I think the moral here is that whether or not the signs are real, reality is what we make. Fate exists if we choose for it to exist... I've been

on the road for nearly two years now and I want to go home – I want a job, a girlfriend, a band. I don't want to see another Greyhound again for a long, long time…"

"You know, in the real world, I'm a total fuck up, but in Greyhound world I'm like a god. Imagine that? After everything, it's the only thing you're really good at…"

"So, fuck it – I officially pass the torch of GhostNomad on to you, buddy boy. I have no idea what's in store for you, but I have total faith in your abilities. This will be the most intense year of your life. I give this meaningless title to you, good sir – yours & yours alone. Do you accept this nonsensical gift & joyful curse?"

Jeremy nods, alive in a way he never considered. As we board I cue the CD; the motor roars & Jeremy hits play. Everyone aboard can hear the high-voltage bombast of duel guitar solos; Sullivan is hopping around his seat head-banging, roaring with laughter, Dragonforce raging: *"proud and so glorious/standing before of us our swords will shine bright in the sky/when united we come to the land of the sun/ with the heart of a dragon we ride…"*

Seattle now, Sunday night at Miss Monster's. I know Clownbaby is going to call. It's been over two weeks of silence, but I know it's gonna happen.

Jeremy didn't even say goodbye – just slunk away like a phantom, hands in pockets & hoodie over head. I walked to my black gravel composition book & wrote the following – 911(x2) 1.11.09: *"GhostNomad just took off down the street."*

The cell phone is on the couch cushion begins to ring. – it's Clownbaby… I step outside, hoping it will mimic the dream I've so long chased. I flip open the receiver and say in a slow, creepy crawl drawl: *"Hiiiiii Clown bay-beeee…"* And do you know what she says to me? *You know what she says???*

The Great American Blackout

The textbook definition of terrorism is the use of calculated violence against any society, organization, military or political system to bend its will (*through fear*) in favor of the aggressor's demands. That's what is happening right now, in Iraq, in 2003.

Kluck and I are watching flower-bud explosions on CNN as the US Air Force dumps 750 tons of depleted uranium munitions on Baghdad. The majority of targets are civilian instillations like hospitals, schools, water refineries, police/fire stations. The Bush Administration calls it "*Shock & Awe*"; the world "*war crimes.*"

The invasion was set to begin on the 3rd week of 3rd month of 3rd year of 3rd millennium, but freak sandstorms kept the Earth's mightiest force at bay for weeks. The Arab world regarded them Allah's monkey wrench of divinity.

The global response is to recoil in horror; in America talk radio DJ's play funny sound samples of weapon fire & clownish bike-horns as cavalry. American media broadcasts yellow ribbons around tree trunks while Al Jazeera the stumps of limbless children. Untold millions protest worldwide, swarming every capitol.

They call this preemptive war "*Operation: Iraqi Freedom*" – we call it "*Operation: Texaco.*" The main prerogative of all ground GI's was to secure every oil field. The scheme doesn't work though – 6 years later & they haven't even had an pipeline running longer then 8 hours, because their constantly blown up by partisans.

The American public do not yet know that everyone in Baghdad – including all USA troops – are already dead from Depleted Uranium Munitions.

See, the Pentagon takes all this used goop from the spent rods of nuclear power plants, packs them inside bunker-buster warhead shells, then dump loads of them on pinpoint targets. Melts steel like butter, but never goes away.

During "*Shock & Awe*", 750 tons of DUI munition rained on Baghdad. For 12 billion years these lethal particles will blow across the region such as microbes of sand – *permanent & invisible.*

While the Pentagon claims this depleted uranium is so safe you can eat it, the reality is it has a half-life of 6 billion years. Inhaling even a microscopic fraction changes the way your body system works, mutates your DNA, renders flipper babies & ultra-violent forms of cancer. The saying is that "*if you live in Baghdad for a year, you'll never be able to have children.*" Whenever our people return home, they'll be bringing untold amounts in their lungs, their skin, their kidneys. When little Billy sits on Daddies lap Daddy irradiates death. Everyone surrounding Daddy is affected. Daddy is a miniature nuclear meltdown on two legs.

In the newspaper on Kluck's coffee table there is a chart graphic printed. It claims that the worst case scenario for this war is 6 months of fighting and a $6 billion price tag.

Today, at Stoner Joe's, it's 6 years later & we've breached $1 trillion. Our armed forces now police a puppet government, regularly blasted by suicide bombers, landmines & guerrilla snipers. 3000+ GI's & 150,000 dead Iraqi's & no end in sight...

Kluck doesn't care about anything, I think. He has no morals. We both talk like we're extras from *Pink Flamingos*, spend hours ranting about the filthiest of ass sex & water-sports, but deep down, I am a gentlemen. I am the nobleman of deviants.

Kluck is 22 and covered in tats; head shaved and face glittering with piercings. His room is a catalog of pirated black & death metal CDR's, like a medieval watchtower of sacred parchments tended by benighted scholars. He hordes everything, especially horror bootlegs & grisly murder footage.

Kluck is my co-pilot on the GG Allin dissemination campaign. I set up a free contest in Real Detroit Weekly where "one lucky contestant" gets both of the new albums from Saliva & Disturbed. Well, they'll get 'em alright, but ye olde Trojan Horse – an envelope packed with Murder Junkies & black/death metal mixes.

We are so passionate in destroying every last trace of nu-metal that we go to malls & concerts like Jehovah's Witnesses distributing mixes as to brainwash the youth one CDR at a time.

Kluck is madly in love with Clarice, who he anally pounds like a mad butcher. He says the key to the heart lies through the rectum, or something to that effect. I've been dating Clarice's best friend, this Greek lesbian with thighs built to shit kids.

The Greek hates men but is infatuated with me. Somehow I always end up with lesbians who've sworn off cock, cause I was raised & educated by women – I'm like a bull dyke with a penis...

Kluck is not a Don Juan Quixxxote. His travails with women are comical at best, often striking out on blind dates. I'll have to pick him up at weird places, at weird times.

For instance, he met this artificially tanned girl at a tiki bar in Pontiac. She picked him up for an evening at the movies & while in line she excitedly pointed to the advertisement of an Ice Cube family film. Kluck sighed: *"I'd rather just masturbate to Passion of the Christ again."* She left him there, 45 minutes from home, in the dead of winter…

Coffee Hoe is a better example. Kluck stumbled upon this MILF at the corner gas station. They had a pleasant conversation regarding the weather, and an hour later he'd spotted her wandering down the street. She came over and asked him to rip a burn CD of *Dark Side of The Moon* then pounced like the cougar she was...

Coffee Hoe starts coming over daily while the husband's at work. Two weeks later she disappears, and then the very angry husband comes by threatening Kluck's father, because he assumed that's who was plugging his wife. When he realized it was some 20 year old kid, he became homicidal.

Kluck soon realized that this man wanted to kill him – this bodybuilding fireman ripped on steroids. Coffee Hoe had left a note saying exactly who she was banging and where he lived, then proceeded to trash 'roid ragers' house. She fled to Mexico but he caught her and after bringing her back he found her with slit wrists in the tub. Barely surviving, she was committed indeterminately.

Coffee Hoe was then in the asylum, trying to pull her wrist stitches out to bleed to death, and the fireman began parking outside Kluck's house for hours on end. Just staring, just waiting, with Kluck hiding inside his room.

Whenever the fireman was busy at work he'd have his cop friends park their squad cars out front. Kluck was fucked as ever fucked could be, and would only leave under the cover of night. He was petrified he'd soon be in jail again, having been running all these years on a half dozen warrants…

Kluck is totally suicidal. He has done more drugs then anyone I have ever known. Over the past 3 years I've witnessed him snort full vials of K, drink hundreds of hits of liquid acid in one slurp, suck down 60 lbs of nitrous in one sitting, eat 10 pills of X at a time. This does not factor in the meth, coke, pain-pills, booze, etc. He should be dead, not burning pentagrams into his lawn & dry-humping the ash moaning, *"Odin, ooh-dinn…"*

My black metal joke name is "Grimjizz The Frostbitten Elite," while Kluck's is "Bullet" (or so he demands I call him). Well "Bullet" wasn't always this grim black metal warrior. I am to blame, mainly, for taking him to Onyx the Urban Priest.

Onyx is the crazy rat man from the trailer park that gives free psychological advice to anyone that brings him booze. He conducts lead pipe & boa staff duels like a schizophrenic John Williams, and he is surrounded by teenage punk kids who think I am the Antichrist. To them I am the John Conner of the promised land. In reality, if I am anything, it is simply the hellfire Ferris Bueller.

Kluck is always trying to out-hardcore everyone, and since he can never out-hardcore me, he instead takes it out on Gothic Jimmy, who we see at concerts. Gothic Jimmy worships any abuse inflicted upon him – this weirdly hunched Arab/Mexican kid that ironically detests Arabs, with rolly-polly cheeks & a drooping bottom lip. His arms are thick from scars of self-mutilation.

Gothic Jimmy says he'd never have sex with a man, but he'd let GG Allin rape him. Jimmy stumbles up to us reeking of whiskey, demanding Kluck punch him in the face. Kluck puts out dozens of cigarettes out on his forehead, before Jimmy starts skull-butting the wall until he's gushing blood... He's now in prison somewhere in Northern Michigan, although we're not sure what for...

Kluck and I hang out at City Club a lot, because we can get away with anything there. It is the sleaziest industrial club in the United States, connected to a fire-damaged Ramada goth-types have flocked across the globe to live in. A penthouse is $400 a month, and most rooms are $30 for overnight stays...

City Club runs until 5am and is packed with leather, bondage bunnies, hacker types, metal fiends, post-apocalyptic fashion; dance floor filled with goths writing like snakes or lurching the zombie sidestep shoe-gaze shuffle.

Since no one wants to be called out as phony, Kluck pushes it hard. He is constantly drunk and starting silly fights; the head of security is a giant black guy who thinks it's hilarious, allowing drastic displays of gremlin nuisance.

We were standing on the dance floor, flashing disco lights whirling, when Kluck went into a trance. He looked as if he didn't know where he was then robotically began snatching empty bottles from ledges and smashing them on the floor.

He was grabbing beers from people's hands, thrusting them down. He crouched, as if in a dream, and picked up two handfuls. He started rubbing fistfuls of glass all over his chest, deep and hard. He grabbed another pile with bleeding hands, washing himself like a bar of soap...

The goth kids were mortified. He kept saying, *"Skin is like paper."* Said, *"I wanna fuck myself with pain."* I was laughing like a hyena as he gushed blood. Security led him out in latex gloves. For weeks his stomach looked like a vicious knee scrape of skateboard collision. But banned he was not.

The depressing thing in writing about Kluck is not so much that I consorted with his likes, but that everyone from the early period in which he sprang have ceased to exist in any meaningful way.

Kluck and I graduated high school the same year, as did the bulk of the East Dearborn kids, better known as the "East Side Crew." Until around 9/11, anyone connected to our tribe were thrown into the chaos of the Detroit rave scene. From '99 to 2001, our lives were a hotel sequence from *Fear & Loathing In Las Vegas.*

9/11 is now 8 years ago, the symbolic death of that world. Huxley did 5 years in Jackson for assault, Eugene is doing 7-15 for armed robbery, Cassum is running from the FBI, Cole's facing life over 160 hits of acid. Heroin addicts, warrant evaders, soldiers joining the war-machine to legally kill people. Anyone left had fled the state, gone to college, or settled on a lazy, stoned family life.

Apart from Kluck, the only one of relevance left from this East Side Crew is Simon, who could also be found at City Club. Simon, Kluck & I – we were always the freaks that hated the other freaks; we were neck-deep in obscure European Metal & the most rugged punk bands in history.

Simon was an industrial/metal type that knew everything about pro-wrestling & horror cinema. Like the rest of us he was a record collector. Simon, Kluck & I abuse the shit out of my guest-list connects for rampant live gigs: *Slayer, Cannibal Corpse, Dark Funeral, Dimmu Borgir, Dying Fetus, Severed Savior, In Flames, Children of Bodom, Type O Negative, Exhumed, Sadomasochism, Danzig, Behemoth, Voivod, Primal Fear, Megadeth, Ministry, BILE, Immortal, Iron Maiden, KMFDM, Suffocation...*

Harpo's was our den – a venue that was so seedy you could openly snort coke off the tables & buy keg booze at 15. No one gave a fuck. Imagine the grimmest, gnarliest, beer soaked ex-silver age cinema imaginable, just run down & crumbling. 3 massive open level floors and a pit area where the most brutal simulations of full blown riots I've ever witnessed took place constantly.

Harpo's is located in one of the worst stretches of Detroit, surrounded by ghetto prairies. The locals see a wraparound line of metalheads with combat boots & shaved heads and think "*nazi.*" People sometimes got shot drive-by style by gangbangers...

See, Harpo's used to be fascist central before the change of management. For years it was all bikers & Nazis, and all the 'hood knew it too. One night, back in 1998 – my first time at Harpo's, no less – an army of these old patrons showed up. I was nearly beaten to a pulp by 250 hammer skins for sporting an anti-swastika patch. I never came back until 2002, but once I did, I was addicted.

The prior Nazi scum really gave Harpo's a bad rep. Tough guys abounded, sure, but that is classic Detroit. The redneck wing of the Detroit male was always thick – lots of apolitical skinhead types, and that right wing Ted Nugent flavor.

The Metro area was packed with Pantera guys, Slayer fanatics, Slipknot maggots, Hot Topic zipper pants kids, mullet-rocker Ozzy guys, obnoxious Juggalos & Korn kids with low-riders/bumping speaker systems & Adidas.

In terms of the wild live gigs you hear about, that much is true. Detroit is insane in its masochistic punishment. Imagine that arena where The Pistons play turned into one swirling circle pit of several thousand lunatics punching, kicking & trampling each other for fun. Detroit is no joke if the people really dig your band...

That I cannot clearly remember much about these endless romps only showcases their dying nature to me. So much of it seems airy... I remember my first metal concert – 1994 & Pantera at their peak, touring *Far Beyond Driven.* Big Phil was like a five star general beckoning his legions, demanded unity & brotherhood. It was galvanizing to me at 13.

Now, at age 22, Big Phil is up on Harpo's stage smacked out of his gourd, embarrassing Hank Williams the IIIrd as he fumbles through the Superjoint Ritual set. People always jump onstage & shake Phil's hand, pat him on the back. He gives that tight-faced nod, that snarling metal viciousness, as if to say the audience is as badass as him. "*Respect son,*" grunted with that meat-head chin-clench...

A gang of kids overrun the stage & hug him like a mob of Care Bears. Big Phil breaks the circle, limber with smack. He says into the microphone, brushing his long hair aside to emphasize his point: "*Hey man...*" Silence, pouting tough. "*I ain't no fuckin' teddy bear...*" Waits another 10 seconds. "*Why dontch you, like... Take yer dick n' stick it in some oatmeal n' just...*" Nodding out from heroin. "*Stir it around or somethin'...*" Gives a little whirly motion with his index finger, brushes his hair, starts another song that he stops 30 seconds in. "*Man... Start it again. They aren't makin' me feel it.*"

The show was over in 30 minutes, 15 of it consumed by his mumbled opiate banter. As the crowds walk out feeling cheated and ashamed, Big Phil grabs a confederate flag from the skinheads in the front row. He ties it around his neck like a cape and starts to Sieg Heil the audience. As we all filter out in disgust Big Phil, our former leader, keeps hollering: *"Skins n' Punks unite! Skins n' Punks..."*

Detroit's culture was 10 years behind, the radio in mainstream lock down, and most local bands were swinging in the dark. The metal acts were Korn Klones, Godsmack rips or Pantera plunderers. If they were attempting death metal, most weren't getting far. The local punk bands were mostly wretched pop-punk aping Green Day, hustling a mediocre Rancid impression or copping the whiniest tunes of Bad Religion. *People actually aspired to sound like Blink 182.*

I was from the down-n-dirty world of grind, thrash & early hardcore – Black Flag, Circle Jerks, Misfits, Dead Kennedys & Cramps. GG was the king of psychopaths, Dwarves the buttplug of ugly, and Rollins the voice of discontent. Anything past Reagan seemed banal to me, lest it be The Hillside Stranglers from Detroit.

Back then, I'd still never even heard the term crust. I didn't know a single train-hopper, never heard of *Cometbus* or read *American Hardcore.* I had no money for *Maximum Rock N' Roll.* I was ignorant of real anarchism, unwise to the Greyhound circuit. I lived in a vacuum, but I believed in DIY.

My return to do-it-yourself guerrilla shows began at a rec center in Novi. In one day I saw 10 incredible bands that annihilated 90% of the local acts I'd ever witnessed – among them Today I Wait, Don Knots, Summer Dying, The Nain Rouge, GANON, Enkaphlin, DemonSweat, & the now world famous The Black Dahlia Murder (*their second show ever, when they were still just nerdy fat kids with poor social skills*).

From that crowd I met a cast of characters which had really propagated an organic scene. All these guys were wholly autonomous from any of the "pay to play" ripoff venues run by shady promoters trying to make a buck.

Dozens of tables hosted upstart indie labels, zines, merch racks, etc. Self prompted organization made easy & dynamic – and no skinhead thugs to be found. Spiraling from that crew I found the basis of all my journalistic efforts locally for the next few years. That's when things really started growing – networks, collectives, promoters. I was grinning like a demented boy scout...

A main hub was the DIY Detroit venue Idle Kids, run by a collective. It was located in Cass Corridor and Detroit city council solidly backed it as part of a manifold urban renewal plan.

Idle Kids' interior was caked in CrimethInc propaganda & a fortress of radical zines, obscure prints & anarchist leaflets. Idle Kids had a team which taught free lessons on how to build computers from scratch, how to rewire electricity, run generators, build bikes. They had attempted a CD store/book shop as well, but the bread & butter was always the live shows. They sold no booze; it was always about the music.

Idle Kids remained a straightedge venue where you couldn't smoke or drink inside. No one was uppity about it; that was just the agreement with the city. You could always chug beer in your car or chain-smoke in the alley. It kept the obnoxious bar crowd away, and it really thinned the herd between metal generations. There was a vast difference in attitude from the punk-rooted DIY kids and the older *Beavis & Butthead* guys – that whole queer-stomping, animal torturing, "*shoot first & ask questions later*" crowd.

The final split came when one of the more popular of the old-guard thrash/death bands headlined a show, whining onstage the entire time 'cause they couldn't get drunk. The guitarist with the corny black metal name went outside, whipped out his dick & pissed all over the wall mural of Martin Luther King. In redneck drawl, he hooted: "*I'm gonna piss on that nigger's face!*"

There were frequent showcases of bands driving hundreds of miles to play for no money – monster bills with 12 acts at a time, be they tech, grind, metal-core, punk, hardcore.

You had a rotating heap of groups: The Decomposition Of Us, Funeral For Rosewater, The Rat King, fordirelifesake, Bloodlined Calligraphy, Caligula, A Waking Nightmare, If Hope Dies, Walls of Jericho, Two Stars Burning Sun, Kenshiro, The Alliance, With Honor; out of State accomplices like HEWHOCORRUPTS, Premonitions of War, From A Second Story Window, Bodies In The Gears Of The Apparatus, Between The Buried And Me, Ion Dissonance, Red Chord, Tony Danza's Tapdance Extravaganza...

These massive shows were always a messy, ill managed affair, but the groups were so workhorse they'd know their cue. No one cared about radio presence or know-nothing managers. All the cornball shit of the early venues I inhabited – Pharaohs, Harpo's, Mosquito Club, I-Rock – they were instantly antiquated...

There was a similar DIY venue called Trumbull Plex, but I'd only attended one show cause the crowd had a snooty anarcho bent. Trumbull Plex was like walking into someone's house uninvited; handbills on Marxism, gender deconstruction & the radical queer scene. I hadn't even spoken and they'd all grimly eyeballed me.

There were other squat venues I never really penetrated – arcane land pyrate dives filled with dirty, mean ass train-hoppers. Most those guys were "*harder-core then thou*" to the point where they grilled you like the scene police. I got into the underground to get away from the bullies – not to prove myself to toothless grunts with studded cliché vests. Some were cool, but still no fun for me.

I was a freak anomaly eyed with suspicion – for wearing a black leather trench (*target for the vegans*), for associating with all fringes (*everyone "knows" that you can only pick one subculture identity*), for having been neck-deep in the rave scene (*dancing with chicks is apparently uncool*).

Above all I was marked as a "sell-out" for my employment at Real Detroit Weekly, the magazine supported by a sundry ad clientèle among the likes of Phillip Morris, Budweiser & the sleaziest of inner-city strip clubs...

For reasons of misunderstanding I was viewed with resentment. Barely a soul knew my idealistic pursuit. Well, I don't buy the argument that punk, metal, industrial, rock, or even hippie-dippy flower power acoustic stuff are contradictory or even segregated movements.

They are all but different layers in a grand design, even if the design itself maintains clashing or polar extremes. All of these items represent a drifting away from the herd, and should be fostered irregardless. While others concentrate solely on stone blocks, I turn my eyes to the fully erected Pyramid.

Thus is the intimate communion of art and struggle, and at the vital center of every youthful movement is communication and creation. Polar effects are solely a matter of perception. 99% of the time these activities inevitably lead towards a larger, more interconnected grass-roots phenomenon.

Instigating movement at all levels to strengthen a larger counterculture design was the ultimate sum of all my efforts. I molested the media to enact these goals and fostered networks as realistically as I could.

But do they recognize the ringmaster spectacle you are establishing with PT Barnum grandeur? "*Punk bands only want to play with punk bands bro.*"

Do they appreciate the living painting which you are expertly unfurling? "*We appreciate your 'psychological impact' order of the bands tonight dude, but can we just, like, play second?*"

Do they comprehend the masterstroke of your mad psychologist scheme? *"So yeah bro, we're like scene veterans n' shit even though we draw like 10 people who all get on guest list anyway. 30 minute jam for $150 bro, this is our manager bro, Duke's old lady. She's even got her own business card n' shit."*

No – you're just some asshole bookie that throws a bunch of random, weird ass bands together, and when it goes against the line of their genre scene purity they bail on you. Then they don't bring anyone to the concert and you're looked at like a thieving douche because the insignificant door money has to go to PA rental...

In those early days of rec centers, VFW halls & dive bars, I'd yet to put the ANOMIE INC tag on a flyer. I assumed the role of the journalist, and it was my mission to plug every Michigan workhorse. Already in PIT Magazine I published interviews/reviews for Saprogenic, Mutilated, Summer Dying, Today I Wait, Black Dahlia Murder, Signs of Collapse, Downtown Brown, Sadomasochism, The Nain Rouge, Parasitosis – the majority I'd popped their press cherry.

During my long run at Real Detroit, I broke hundreds of bands locally, in terms of press. This merciless Hoffa routine served to maliciously inflate my anxiety. I was never comfortable anywhere – I always had to play journalist guy or scene politician. Always talking business, rambling well-constructed, self-selling shtick...

While perpetrating this immense blur of activity, I would spend my free time away. My life was a carefully plotted ying-yang of public rallying & solitude. Socially I mixed with a half dozen groups all fairly unconnected. I tried to pull many of these people together for years, but it was anticlimactic...

Kluck and Simon, for instance, were self-contained. Onyx and his trailer (*with a cast like Skinner, Brandon, & Dr. Santiago*) was also a locked reality. You had the remnants of the East Dearborn crew I'd occasionally visit, but also this group in the Northern Suburbs where Stoner Joe originated. Those are whom I spent my daily interaction with – fun-loving stoners into bonfires & disc golf.

I'd met the Northern group when I was 19. It was my infant attempt to start somewhere totally fresh, knowing I'd eventually attempt the same in larger cities. I took a job as a line cook and soon found myself at the 24-7 diner where everyone hung out in the area.

In that 5 month period in late 2000, I distributed dozens of composition books declaring the genesis of our personalized Neo-Beat Generation. This seduced explosion of autobiographical novels inevitably led to a not-so-viscous fight club that was rather slapstick.

These activities imbued a strong sense of tribe, culminating in a commune of sorts – a huge apartment above a Nextel building that had 8 rooms, 12 people, 4 dogs & multiple bands practicing there. Since it was commercially zoned, we set upon the creation of a monthly mag called "*Fuck Detroit Weekly*."

The project never got too far, and they were evicted by Summer 2003. Today, at Stoner Joe's, the remnants show up every Saturday for a massive bonfire. There are a good hundred of us, I'd say, but they are now grown men & women with careers, engaged or married with children. And here I am, "*Revolutionary Ryan Bartek*" whom they liken to The Mole, still furiously refusing The Grid.

**Your friends only believe in you so much as they know you, and what is foreign to them is alienating or incomprehensible. They confide in you because they detect themselves in you, and suffocating this sort of empathy causes irreparable damage.

Rarely was there an accomplice who engulfed the full portrait of my existence; few knew the *meta-physi-spiritu-ectual* undertones behind my wall. Many from the East D clan were enraged that I wrote of it as "*a life in the gutter*." They never understood that quintessential Beat Notion – glorifying the sludge of bottom-rung Americana…

Even as a child I felt a grown man; at bottom I felt a reincarnation. Until 7 I'd no friends my own age, and most every male child I'd end up street fighting somehow. My early companions were Nam/Korean War vets, grizzled auto-workers & failed musicians that hung out at smoky Detroit bars with my mother's ex-boyfriend. 6 and surrounded by cabbies, chop-shoppers & ex-cons.

My best friend was my grandmother, who I watched rot like a still projection of moldy fruit. Locked for two years in a room with an emphysema victim eaten alive by cancer – this defined my level of intimacy among my common man. I developed apart…

The other children instinctively knew I was not one of them, lost in my own dream-state. I could at any moment switch from quiet child to arsonist, vandal, attacker...

What of my teen years? An internal Hiroshima equally fueled by the brash hooliganism of my psychotic friends. From 13 onward my life was tribute to revenge – and there was no villain of cinema with whom I couldn't identify…

The Old World has been laid to rest, and I am left with echoes. I shake it off and walk the empty streets. It is the sense of liberation I had riding my bike as a child. While all the adults were at work, the real world was pulsing before me. Without questioning the impulse, I'd explore the backyard of a depopulated home. I'd go through garages, sneak alleyways...

The discarded world was the one that entranced me. I'd rummage through garbage cans, befriending plastic artifacts. I'd act more an owner to the house cats on the street then their proper master. I'd sit alone in fields, communing organza. While the other children played baseball I'd wander the strip-mall, dissecting the meaning of adult femininity. I'd sit in lobbys & watch men banking. *Shopping malls. Architecture. Empty swimming pools in winter...*

I am the embryonic GhostNomad, confined to doll house terrain. I determine the habitual instincts of fellow man, recording notes real or imagined. Like an astronaut I clomp though aisles of convenience never seeing people only systems of calculated reaction – *pulpits of retards cannibalizing children, liquidating vulgarities... The destruction of ignorance as if I were the empty space... Quintessential existence absorbed & deluded, malformed & unfocused... Terror of sleep, fear of day-walkers, lust of dreaming... The immortal presence of childhood deleriums seeking oracles of communion... Deaf and blind parades choking the arbitrary fallacy, severing the foreskin of existence...*

The other major group were at "Thunderdome II," in Royal Oak. The first Thunderdome was Neil P's house, the singer/guitarist from Downtown Brown.

Having dropped out of art college to play rock n' roll, Neil's homestead was soon filled eccentrics. After Lisa's suicide, our mutual friend Zoe ended up living on Neil's couch in raw, post-funeral mourning. He was always was a sucker for the damsel in distress, and it was Lisa's tragic end that birthed our mutually intertwined paths...

Neil and I, our grand vision of the future was cemented during a leviathan party at Thunderdome. We sat upon the front steps splitting a gallon of Jack Daniels, confirming each others' truths like grizzled pyrates. As dawn quieted the snoring, body-strewn lair, I unsheathed the album *Condition Red* as the sun hit the CD, filling the room with prismatic light: "*Welcome to the glory of Iron Savior.*" Into the stereo it went, blasting "Titans of our Time" with the velocity of an Andromeda-hurled comet.

We keeled in spastic laughter – track after track of the cheesiest, intergalactic German power metal imaginable. *Warrior steel, the lion inside of you, the riding of intergalactic waves upon The Thunderbird...*

The divinity of our mission befell us, for Neil and I had discovered the soundtrack of *The Acropolis*...

The punks in the 80's had Reagan, and those panoramic Dead Kennedys news-clipping spreads spoke more to our heritage then any modern device. We were well in the Post-Clinton age, right at the introductory helm of The War On Terror.

Instead of Khomeini we had bin Laden, for Gorbachev we'd Saddam, for Goebbles-drunk propagandists we had Karl Rove. Homeland Security, "Terror Alert" color codes – Nostrodamian apocalypse scorched the horizon...

If the punks of the 1980's had forewarned the apocalypse, then we would instead freely admit we were already there. Out great protests came not in the form of doom-saying, but in the glorification of the *Mad Max* aesthetic. *The Acropolis* was here, and banshee-shrieking, leather pants power metal was its anthem.

Neil soon got so neck-deep into Manowar that he refused to play live until the audience sat through "The Crown And The Ring" like a sermon. Many of the attendees to the Downtown Brown shows would kneel before the booming PA, like crusading knights...

It was the dawn of The Acropolis, and soon we would be living feudally, combating each other for stockades of gasoline and water. We would wear neon headbands, spiked football pads & slide on Nintendo power gloves to battle radiated mutants in the desert wastelands. The Nuclear Hordes were approaching, and for heroes we had Beastmaster & Swayze in *Steel Dawn*...

While Neil maneuvered his group like chess pieces on a board of venues, the oddball gravity continued to suck in freaks of all varieties. The theatrical vibe of a DTB show appealed to a slew of age groups. With their small-stage arena-rock presence of pomp & gimmickry, nothing ever got stale. The crowd's enthusiastic ideas often determined the ongoing pranks and tall tales of urban legendry.

Neil was ringmaster – a pudgy, boisterous loud mouth with a raucous laugh endlessly bantering on the microphone. His targets were always the abusive, the ugly, the deprecating. He represented the slapstick death of the mainstream choke-hold. Every thing he ingested was unveiled like the hieroglyphs of a living cartoon.

There were moments of supreme cheese – the bi-annual Satanic Sunday showcases, giant foam cowboy hats, robot costumes, mullet barbers, 80's garb, piss drinking, minor pyrotechnics, the dumping of cream corn all over the body and audience.

It goes beyond causal stupidity when a wholly new vocabulary is invented in result. It is one thing to be a novelty act – it is another to actually have tunes as well. The Downtown Brown whom I tour with today is a vastly superior machine, hopped up on Zappa, Ween, AC/DC, Fishbone, Dead Kennedys & Mike Patton + Van Halen solos...

It is the summer of 2003, and there is nothing else to be considered but merciless grunt-work & expansion. Thunderdome II is functional in Royal Oak, easily identified by the 600 lbs gorilla statue on the front lawn.

The inhabitants are a wild roll call of Flannigan, Coop, Torino & Davis. As we toil on projects everyone adds his own particular flair – Flannigan the organizer, Torino the architect, Coop the electrician/soundman, Davis the philosopher, Neil the Musician, Bartek the propagandist...

Thunderdome II is like a battle command HQ, where Flannigan & the boys gear up for the big spectacle of summer – *Save The Vegetable III: Butchered Under The Big Top* at the Theatre Bizarre. Not a stab at vegans so much as a ridiculous cause, the premise is that *yes*, you betcha – *plants have feelings too*. The monstrosity of slicing those wilted flowers apart, of digesting pepper slices & eggplant slabs – well fuck you monsters, we'll just stick to veal cutlets & roasted pork...

At *Save The Vegetables* no plant life is to be consumed – nothing but bloody steaks, gooey pork, charred burgers, yummy tripe, brain matter & Rocky Mountain Oysters. Amidst this cauldron of burning flesh we have the greatest carnival themes. Davis will run the dunk tank with a cow-disguise.

Neil P, globbed in clown makeup, runs the "*whack the pins & win a mutated prize*" while sporting a butcher's bib caked in plasma. All the stuffed animals are half-melted or dental-floss stitched into half human/half-alligator oddities, Siamese cabbage patch twins or flesh-wrapped robots...

While Flannigan deciphers the game plan like a boardroom presentation, he also organizes the death match wrestling sideshow where he will battle "Public Enemy" for the heavyweight title. Flannigan enjoys being thrust through tables & mashed in broken glass, or Irish Whipped & snowplowed into a turnbuckle...

Coop fashions the electrical grid and sound system, while Torino fashions the life-size paper-mache Pig Warrior statue that will rise in the middle of the festival like a sentient guardian...

Even though Save The Vegetables is the ultimate annual gathering of our tribe, Flannigan also hosts Death Metal Ping Pong where table-tennis carts are pushed into the mosh pit – a tournament of short-shorts & tube socks to the soundtrack of guttural annihilation. We live this Merry Pranksters/Marx Bros vibe of community. Flannigan & Torino have also been collecting Mopeds; they barrel the streets like a zany scooter armada with over-sized helmets & jet fighter suits…

Recently they hosted a "science fair" in which someone rented a ghetto warehouse & pumped it full of fog & strobe lights. The crew spent weeks preparing exhibits & the night of the "party" they became mad scientists in green lab coats, having built life-size projects in elementary school style. There were giant brains, scrambled memory chambers, trans-dimensional speaking devices – *Mr Wizard's* hybrid planet…

Even with all this going on, I still can't get one group to intersect with another. The Idle Kids people are their own world, the Thunderdome folk their own tribe. The Northern Suburb stoners don't budge, the metal guys – forget it.

The punks are confined to their dingy dive bars, the gothy types City Club elite. Kluck and Simon, can't get them to do shit. You can't lead a horse to water, but why not freaks to the freaks?

Save The Vegetables is turning that tide. Despite the gimmickry, it's all about the two-stage lineup of a dozen bands. When Neil & I teamed up, we both had a vision of "The Coalition" – to unite every weirdo band on the common grounds of strangeness.

The Amino Acids are one of the main destroyers in the arsenal. They are raw surf-punk space aliens that crashed into a bowling alley in the late 60's. They wear smiling face-masks beneath white stockings that they pull over their heads, giving the impression of cranial bowling pins.

All of them wear black uniforms & remain mute. The "vocalist" speaks through a theremin, and communicates by lunging into the audience, slamming into people & rolling around the floor. They are ear-bleedingly loud & have a half-dozen TV's onstage showing clips of sci-fi cheese, horror movie footage, porn & confusion. By the end the TV's go flying into the pit where smashing glass flings wildly, people beating them with baseball bats, concert ending with the rank of smoldering electricity

The Amino Acids are disciples of the Church of Subgenius, the faux-religion that Devo had a heavy hand in. J.R. Bob Dobbs is their savior, except he is the prophet of Slack. Dobbs is a door-to-door vacuum cleaner salesman from the 50's. His prophetic declarations run in circles & the logic adds up to: *"Do what thou wilt just don't be an asshole, 'cause everything is one big joke anyway."*

The leader of Subgenius is Rev. Ivan Stang, who beget it in the

1970's. Amino Acids had him come to Detroit at their annual "Subgenius Devival," giving sermons in Slack-Pope regalia...

Then you have the Koffin Kats, who are now one of the biggest psychobilly bands on the face of the planet. In 2009 they are a household name & staple to Greasers kids.

Today they are on tour 300 days a year, but back in 2003, Vic Victor was our pompadour king & riding his stand-up bass like a surf guitar. The Koffin Kats jammed the most creep-tastic boppin' rock with that raging punk edge, laying down tunes like a Frankenstien Chuck Berry...

Or the Bump N Uglies, the notorious punk outfit that runs the IWR (*Independent Wrestling Revolution*). Bump N Uglies are the "rock n' wrestling" champs & have their own league which has brought names like Jerry "The King" Lawler & "Hacksaw" Jim Duggan into town.

They perform in tights and their shows end in brawls. Before the last song is played contenders from IWR jump onstage and drag them into the pit where chair shots are taken, body-presses slammed. They were banned from the State Theatre for putting someone through a flaming table covered in barb wire...

Rubbermiilk Orchestra, who first had this quasi-Droogie visual aesthetic then morphed into a fly-by-night, fuck everything whirl. The bassist was the lead, this maniac black dude from South Chicago that could go head to head with Les Claypool.

I've never seen anyone play like him – this slap-bass, post-punk, proto-trash blend. He'd go under different aliases, sometimes wearing wigs or suits, or just football jerseys; he was 27 & had 6 kids. Behind him raged a thick wall of experi-noise somewhere between late Black Flag, Daisy Chainsaw & Primus. Screeching dissonance, merciless in its application...

And then MAN Inc, who went on to become a European sensation. MAN was a one-man band – a guy in a suit & tie venting with a beat-red face. He had a bass & a kick drum only. His lyrical rants were total Bill Hicks action...

Then you had the Juan Valdez Love Machine, which were the ultimate in Zappa worship. They were astronauts of the Mike Patton galaxy surely, but their ensemble was vegetable obsessed, funky, heavier metal parts chimed in with a punk edge. They'd go the full distance with costumes, pranks.

I sent their album to Alternative Tentacles around this period, and 4 years later Jello Biafra wrote me an email wanting to sign "*us*" long after they'd broken up.

When I told Juan Valdez about it, they said to lie and confirm it was my old band so I could try and pawn A.K.A. MABUS off on him. Never heard back, but at least I can say I helped them make Jello's personal record collection...

The roll call goes on an on – The Farley's, The Impaler, Motor City Burgers, The Jollys, 45 Cents, Vietnam Prom & countless others. Neil keeps feeding them all to the public because Downtown Brown won the lucky lotto draw after playing the Hamtramck Blowout fest. Metro Times (*Real Detroit's competitor*) awarded Downtown Brown one free year of advertisements – 52 weekly blocks to promote whatever the hell Neil felt.

At this point he's making a mockery of it, sending in pics of squirrels with slogans like *"The Coalition Owns Your Soul."* Neil abuses it so fanatically it's the last time that gift is ever doled out...

***August 2003, and the nightmare bus depot with corn blue ear-muffed Wendell is but a turgid footnote in frigid history. I am now a porter at a Ford dealership, running around a car lot the length of a football field every day.

Whenever a vehicle needs to be summoned, I hop inside sweat box interiors, searing my flesh on the leather contours of driver seats. By early July, every car is a scorching 110 degrees of a hotbox womb...

When I broke it to the bus depot management that I was quitting for a porter gig, they looked at me as if I were insane. *"Give up 7 days paid vacation??? You fuckin' crazy?!?"* They'd long turned on me anyway. It took months to find a job, and this gig isn't such a grand payoff. Still, I can reenter the daylight & go to concerts at night – the point of my existence. My coworkers are now rocker mechanics, or hard-drinking country boys.

Earlier one of the mechanics shouted for me to get in the back of a squad car some cop had brought in. Once I hopped into the containment back seat with its steel grating he just drove it to the back of the lot & parked it, trapping me inside a cell on four wheels.

He came back 10 minutes later, laughing his ass off, then threw me the keys: *"Take it for a spin, just don't tell the boss."* That was weird, cruising a squad car around Woodward Ave & watching the drivers in front of me get shaky, glancing in the mirrors nervously, like I was going to pull them over...

My days at the porter gig are spent on my feet, or idly standing by the garage doors where I have a little metal stand that I can hide newspapers. The boss is scum. The original guy who hired me was replaced by a mean, ugly, self-loathing orthodox Jew. He looks like The Penguin but is 6 foot 5 with a lumpy cellulite ass, scowling face & beak nose.

Anything an employee can take delight in he's banned – newspapers, computer solitaire, music radios. He's shortened breaks, changed the dress code, makes everyone work extra hours, keeps firing people erratically.

I get to drive customers around in the parts van and rock out to death metal, the only thing that really keeps me here. Once boss man caught onto my freedom he grumbled arctic bird noises & jacked the CD's. When he looked over the Monstrosity album with the demon skull & burning pentagram he became unnerved.

When I was napping in my car during lunch break, he actually woke me up to complain about a too-close parking job. He pointed hatefully & grunted: "*I can't even stick my dick between 'em.*" He waddled off fuming with half man, half penguin swagger…

The other porter I work with is an old Jewish guy who has a really heavy gay vibe, or just some creepy sexual thing going on. He used to run an ice cream store for 30 years before retiring. He's a total pervert & talks about fucking his 63 year old girlfriend all day, the wonders of Viagra. He got my phone number through office paperwork and now he calls me at night, just to talk about pussy.

One lady came in, saw him & started bawling tears. She went into a blind panic, and collapsed at the customer desk. She told The Penguin that she hadn't seen him since she was 6 – that he'd tried to drag her into the ice cream vault to sexually molest her. She ran away & never told anyone, harboring this awful memory. She was positive it was him, beyond any doubt…

It is at my little metal desk, ducking The Penguin, when I can barely wait to clock out to go see The Stooges reunion at Pine Knob. As I'm humming "TV Eye" the power in the shop goes down – even the emergency lights don't flick on. The salesmen are perplexed, because their cellphones aren't working either. The radio is inoperable static, the street lights on Woodward dead. The televisions don't work; even the battery operated break room one with rabbit ears brings up snow…

The bearded, disgruntled NRA guy from the service desk gives me "the eye." He's a Rush Limbaugh fanatic & carries a machine gun in his trunk. We've been talking about al Qaeda's recent threats all day, how they've declared Americans will soon know what it's like to live in Baghdad with primitive conditions devoid of power, heat, electricity.

NRA guy gives "the nod," punches the clock without informing The Penguin, then heads for his fortified compound.

Everyone is on edge with that same vibe of 9/11 – eerie calm, clear blue skies. Driving home there are snakes of cars wrapped around the gas stations, even though they can't siphon a drop. People hound liquor stores & supermarkets, the animal impulse of survivalist consumption.

I make the apartment & the only thing working is my telephone land-line. No one locally can be dialed – even my New York contacts are stifled.

I find an office number for a metal label in Washington State. The owner tells me that something is seriously wrong, that the entire East Coast is down. There is a live CNN chopper broadcasting a building in Manhattan on fire, and early reports claim car bomb-like explosions outside nuclear power plants.

That sinking feeling creeps in my blood, and the phone-line goes dead. This is not any kind of normal shortage. Radio towers do not die; satellites do not fail. There is no such thing as a blackout that takes down half the United States. There may seriously be a series of nuclear meltdowns. I am instant Mad Max with nothing to show other then road flares, a bowie knife & a quarter tank of gas...

I borrow the neighbor's bike & roll down to the Phallus House, which I assure you, is not a gay bar. Phallus is a band (*kind of*), and Jesus The Anti-Savior is like their Captain Kirk. Jesus is the republican protégé of Kurt Cobain.

I think the heartless capitalist conservative talk is mainly to create a stink, because at bottom Jesus believes in nothing. His IQ is Lex Luthorian, and no matter what you say, even if he agrees with you, he'll aggressively refute it.

He talks like a used car salesman, pitching abortions & wars. He thinks America should plunder more, incite more wars, 'cause raping the 3rd world like a slave plantation is beneficial to him.

Christ gets his martyr-like glow from his chin length, blonde surfer hair & finely groomed goatee. He is still entombed in the Seattle whirlwind & claims Nirvana is the greatest band in history. His living room is draped in Melvins, Soundgarden & L7 posters, Red Wings & Tigers paraphernalia; the lamp-shades are covered in coat buttons & animal bones.

His girlfriend has a hazy Courtney Love vibe & wanders about in a rag-patch skirt, writing letters to Kurt Cobain's grandpa who she befriended years ago.

Phallus aims to be the best/worst band of all time – this raging, screaming, dissonant horror intertwined with The Beatles. Phallus have only played live twice & cleared the room on both occasions. While Jesus perverts the Fender, Krooner dabbles the bass & their drummer stumps along with down syndrome finesse.

The Phallus house is their practice space & home quarters. It is also the HQ of a diabolical project which is so secret it doesn't even have a name. Jesus is the Fuhrer of this agenda – to absolutely destroy EMINEM by any means necessary.

For months now they've been trailing Marshall Mathers – pranking him, vandalizing his house,; leaving lewd phone messages, picking through his trash...

Everyone hates Marshall in The Phallus House. True, he may have *"mad skills,"* as they say, but the beef is in the raging forgery of his background and disgusting nature of everything he represents. That he mutated from mullet & Judas Priest shirt (& *Juggalo*) into a durac-sporting tough guy 50 Center is beyond laughable.

See, he was cool with that Priest shirt. Early on, he was funny & clever. But when he started pistol whipping to flex his rank masculinity... *now you're fucked* – now Phallus is gonna ream ya.

Had he just stayed a Doctor Octagon imitation, no one would have came out against him. There are always the haters of success – and Jesus is no stranger to finger-pointing, ludicrous hatred – but when EMINEM erects a Ponzi Scheme of capitalist triumph based on deception, delusion & fraud, you're damn sure he's got it coming.

Jesus & the boys began their campaign by making 200 fine-print invitations to a fictitious party at EMINEM's house on 32 Mile, promising a full bar complete with dinner & a personal performance so as to welcome his new neighbors into the Mathers family. They mailed these letters to every house for a quarter mile within the vicinity of his mansion, hoping to turn the entire neighborhood of rich honkies against him.

The Phallus armada began stalking Mathers studio, slapping gay rainbow stickers on the entrance. They glued plenty to his Escolade, making sure that everywhere he drove in war-zone Detroit they'd know he secretly begged for cock...

They left trails of Twinkie wiener sandwiches around his compound, hundreds like Hanzel & Gretel in cold blooded revenge for his arrogant treatment of Weird Al. Over a silly edited fake interview handing Marshall a Twinkie with a hot dog in it, EMINEM threatened to assault Yankovic. What kind of douche would beat up the creator of *UHF*? A colossal one, that is – one who should be driven from his home by peasants with pitchforks & torches...

Phallus started their drive-by water balloon campaign on this recording compound, nailing all of D12. Next they stole an 8 Mile street sign & glued it over the 32 Mile one to make sure he felt more at home in his rich white person neighborhood.

Best of all, they spent $50 on giant packages of M&M's and dumped them in the back of Marshall's Escolade on a scorching summers day, ensuring that the gooey treats would melt all over his leather upholstery...

Following week, Jesus heads to a dive bar – at the counter is Kim, EMINEM's ex-wife – right after Marshall pistol whipped the guy he caught making out with her too, then had to pay the guy off in court to the tune of one million $$$. Well, Kim was there at the bar, and Jesus knew it was her for sure having obsessively studied her pictures like a world class assassin targeting a hit,

So Jesus wanders up with his handsome blonde surfer looks, starts hitting on her, buying her drinks. She's playing with his hair, all about it, closer to sealing the deal.

Kim goes to use the bathroom & then Jesus, in a moment of humanity, remembers his girlfriend. Love defeats the demon, and Jesus walks out: *That would've been the kicker huh? I could have totally fucked his wife – just rammed it right up her ass, hahaha! That would've been the cherry on top – to drive up to that 32 Mile mansion & scream: 'Hey you – yeah you, fake whigger piece of shit – I just fucked your wife up the ass!!!'*

I roll up to The Phallus House and Stew Goat is in the front yard. He is a nuclear engineer of sorts and says that there is no logical way the power could shut off to this scale. Says all initial reports indicated car bomb explosions & a time-line of events that don't add up...

The radio towers kick in with generators, but there is no answer other then Marshall Law. Anyone caught looting would be sentenced to 10 years in Federal Prison. Locals hang out on porches, speaking frightfully. Bin Laden is on the tip of every tongue.

Jesus, consequently, is in jail. There was a rivalry with their neighbor who wanted them evicted. A few weeks ago they'd all gone to sleep, and were wakened by a mad beating on the door – flashlights & shadow figures peering through windows. They knew it was the cops, but refused to answer & called 911 on them.

Jesus did the emergency line talking, saying burglars were at their residence. The cops showed up to find other cops outside, and both parties knew the punks were in there laughing at them. Still they never opened the door no matter how hard the pigs beat; the neighbor apparently called in a noise complaint.

Earlier today Jesus went to court smug & knowing all the legal loopholes. He represented himself in court by writing down a series of numbers that annihilated his case.

The judge was infuriated. As Christ sat grinning, the judge broke the law anyway, dismissing his legal mumbo jumbo. Then the cops trotted out the supposed 911 call, which was heavily edited. It was a blatant frame job and Stew Goat sat befuddled as Jesus was carted away by laughing pigs.

As Stew Goat & I decided over a definitive course of action, Jesus rolls up on a bike. He'd sat in the cell all day long while his jailer kept apologizing for the set up! The cops thought it might be a terrorist Armageddon and they let him go prematurely! Not without a future court summons that was illegal and eventually dropped.

Two days into The Great American Blackout and no answer why any of this is happening. Looters are in the supermarket, pick-pocketing everything. The roads out there are dead...

In Jesus's backyard it begins raining heavy. Sticky & stinking, I wash myself with rainwater in my boxer shorts as the hate-filled neighbor gazes from a window with unrepentant fury. I make sure to take an extra long time washing my leather Cheerio pointed directly at his window.

BAM – the power resumes. Jesus is convinced he is going to prison, packs his bags & runs to Colorado the next morning... Later that night, I attend the *Bubba Ho-Tep* movie premiere and meet Bruce Campbell. Not much else to add except the strangeness of surviving a possible terrorist Armageddon & who is there to greet you at the finish line but Ash J. Williams himself?

Days later, al Qaeda claims they took down our entire power grid & cost the government $10 billion dollars over $40 bucks in car bomb fertilizer. They claim every country involved in "*The Coalition of The Willing*" will understand the plight of the Iraqi people, and what it's like to be reduced to the Stone Age.

One week later & all of the UK goes down for 3 days in the worst blackout since the Luftwaffe raids of WWII. The next week, Spain goes down for 6 days and abruptly leaves this "Coalition." The next week, in the USA, 4 men are arrested on 4 different flights armed with box-cutters.

No mention in the press anywhere except Drudge & my column in Real D. And as a result of freaked out readership, editorial formally strips my Chief Political Correspondent entitlement...

Coach Snake Rides Again

It makes me wonder how much of my life, at least subconsciously, has been spent in the Zombie Apocalypse. I dream of reanimated cannibals more then I do of sex.

Uncle Ron says it's healthy. Everywhere he goes, he also envisions having to pick them off – how best to secure the house, the finest weaponry choices, contingents Alpha thru Omega…

Uncle Ron knows everything, just like Claudia. We call him "Ronstrodamus." We pose conundrums both on stage and in casual talk which no Aristotle archetype would dare confront.

"*Uncle Ron,*" says we, "*If 15 SS officers are spinning grapes to the soundtrack of wolf howls, how many placentas strip the plutonium of dyed red pistachios?*" [I'm actually texting him right now for the response, and…]: "*Iran's nuclear test facility.*" BRAVO!!! Well done!

Uncle Ron is also referred to as the "Polish Charles Manson." He is large & commandeering with a thick black beard & long hair. His shabby wardrobe is of torn D.A.R.E. shirts, untied Caterpillar boots & cutoff denim shorts.

He is an irrepressible, towering mammal. He cradles his backpack like a prize possession, and it is always filled with pixie sticks & Crayola markers. He is like a deranged adult child whose development was stunted by LSD.

Ron gets frightened by too many humans at once. He masks it through a cloud of pot smoke, and when feeling threatened grips his old high school ID card for luck. He always carries it, just in case he might ever "*need it.*"

Uncle Ron is missing 6 years. From age 7 until he started eating acid at 13 – this period is a blank. The last thing Ron remembers is sitting at the dinner table with his family.

He was eating green beans when he watched Turok from *Troll* 1985 creep across the hall. Turok stopped to acknowledge him, then continued into his bedroom. Ron left the table without a word, and Turok was waiting by the closet. Troll slipped into the darkness of coat hangers, and young Ron began following, closer & closer…

Next thing Ron remembers is being 13 years old & tripping on acid in his basement, eating blotter up to 5 days a week over the next few years & repeatedly watching *Troll, A Million to Juan & Killer Klowns From Outer Space*. He got neck-deep into Ween, Frank Zappa, slowly morphing into one of the most technical bass players I've ever known…

Ron's dad perished about the time of the Troll amnesia, but his psychiatrist attributes it to possibly being an extraterrestrial/inter-dimensional life-form communicating to him based on the child's psychic language of familiarity…

Like Clownbaby, Ron is part of the alternate dimension Detroit if I'd never left. He had an audition for A.K.A. MABUS the very day I threw in the hat. Now he is the bassist of Downtown Brown, of which I am Coach Snake. All 4 of us live in a van for 5 to 6 weeks at a time. While the boys shred their set, I hound the merch table.

I have been nearly everywhere in the continental United States with them, minus that stretch north of New York State. Some bands are professional entertainers – Downtown Brown are psychedelic mad-dogs distributing confusion.

Despite the rigorous attempts of internet & magazine promotion, the fan-base consists of random freaks that have done way too much acid. They come out the woodwork & drag us to strange homes filled with cabin fever castaways.

We are not a band – we are speed-freak Argonauts sailing black tar. We just completed a 4½ week tour, our second this year. The last show was 9/11, in Pontiac, and I had nowhere to go afterwards except Stoner Joe's. That's why I'm stuck in Michigan.

The thing with touring is that reality becomes malleable; your daily existence is held hostage by random draw. The gigs are always there, but the real adventure comes from the secret ports of promoters & allies who wave you in like landing aircraft. It's always random, and many times the air is thick with bizarre hostility…

The only constant are your traveling companions, who in this case are Neil P (*Grandpa*), (*Uncle*) Ron & Danny Glover (*Cousin Don*). Glover takes the wheel in between bouts of "*emergency dating*." He is 22, bespeckled, drinks like a fish & has the shroom appetite of Syd Barret & the perversion of 30,000 Vivid Videos.

He makes an excellent onstage fake tranny named "*Daniel Nova*." No one got the Jeffrey Star reference though, so Glover morphed it into "*Macho Sledge: The Hetero Hammer*."

Glover's childhood was spent committing random acts of creepiness – he was the klepto king, an arsonist, and just as freakishly adamant about wandering into unlocked homes just to have a *look-see*. He is the advice man for all romance matters. If something is immoral, you can't count on him to high-five you from embracing its sheer thought. His enjoys researching serial killer pathology & reading the works of Kurt Vonnegut. Blame him for all the Billy Pilgrim references…

**The tour earlier this year took place Feb 22nd to March 27th, 2009. I had spent all January licking my wounds from the Anticlimax Leviathan of 2008 – just isolated in Seattle, waiting for summer when I could travel again as a freelance journalist.

The economy had melted with the collapse of Wall Street, and the idea of seriously starting a new band with long-term, die-hard ambitions midst this background of financial chaos seemed not only futile but absurd.

I wanted out of the computer-hypnotized writer guy life, so I'd made one final push to sort out all my loose ends. I spent a week revising contact & email lists, then dug through every scrap of paper I'd saved with phone numbers, emails, etc.

In the final pile of notes a tiny slip of paper fell onto the carpet – a MySpace profile link, written in cursive. Quite literally, my last "loose end" before leaving on tour was to hop back online, add whoever it was then run out the door for Detroit.

I'd been at Greyhound less then two minutes when a shaky black guy asked to bum a smoke. He was going to Grand Rapids, three hours north of Detroit, which meant I was in custody of him for the next two & a half days. I didn't mind so much, seemed ok... *until the Jesus stuff.*

He'd recently witnessed his best friend blow his head off with a shotgun, and now he was going to the dead-center of Michigan to sit in a field for 3 weeks of praying & fasting because the longitude/latitude was perfect to channel the light of the holy ghost. He believed it to be the center of the world...

He started talking about the Great Spirit filling him, and how together we must fly across the land upon that magical Greyhound spreading the gospel of Jeebus. The bus would in fact sprout congregations; our unity would flood God's glory into the heathen vastlands. I said I needed to use the bathroom then vanished through the back exit, taking the last bus home...

I parted the next morning without hassle. The first smoke break was Tacoma, and I was three drags in when she made herself known. *"You know, when you said you lived on these things, I didn't think you actually meant it."*

That Snake Plissken quip was coming from the MySpace girl herself. She'd short black that was hair frayed & frizzy & red & white scarf wrapped around her neck.

I immediately thought she was the Japanese foreign exchange student I met from the prior ride – that long run with Dr. Jeremy Sullivan during the freak snowstorm. I asked her if she still had the digital photos of our trip, but she stared at me blankly.

No, this was not the Japanese girl but someone else altogether; an Irish/Black mulatto I met on the bus nearly a year ago, which makes the next bit downright creepy.

See, there is no way possible that the little torn piece of paper with her MySpace link could've been situated in those notes. This particular girl – I'd met her in Billings, Montana 9 months prior, when I was first moving to Seattle.

Her name was Holly Doom, and she was nerdy & pimply back then – a high-schooler deep into metal with very few friends. We spoke for a quick 20 minutes before her bus shipped out. Now she was 19, clear-skinned, full-figured & a pinprick away from exploding into unbearable, scorching hotness…

This was divine, because there is just no way it could've fallen out a paycheck stub from last month…

I explained to Holly Doom the peculiarities of this absurdity. Stroking our fingers beneath our chins like college professors, we debated the conundrum. I told her, *"There must absolutely be a reason why I am meeting you, after all this. There must be a clear definition of fate, of some grandiosity hanging in the balance. What could it be Holly Doom?"*

We locked eyes & lunged at each other & camouflaged by a quilt as we made it on the backseat. I never had sex on a Greyhound, let alone sex with a black girl, let alone sex while driving through Idaho. No one seemed to notice or care, save for the toothless old woman with the cowboy hat who pretended to sleep, smiling with one eye partially slid open, just smiling, smiling at purity…

Barely a week later I was on the road with Downtown Brown, and we had narrowly evaded home invasion charges. In Louisville we met the ex-bassist from The Necros, that legendary Ohio punk outfit from 1978. He offered we crash at his place, and we followed him home via the freeway.

He pulls into his garage, and we take a moment to finish the blunt we'd been passing. Barreling out of the van, Uncle Ron & Danny Glover began pissing on the lawn.

We get our duffelbags & blankets, all 4 of us are trying to break into the garage, the side door, muttering things like *"I know they're in there."* Yet as I fuzzily look into the window, eyes blurry from drugs, I see a middle aged man cowering behind drapes, frantically calling the police.

In our confusion we'd trailed the wrong car home. We actually stalked a family to their front door in a white molester van – these sweaty, hairy men on drugs trying to barge inside their house under the cover of night. Pissing on their lawn, eyes glazed from drugs... We fled with Olympic speed and as we hit the freeway ramp 12 squad cars flew into the subdivision, lights & sirens wailing. We sped off laughing senseless...

The next night in Tennessee I shaved a Mohawk into the head of a mother of two, and the following eve we stayed at the apartment of Lynard Skynards' keyboard player.

By Friday, Feb 27th we'd been booked at an LGBT art commune in Little Rock called "The Lazar Pussy." It was a massive Old South mini-mansion venue with nothing but Cowboy BDSM images hanging on the walls. Cocks everywhere, leather caps & Big Bubbas' in denim overalls...

Overnight we'd went from gay land to the Rockstar Bar in Fort Worth, where a mural of Troy Aikman riding a buffalo in full Dallas Cowboy get-up was hand painted. Which, if you ask me, was far more homo-erotic then anything from the previous night.

The Pantera guy crowd weren't digging it; we sold nothing, packed up fast & gunned for Norman, Oklahoma where our crust punk clan had set us up in 15 room, 3-level mansion – the infamous Fortress Andromeda. We slept in 30 degree temp watching our breath like dragon steam. By morning we'd dumpster dived a feast...

48 hours later we crossed the Hoover Dam and into Albuquerque, where Beefcake In Chains front-man *(& occasional porn actor)* Steve Eiland let us stay at his house.

On Steve's desk was a CD case from the son of the guy who painted the Guns N Roses *Appetite for Destruction* cover. His father/artist had recently died, and the son made classical CD mixes to ruminate over his father's life. I sat embracing them; stoned, darkly transfixed on this private current from the skull-headed-crucifix-GNR master...

10 hours of desert later we popped "Hotel California" in the CD player as we crossed the state line, entering the West Coast universe of tropical slop. LA was a messy affair, a small backyard party show & a 4 day "vacation" which equaled a money pit.

We recorded with hip-hop artist WAX in his studio & made use of our buddy's medical marijuana card, stocking up on Strawberry Kush & Blueberry Randazzle...

In Austin Texas, Billy Milano *(from S.O.D.)* cooked us pancakes; at the Alamo they told us the basement had been moved to the attic. In New Orleans we arrived just in time for St Patty's & played for gumbo swamp kids who were break-dancing to DTB's groove. Tallahassee was a nightmare – the "Meat Castle," as we dubbed it. It was an open-sky bar called Bullwinkles, built like a King Kong bamboo holding cell.

A $7 cover fixed you endless free booze, and they'd arranged for DTB to perform an all-cover set for $300 in front of all these white hat, scumbag jocks & artificially tanned women. All forms of dirt-bags between 21-50, force-feeding college girls booze like sheep in shameless, sex-a-holic rampage. We sold not one disc & had trouble even giving out free bumper stickers...

The last gig before Detroit was Greenville, North Carolina. It was another anarchist space called THE SPAZZ HAUS. Kenny stood out the most, like a disheveled *Beetlejuice* in his mid-20's carrying around whiskey jugs he'd nonchalantly stick his dick in & start filling with piss. It was so common that no one would even acknowledge it, circles of 30 in deep conversation just ignoring him as he piddled away...

Saint Marvin

Zelda is handcuffed to my bed, laid naked upon an American flag. The room is dim save for the flickering of candlelight, her eyes blindfolded taut. Like a human tapeworm her tiny body wiggles in slaughterhouse ecstasy...

I am the peak of Aries, the ram gone asunder, breathing fire like a dragon. Like a Tzarist saber I wield a 10 foot electric dildo with 12 alternate speeds. Beneath the jelly tip whizzing like a dervish are a stretch of pearls encased in thin plastic. They wriggle and bounce, spinning 180's & 360's. The jutting cusp works as flickering tongue, pinching the clit & thwacking it delicately at several hundred horsepower. I will tune her as Pep Boys does the engine of a Trans Am...

In person I am shy, awkward with women; in the bedroom I'll strip naked at the drop of a hat, work on them like a surgeon. There is nothing I won't do – there is nothing I won't let them do to me. *I am a monster, but I will forever be their monster…*

With Zelda I am the bleeding wound of love stuffed with salt and lime, rainbows & cocaine. She tells me everything, hides nothing. She is the most beautiful creature I have ever laid my eyes upon, a faerie person with delicate wings tip-toeing through Armageddon. She sprouts flowers with her toe-taps like mother Gaia on radiation-caked knoll...

I have been waiting two long weeks for this moment – 14 slow-motion, dark trance days writing frantically, calling obsessively. It is the last stand of Fiji, and if I don't capture her now I shall lose her forever... Linda told me that all you need to fix any relationship is "*2 hours and a pair of handcuffs.*" Well, why not 5 and the finest reefer, wine, pizza & beef stroganoff? Why not a lavish, romantic assault of licorice, *El Topo*, banana muffins, Glen Miller, *Julian Donkey Boy* & *1999: The Bronx Warriors*?

Zelda's not getting away this time – not after two years of incessant boomerang. She'd been bouncing between her boyfriend & I this entire time. They break, she comes to me. She disappears, they are happily reunited. Or she just plainly cheats on him…

2003 has been dominated by her figure. Once Lana took the plunge, we clung together with magnetic force. The first portion of the year was spent with her on the weekends, but soon she started drifting. It's no longer clear the sequence of events, except her on/off again boyfriend came back around. Not that it had ever stopped us before...

It was the 13th go-round, I think, when I'd called her after a great deal of silence. It was approaching November & boomerang boy had moved to The South. I was tired of playing the games, ready to commit, for in Zelda I saw the crucial velocity of my life. She was my partner in crime, the jester to my crown. Had she made a big enough stink I would have married her on the spot.

So when I learned she was about to run away to California with some guy she'd just met, I exploded. She'd been with him less then two weeks – this dread-locked doofus convenience store clerk that was a *hardcore Juggalo.* So square, so L7 – *sooooooo fucking LAME.* Every inch of his body covered in Joker's Card tattoos, his vehicle splattered in Insane Clown Posse decals.

Was I, the KlownFührer of Demon City, to lose the love of my life to a putrid bologna minion? In blind vertigo I thrashed my apartment, beating my fists into the floorboards until the skin punctured & bled.

I totally unraveled, throwing myself uncompromisingly at Zelda. I was a non-entity at the porter gig, rushing to the locker room every 20 minutes to fill notebook pages with dread & despair. I'd pace around the lot talking aloud as if Zelda were present, trying to *feel out* the future conversations.

I made no attempt to rationalize myself to my co-workers, and they all thought I was talking to phantoms. They began chatting amongst themselves in hushed tones & freaked glances…

Zelda, on her own part, stayed the distance. She knew I was flying off the handle. Her non-committal back & forth of phone banter helped none. The verbal yo-yo – telling me all about him, talking about us. No definition. I was just this demon in a hole on which she poured gasoline, snickering with a lit match in hand. She kept me on a leash frothing like Cerberus, hot with volcanic carnality. If I were to lose her, I'd completely lose my mind. The countdown was on – come Friday she'd be *MINE*…

I awoke like a samurai primed for the showdown. I sketched my own Kama Sutra improvisations, since those manuals weren't hardcore enough – *The Indian Ariel-Barrow, The Full Frontal Lobotomy, The Nagasaki Leg Stretch*. I went to the leather store & picked the most over-the-top beast of a vibrator available – handcuffs, jellies, blindfolds, the works…

After I dropped the last customer off in the work van, I was called into the office and fired without explanation. The Penguin nervously coughed & looked fearful, like I'd go postal & start firing bullets. I grinned & gave Oswald Cobblepot two thumbs up, leapt out the office & rushed to my car. I cranked the engine & flew…

I flung the car to the roadside & dialed her number on a pay phone. She wasn't answering. I took the freeway towards her home and once in range stopped at the convenience store where ICP guy worked. The schmuck was at the counter.

I slapped down a dollar asking for change, and with every bit of psychic fermentation stared through his soul: *"You have no idea who I am, but I'm about to gut your girlfriend like a trout. With the brute strength of a gorilla I will give to her the orgasm which is so apocalyptic that it will forever end the need to fuck again."* He shakily filled my palm with quarters, vaguely registering that my madness in fact had some random thing to do with him...

Zelda was drunk, trying to squirm out of it, but I wasn't taking no for an answer. Next thing I know she's in the passenger seat, and I'm driving her to vaginal doom. She's struggling to stay awake, telling me that I saved her life. That if I hadn't threatened to walk away from her eternally, she would never have quit snorting heroin, and that she loved me more then life itself... You're not getting away – no, not this time. You are mine mine mine _MINE_...

**Lana is no longer part of the davenport, commenting on absurdities. Zelda is not stretched out on my bed, flipping through lingerie magazines. I cusp my ear to pick up her reverberations, but no one is describing the page-by-page play of the pretty girls. The apartment is cold & empty; I am howling to the gods of literature...

It is said that no writer completes his first masterpiece until the age of 25, unless you are Rimbaud or Lautreamont. I am the freak anomaly, the spacious vector where all things collide in mute panic. Married to the computer, intimate to none but an ocean of black java, again I am severed from the human world with no conception of time; cold as Antarctic hop-scotch, calm as a tri-centennial redwood...

The screaming phoenix has left me shrapnel. I hurl across the galaxy in all directions without center, without grip. I've been up 56 hours, pushing out 60 pages in one blast. This book is my autobiography as much as it is a letter to Zelda, as if by cataloging my wealth of experience in one frantic outcry I could make her understand – that I could somehow complete the job in a few weeks & lob it in her direction like a missile of information. That she would rip apart the FedEx package, gobble it whole, wrest herself from those putrid Juggalo arms & flee back into my tormented clutch...

As if any living woman actually works this way. As if any letter of desperation in history has had that effect. Once a woman seals her affection to your advances, you can claw at the walls for eternity but no amount of slashed fingernails so much as adds up to a Hallmark card in return. And we all know the golden rule – *that the best man never wins.*

This book I now write actually began for me on September 13th, 2001. The first line: "*I now stand motionless before a vast audience of none; a theater of tragedy thrice-removed from mankind's base conception of malicious irony.*" It had been gestating since birth, but it took trauma to unleash. Zelda had confessed to me her secret heroin lust & I stumbled onto to the porch in shock, gazed into the night sky & told god if he had any balls to bring on the apocalypse. The next morning, planes were flying into the WTC…

I wrote off & on for the next few months, combining it with years of completed annotations & minor passages. The skeleton was comprehensible but the task was daunting. I set it down when I ran out of juice & waited for the right moment to finish the job – the perfect death sentence to purge finality…

That spiritual dismemberment has now arrived. It is December 2003 and I am attempting to convey *the whole man*. With every line I get closer to completion, only to unearth 100 uncharted directions. I cannot fail in any vein of communication – no character must be left one-dimensional, no subtlety overlooked. Expansion, contraction, distillation – a marriage of heart and action, a myriad web of fates…

I've been holding off of resurgence into economic life. I have just enough saved to make rent, to keep the coffee supply on hand as well as a cupboard of soup cans & noodles. Even if I were to nab a job, I am in no state to make it work. No one hires a soul in November, and the Detroit employer is squeamish of the neurotic...

{...*DRUMROLL*...}

MOO-HA-HA! Fortune reversal! I now qualify for a glorious unemployment – *26 whopping weeks of $250 tax-free checks!!* It's called M.A.R.V.i.N [*Michigan's Automated Re-employment Voice Interactive Network*]. See, you get hooked into an automated system that you can only access from one specific number. You have to call once a week, go through a number-punch system, answer a battery of questions, and then you get the automatic mail-out.

It's intentionally set up as haphazard mess so if you hit one wrong button wrong they sever your pay immediately. The system is rigged unless you are crafty enough to maneuver it.

I was set for the full haul, but I still had to go through a half-dozen M.A.R.V.i.N. calls before the first check was even sent out. If I could somehow push 12 weeks of zero income, I would have a check sent out for around 3 grand with another $2,500 to follow.

With the scorching cost of living, I had to find something under the table. I began by posting "leaf raking" ads at hardware stores, but that was useless. I called sperm banks but I did not have a college degree, so no one wanted my dunce jizzom. I entertained the notion of being a male stripper, but I just did not have the physique. I contemplated selling grass, but my friends had better connections.

The last customer before getting axed at the porter gig was the owner of a taxi company. He explained that all his guys were snakes & could use a clean cut kid like me on the crew. After he laid out the perks, he slipped me a business card. He got out the work van, then leaned in.
"What did you call your boss again kid?"

"The Penguin – you know, like in Batman."

"Haha!! Damn straight!! Fuckers got a beak nose n' everything!! Guys a real motherfucker – I've brought 'em $1000's in business now, n' he still treats me like a nuisance. Well I got no problem stealin' that sunuvabitches best man."

If I've ever been a sucker, it's always been for positive reinforcement & praise. Which is why that very man's business card has been sitting on my desk for over a month now, just beckoning me, just awaiting the right amount of insanity it takes to accept such an offer. And if there's any one thing I've always excelled at, it's making horrendous life decisions on a spontaneous whim...

Blank Dice & Blind Prostitutes

The law of karma portends that all reversals of fate come in a series of 3 – in my case its perpetual maelstrom.

Last week I was stuck in the boonies at Stoner Joe's with no food stamps or dumpster diving spot, no public transit – just walking to Wendy's & living off a couple $1 hamburgers per day – back to Ramen & black coffee, "The Detroit Diet."

Now I'm being handed my old life back a thousand fold – if only I can STOP.

Clownbaby knows I'm writing a 500 page epic in which she is a star. She really doesn't know what to make of me, honestly, but I see through her with x-ray vision.

When we collide it's like two cabin fever isolationists thrust together with centrifugal force. She writes & says she's about to dump her boyfriend, lists a comprehensive analysis of why – the main jib is he's symbolic of some abstractly incestuous relationship with her stepfather.

All men sucked into her trapezoid are symbols of bizarrely wrong infatuation. Everything about Clownbaby is tinged in the language of rape, cancer, insanity… I love her as no other, but will never reach her.

To her I am some transient therapist, a near-imaginary friend she partially wants to erase. I shatter like glass before her; had I the power, I would kill everyone who harmed her…

Whoever it is that calls, it won't be Clownbaby. I know this because she is impossible – because she is the ultimate woman and therefore has to be...

At the end of her missive she mentions hanging out with someone whom inspires her greatly, that in lieu of this she may attempt to write her own book, which in any sane world would win the Nobel Prize. Her writing is that of a child, yet in person her dialogue is earth-shattering. Her pronunciations are acrobatics – astonishing feats of linguistics that Dostoevsky would give a testicle for. In one paragraph she unravels the codex of all…

Stoner Joe leaves for his 5 day camping trip & drops me off at the bus. 3 hours later I arrive to West Dearborn where I nab my stepfather's Dodge Skylark from the auto shop. I then head to Ferndale where I'm to rendezvous with Kaitlin (*my high school sweetheart*). The plan was to see *Public Enemies*, the film with Depp as Dillinger. She is incapacitated with stomach problems & I go it alone, even though the movie starts in 10 minutes.

I decide I'm already late, so why not get some drive thru burgers? I make it to the theater and the only guy in line is a staff writer from Real Detroit Weekly.

I slipped by but then trotted backwards in a slow motion crawl. Immediately he jumped on the subject of me coming back to work for them. They just fired their music editor, and despite having no contact over 4 years, I was somehow a top-shelf candidate…

4 days later I'm in editorial meeting with the publisher, unveiling my presentation. Not that I really want this job or to stick around Detroit, but I go through the motions anyway.

They were fairly bowled over by my digital/print combo scheme – an army of interns running around with video cameras, filming shorts for a multi-pronged web-cast. I dubbed the project "Detroit 2010."

In the end, we'd unveil a 3 hour "best of" comp-reel at the local art theater with a great hullabaloo. Vastly impressed, they claim they'll be in touch by the end of the week…

It is 6 days later now, and I've yet to hear any word – which means they are seriously considering me. The publisher is apprehensive yet still encircling the bait. It's like Vince McMahon bringing back Hogan's N.W.O. – desperate times breed bold decisions, and slam-bang flashy trumps in the end...

**It is Sunday night, the 4th of October. I just spent an hour on the phone with Sage, a long lost pal from the Rave era. In 2002 she'd fled to The Bible Belt; I hadn't spoken in 7 years.

One of the first things she says is *"When I tell people about the way were, our crew, no one believes a word of it. These people think they partied hard in their youth, but then I tell them about trash bags full of ecstasy pills & briefcases of Special K, everyone thinks I'm a pathological liar..."*

The last I remember of Sage was hanging out after she'd broken up with her long-term boyfriend. She was single and interested, since I was the only one in our rave crew who was basically a punk rocker at heart.

Sage wasn't some toothless, grim crusty by any standard. She dug on Rancid & Dropkick Murphys, had the cliché stars tattooed on the elbows – no anarchist warrior by any means. It was that crushing elitism which drove me from Sage way back when.

She was gorgeous, of course, but I never made a move – she didn't dig metal, was neck-deep in pop punk & Jesus Christ.

But here now is Sage again, unbelievably gorgeous Sage with her narrow face & cold blue eyes, that short blonde-dyed hair. She is heavily tattooed, single, twice divorced (*from the same husband, no less*), working as a bartender in Raleigh.

She is through with America & taking care of a second DUI before jumping ship to London where she has 4 family members with duel citizenship.

They are offering free rent and a base of operations to whoever she brings along. She is ravenous, seeking to hire me like Rambo for a mission up hostile Cambodian waters. There is now a lengthy fault in the concrete of Fortress Europe…

The question of Sage defines the digital conundrum of our era. Imagine the gallant knight galloping his trusted steed, rightfully earning his fair maiden through bravery and heroism.

He slays, he conquers, he vanquishes dragon & human foe alike. He bows before her simplistic in his adoration. Her beauty is all defining. She is a symbol, a prize – a classical epoch of a more basic formula…

But what if said knight were privy to our current dimension? What would he say to the fairest of maidens if as he galloped forth towards her castle Blink 182 were blasting from the elongated tower? What would Romeo be reduced to, had Juliet clutched the reigns of Facebook to spend hours digressing only the most banal of household chores? What should Gwynnivere morph into if aided by the rapid-fire communication of the Blackberry?

In a magical world Sage would've been my fair maiden in tragic repose. I would gallop towards her, stallion raging & sword unsheathed, ready to decapitate any aggressor upon her purity…

***It is Sunday, October 11th, 11:03am. Stoner Joe & his girlfriend cook breakfast that fills the house with thick smoke. Obama won the Nobel Prize, Black Dahlia Murder debuted 45 on The Billboard, and one of the physicists currently trying to rig the black hole in Switzerland was arrested by Interpol as an al Qaeda operative…

Despite formatting the C: and reinstalling everything thrice, this monster Trojan is still ransacking my laptop. I type five words & the cursor shoots midway through some random paragraph. The battery reads 949 hours & 12 minutes…

I'm jumping ship for North Carolina. Sage says she'll have somewhere comfortable but it's still a 6 month window for departure – I'll have to work full time & she has a 90 day DUI sentence.

I've no wish for Raleigh, but if I stay in Detroit I'll never get out. Stoner Joe's would be $400 rent a month + utilities, and then tacking on cell, food, gas, leisure – even if I worked 60 hours a week I'd only be saving $200 per month.

Fate has handed me back my old life, the supped-up version of it. The remnants of SASQUATCH AGNOSTIC are moving into Stoner Joe's, converting my current room into a recording studio.

Real Detroit Weekly wants me back. The trailer is now a mansion. I have a new car, free of charge. The Theatre Bizarre is in full swing. If I stick around much longer, I may get the girl back...

Yet is completely meaningless, a dogged farce. I am intentionally aborting the life I once so struggled viciously to achieve in order to expatriate myself to France.

I look at all with final eulogies, prepared for the next freight out of Dodge. My fate might as well rest in the hands of a complete stranger, because for all intents it does. *Say la vie mon petit Clown-bay-bee, like a heartsick banshee into the great unknown...*

Just Another Motor Rumbling The Motor City

The thing I most remember is the steam of black coffee hitting the frost-thick windshield, melting small patches before the defrosters axed the rest. The second was the smell of the taxi cabs, that gas station deodorizer liquid. The third was Jim Reeves off a warped cassette. The 4th was a guy named Lumpy Paul.

He'd sling right in the backseat like a Dalmatian on a Sunday cruise. Half-puckered lips barely restraining the drool slobbering from his misaligned jawbone, this ticking time-bomb of human loneliness would gyrate with choppy movement. His impulses didn't quite reach the nervous system as quickly as before, when his skull wasn't a fiberglass mesh screen mingled with recyclable plastic.

20 years ago – and a week before marriage – Lumpy Paul attends the 1984 World Series. With Detroit as the new world champs, Lumpy Paul gets in his truck piss-drunk & hits the freeway. He's blasting Skynard free as a bird, zipping down I-75 when he spots this patch of fog.

Confused, he speeds up, then at 90mph slams into an overturned semi truck that's leaking the chemicals which are causing a vaporous, poisonous mist. Like seat-belt deprived crash test dummy his face shoots through the wheel straight into the dashboard, smashing his skull & breaking every bone in his body. Half his teeth come flying out with his right eye, leaving his brain totally exposed. The doctors are amazed his heart continues to beat.

Lumpy Paul goes into a predictable coma, and the prognosis is that if he ever does wake up he would be a vegetable cursed with total paralysis.

Miraculously he snaps out of it 9 months later, regains 70% of his motor function through intense therapy, and is reconstructed piece by piece like a polyurethane Lee Majors. Ever since, Lumpy Paul has traveled to high schools telling his story & preventing teens from jumping behind the wheel plastered.

Paul is surprisingly sharp for his condition, but tells the same corny old jokes: *"Did I tell you about my dickydoo award?"* And of course I grit my teeth & remain polite, even though I've heard it 40 times. Not that I have anything against him, but AAA is picking up the cab fare. Just like the rest of them – this assorted legion of burn victims, paraplegics, amputees & worse – there is no chance of a tip out. Medical slips are static, and the asylums never slip a $10 spot. As a cabbie, the tips keep me alive. Lumpy Paul slurps back saliva, and out it comes: *"My Stomach sticks out more than my dickie do."*

As a fledgling Cabbie you were soon introduced to facets of this employment never before imagined. Since there is little money in picking custos (customers) off the street in a bleakly impoverished metropolis such as ours, your pockets were lined from insurance companies or the judicial scams.

Lumpy Paul is a prime example – he paid for the premium insurance, and they were legally bound to assume responsibility for everything. But with capitalist health care it's cheaper to taxi patients from hospital to hospital then it is to call an ambulance. About $900 cheaper on average. *Which is why I'm the guy mental asylums call when they need to transfer insane people to other insane asylums.*

My first day I was paired up with a burned out old cabbie who was told to show me the ropes. He'd no intention of giving me the secrets of the trade; this company was rife with sharks circling the same dispatcher. They all hustled, they all pulled low-blows & pick up other's customers when they caught it off the CB.

We went to Kingswood Asylum on 8 Mile, buzzed the intercom, and like a prison the barbed wire gates rattled open. Armed guards blockaded a series of doors unlocked by buzzers. In the waiting room the receptionists hid behind bulletproof windows.

As we wait the old cabbie explains how he hates driving these people alone. About one time when even though guards were present to hold back a violent patient, the woman got free & started beating the shit out of them in the back seat. When a guard tried to tranq her she pried the hypo from his fingers and tried to stab the old cabbie as he was blasting 75mph on the freeway.

Tells me about how he had to chase and tackle a patient attempting to escape. Tells me about driving dead silent maniacs that had enacted Micheal Myers scenarios. Tells me about how his wife just died of cancer, how hard it is to wake up alone after sleeping next to the same warm body for 30 years. Tells me he might just park the taxi one day & sign up for a Kingswood vacation.

The guards haul out a woman in a straight-jacket that isn't so blatant, but it is what it is. This middle aged woman, frantic, was like an obsessive compulsive that always needed to do some chore – such as scrubbing the toilet over & over & over. The guards discreetly explain she might piss herself, so I have to put a stack of newspapers on the seat. She keeps asking about her cats, where are her cats, she has feed them, they aren't safe without her, she just needs to get to her cats and everything will be fine.

The company has me go solo at noon. They toss me the keys to a 1992 Lumina with 228,532.1 miles, and off I go jamming classic rock & old-school Motown (the *only way to roll in a cab*). I only had a few gigs that first day, carting around hospital outpatients.

Later on the hospital called on me to dump off an enigma, since she was babbling incoherently. They didn't know what to do with her, didn't know who she was. but in her pocket was an address.

I drove off and began asking her questions, but she was mentally insane. Like completely gone, babbling in dementia. She didn't know who she was or where she was going. I took her back to the hospital. They said there was nothing they could do, and she was now my legal responsibility. They essentially said *"tag – you're it."*

It was so inhuman, so undignified. Throwing a crazy old amnesic woman obviously eaten by dementia into the street to die. Even worse pinning her existence on me! I took her to the address on the mysterious paper, and luckily someone was there. Sheer luck.

It was in spite of the ugly character of our gangster health system that I got so attached to playing the role of the good Samaritan – the noble cabbie with a gold mission. I was centered on guiding the wayward souls back home, like the ferryman on the River Styx.

It seemed that the days I tried to make money I'd walk out with $50 or $70 under the table after a 12 hour shift. When I'd just do the work of karma, I'd bank – or just fail miserably. I'm not manipulating divinity assumptions here, but 70/30 isn't bad odds.

My income intake was based on our sliding scale payment. Here's the basic racket – you "lease" a car and "pay" for the insurance with a percentage of your overall day's intake (*the book*). The more money you make, the more they gouge – but at a certain point you bust through their scheme & start to make the big bucks.

The scam ropes you into a full 12 hours. The cab company pays for the gas and they have no claim over your tips, though you do have to report a minimal amount like a waitress. Even though you are under the table & "renting" their cab, they still have to report earnings to the government. But for some reason they do not have to report your social security number because you aren't a real employee. Just some weird loophole they exploit.

Also, the cab meter isn't accurate, nor is it recording anything for them. They never have a clear idea of what you've really done. If people pay you with credit card you do not swipe it in anything – you write down the numbers & hand them a receipt.

Keep in mind this is Cab world before GPS & I-Phones, so you had to have a street map & memorize your shiznit. Being a guy that would drive every inch of Detroit as a hobby and knew most suburbs like the back of my palm, I was made for this hustle...

Due to the weird rules with the book, the first day they screwed me. I worked nearly 10 hours, and I somehow owed them $12 bucks. I was pissed, but they assured me that I'd bank tomorrow. I should never have gone back, but I was hooked. It was the sleaziest, most fucked up & dangerous job I could ever dream of.

Well, come back I did, walking out with $120 cash. The next day $100. the next $65 – it was scattered. I could go home with $40 bucks, sometimes $200. Overall, I was making about $400 a week on 4 days of work, and plenty of time to complete my secret literary masterpiece *To Live & Die on Zug Island...*

In cab world I am the master of the River Styx, covering the asses of poverty. The hospital dumps this ghostly, white-haired black woman off on me and I take her to the trailer park where Stoner Joe lived.

She got out of the cab in her open-back gown, floating about like a phantom. She had no money, she didn't understand what was happening. If I took her back to the hospital the vultures would just toss her back into my cab & tell me that it was my responsibility.

When a trailer door finally swung open, I was relieved. The guy was obviously broke, so I drove off without demanding the $40 bucks owed... *One man is released from ER having been shot twice in the chest & once in the head. Miraculously he is fine and goes home free of charge...*

Another flags me down on 8 Mile – he is mad, babbling a frenzied tale of his wife being murdered, his child kidnapped 7 years ago, something like that. He just needs to get to Pontiac & I oblige, and he continues muttering to himself, at intervals either weeping or communicating with Satan...

New Years Eve & I am cruising through the dead zones of Detroit on my way to Kluck's house. Zipping down I-94 I'm about left-lane it onto the rising split freeway of I-10 (The Lodge) so I can hit I-75 South & short cut to Melvindale.

As I get on the turnpike that's hoisted 20 feet into the air I'm blasting 70mph towards a smashed car that is blazing away on fire dead in the middle of the thin highway corridor. With the flick of the wheel I dodge the incendiary roadblock & zip past a concrete barrier. Another of 9 lives down...

Kluck's party is raging – Onyx is with some punk rock hoodlums from his trailer park, one of which is this crusty chick with liberty spikes. She has a crush on me, but she is totally gross. For a month I've been deflecting her hideous flirtations. To seductively lasso me in, her first instinct was to relate this story about how she'd deep-throated a human turd. Even Kluck wouldn't touch her.

On the other couch is a girl I'd never met – quiet, shy, artsy with finger-less striped gloves & a night watchmen coat with the furry blue lapel. We hit it off quick. This was Mandy. She soon came to visit me in her busted up van with the legion of figurines glued to the dashboard.

We got cuddly, and her stomach had sagging skin. She was once hugely obese & starved herself rapidly. I took her to Thunderdome II, everyone liked her. We disassembled weird toys and glued together pigs & crocodiles. We drew pictures, sliced up advertisements into strange collages...

Deeper into Detroit I ventured, further into the wastelands. I began having visions of a book I'd write called *The 120 Days of Sodomoski* – the woeful tale of a Motown cabbie who was a sexually repressed orthodox Jew. His arranged wife leaves him due to a loveless marriage & when driving his cab to a make-out point hilltop intending to put a bullet through his head.

As he blindly fishes around for his handgun on the backseat floor he instead finds a copy of Marquis de Sade's *120 Days of Sodom* that a random customer left behind. He reads the first few lines, then blasts half of it. His life's calling discovered, our forlorn character launches into an erotica rampage in which he's then rampantly fucking all of the mental patients he's been carting around.

Eventually he impregnates one who just so happens to be the niece of an Italian mobster, and finds himself in a shotgun wedding with La Cosa Nostra. This leads to colossal hi-jinks, climaxing in a bloody crossfire with territorial invading Yakuza & the Ukrainian gangsters running his cab company...

I was horny, if you couldn't tell. And reading The Marquis with ever growing fascination, feeling like a man who's scrotum was about to burst. I entertained this absurd notion of an asylum dating service on wheels, this swingers club of paraplegics, this multi-sexual bathhouse of burn victims and amputees...

Ethel though, "The Man Eater" as the dispatcher called her – she was burnt crispy like Freddy Kreugar. She had insurance taking her for skin grafts but the rest of the time she was having drivers chauffeur her for groceries. Not because she needed food, but because she had crushes on them. She was so lonely. One day when she called for me to chauffeur her around aimlessly, I didn't bother to charge her anything...

Mandy comes over. We watch *Twin Peaks* together. We cuddle on the couch. We eat breakfast for dinner. I am happy.

I get dispatched to a brain surgeon that has a patient under anesthesia on the operating table – he's forgotten all the x-rays & schematics at another hospital!! I break every traffic law one can think to defend this mans poor brain, dart inside the hospital, snatch the docs & zip out back to the operating room halfway across county. I zoom back in breakneck speed, park in the handicap spot, bolt inside to the surgery room, hand it off and... *motherfucker doesn't even tip me*.

I think it may have been the day that started off with me driving the 16 year old Juvenile delinquent to her court ordered drug awareness classes, the one on the tether that was trying to get me to fuck her in the back seat. I'd picked someone up to bring him to an auto dealership, and the cab rumbled like a Romanian space shuttle.

I dropped him off, went back on the freeway then at 65 mph the front tire just flew off. I skidded perfectly onto the shoulder, cars zoomed past, and I watched the tire roll straight down the highway...

I knew it was time to quit, but I was addicted. The signs were screaming loud as they could be. After all, I didn't need the money – the promised unemployment of Saint Marvin was to come any day. I resolved to hang up my love affair with the meter.

It was early February, and I was taking a physical therapy patient to her appointment – this fat black lady that was mangled in a car wreck & had a jigsaw spine. She must weigh at least 250 lbs.

I could barely think of much else that morning, other then the fact I would finally break the curse of Black Valentines, since I'd never had a girlfriend let alone a date on that lowly holiday. It was always something – a tragedy, a nightmare, some black hole I slipped through. But now I was with Mandy; I would win this time.

We pulled up to the traffic jam on the freeway – at least 50 cars were idle because of an accident. As we sat there with talk radio on the dial, right-wing meat-head disc jockeys finally admitting our nation had made a very serious mistake in Iraq – I felt that deja vu tingle. Everything screamed "*jump out the cab – now*." Instead I tensed up, gripped the wheel, then heard the skidding tires...

They say that your life flashes in front of your eyes right before you die. Somehow all I could envision was myself playing spades in a smoky room.*

!!!WHAM!!!

It happens in slow motion. I feel my shoulder blades crack; my ribs slam into the steering wheel as the cab accordions into the next car which hits two more ahead of it like a row of dominoes from the sheer force. I fling back, nail my seat, bounce back directly into the airbag which opens too late & explodes in my face.

The fat black lady, like a tsunami of brown sugar, cannonballs into the back of my seat with all her inertia, cracking my spine once again. She ping-pongs around the back seat & hits me twice more. I snap out of the slow mo – the dash board is smoking, the car might blow up. In shock adrenaline I get out the car, stumble around. Cab is wrecked...

A driver who fell asleep at the wheel had rear-ended us doing 70 mph in a Volkswagen Rabbit. A guy from the cab company shows up to handle it, because there's no insurance or registration in the glove box. The cab people take me away, and I don't even file a police report. Still in shock, I drive home. I lay down on my bed. I go to sleep...

The pain wakes me, like needles in every spinal vertebrae. Like I've just had the shit kicked out of me by the entire cast of Monday Night Raw. I can barely move, I can barely walk. I can't go to the hospital, because I'll be put in jail for scamming welfare. Just stay down, just rest. Give it a few days. Everything will be fine. Saint Marvin must never know...

Four days later, I'm still a wreck. The pain in the middle of my back is so bad I can barely walk. I drag myself like a cripple to the mailbox and in the pile of CD promos is a check from Saint Marvin.

I rip it open – $2,250 dollars & another $1,250 to come with weekly $250 checks!! I start belly laughing & fall to the floor, rolling around the piles of mailings as if I'm a shipwrecked man being cast a rope from the yacht of the Swedish bikini team...

I cash the check, get EMG pickups installed in my Ibanez & swoop up a full guitar rig. I call the cab people and tender my resignation and eat a hearty Middle Eastern dinner of swarma & hummus & falafel & then pick up Mandy for a night on the town.

We go to the bar and she wants to dance to the jukebox, but I'm in so much pain I'm in a pissy mood sulking at the table. Mandy gets dark herself, feels insulted. Starts shouting & makes a scene. Wants to be taken home. I drop her off, we part disgruntled...

I don't talk to her for a few days, though I'm not thinking it's the end of it – I'm just wigging out on pain pills someone mercifully gave me, trying to figure out what to do with this spinal injury. Maybe if I just take it easy, just keep writing, it will all go away. It's not as bad as it was the first few days, it's... its February 12ᵗʰ, 2004, and in two days Valentines.

Mandy is on the phone, breathing heavy. She's crying, not saying much. I ask where she is – gotta force it out. She's at home; I ask if she wants me to come there. She's sobbing, takes a minute, then says to get there soon.

It's a 50 minute drive, dark and in the dead of winter. It's hard for me to turn the steering wheel because the pain is jutting through my ribs. It never stops radiating my upper torso, and there are sharp pains whenever I turn funny.

I pull up to Mandy's house, and her mom is bringing in flimsy bags of groceries from the car. Mandy is standing idly in her front yard, in the snow, in some other dimension, holding a bottle of half drank red wine as her visibly pissed off mother pays no attention. Mandy is completely disoriented & slides into my car.

I start driving, asking what's wrong. She doesn't talk. I start to catch on – *"Did you eat a bunch of pills?"* She nods.. *"And you just just slammed how much red wine?"* *"Second bottle..."* She gives me an ashamed look, a crazy look.

Then I notice the blood on her jacket. I grab the sleeve and pull it up. She's ripped her wrists wide open, and she's bleeding to death in my car. I start to panic. She won't tell me where the hospital is, I'm yelling at her, very angry: *"You don't get to do this to me – you don't fucking get to kill yourself in my car – fuck you, you fucking god damn, fuck, shit, fuck– where in the FUCK is the hospital!?!"* She won't tell me – she's trying to die, trying to make me suffer as I zoom through suburban streets at 50mph...

I fly into a gas station & the pump man points me the way. She's nodding out, comes to, tries to drink more wine but I grab the bottle & chuck it out the window. She's bleeding all over the seat, all over the floor...

I park on the curb & drag her to the reception desk as she fights me with dying strength. The medical staff rushes up and whisks her away. She gives me this final look as if I am a monster, as if I just killed her.

I go back to the Mercury Sable and calmly drive to the local band metal show. This band had been trying to get me to a gig forever, to write a piece on them. Because even though I've shut off the world for months, I am still the famous local metal journalist guy. I walk into the venue, re-assuming this stale role, and band guy comes at me with a demo.

Haunted, I explain what just happened, that my girlfriend just tried to commit suicide and I had to throw her to the vultures. Band guy stands there with the demo, unsure how to respond. I snag it & say I just need a second to collect myself, that his band rocks & I really want to be at this show.

I sit down on this couch and the band guy tells the other band guys, and soon everyone at the venue knows and they are all looking at me funny. The musical performance instantly cures me. I totally forget what just went down. I mosh around the pit with the other drunkards. We shout things like *"SLAYER!!!"*

Mandy's brother calls me. Says that she tried to escape and it took 6 grown men to hold her down. They put a mask over her face & sucked the booze from her stomach by tubes down the nose. Stitched up her arms nice & good, saved the day. Had I arrived any later, she would've died. Then the brother tells me exactly where she is...

I sluggishly climb into my car & drive down 8 mile, pulling up to the front gates just as I've done over & over as a taxi driving the crazy people around. The armed guards don't even ask to see ID – they all know my face.

Like my mom, like the bus depot g-thugs, the workers of Kingswood Asylum call me "Ryan." The receptionist thinks I'm there to transport a patient – they buzz the prison-like doors, and into the catacombs I go – horrifying corridors with chipping paint & bugs on walls, straight to the rec room for a scene out of *12 Monkeys*.

They sit me down at the long table where crazies are doing art projects & playing checkers. A man spills a stack of Doyle playing cards all over the floor. I help him pick them all up, but then he spills them again. I help again, he repeats. It's obvious his is his life – just spilling his cards, nearly picking them all back up, then spilling them again without any disruption of flow.

They cart out Mandy – she has white gauze wrapped around her wrists, brown with dried blood. When they left her alone on that first night, she tried to pull out her stitches to bleed to death.

Mandy sits down, smiling, She is so happy to see me. She puts her hands around my clenched knuckles lovingly. "*You came.*" "*Yes honey, I'm here. We're gonna make sure you get the help you need. I'm just down the street, you know. I can come visit you anytime. I'll make sure you are ok.*" "*You're not mad at me?*" her insane eyes, bubbling with love as if they are about to cry. That feeble, wobbly grin. "*No baby, its ok. Everything will be ok...*"

They buzz me out the doors & draw back the barb wire gate. I drive down 8 Mile with it's gray skies & grim buildings & junkie prostitutes & street demons that will shoot you for your tennis shoes. I pick up some upholstery cleaner & cruise back to 9 Mile where my apartment is. I park out front, go into my empty apartment. I fill up a bucket of warm water, pour in the orange cleaner. And then I spend Valentine's Day scrubbing her blood from the floor of my car...

A week later, maybe. I'm at this death metal concert – Severed Savior, Spawn of Possession & Saprogenic. Just trying to return to what I once was, just focus on extreme metal which never tries to slice it's arteries. The other night Mandy was released, and I told her I couldn't do it anymore...

Something about this show, this moment – I just walked out. I left mid-gig and drove right to Onyx trailer. He sat me down cause he had a serious question for me: "*Just tell me the truth, honestly... Are you The Devil?*" Onyx is borderline schizophrenic – he gets things into his head, the same as his wife. Both think I'm potentially The Antichrist, if not demonically possessed...

The punk kids at Onyx trailer shave my head into a mohawk & dye it blue. It's a sort of rebirth for me. I go home, spike the 'hawk with pomade, grab a bottle of whiteout & make myself a new t-shirt in crooked capital letters – "I

Hate Kid Rock."

I get an email from a DJ at the big FM rock station – loves my column & the reason they've been plugging European metal shows with big swooshing ads is because they were testing the potential audience demographic off the band suggestions from my writings.

The DJ says that's why they've been playing a ton of death metal on the midnight program, just to see what would happen and that the listeners were digging it. Says he wants me to guest spot, to host the show for an hour & play whatever I want – the biggest hard rock station in Michigan handing me free reign!

Days later I was live On Air & the show was a huge success – one of their highest rated broadcasts! Afterwards, people are regularly calling in to hear more Bethlehem! *On Detroit radio!*

The show went so well, in fact, that I was brought on to host the local band hour that following Sunday, and recorded a sound byte that continued to get airplay on one of the biggest rock stations in the nation: "*This is Ryan Bartek and you're listening to...*" I began funneling all sorts of local albums to them, getting very deserving bands in-studio guests spread out over the next year...

The storm breaks & I finish the book. At Onyx trailer we have another lead pipe duel but I break some kids finger by accident & he's rushed to the hospital. Once he's gone an awe-striking Aurora Borealis lit up the night. We lay on the ground as if watching the static on a TV, except it's green & magnificent, like the semi-truck possessing cloud hovering over earth in *Maximum Overdrive...*

**Clapping, clapping – the entire place, that is – all of Idle Kids packed with the roll call of brilliance that surrounded us in those glory days. Downtown Brown, the Thunderdome Crew, The Koffin Kats, The Amino Acids, the Theatre Bizarre people, The Coalition...

A standing ovation for all our hard work & the applause thundering the rafters. Mr. Will, the director of *DADBOT: The Motion Picture* takes a bow before the crowd. He gazes over to me with those same sort of bubbly eyes Mandy gave me, overjoyed that he's finally being recognized...

This was the debut of our first independent movie, and we let the 2 ½ hour cut roll projected against the grainy concrete wall. The EQ blared lopsided levels, the audience got the sarcasm without fail, and those who shouted like happy hecklers did so riotously...

DADBOT: The Motion Picture – all it took was 2 years, a $1000 dollars, lots of sweat & a hernia for the director. The rough cut, Mr. Will said, was 5 ½ hours long.

DADBOT I always described as "*The Walt Disney Family Film From Hell.*" Imagine a Saturday night made for TV movie, with kids in their full body pajamas, gathered 'round the old rabbit-eared analog TV set in the late 80's. The Disney castle logo begins, with its budding luminescence. The American audience of 1987 is revealed this sparkling world...

There is a scientist living alone with his son in the suburbs of Detroit, his wife having passed away. He has moved them to a new city to start fresh & has taken a job at a robotics firm. He's been working on a quirky, lovable robot with personality and his son just enrolled at a new high school.

The scientist soon meets his son's science teacher, and they hit off a quick romance & are soon married. The company the scientist works for, in typical evil corporation mode, want to use the robot for dubious purposes – whether it be military, or for sweatshop labor – and the scientist is wholeheartedly fighting their advances so it may be used for the betterment of mankind.

The full cast of stereotype characters are introduced – the fumbling next door neighbor, the Scientist's best friend, the local pastor, the doting policemen who travel to high schools teaching kids the dangers of drugs, the 80's tech vest juveniles that ride around their bikes like the mob from *E.T.* At the corporation you have the old executive, the sleazy hot shot that wants to run the department, the Chinese assistant, the military man, the sheik, the wheelchair bound money man...

After 30 lighthearted minutes, the Scientist is brutally murdered under confusing circumstances. While he wanders about holding his brain from spilling out his cracked skull, we see the flashes of his own thoughts midst his dying moments – chiefly violent explorations of his secret blood-lust where he is envisioning himself torturing and killing his own friends & coworkers.

Because he is so deranged he has to just suck the last of his torture thoughts out of his sick mind before everything goes black. The scientist makes it back to his car, his wife discovers him bleeding in the backseat then rushes him to the ER room. En route he dies next to the robot, his soul becoming magically trapped inside the machine (*maybe*).

The movie then becomes a cross between a silly comedy & a psycho-sexual psycho-drama in which this man – who may or may not be in the robot – is slowly trapped in hell & watching his life fall about around him. His son, who was forced to live with his own teacher after they'd gotten married within 2 weeks – is a rotten bastard doing very disturbing things.

He's also angrily dealing with his own repressed homosexuality, which he could not ever deal with before because his father was a Westoboro-style hellfire homophobe.

The film instantly becomes more about the sleazy corporate hot shot guy then anyone. Initially he' introduced as a villain, but then the film becomes instantly sympathetic to him.

We have to sit through a large montage of him having to deal with his mocking parents, his failing relationship, his attempts to run the department. The military man (*played by me*) is like a big idiot child & totally lovable, and that the military thing is really just a weird gay fetish because he's totally a Bear Cub playing dress up.

With the cops hot in pursuit of the killer, the lead policeman is having a nervous breakdown acting out the cop TV programs he watches in the most pathetic of all natures while his partner constantly berates him. It gets so bad he collapses from stress because Santa won't write him back, because he knows he stole his Uncles porno magazines.

Meanwhile the teacher is now plainly shown as an airy buffoon, involved in ever-enraging shouting matches with the son. After a giant fight, the robot finally comes clean that he actually _is_ his dead father (*maybe – it isn't clear if the kid is just hallucinating it all*). The sleazy hot shot hires the wacky next door neighbor (*played by Neil P from Downtown Brown*) to spy on them because he wants the robot & the kid won't give it up.

The neighbor invites the kid over and tries to persuade him to jack off together while watching gay BDSM porn. In the stacks of garbage on the floor, mixed in with hideous pornography, are bloody schoolbooks schoolbooks collected as trophies.

The silly next door neighbor is indeed a budding serial killer who's been abducting, molesting and murdering children through the neighborhood. It is he who killed the young boys father, though the son never catches on.

When hot shot realizes the kid thinks the robot is his dad, he uses a program to override the robot (*possibly freezing the dad in electronic paralysis*), thus using remote control to talk directly to the child & play up the (*possible*) myth that this robot really is his father in a very heart-wrenching, shameful power play in which his moral consequences come front & center in the anticlimactic finale.

By the end of the film, it is finally revealed that the scientist was trapped in the robot all along, and has gone completely mad stuck in this nightmare of his own creation...

We really did something epic here for shoestring that has never quite been replicated. The entire tone of it, the placing of ideas, the rapid fire alterations of the characters – yes, it had its problems (as all zero-buck B-Movie's do) but it was still incredibly effective & fun.

Reactions were always strange; viewers that "got it" didn't think they were "getting it," and complained about things they were interpreting correctly because they weren't used to ingesting this sort information. They weren't sure if they were supposed to laugh at times, which is what was intended.

They couldn't figure out what was comedy, and what was serious – which was the point. The whole thing was appropriately sea-sick & deranged – packed with so much between-the-lines info that the casual viewer hated it, while the film freaks totally dug it.

Because *DADBOT* had so much heavy gay commentary going on, it really alienated the general crowds. But Mr. Will made this film as a way to slowly lurch out of the closet. We did ok on the queer front, with a big write up in the local Detroit LGBT paper, but once anything gets that queer tag on it, it's thrown into a segregated cauldron & stuffed on shelves with pink triangle markings.

We started showing *DADBOT* downtown at this place called The Puppet Art Theater, a puppet show place run by Russian immigrants that little kids would get to travel to during field trips at school. It was perfect ambiance to tack on the childhood fantasy aspect before throwing them in a dark room to watch such an evil film. We had a handful show up twice a week, but ceased this activity after a few months. It was just so deep into Detroit no one would come – plus it was tough to find & even harder to park.

So we tried the film festival circuit but it was rejected because most would only watch the first 10 minutes then eject the VHS thinking it was a crap family film, not even bothering to read the press release.

Also Mr. Will wrote a messy press release that started off talking about the Scientist's kids' jack off room (*alienation at it's finest*). This ensured no one would so much as review it, especially since we didn't have a DVD for sale & there was no YouTube in existence yet to promote it.

One festival we did was in Oklahoma, this town called Muskogee. There were crazy showdowns with tornadoes, and a strange run in with the actor who played the weird naked Indian in *Wayne's World 2* because he was like the guest of honor.

The fest awards were rigged by this wannabe Hollywood producer though – this string-bean lesbian that made her own starring feature film where she was a karate hero.

There was heated exchange between our film-making groups at the high school across from the cornfields where we were brought to talk to the students. The karate lady was telling kids they had to buy $20,000 permits, and we were slinging the gospel of DIY guerrilla film making.

One of the kids pulled us aside & wanted to make movies, thought we were cool, etc. We told him to come Saturday for the big premier. Saturday comes, and we've got this tiny pull-down screen at a room in this college. A bunch of punk kids drove for 100's of miles to attend, and we ended up hanging with them that weekend.

Anyway, we start the movie to a capacity audience. Early on, everyone is digging it. But then the very second the scientist gets murdered, they start to filter out. Then the gay stuff, the swearing, the constant swirling abyss of doom. By the end of the film, there were like 10 people left – all whom gave a standing ovation.

I was standing outside the door towards the end. Before the lights went up, the high school kid rushed out the door without saying a word then hustled down the stairs. I walked to the balcony window, and I watched him run to his pick up truck, start the engine, zoom over the grass median, then fly out the parking lot...

I returned from Oklahoma only to end up on another trip, this time to Manhattan – my first New York excursion & playing up the famous music journalist guy thing. See, there was this band called Brand X. I showed them a little attention, and they pounced on me like crackwhore spottin' a nickel.

They were just some mediocre poppy rock band that sent me a demo, but then I met the bassist who was super cool & had just kind of joined them for something to do because he lived in the Styx & knew them from high school.

Thing was, he was bored as shit playing in Brand X, but he knew he'd stumbled onto a sweet deal that he wasn't quite ready to walk away from. The other two members of the band were the sort of guys playing strip clubs & "rocker" places with booby advertisements. They had fo-hawks & too much cologne & the cocaine thing going on. They also came from a band called BoringMcDoodleFace that were kind of like Primer 55 without any testosterone whatsoever.

Back in '99 they inked a deal with this huge label & recorded their debut album *Hit Play & Zzzzzzzzz*, which got a lot of exposure at the front counters of music stores all over Detroit.

The first week of release they performed live on this big syndicated wrestling TV show, and were set to head off on this huge stadium tour with Puddle of Creed. Thing was, with these "rock star contracts" the singers get like 60% of the money, because they are being groomed as future products more so then the music itself.

BoringMcDoodleFace fell apart bickering over money within a week because the singer wanted every dime he was legally owed after a 20 audience gig at some empty bar where they walked out with like $30 – and then they quickly blew the rest of their mega-contract advance on huge bundles of cocaine. *Hit Play & Zzzzzzzzz* tanked cause it was crap, but they were still under contract.

For some reason the moguls kept them on the hook & pawned them off on this hot shot producer who was starting his own label. So this new incarnation of BoringMcDoodleFace (*now known as Brand X*) were trying to woo me for press, and invited me to hot shot producers studio in Manhattan. *Why not?*

The hot shot producer (*who I keep calling "Rich Uncle Skeleton" in reference to a long dead inside joke*) was the real deal – and extremely wealthy, having produced names including Rod Stewart.

He also owned this 13 million dollar building we were staying at, right in the heart of Manhattan. What he saw in Brand X I had no clue. He was screaming at them to lose weight & be pretty boys like the soulless commercial advertisement they were.

He took us out to a fancy restaurant where everyone had suits. This huge bouncer at the door with his white ear-piece looked at me like the scum of the earth, with my giant purple mohawk & death metal t-shirt with the rotting zombie demon face & my cut off camouflage shorts & army boots all scuffed up.

The bouncer tells me to scram, but Rich Uncle Skeleton gets in his face and says: "*He's with me.*" The bouncer lets me in & we eat dinner at this long table with silk napkins & wine glasses & businessmen that probably hung with Mayor Giuliani – all hawking me like a dog spewing tapeworms...

I woke up the next morning and climbed onto the fire escape without my shirt on, purple mohawk dangling in the wind as much as plastic chunks could. From this vantage point you could see the long stretch of this intense Manhattan street jutting down 13 miles to the ocean like a road of hollow mountains, sun slowly rising like the nebulous of an atomic bomb. I kept thinking how most of The Third World would kill to be in my position, to see what I am seeing right now.

It was the sort of view men have dreamed of over a century when envisioning The New World – the infinite corpses of men who died on the floors of sweatshops just to harness for one moment this vision I could not allow myself to take for granted. Yes, I was grateful to see this sight – but it was even more fulfilling to know that no matter what this world could throw at me, no matter how many hot shot producers came forward or fancy dinners I was taken to, no amount of money could ever buy me.

More then anything, I was grateful that I was still young enough to slide down that fire escape of wealth & privilege and just cast myself into the mire of the ant people. To sit on porch steps drinking 40's with Brooklyn hoodlums, to bullshit with Arabian cab drivers; to volunteer for soup kitchens in Harlem, to play chess with old Jewish men in Central Park.

To get as far the fuck away as I could from all the Brand X's & Rich Uncle Skeleton's of the world & just go on with my happy day of feeding the pigeon swarms scampering like rats across those glorious, filth-caked streets...

I returned home to find Saint Marvin out of steam & willingly became a taxi driver again. I was a meter junkie; my back was still wrecked though. The pain reduced in scope, but sitting in a driving position, turning my head – the pinch was unbearable.

I started dating this girl that knew some of the Thunderdome crew. She was shaky 'cause always drunk – but a happy drunk, and real strange. She was a home care CSA – an end of life nurse, closing the book on a new client every week.

All this death surrounding her, yet it did not phase her. She lived in the same neighborhood & had this big white dog we'd walk at nights. She was really into Mike Patton & The Melvins; she'd dated this one guy for 7 years straight & had been single for a year. It didn't last long though, 'cause we couldn't hold a conversation...

It was a calm morning when the door knocked – Lana, first I'd seen from her in forever. She was beautiful – I'd completely forgotten how much so. Skinnier though, and with an even fuller figure. We went out to breakfast, and it was like old times.

We came back to my apartment, and I realized I didn't want her to leave. Really, all I had to do was flick my fingers and it would be willed. She wanted to stay right there, but had some new boyfriend. "He" was clearly not the two of us though. She got nervous, then bounced. She vanished totally afterwards, leaving me in nostalgic disarray. She'd be back, but in what form I did not know.

I couldn't help but feel this really was the woman for me, that I'd been a fool to cast her out. For a second I thought she was just going to move in again. For a moment, I saw a future expand that was gone again in an instant. I could have fought for it, but I didn't.

I never asked my parents for shit. I grew up poor, but my mom remarried into a little money – they were always trying to do stuff for me, but I refused out of principle.

My stepdad was a retired cop & 'Nam vet, a super right wing Reaganite, even though he knew the Iraq invasion made no sense. It was horrible military strategy, through & through. Still, no matter how much he hated everything, he cowed along with it 'cause of the Fox News war drum propaganda, same as mom.

They hooked me up with chiropractic & the doctor cracked the fudge outta me. I was lucid from the resetting; by the time I got home my muscles had swelled all over my body. I started hearing all sorts of chaos in the streets, people shooting guns. I thought it was World War 3 but The Pistons had won the NBA championship. Detroit went stark raving mad with jock testosterone.

I sat in bed the next few days. Although the doctor said "*just take it easy*," I kept squirming & cracking my spine 'cause it felt good. This was a really bad idea, because I healed funny. I ended up a jigsaw of new aches & pains – although at least I could walk...

Irish shows back up – a major character from my past. Back in '99, he was my right hand man – a kid from a broken home with a violent, abusive father. At 15 he was wise beyond his years.

Problem was this cop from my hometown hated my guts – this same cop was buddy buddy with Irish's father. After Columbine, that cop placed me atop the "possible shooter list" of Dearborn & was leading the witch hunt against those fitting my profile.

Piggy pig was gunning for me long before Columbine, 'cause he had a vendetta against punk & metal kids – and especially anyone with a Marilyn Manson t-shirt, whom he viewed as the ultimate degenerate scourge ruining teens of the nation. He'd first targeted my high school group in 1998, pulling us over without cause & searching us spread eagle against the van.

Graduating in '99 – being unmistakably the "Trench Coat Mafia" archetype – I personally felt the ensuing Columbine sting. My mom was nearly fired from her job 'cause the way I dressed, my (*former*) best friend & I were placed atop the police list of possible copycats, and I had cops parking outside my house at night – not to mention all the weird clicks & sounds on my land-line phone.

I'd a number of friends harassed by the police. Some cops shook kids down demanding info on me, street or pulling them over without provocation & searching them illegally.

Another friend had his car seats torn apart by cops who literally sliced into them with a switchblade looking for explosives or drugs. This harassment is ultimately what drove me into a more underground existence of night jobs &

reclusive public appearances.

While I'd moved onto an adulthood of full time blue collar, that same cop realized I was now hanging with Irish, who was in & out of mental hospitals for disagreeing with his parents' views.

They caught him smoking weed, found out he did acid & shrooms. The cop convinced them to export their son to this boot camp school in NY State where he'd have no contact with his family or friends until age 18. They locked him up & threw away the key, because he was my best friend – erased, as if he never existed.

2004 now, and Irish shows back up like a freshly-thawed Austin Powers. Like a resurrected person trapped in time, he wants to know is if Korn is still together, if Slipknot put out a new album. What movies should he watch? I take him to Blockbuster Video, but all aisles are now DVDs. This look he gives me...

Irish was still filled with visions of the apocalypse – always about 2012, about how the Iraq war ties into everything. He was always into Jesus, our big rub. And while we tried to bring him into our newly existing group, he stood back due to the satanic heavy metal stuff. Mostly he was apprehensive to seek us out 'cause he wasn't ready to confront who might be dead or in prison...

Across town, "The Coalition" blossoms. One of our main players on Detroit's East Side (*like Roseville, Grosse Pointe*) was Punk Rock Steve, who ran a notorious party squat called The House of Beer packed with bottomless kegs & underage drinking.

After the HOB was evicted, Punk Rock Steve got this bright idea to found a company called iamsickandtiredofwhitegirls,com – the joke is, well – it's just a funny name, and attention grabbing. He promoted bands through it, crazy pranks.

He'd have men dressed in full yellow chicken outfits handing out free t-shirts & bumper stickers at malls. Black women would stop and get their pictures taken with the chicken. This zany slogan properly offended everyone, even though most the girls that hung out at these events were, in fact, lily white.

Punk Rock Steve has this grand vision – the "Pimps & Hoes" party. He rents out this giant ballroom in Mt Clemens & the prank is such – all the guys dress like pimps in over-the-top get-ups & sling their hoes alongside them.

At the door they hand out all this fake money printed with a crazily grinning Steve as their mock President, and the goal of this party is to trade their dates to one another with this fake money.

To coerce the girls to play the prostitute part in doing all sort of bizarrely dirty things for this Monopoly money, in public, for all to bear witness. Punk Rock Steve actually flew in Ron Jeremy to be the grand master of ceremonies, so now The Hedgehog himself was a blood brother of The Coalition...

I see all the fake tanned orange women rolling around the floor like hogs, lifting up their braziers desperately & drunkenly grasping for wads this fraudulent cash. I watch them play tug of war over these useless dollar bills with their tits flopping out their scantily clad dresses. And then I see Steve looking right back at me with this insane grin, those raised eyebrows & I get the joke.

All these fake tanned orange women – none of whom are remotely getting the joke at all – all these awful, soulless, perfume-drenched pre-madonnas who can only be seduced by real greenbacks & never real truth or affection.

These human pigs are in fact ripping off all their clothes, going hog wild for these worthless wads of paper that are nothing but a fleeting status of retardation. Yet try as they may to win the day, to be the whore queen of this vile prom, there is no Benjamin Franklin on that Federal Reserve Bill – just Punk Rock Steve's grinning insane face...

Steve kept the whitegirls.com gimmick going for two more years, and threw a second sold out Pimps & Hoes in which he again flew in Ron Jeremy, as well as Bridget The Porn Midget. Then one day, for no particular reason – with all of the Detroit media completely buying into his scam & promoting him wildly...

Steve decides to commit career suicide. He attaches a photo of his cock to an email & sends it to every person on his email list. If I remember correctly, there wasn't even a message – just Steve grinning like a maniac with his big old floppy cock for all to see...

Punk Rock Steve is in Cambodia now, married to a gorgeous Asian surgeon. He's all fucked up from Multiple Sclerosis, and doesn't know how long he'll hold out. He's turned into the revered white man of the village, has all these Facebook pics with smiling children of the region who adore him like an immigrant Mr. Rogers.

He's working on a documentary to expose to the world the abuses of sweatshop camps & spearheading the effort to create a vast network of DIY Third World medical shelters.

Punk Rock Steve is a true living legend & noble hero – yet sadly Detroit will remember him as the guy who sent everyone an email of his big old dick. But I remember you Steve, I remember…

One funny story though, before I move on. One day Steve calls & says they are doing a big photo shoot for that first Pimps & Hoes party. Says everyone is meeting at the fountain at Grant Plaza, while the huge free rap festival is going on, as to prove to the people of Detroit that his website is not racist.

He's got a full page ads that will be running in both Metro Times & Real Detroit to prove this point, with all our smiling faces showcasing that it's just a goofy prank.

To cause a stink, I dust off the I HATE KID ROCK t-shirt with FUCK EMINEM on the back in big white letters. I spike up my blue mohawk & head off to the fest downtown.

I walk into the pulsating crowd but no one is at the fountain – and I realize every g-thug in Detroit is eyeballing me like they wanna shiv me – like all 20,000 people at this free event.

As I walk through these crowds even the cops are gritting their teeth, shaking their heads. I walk through a mile of voices shouting, "*Why you hate 'Em* dawg?' Why you hate 'Em?!?" & "I'll kill this cracker ass muthafucka" and all this & all that & just keep smiling, keep moving forward, knowing I'll be dead any minute...

I'm almost to my car when this group of like 10 black girls start yelling at me: "What the fuck you got against Kid Rock you motherfucker?!?" I turn around & shout back at the whole bloody lot of them: "BECAUSE HE RAPS IN FRONT OF A CONFEDERATE FLAG." And they all just stop completely, just dead in their tracks. The noise dies. All have this look, this dawning awareness. And the lead girl calmly says: "good point."

I get in my car & go to The Magic Stick, where I am interviewed for a music documentary called It Came From Detroit. I go home, relax on my bed, and then I get a phone call. It's some angry guy, yelling at me from the other end. I hear someone crying, and I recognize her tone – it's Lana, sobbing heavy.

The psycho boyfriend starts threatening me, the whole "you tryin na take mah girl?!?" babble. And I tell him, calmly, "Look man, I don't want anything to do with that crazy fucking lunatic, she's all yours." He stops, thrown off, then starts up again. I repeat myself, calm as ever.

And then like the black girls on the sidewalk, he adopts the same perplexed attitude. "Well, um..." And I go "Yeah man, fuck her silly – pump her full of jizz & shit out all the kids you want. Marry her, by all means, be my guest – I'll be your Best Man if you really want." And he's like trying to process it, and is like, "Yeah?!?" And I'm like, "Yeah man, all you." And he's like "Well... um... ok then." And the receiver goes: CLICK.

***Kluck is now living on my couch, hiding from the police. If apprehended he's looking at 2-6 years in prison. Years ago Kluck did 6 months for viciously assaulting a high school quarterback & his father with a baseball bat.

He was on smooth-sail felony probation until recently pissing dirty. Compounding the situation are 4 outstanding warrants his case worker had somehow overlooked and he never bothered to mention, trying to outsmart the courts.

I hadn't seen him in awhile. He was in the asylum, then rehab, then some other facility, but to be honest it's not clear the time-line of these detainments because from hereon out there were always so many that I completely I lost track.

Kluck's been neck-deep in heroin land for nearly a year. It's one thing to turn your girlfriend into a junkie – her cousin even – but now he shows up from total obscurity with Mandy, who is nodding off and having trouble sitting Indian style on my floor.

It was the first time I'd seen her since Kingswood & she was blasted, having shot up with Kluck. Scumfuck goes about his usual banter, commenting on Gorgoroth & Dying Fetus, totally oblivious to my dismay. That this would upset me never occurred to him.

Thing is Kluck knows he is a monster – he just doesn't care. It's all one sick joke to him. He is the clown of death, yet not a muse remotely appealing in his satire. He is a vile Pagliacci reeking the grim stench of spent needles & stale vomit. Passed out in human waste – gimmicks untouched & balloons unfilled – the children pummel his wasted cadaver with his own floppy red shows, berating his insolence. He is the opium Gacy that crowbar-pries your front door not to murder but instead continually shit in hostage mouths...

I'm not sure why I continue to shield him. Perhaps it's because I really think I can help him somehow & get my forlorn friend back. Maybe it's just because I'm still listening to all this GG Allin bullshit & want to play it up.

Maybe it's just because I'm not strong enough to say fuck off, or I just can't throw him on the street because, at least mentally, that would be calling the cops on him.

Still, I make him buzz off because I have a hot date. This girl I knew back in high school that always had the industrial freak look but was still on the swim team & got good grades & would've been a cheerleader otherwise.

But here we were in 2004, and still she was wrapped up in Trent Reznor and Marilyn Manson – just everything, all the time, forcing them into so many sentences and descriptions where they need not be. But she sure had legs & knew how to work them in the way only ZZ Top could describe. She was also performing sleazy burlesque at this industrial club nearby.

I knew it was over when we were riding in my car & I put on the classical station. We were cruising along with Beethoven for 20 minutes and she said: *"What is this?"* And I was like, *"Something awesome."* And she's like *"But we're... listening to... classical music."* It was over right there, then I gritted & inserted *Holywood*...

Next night we go to this industrial club called Mephisto's in Hamtramck – a classy 3 level ex-mansion with dance floors & pianos & live shows & full bars & this BBQ area where tonight there is an oil wrestling contest with all these hot industrialized goth girls & my new girlfriend is leading the pack. I should feel Mr. Lucky, 'cause every dark-apparel dude is gunning for this chick.

I'm outside in the BBQ tiki yard brightened by sharp red lights like a photo developing room. All of these industrial pre-madonnas are sloshing around in this tub of sex oil & my "girlfriend" is beckoning me to jump inside with the curling finger, laughing, laughing – they all are, all of them – all trying to suck me in like harpies, like sirens seducing studly to get soaked in oil while all these other gothy guys are standing around totally jealous.

But I look down at that rippling oil in the tiny inflated pool with Donald Duck & Mickey Mouse heads on the side & the oil is now crimson red from the outdoor lights and in my mind it instantly becomes Mandy's blood spilling out from her arteries.

The hottie goths are doused in her blood, dripping head to toe, drenched in suicide & despair – it rolls over me like a construction truck. Instead of jumping in with gorgeous vixens, this hallucination of suppressed anxiety overtakes me & I simply turn around – I walk out the exit, I just drive away. I leave. I go home.

The days pass, and I just kind of blow her off which leaves her confused without any resolution. Then all the other gothy chicks think I'm a raging asshole – I start getting all these looks at Mephisto's & Luna & City Club & no one talks to me anymore & their eyes read *"you broke our diva's heart – burn bastard burn!!"*

The smoking hot burlesque model with the shiny juggernaut legs moves to Hollywood. Within a week she becomes lead advertiser for one of the biggest strip club franchises in the world – keyed into LA power, hanging with Korn & Tool & Lemmy.

Any other man of my persuasion would've run off with her in a heartbeat. *Jackpot right?* Bright future amidst the golden boulevards of Melrose living gothly ever after? Yet all I could see when I shut my eyes was the fire escape at Rich Uncle Skeletons...

I quit the taxi gig soon after – it was too painful to sit like that anymore. One more bad accident & I'd be a cripple for life. I was once a speed freak freeway demon – now I was squeamish at even 25mph, trying to stomp on the imaginary break pedal of everyone's car while in the passenger seat.

The fat black lady from the accident got $250,000 in the court settlement; I myself am resigned to shoddy chiropractic quacks charging $20-$70 a pop. I live in screaming pain with a jigsaw skeleton that mimics a bowl milk-saturated of Rice Crispies – *Snap. Crackle. POP.* Such is my fate. At least until I escape to Europe where they have fancy socialist health care. I'll get there. I have to – Miller made it there on $10.

Kluck finally turned himself in, getting 6 months for all warrants combined. That night I'm contacted by this metal band called Dissonant from Northern Michigan that had just put out their debut, and they had this big magazine wanting to do an interview but they had no writer to assign.

They recommended me, the editor sought me out, and next I know I'm on the roster of AMP Magazine, one of the biggest in the USA. But I'm so jacked on pain pills I completely forget about the gig, and it never occurs to me to publish anything else with them...

Another weird night. 4am, I'm sleeping, then this mad full-fist pounding erupts on the front door – maybe some dope dealer that got burned by Kluck, or the cops with a warrant? Perhaps Lana's psychopathic boyfriend in a delusional rampage??

The beats keep going; I peek out the blinds – someone is crouched on my lawn, curled up into a ball. I grab this fake toy rifle that looks authentic in the darkness, swing open the door & point it – *"WHO THE FUCK ARE YOU?!?!?!"*

Candy throws up her arms, terrified & crying – this 23 year old girl I had a short fling with last year. She was kind of dykey, wearing cowboy hats & listening to nothing but Led Zepplin – the same songs, over & over, randomly mixed on 30 CD's...

Well, Candy was back to dating, and that night she went home with some indie rocker that lived on 7 mile. Maybe his nut-hugging jeans were too tight & it bottled up too much semen over the years of lame dress aesthetics, because he tried to rape her.

She wrestled him off & nailed him with a cast iron pan, then ran through the ghetto straight to my apartment cause I was closest.

After Candy tells me this story she calmly climbs into bed, clasps my body & starts bawling her eyes out. I stayed wide awake in early morning darkness, just stroking her hair.

Maybe we could be real this time. I gave her a ride back home, and she soon was on her way to Virginia to start a new life...

That week I finally inked a deal to put out my first book, *The Silent Burning,* by a small book publisher from Detroit. I'd been making stapled-together Kinko's versions & selling them for $5 bucks around town as *Abortive Pulp Manifesto.*

Long story short in 1998 I started a book of short stories, journal entries, poetry, etc that was like a diabolical whirlpool of *Naked Lunch, Eye Scream, Negative Burn, Downward Spiral, Catcher In The Rye, Howl, The Wall, The Satanic Bible, The Manson Triptych* & whatever other crazy, black-hearted, revolutionary nihilist gibberish I could cobble.

Elitist Publications was a small print label based in Detroit, and the young guy of the older money man was intent on dropping my unparalleled tome of hatred on the city. He swindled them into it, despite great apprehension.

It was a solid deal, a five year contract – just make the money back & then we go half/half with no other strings attached. All I had to do was get them the layout & we were good for a 300 print run in which I had final cut and was not monetarily responsible for advertising. They would pay for the ISBN code & legal jazz.

I had no illusions of it being any kind of success for at least 5 years of circulation anyway. So sign away I did...

Big Ocean // King Leviathan

There is a monster in Boca Ciega; it slithers black waters, this prehistoric serpentine. Eyewitnesses judge the aquatic demon to be at least 60 feet in length, bobbing from depths to haunt The Bay surrounding this quaint Florida Key. The locals – mostly a retired & elderly lot – have nicked the name "Bessie."

A 78 year old man was first to have caught glimpse of this black-skinned, whale-sized prehistoric eel. Every afternoon, beyond the fencing of his backyard, the leviathan submerged over rippling waters. With a HI-8 video camera, he'd caught it bullseye, and the local bike-riding pre-teen hooligans showed the geezer how to post it on YouTube.

Bessie soon became the terror of this tropical community, the hushed freakishness driving the misty streets vacant at night. Dead quiet it was, leaving nothing but purple/black sky reigning silent above luminescent homes which appear to be constructed on floating islands. Nothing but silence and the buzz of hydroelectricity crashing on the powerful Gulf shore beyond our subdivision.

Within weeks came the cryptozoologists. First the Japanese for prime-time Tokyo TV, then the Loch-centric Scots, some misplaced monster hunters & camera crews from National Geographic with their sonar devices, high-speed boats & technological rigs...

Not long after the kraken had arrived, I showed up as well for the Thanksgiving feast of 2009. It had taken 24 hours on a Greyhound to reach Florida via North Carolina, where I'd just sneakily weaseled from the grip of Sage. In Raleigh it had come to a point where even I questioned my repudiation of Christianity.

When you're surrounded by an entire population that believe in one nonsensical thing as undisputed fact – when they base their entire lives around it by attending prayer meetings, bible studies – you start to question your own logic.

Thus, I had to return to heathen, beer-drunken logic. Who else to turn but Linda? She'd protected me with safe harbor throughout my adventures of recent years. Drop into Detroit, come sleep on my couch – no questions, no demands. Drink my coffee, eat my leftovers, tell some jokes & entertain me – see ya again in 8 months. Cheery ho.

We go way back –, Linda used to live with Stoner Joe at the same trailer park many moons ago. That was back in 2003, right after she came back from her original Floridian escape attempt. Thing is she loved it – just existing on a boat somewhere deep in the South. After 6 months, for whatever reason, she just kind of floated back. Missed her friends I guess.

Was going to leave again shortly, but got stuck in Michigan another 6 years.

That's what Michigan always procures somehow – involuntary, social-driven prison sentences forged of quickly drained bank accounts. Once you pop your head back in, the drunks tackle you with card games of euchre in smoky beer-stink rooms, bonfires & weekly quasi-Thanksgiving dinners...

The black hole of Michigan & nothing to do but drink, drink, drink. And then you fuck it up on a rabbit-quick hair-trigger, so low is the drunk driving breathalyzer score that even a mouthful of alcohol based mouthwash gives you a DUI. What starts as a weekend vacation becomes a 2 year tether or halfway house scam where cops make you pay for every slice of "correction" they bestow upon your doomed fate.

And then you can never pay their charges 'cause no jobs & even if you find a gig it never pays enough & you get charged interest & they lock you right back up because you are broke...

This is why Linda finally lopped off the Midwest's head in a stunning, Olympian strike. One year with the new boyfriend & the common goal of escape had culminated in all of their possessions boxed & loaded without telling much of anyone, lest the hordes come with Euchre decks & whiskey.

As we packed Linda's belongings in the U-Haul her father – who has always looked at me like an absurd mooch (*yet finds me highly amusing anyway*) – dropped a $10 bet saying I'd end up in Florida not long after. With a big old grin, he declared that I would be there to mooch off his charming daughter within a month, at best.

I laughed at him and said "*never in a million years, Bub.*" Linda was free to live her life as she saw fit. If I was to head anywhere, it would be Seattle. I would freeze to death on the streets before I went to turgid Florida. *But then came The Bible Belt...*

Soon as they departed, I got dumped off at Stoner Joe's & began this book. Before long it was approaching winter, and every stronghold I had in America was in bad shape. It wasn't just the record-shattering sub-zero temperatures or record unemployment – no one had a spot for me. Usually it was no problem to find a couch or a floor to unfurl a sleeping bag, but all the main people I'd ask had either fallen through the cracks themselves or were already sheltering too many people. Everyone was borderline homeless & I was tardy to the party. In the end, Florida it was out of short term convenience, logistics, and curiosity of experience. As I walked up the long, winding path to Linda's new residence, I felt uncertainty evaporating with the blazing Floridian sun...

Sage's apartment seemed like another dimension. She'd secured the bottom floor of a colonial home across from the commerce center of Raleigh & by the college. It was a Southern slab of Americana –firewood chimneys & gutters clumped with orange & red leaves.

It hammered this classical "writer guy" streak in me, imagining myself in this Civil War-era apartment at a long oak desk & scribing Emerson logic in longhand form whilst intoxicated by the musk of fireplaces...

But then on the bus, on my way to find a job, I listened to a doting grandmother gumming slipping dentures. Quite loudly, without care, she jump-started a tirade against *"President Nigger,"* while her rosy-cheeked Americana family and Boy Scout kiddies laughed heartily, like a Family Circus cartoon strip, whimsically baffled by the insurgency of African-American politics.

I stepped off the bus to wander about, honing in to dialogue. Friendly looking white people everywhere and just behind their facade of civility lurked eruptions of fag genocide, detestation of Negroes & prison vendettas for hippies – and all of them sporting a shiny gold cross 'round their neck...

Sage sits me down, tells me she scored a new boyfriend – some Southern Bubba that plays in one of GG Allin's old bands, except he's like this Christian purist. She doesn't know who GG is, never heard of him, the violent king of toilet rock who waged war with the world and thieved young children into his carnival of excess. His point was to take the limits further then anyone ever had – shitting on stage, rolling around in it, eating it, fighting his audience, sometimes sexually assaulting them.

He was a cross-dressing psycho born of a bad acid trip and mis-wired brain chemistry; he wanted to destroy all religions, kill everyone that posed any sort of authority, and rape the world to teach undefiled strength after victimization. GG Allin was the enemy of civilization.

To Sage, punk rock is Green Day and Rancid. Says Southern Bubba is gonna burn her every GG album, that they're gonna have like this GG marathon. I know it's going to be a slaughter of heartbreak, and he's coming here to stay with us for the next two weeks.

So I go to try and find a job. All of Raleigh is plagued by grown men walking around with resumes in their hands, moaning like zombies. Even the day labor place, which regularly hires any bum off the street for *"pick up that box & put it over there"* caveman opportunities, is booked solid for two years. Swallowing my pride, I approach Burger King. The manager sits me down in near tears saying he'd received over 200 applications in the past four days.

GG guy soon arrives and he's pretty much my 19 year old clone, except he's around my age. We go to a local punk show where the singer of the band interrupts the bar to preach the glory of Christ. Big Bubba explains to me that GG wasn't at all what he promoted himself as, how he was a very polite & misunderstood person, and that everything was basically an act and GG was loaded with money the whole time.

Says he's good friends with GG's brother Merle & that Merle actually wanted him to sing for The Murder Junkies but he couldn't bring himself to sing the anti-religious stuff – especially *that 'Highest Power' song*" (which, coincidentally, I'd recently recorded a cover of with my grind project Sasquatch Agnostic).

Big Bubba and I are left alone while Sage is at work. He talks about how the country is headed for revolution, all this InfoWars sort of libertarian talk. About how he hasn't had sex in 5 years because it has to be a Christian girl, and even if the sex wasn't recognized in marriage it at least had to be pure in the eyes of The Lord.

At night, I fall asleep to them reciting Bad Religion lyrics to each other like sermons – like alter boys repeating *our father, who art in heaven.*" It's extremely creepy, but even more so the fact that they are repeating anti-Christian songs and warping them into pro-Christian ones somehow, all while ignoring the screamingly obvious fact that the band itself is called BAD RELIGION and their logo is a Crucifix with a BIG RED NO SIGN canceling it out...

On Thanksgiving weekend, as Sage visits GG guy on his family farm, I leave a thankful parting note on her desk which by the end rolls into an explanation of The Gospel of Judas. I thanked her for everything, wished her luck, but I wasn't the one to take her across Europe. She needed Orlando Bloom, not Jack Sparrow...

Big Bubba had pretty much begged me to give at least 6 months with her anyway, because he was falling madly in love. He dug all her friends – especially the Christian Marine on holidays from Iraq. He bought him a GG back patch, and the marine said he'd sew it onto his military uniform when fighting the Tikrit insurgency.

So I let him have her, and he made all sorts of empty promises about making me a merch guy for some high profile metal/punk bands.

I wasn't gone for long when he fucked it all up himself by showing her his Hitler Youth knife. He took her up the farm attic & led her through his scary collection of *you know I'm not into Hitler but they had really cool tanks & – HEY, let's go downstairs & watch the 'Hated' documentary."*

On came the infamous GG movie, the violent crowd attacks, shit spraying & vomiting, the sexual assaults on the audience & cell visits to John Wayne Gacy, the endless rants about fucking young boys, donkeys, dogs & his brother. So that was that...

In my absence Sage was sentenced to two months in jail for her DUI charge and went solo in the UK later that summer. The jailers let her out in 3 ½ weeks because they have no budget to keep people any longer...

Oh Florida, the swinging dick of the United States... Earlier in the year we had a tour stop in St. Petersburg. We headed to the coastline we always hung at when rolling through that area, which we'd dubbed *"Grabbleton's Beach."*

If I ever lived in Florida – had I any choice of tropical paradise – this would be the locale. I would sit here content from dawn to dusk sipping Margaritas & playing acoustic ditties...

As Uncle Ron spotted UFO's in the skyline, I myself floated in Gulf currents. I pleasantly reminisced about all the great loves of my life. I imagined, rather magically, stripping them from my soul & letting their elements drift into the sunset. I concentrated on their subconscious dismissal, begging the wind to carry them off...

Yet as I purged, I felt the breeze flow their memories into a neighboring city. Deep in my gut I felt them create a new destroyer of a woman though my own inadvertent spell weaving. Like a lab experiment gone haywire, I felt her assembled like Cobra creating Serpentor with strands of Mussolini, Stalin, Napoleon. Somewhere, within miles, I felt this mystery woman take shape. Let this delusion drift into the sunset, I thought – let this surreal malarkey remain infused amidst these scorching white sands of tropical bliss...

When I took the bus from Raleigh, not having the slightest clue where Linda was now located, I discovered that the one place in all of Florida she'd decided to move was three blocks from Grabbleton's Beach. That it was plagued with a sea monster was expected – that the only way onto the island was a bridge named ROUTE 666 was not. Of course – the only route to my new home was by crossing over the Highway To Hell.

The legal title of Grabbleton's Beach was actually Madeira Beach, and it's history only added to it's inherent magical properties. See, this Florida key was actually *the* Treasure Island of Pyrate Lore. As in the same location from all those mythological writings, even if long picked clean of buried booty.

These days, it was a tourist resort that remained a ghost town until spring break sent rich white people marching towards it like lemmings clutching wads of greenbacks.

However, it must be noted that in the early 20th Century a hurricane actually ripped the island in half, creating two separate communities now pieced together by a short bridge.

Since we inhabited the northern chunk of Treasure Island (Madeira Beach) and not a job was available on any stretch of the land – it'd appropriately been nicknamed "Poverty Island."

The irony of it all! Ryan Bartek – the shabbiest, most pathetic land pyrate of the entire lot – washing ashore broke & stranded at this mythical locale! Even when the winds of fate throw me into this cauldron I don't even make the cut to Treasure Island!

From across the bridge the ghosts of Blackbeard & Davy Jones flip me the bird, laughing at my ineptness. No matter – there were plenty of turkey leftovers & Linda's father just laughed, passed me a joint and told me to keep my ten bucks...

It was over this Thanksgiving weekend, marooned on the anti-Treasure Island, that I became famous almost instantly – at least in the most profound underground sense.

As you will read throughout this book, I had long embarked on a Sisyphean struggle to be considered a serious artist, or at least get a little love from the press – same as every artist, no matter what they tell you. Did a book, a movie, a few bands – wrote articles for some big magazines– but everything drastically changed the moment I crash-landed on Poverty Island.

As you will learn later on, throughout 2007 I traveled the USA gathering material for a road book/music journalism expose called "*The Big Shiny Prison.*" The following year I spent a Herculean effort trying to get it released properly, but I gave up when Wall Street collapsed. The print industry was destitute.

Had it not been for the situation at Sage's, I would never have simply put the thing out for free. It just kind of came in a flash to me – why not just post the PDF as a free download, plaster the press release everywhere, and notify every person on the giant list of email contacts I'd amassed over the past 8 years that it was time to cash in my "Scene Points" and call in that magic favor I was duly owed?

So I did just that, not expecting much in return. After 7 days of promo push I left North Carolina. In Florida I was finally able to get lightning speed internet to really observe the damage. Maybe it was luck, or perhaps just heavy metal people dodging their families on Thanksgiving by doing busy-body work behind computers, but I soon realized that almost every major underground news service had posted the download link. I was son major news threads next to Iron Maiden & Rob Zombie & Judas Priest, Rammstein & Danzig &...

The downloads kept coming, the interview requests, the weird letters from readers. Then America Online interviewed me, Fangoria gave press – bands I worshiped as a kid started writing to tell me how rad the book was. It just kept going & it still is. I became a made man the very second I'd given up all hope...

But I was still stuck in Florida with $250 to my name, and it was the lowest moment of our ever-growing national depression. I needed a job, and fast. With a bicycle I rode up & down the coast, applying everywhere to no avail.

Since hitchhiking was illegal & it was approaching the gruesome depths of winter, I took a job at the only thing I could find – Fast Food Franchise XYZ, one of the lowliest of them all, which I am forever embarrassed to have assumed...

The "restaurant" was generally abandoned, forever in slow motion. The only reason it stayed open at all was because during Summer Break it was a gold mine.

They could only give me 15 hours a week at minimum wage I'd stand around like a chump in their little uniform listening to jukebox pop radio & being punished by Don Henley. Like a prisoner with a little black spatula, I'd stare vacantly out the windows towards the glorious ocean across the street. That depopulated, wondrous Grabbleton & the cobalt skies which accompany it...

What I was, at heart, was lonely in this bizarre sideline of an adventure. Again I was free, but took it with silent reserve. To avoid the black magic woman I was subconsciously convinced I created when floating in the ocean, I tried romance.

Holly Doom started calling me out the blue, having just been released from a mental asylum in Pennsylvania. She wasn't crazy though – her army guy boyfriend had called the cops after she sliced herself up for fun while drunk, and once out she retaliated by stealing his secret big black dildo & posted its haunting specter on Facebook for all his homophobe friends to see. Holly starts calling me all the time, making plans for when I come home to Seattle.

There was another girl, one I met in Michigan at the last second. She'd started writing to us planning a visit, but I didn't make much fuss about it. I knew the Detroit trap and after all, she wasn't Clownbaby – just some girl who got drunk & had me rub her back. Plus she had a kid.

But I had no qualms being her vacation man-meat. Days before she was set to come after a month of flirting online – they discovered cancer in her breast & lobbed of her boob.

The desperate 40 something totally hot Vietnamese woman that worked at Corporate Franchise XYZ was pining for me. She'd say things jokingly in her accent: *me love you long time, hahaha.*

Things got awkward because our obvious mutual interest and I fumbled my conversation with her. The head manager thought we were fighting and forced the Vietnamese lady herself to write me up because we were too shy to explain the situation – on the day before Valentines, no less, when we had a date scheduled and I was sure to get laid after 5 months of no play. Well she wrote me up, then never called me. The 29th year in a row without a date for Valentines.

At all local bars the women were grizzled biker chicks, or "oceanside preppy." Some just looked like mummies from chain-smoking. I started thinking about the girl I shaved the mohawk for on that last DTB tour – the pretty, young mother of two children that hated her life in Tennessee. Maybe I could have a cute pen pal.

Neil P broke it to me that two days after we left she blew her head off with a shotgun. And our other friend from Detroit that was present in that same room that day – the one who'd moved from Detroit to start all over in Chattanooga – she'd hung herself as well.

There was another girl from Michigan, from back in high school. She was living near Orlando with her brother, trying to escape Detroit. I hadn't seen her in years & she'd developed into quite an attractive adult. At least she could understand me.

She pledged to visit me, but first she had to go back to Detroit to visit family. Then she would by 100% liberated, scot-free forever & ever. Oh yes, she would be coming. And nothing in me would be able to tell her to leave.

Three days into her visit she was brutally raped & thrown into a trash can. The assaulter tried to rape her friend as well, planning to murder them both. When some random guy overheard them the attacker ran off. She lost her mind, then after the trial moved to Portland & started dating her cousin...

Despite all this bad noise, I was in a decent place mentally. Once I'd gotten settled in after Thanksgiving, I downed the mushroom cap Sage had left me on the table. I wandered to the beach at night, while locals were having bonfires on the shore...

The hotel resorts turned into Tripoli, and the crashing waves a living blob. I felt the Lovecraft vibe emanating from the powers of the deep, like Cthulu was beaming thoughts into my head. I kept making myself vomit, because I wasn't ready… I walked back to Linda's becoming the tropical fauna. I started lurking the subdivision and a tiny white kitty cat wandered up to me. As I crouched down to pet it, a squad car rolled by shining its lights on me. I thought I was doomed, but it kept on rolling since I acted unafraid.

Once the pigs were out of sight, I scampered off to a lot between houses to gaze across the Boca Ciega bay – but then I saw a big black thing slithering in the waters, and I ran back to Linda who was smoking a cig on her steps & explained to her that dinosaurs were after me. She started laughing, and explained Bessie...

I went inside & hid from the prehistoric monster in the bathroom when T-Birds line from The Crow hijacked my head: "*& abashed there the devil stood, and felt how awful goodness is.*" I started imagining my friends all over the world, and I was attacked by love. I started crying, beleaguered by affection... I made it to the couch & was huddled by the dog who knew I was in darkness.

When the visions let up, I went back outside, smoked a bowl & melted in the chair. I had another vision of myself from earlier this year – this haunted figure wandering around Seattle, empty eyed, moaning "*Clownbaby, Clown-bayyyy-beeeeee*" like a Lazarus entombed in damnation. When this phantasm approached me, I told it to "*go that way – she went that way – there, off in the distance.*"

I saw & felt my own cursed apparition stumbling off into the night searching for his lost love, for the impossible way to make an unrepairable situation right. "*Poor bastard,*" I thought, "*I'm so glad I'm not him.*" Then I began laughing in rebirth, and melded even further into the plastic chair & the palm trees & the insects & the nocturnal kitty cats & the pyrate mythology & forgotten dinosaurs...

As my 29th birthday approached I knew I had to flee to Seattle and raise $4,000 to travel Europe for *Big Shiny Prison Vol. II*. I wasn't thrilled and the stakes were sky high. One thing dawned on me like lightning – the only thing that could prevent my escape to Europe was impregnation! I needed a vasectomy, not career training.

Somehow I'd landed in the only county in the USA with a free vasectomy program!! So I did it – I got neutered. As Henry Rollins penned: "*The race of my parents must end.*" No shortage of single mothers with kids, if inclined... The "operation" was numb, clip, done. They pull your tubes out like spaghetti noodles & clamp 'em with staples. And then…

…all I had to do was stay put & refuse to Linda's insistence with blind-dating her co-worker... You know who I'm talking about, 'course you do. The Serpentor of ex girlfriends past & present – *the bizarre woman child I will forever know as Mistress Maam…*

March Of The FilthPimp

The following tale is of a wound which is no longer an affliction, and a central figure that has long subsided any relevance. It is the story of many such figures, intertwining through an era that is now so distant it seems I never lived. I am the critic of this film rather then the star of the celluloid, and it is not her silhouette that festers but rather my own reflection. Rest assured, not one bad word against you will be recorded. I will cover your tracks, rearrange your physique; I will dissect your genetic sequence & fry it like scrambled eggs. I will recreate you not in 7 days but in 7 pages. I do not chase your ghost, nor do I sulk in your memory – I am merely purging every last trace of the man who once was. I am not your enemy, nor was I ever. I will leave you nothing more then a blurry face & impenetrable force field. Not a soul will know that I even so much as shook your hand...

While this heartfelt guarantee extends to all parties exemplified in this literature, there is one in particular who gets preferential treatment. Dearest reader, you may tell that this individual does not like me very much. Like many, she was the kind of soul with quick-defenses – where the slightest wrong turn of a phrase could be skewed as a personal attack.

It is because of this knee-jerk reaction that no matter the absurd lengths I'd gone to redeem myself, still I remain some distorted monster in her eyes. The great tragedy is that I did nothing to provoke it. One thing let to another, and then catastrophe.

To be honest, I wouldn't extend an olive branch to the 2005 me either, if this is the person I conjured when trying to envision the radically different incarnation now writing these words. No matter how charming my motivations were, I was still an Aries egomaniac.

However, what most never comprehended is that this egomania – this over-the-top, highly animated super-villain cunning – was one of my greatest art-forms. Everything was imbued to the living painting I was rendering; Detroit was my canvas, and propaganda my tool. But some people, they just never got the joke. Or perhaps they in fact did, and ran screaming – which made it all even the more joyous & zany.

In 2005 I still looked the industrial guy part. Ranting like Bill Hicks on speed, a black leather trench & fingerless gloves – blue mohawk slicked straight back, wracked with spinal trauma & abusing pills whilst chasing that candy with vodka...

I had a jet black 1995 Ford Thunderbird with a Judas Priest decal on the rear windshield & hot-wired switch that shot the thing up to 120 miles an hour like *Mad Max* so that at night I could roar down the emptied freeways of Hell City like Darth Vader in a Tye-Fighter. I had a hood-rattling stereo bumping LAIBACH, VNV Nation & Front Line Assembly – I'd a wide satanic audio spectrum of blackened death metal grindcore holocaust & zany tunes by Devotchka & Gogol Bordello.

Always a lit Marlboro dangling & ranting the New World Order, always sky high on a power mad press scheme or obsessively compulsively cutting the tags off every item of clothing. Always distanced and hateful with cold, crude, Darwinian ambivalence & self-masturbating puppet-mastery Machiavellianism…

See, when I was 7 years old, I saw Tim Burton's *Batman* on opening night. A tiny little boy in the very front row & that Goliath screen above stretching for miles. I was intoxicated by Jack & said to myself, *"This is exactly what I want to be when I grow up."*

And in 5th grade, in Elementary school when I started to slip, I would come home every day & watch Paul Dini's animated series. These were my friends as a child, all these maniacs that would be rounded up by Batman & locked up in Arkham Asylum week after week. And I knew that when I grew up, that was gonna to be my circle of friends, and that Harley Quinn, the hottest woman in fictional Gotham, would one day be my blushing bride...

...but The Joke was always that I wasn't The Joker.

In the little kid game I played, I was another character entirely. In accordance with Freak War among the madhouse – I'd thieve not only Clownboy's empire but his female companion as well. I'd run the asylum with an iron fist & bring Batman to his hockey-padded knees. But no one would ever figure out this secret supervillain identity, because to explain The Joke is to ruin it...

So where was I? Oh yeah – General Lee, the singer of FILTHPIMP. He could give a fuck if I wrote about him all day long. He'll probably microwave a bag of popcorn & dig in to these words like it's Superbowl Sunday. General Lee & I, we were both scumbags. It was a different sort of scum-baggery then with Kluck, which was more a real sickness type sickness. We, at least, had heart.

General Lee was a cartoon heckling everyone & everything. He was a porn store clerk for years, filming *Jackass*-like stunts whether it be taking a baseball bat to the balls or pooping in a frying pan & stinking up a kitchen for weeks with shit steam.

He was all motion – extremely hyperactive with lots of tattoos. Dirty like a dog, he was the sort of physical guy that would wrestle around with his friends and always be covered in scabs & bruises. Guy was a freak comedian between crust/grind world, industrial world & blue collar existence, working 3 jobs at a time. No matter how pompous I got, he'd deflate me with a few jabs...

When I first saw him perform live screaming for a local metal band, I knew he was the right guy for FILTHPIMP, which I'd vowed to finally get rolling. Thanks to all that MARViN money, I now had pro gear & a full rig.

We spoke a little beforehand, but all of this roots to one weekend in particular – a BBQ at his folks house where he, his girlfriend & their child lived...

I walked up the driveway to the garage, and while the meat charred on the grill Lee was blaring The Jesus Lizard. Lee's girlfriend Shanna was in a foldout chair next to one of her best friends, and then I looked over at that best friend & I saw [][][] for the very first time.

She was wearing a Ministry t-shirt, a dirty ripped up white one for Jesus Built My Hot Rod, and her soul just glowed so bright I barely noticed anything else about her until I caught those hypnotic eyes burning a hole through my head. She was...

Say it, say it...

She was...

Come on...

A black girl.

Liar.

Yeah, she was totally black.

Charlatan.

She was totally black, with purple hair & face piercings, and she just... [][][] just glowed in a way that no woman had ever glowed before, and I just spiritually felt her as this psychic powerhouse screaming two intense distinctions. She was like a thousand miles of frozen concrete encasing a blinding supernova.

I knew I'd be cursed to chase her until the brutal, bitter finale – fangs snarling & claws gnashing – until every finger was nothing more then a stub of bloody pulp from trying ever so desperately to tear through that impenetrable, ever-regenerating concrete shell. She was single, with a daughter – a madly clever girl of 4.

While General Lee & I went through CD's pointing out our mutual tastes, what we wanted to accomplish with the band, he started to mention his legal difficulties.

Basically, the couple had found a dog they knew was some other families, but his girlfriend was 7 months pregnant & rather then face the wrath of "*crazy pregnant bitch,*" he just let her keep it.

They moved from elsewhere onto this new area, and when the dog got a nasty infection they took it to the vet. The dog had been injected with a microchip and Lee was arrested for felony theft of a show-dog.

He was in the process of fighting it in court, and the rich yuppies had made a finger-pointing hellfire scene at the preliminary hearing. *"These fucking people man,"* he said, exasperated: *"It's like why the fuck are you doing this to my family?"*

Lee was to get slammed with an avalanche of fines, community service & probation simply because he didn't want to take any more guff from his kinder-blimped woman. The defense enacted was they thought the dog was lost, and assumed it was a good deed caring for it.

This situation would be the content of our first song, but in the lyrics he'd just ransom the yuppies & send them different parts of the dog until they sent him the $$$. But at the end of the song he just sends them half a dog in the mail anyway, just because.

We made a chart of all the song subjects we needed to tackle – a blistering critique of the Iraq War filled with *Rambo* samples, a tune about the fascist straight-edge goon squads that would jump people at concerts for smoking joints, some mocking ditty to poke a little fun at the basement dwelling Dungeons & Dragons nerds.

We went up to his bedroom to dig through some old lyrics he'd stashed away & I asked if I could check my email. As I'm pulling up the internet explorer, I notice the messenger's nickname. Then a big old bell started ringing in my head – the mystery online chat from a few weeks ago that started hitting on me, saying she knew a friend of a friend. She was trying to get me to rendezvous in the dead of night.

As you know, I was quite lonely, so I tried to get this anonymous person to meet at a late night Coney Island, but they flaked out. In fact, had Lee not invited me to the BBQ, I would probably still have been hanging around my house hoping this mystery girl would magically pop up on my computer.

When I put two & two together, I said *"Hey Lee, oh this is cute – your little sister has a crush on me. She was like writing me last week, trying to get me to come hang out."* And then he stops shuffling through his papers, gives me this look. And then we both realize it's Shanna, the mother of his child.

At first, I think he's about to flip out in jealous guy mode like the majority of Detroit males. Instead, he's more entertained then anything. Then he wants me to be, like, this spy, to keep it up, to save the text logs & show him everything. And I'm thinking he's trying to dump his girlfriend off on me, because they are both miserable together...

[][][] is like Shanna's ex-girlfriend. For two years Lee was the graveyard shift porn store clerk at this giant strip club, and [][][] was one of the elite showgirls of the era. He started cheating on Shanna with her, pretending he was single.

After many months Lee was finally caught red-handed at this house party that both of the girls had randomly attended. They quickly realized what was going on, and instantly started to bicker with one another. Things started to get heavy, and Lee was certain the police would come.

Yet within 3 minutes their angry yelling turned into mutual respect, and instead of grappling each other in a ruthless cat-fight, they both dumped Lee on the spot, leaving him to a romantic nervous breakdown of sorts.

For the next few months they tortured him like a human yo-yo, as if he were a human voodoo doll. Eventually Shanna relented, since they had been together since the age of 15. But [][][] was now permanently in the picture, and Lee was cursed to be melded to her unwanted presence.

And now I'd been thrown into this bizarre soap opera, with Lee handing me a plate of BBQ ribs grinning & expecting to hire me as a private eye, Shanna harboring a secret crush on me that I want nothing to do with, and this [][][] girls' eyeballs drilling through my skull with the zest of a Bush family member on sacred Alaskan wilderness...

I loafed around the house that entire weekend hanging with the girls. Lee would be busy at work – he'd come back, and we'd all ignore him. These two women and I had started a freaky clique, and Lee was happy to see me get embroiled in his personal world. He wanted me anchored to it, because our band would flourish.

I went right back to taxi world, and the next weekend I was over there once again, hanging with the girls. I was completely infatuated with [][][], and I didn't really mind that she had a kid.

I was starting to think the sort of thoughts most men my age begin to consider around 23. Maybe it's just genetically psychological – that you're supposed to start building a family, planting roots. Maybe this is what we were all doing here, because that concept was heavy on Lee's mind. He didn't just want to start some band – he was looking for a business partner & sense of family that would blossom.

That Sunday, I kept telling the girls there would be a triumph of a radio broadcast that evening. At 9pm, I clicked on my car radio & what went down was legendary. See, the previous Sunday I'd secured a guest appearance on the local music hour for Flannigan to promote Save The Vegetables.

Despite the DJ calling him directly & affording a host of pleasantries, the receptionist wouldn't even buzz him in. For 30 minutes he hung outside like a leper. Once inside, the new asshole DJ pretended like he didn't know him & made him sit on the hallway couch. He finished before letting Flannigan in.

I wrote a nasty letter to the d-bag DJ knowing he'd take the bait & read it on air. In the email I completely decimated him & his fraudulent business of plugging his friends' bands, sucking ICP's ass & giving the local spotlight to endless Puddle of Creed bands. I explained in acute detail the fool he was, and related exactly what every musician in Detroit was thinking.

Like a chump, he read it word for word – breaking down every sentence & devoting 35 minutes to shit-talking me. By the end he was accusing me of being racist, of being a closet fascist, all sorts of blatant garbage. As ass-head ranted furiously, I kept doing cartwheels. The scummiest DJ imaginable was making me sound like the coolest guy on earth, and everyone in Detroit was hearing it.

As for the DJ, so many people wrote in with nasty letters defending me that it swamped the stations' inbox. So many people dropped bombs that the DJ was officially disciplined.

He was soon pulled off the air due to his continued shenanigans, which led him back into the mire of pathetic attempts at becoming some local personality by hosting crap-tastic gigs packed with bands like Brand X at seedy strip joints that no one who gave the slightest fuck about music ever attended...

As summer drew to a close, I needed out of my apartment. Not only because I could no longer afford it, but because of all the memories I wished to negate. Thunderdome II was being illegally evicted, and Moses (*their handyman*) needed to jump ship.

We hatched a plan to become roommates, and many face-palmed themselves. There was widespread sentiment that we were the two worst people you could pair in a living situation.

We were both always fucking everything up in one way or another, like mischievous gremlins running around the Theatre Bizarre or Save The Vegetables. Somehow we both had the misfortune to be clumsy – shorting fuses, accidentally breaking lights, relaying incorrect info. It's not that we didn't try, we were just prone to slapstick.

Thrown in the same rental situation, people assumed we'd flounder about like Harpo & Chico without a Groucho to managerially steer the course...

We moved into an apartment above this old barbershop, like an upstairs flat with two bedrooms & a decent sized living room. The floor was sagging, because the building was elderly; it even had a bathroom with one of those 1920's middle of the floor bathtubs so deep you could float in it.

The barbershop was directly next to an intersection light & busy gas station, so monoxide & petrol fumes would drift in through the windows heavily at rush hour, which would send Moses up the wall because he was hypersensitive.

The barbershop was perfectly stationed in an area where no neighbors would call in noise complaints as FILTHPIMP auditioned members or practiced. Lee always hated the name though, but I was adamant in using it. He said that people would think it was some nu-metal rap rock thing, whereas I could only envision merchants of sleaze peddling scary ideas in a kinghell attempt to corrupt the youth. The album was to be called *A.K.A. MABUS*, alluding to our mock status as Nostradamus' Final Antichrist.

Jump to October. [][][]'s prior boyfriend had cleaned up his act & was moving to her area. Even though I had a giant thing for [][][], she'd been with this other guy for years. The little girl actually thought it was her real father, and neither of them did anything to dispel the myth. The guy was ready to slip the ring on her finger.

I began a new job as a line cook at Pizzino's, a fine dining restaurant that was the big mafia hangout of the 50's & 60's. The remaining gangsters were elderly & dying, sucking spaghetti noodles through their toothless gums.

The owner was 80 something & on his way out. His daughter assumed the role of manager & was trying her best to save this failing business but had no idea what she was doing.

She was smart enough to hire Chef Frankie though, who hired his entire high school crew. I was one of the only guys that stumbled in looking for a job randomly.

It was a crazy roll call of characters that don't really need to be elaborated on, but as I worked with them all I could only envision them as a reincarnated crew of pyrates or cowboys that I was once a part of in some distant past.

One of the cooks was a golden boy – the nephew of an excessively wealthy family that owned a mega-franchise with restaurants all over America. They were hashing things out to start a new national chain, and we were all going to be hired. Frankie proudly explained that Pizzino's was the upstart nucleus & this crew was expertly crafted to dominate the market. We'd be set for life...

I went home glowing. Moses was up late, watching this random video tape of weird clips that the Amino Acids had cobbled together. Just another VHS left on the floor of a venue after we'd smashed all the TV's at the climax of their set. Moses pulled it out the busted VCR, reeled it back together.

Immediately it cut to this hand-held camera segment. I heard the laugh, and I knew it all too well. There was a man with a hockey mask revving a chainsaw, talking in a strange squeaky voice: "*I'm gonna cut ya – I'm-a-gunna-cut-ya*" while this girl was strapped to a table, giggling crazy, half-mummified by VHS guts – *Lana*.

Why did the Amino's have this? Who was this guy in the Jason get-up? Where in the fuck could this have possibly come from? Then everything lightened up. With the fuzzy blast of THC, I remembered her clearly.

How beautiful she was, how much I truly missed her. I recalled that scene at my old apartment when she appeared from obscurity. I had to seek her out. And then the video jump-cut to *Rudolph The Rednose Reindeer*, the bit where he meets the Abominable Snowman.

I called the Amino Acid's drummer, and he tells me it isn't clear where the segment came from or how it got on the tape. But he says I should know the guy in the Hockey mask, because it's Stanley Pluto, one of the photographers from Jam Rag...

SHIT – I totally neglected Jam Rag, haven't I? How these most important of details slip my mind ever so frequently I will never know. Well anyway, alongside Real Detroit & PIT Magazine & a gaggle of web-zines,

I'd been itching to get a print magazine going in Detroit where I would have full sway over editorial. Something heavy-handed that would propagandize the bands in The Coalition.

There was this tiny mag called City Monthly that the publisher was fumbling, placing classifieds for an editor because he was close to throwing in the towel. Flannigan & I met with him and unveiled a number of concepts.

He took the bait, I tapped some writers to furnish some pieces, and we were good to go. Unfortunately the only advertiser I could come up with was this ultra-Satanic black metal label. The publisher squirmed & gave up, and I was left with all these Detroit-centric articles that had no home.

Real Detroit was precarious, because the editor who backed me for years had quit and now there was a new editor who still supported me yet the indie rock scenesters were trying to push me out the door. They wanted a White Stripes clone paper. The bottom line though was that I still got more mail sent to the office then any other writer, and I was still very popular with the readership.

It got so bad, in fact, that I was looking to City Monthly as a way to jump ship, because I was still anywhere but done with my hostage situation on the media. At least until FILTHPMP was operational, when I could just dive right back into the music scene trenches like a metal/punk mercenary.

I caught wind that Jam Rag was looking for a music editor. For 20 odd years, it had been the premier underground rock mag of Detroit. It was totally independent, had no strip club or cigarette ads, and a huge political bent because it's owner Tom Ness was a revered left wing activist who ran for Senate as a green party candidate.

They were tied into all sorts of anarcho/socialist circles, and all the old guard freaks looked at the paper with reverence, even if the layout was old-school & the writing had been less the impressive for the past decade.

Problem was that Jam Rag was deeply in debt to the tune of $30,000, and their long-time printer just couldn't overlook it anymore. They needed money or it was a total bankruptcy.

So it was one of those moments where I saw myself desperately needed in a specific place and time, in a particular manner that only I could salvage, and that it was time to use the full weight of my career & exploit some underground politic wrangling.

There was one other issue though that was thoroughly unavoidable – Tom Ness was now Stephanie Loveless. As in he went from a notorious womanizing polyamorous loudmouth to entirely bypassing even a bi-sexual infancy or the early stages of cross-dressing.

Instead, Ness went the whole hog & started living as a woman immediately, gobbling hormone pills & writing a series of emails to his world media list describing in graphic detail his slowly budding synthetically induced breasts.

Furthermore, he released a Jam Rag special issue in which he interviewed his new self as if his old self were the journalist & this new incarnation the interviewee.

This was Detroit, not San Francisco, and things did not progress so stealthily. Bear in mind this is late 2004, and non-vulture capitalism print media is on it's last legs. Within a week, 70% of the advertisers dropped off, half the writing staff quit, and there was simply no money to pay anyone.

Ness's heterosexual wife of 15 years begat a short lived nervous breakdown, and his parents completely disowned him. Even the gay scene didn't really know what to do with him.

So Stephanie Loveless calls me over to discuss the paper, and I decide I might as well just steer this thing into it's final grave with dignity. Maybe we could stabilize it, but I had no grand illusions about it lasting more then a year. Furthermore, it put me dead center in the underground & reaching a whole new audience of old-school Detroiters that would never, ever find my "*diamond in the rough*" writing in Real Detroit's pages...

It was time to strike hard, because the whirlpool of live music I'd succumbed to had grown so intense I wasn't quite sure what else to do with it. Before moving in with Moses, I took this gig as a bookie for a bar on Woodward Ave. The owner was this old rocker chick with big hair, and no idea what she was doing.

Dinky stage, no PA system, no budget drafts & the cheapest beer at $4, she mainly booked crap cover bands & was seeking the right guy to book Puddle of Creed bands. But she told me "*you just book it & promote it & bring the PA & I'll give you $40 under the table & you just divvy up the door money as you see fit.*"

The first big show was a killer lineup – the surf punk Amino Acids, the rock slicers The Whiskey Diaries, noise-punk legends The Hillside Stranglers, experi-doomers LIGHT & the post-apocalypse themed Wolfbait which was like Turbonegro dropped into *Mad Max*.

By the end beer cans littered the floor like bullet-casings on the beaches of Iwo Jima. The owner banked, everyone got paid out, and from then on she just let me run wild. She was wise enough to know the law – *money talks & bullshit walks...*

I started doing gigs every Thursday, sometimes Saturdays. Although I should've just stopped to concentrate on my own band, the volcano I was fermenting here would surely pay off when I began booking FILTHPIMP. We would raise our black flag & sail our ship into every available port, assaulting every audience with sonic destruction.

The bands came fast & furious, expertly arranged into dynamic motifs. I grinded through all of them like a meat machine – *Saprogenic, Mutilated, Kenshiro, Nain Rouge, Joiya, The Potions, Serrated Edge, Eggslave, Lame-O, Return To Dust, M59, Midnight Thud, Christpunchers, Circa: The End, Bazooka Jones, Signs of Collapse, Whiskey Fistfight, The Dawning, The Jollys, Gas Chambers For Christ, Stab Stab Die, Eudomania, Highbinder, Omission, I The Sky, Stash, Uriel's Proxy, Kill The Beast, Small Town Revolver, Alucard, Zero Dependence, Jibilian,*

Firewerk, Quit Your Life, Tentacle Lizardo, Rubbermiilk Orchestra, GANON, Malpractice, The Red Shift, Today I Wait, Mean Mother, Goodison, Justin 6.7, Eat Your Heart Out, Comrade Kilkin, Letters In Binary, Tabula Rasa, Shorty Brown, Facture, Troubleman, Johnny Mundane, Lobby Rats, Orange Robot, Imp Villains, Absinthe Ava, Helvetica, Detroit Crunkstar, Heroes & Villains, Wizards of Hope, Blackbird Suite, Otto Vector, Fight The World, Stare Into The Sun, The Questions, The Chasers, The Hadituptoheres, The Book Was Better & Coke Dick Motorcycle Awesome...

Somewhere amidst this blur, gleefully sipping vodka/cranberry & taking in door money, the young guy from Elitist Publications shows up. He's got a cardboard box filled with the first edition of my debut book *The Silent Burning*.

The release party is set to occur at The Magic Stick on January 5th, 2005, as to ring in the New Year correctly. Amino Acids are headlining the gig as their own record release party, the Bump N Uglies are about to unveil all sorts of new wrestling showcases, and MAN Inc is about to head off on his first big European tour. Everyone is about to win.

I take one look at the cover, barrel through the pages, and I realize the disaster I'd stepped into. Now, I'm not taking it out on him, because it's my own fault from denying the raging fact that any time I ever put anything in someone else' hands it always goes horribly, horribly wrong. Doesn't matter what it is – *it's always fucking something...*

The young guy visited the print company in September, and they told him unless they immediately began that day, there were just too many other projects in queue & it wouldn't be done in time for the release party. He said *"no problem,"* pulled out the disc I gave him, but they didn't think to select the "show all files" button on the computer.

Thus completely overlooking the final product I'd spent 20 hours arranging through Adobe Acrobat – not to mention the high-resolution cover art that accompanied it.

Thinking I'd shafted him, he immediately went ahead & hired the print company to make a brand new Adobe Acrobat version of the book themselves – based on the third-from-final draft he had sitting on a floppy disk I gave him months ago when he initially inquired about the project.

He then paid the print company $1000 to tailor this mauled version which was a mass of spelling errors, missing content, and gigantic gaps in text. This was trumped only by the shoddy, grainy packaging which took the classic black & white RS Connett cover art & then rendered it pumpkin orange (*my least favorite color*) from a low-res jpeg.

They modified the image itself against my consent as to darken the *"fish cocks"* in the background, which led the print company to tack on an extra $500 bill. This raised the overhead cost to a whopping $3,000 that I was now responsible to recoup.

These huge errors were so blatant I knew few distributors would take us seriously. Furthermore, I did not feel comfortable promoting this product, let alone promoting the subject matter of the book itself. I was heart broken that after all my impassioned effort I had a steaming pile of shit that would contractually haunt me.

I was calmed & told not to worry, because both Barnes & Nobles and Borders would be picking up 5,000 copies each just to stock in their warehouse. With the 2nd printing, all would be set aright. The book hadn't even come out yet, and the deal was a wretched stand-off. I kept my mouth shut & agreed to promote it anyway, 'cause If I made a scene it would spiral into oblivion...

The next week, he secures a promotional spot in this prestigious Detroit literary magazine. They agree to run an excerpt online, to shine a floodlight on this promising monumental work that is to theoretically launch me towards being considered a serious artist once and for all.

Proud of his wrangling, he send me the link. I open it, preparing to be floored with victory. Without consulting me, without even asking what I think should be the flagship promotional item, he selects one of the last things in the book I would ever want to be dropped on such a spotlight.

It's this soliloquy from a scumbag character, supposedly a football jock. Yet the way the magazine frames it, it inadvertently makes it sound as if it's my own voice without any reference, thereby leading the whole of Detroit's fancy lit community to believe I am some sort of ignoramus monster: *I've waited all this time for it to come out of your mouth: the abortion speech. I've heard it countless times before. It's become so fucking cliché. How your mother had the tears of Christ in her eyes as she drove you to that clinic. What those tools felt like inside of you. You wanted it gone; it would have destroyed your life. Now I hold you tighter, telling you it's ok. How bad things happen to good people. You look so calm and safe pressed against my Varsity jacket... If only you could hear the torrent of hideous laughter inside of my head. Now I know that I can fuck you all I want and if I slip up I can pay you off and throw you away like the worthless piece of shit that you are. Stupid bitch, get on your knees – it's all your good for...*

Gunning for spoken word gigs to hype the book release, I get talked into throwing a Saturday showcase at Small's, one of the bigger venues in Detroit.

I was urged on by this guy named Tex (*from Country Bob & The Bloodfarmers*) – an old school rocker with a Southern accent & cowboy hat doing a Cramps meets noisepunk thing with a country flair. He digs what I'm doing with the PT Barnum ringmaster aesthetic and wants to hammer together a bill with lots of intermissions & call it "THE HELL HARVEST."

We get the singer of this GWAR-like band called Halloween to host it, all make-up smeared like Satan with a huge 10 foot spike cock dangling off his codpiece. Downtown Brown headline, and the others are a loopy cocktail of Country Bob, Signs of Collapse, SNAKEOUT & The Nothing, with some comedic intermissions.

When I sent the list of bands to whoever does the advertising at Small's, they thought the descriptions of the bands I'd run below their names in parenthesis were somehow bands themselves.

So where I had this bill that if clearly promoted would pack at least 1000 easy, they instead ran an ads declaring Downtown Brown is playing with Chocolate Funk Turbo Doom, SNAKEOUT, and High-Octane Psychobilly Madness.

The show begins. First up is Signs of Collapse, who are among the greatest tech metal bands ever to emerge from Detroit. The older punk crowd is slaughtered, half of them walking out because S.O.C. are just so fucking hardcore.

Before the next goes on, I have Nicholas Steven Pobutsky do a comedy routine. The joke is that he's supposed to be like the worst comedian in the world, dragging it out & rustling up hecklers & sluggishly farting around stage until people scream for his blood. They don't get it, they think he's awful in a serious way, but those of us who do are on the floor.

Next up is The Nothing, a bunch of awkwardly social artsy crusty punk kids who play this pretty instrumental music with cello & piano, that randomly bursts into metallic heaviness that is just screechingly decimating. The crowd adores them, then the GWAR guy does a little comedy routine about banging chicks in hell.

The Bloodfarmers rock their set, and up next is my spoken word which will be followed by SNAKEOUT & Downtown Brown. I walk up to the podium with a cigar clenched between my teeth. There are a sea of smiling faces before me, all excited to hear something from the big book which will soon launch me to serious artistic reputability.

"Hi everyone," I tell the smiling faces – *"This one's called 'Bob Sagat Raping The Olson Twins On PCP.'"*

I clear my throat, and begin: *"Son, I'd like to take this moment to reassure you that you were the biggest mistake of my life. I know you're only four years old and I know it's a lot to handle, but I want you to fully understand that all of that Saturday morning nonsense about storks parachuting babies into suburbs is complete horse shit. In school your teachers will use terms like 'the miracle of birth' or 'the wonder of life.' They've got it all wrong, it's just shitting out a kid - a bloody pulp substance that lives and breathes and constantly shits and costs lots of fucking money.*

They'll lie and tell you how unique and special and important you are. They'll tell you that you can be anything you put your mind to. They'll make you think that you'll become a movie star, an astronaut or maybe even the president someday. But you won't. They let you graduate before you realized you've been primed for a future of casual slavery. You'll quickly learn that your public high school diploma is just another piece of paper to wipe your ass with. No job you apply for will ever ask for concrete proof. The teachers who deny it were taught the exact same bullshit but went on to college so they could recite it all over again. It's merely the traditional product placement of yet another unnecessary institution designed to drive you into endless inescapable debt.

You see it's all part of a larger system of misery. Public school is the cornerstone of all social control mechanisms. It is a system maintained to shatter the spirits of the youth who've just begun to articulate clearly in complicated symbolic language, as well as starting to master complex physical and mechanical tasks. This is when you and millions of other displaced children are forcibly kidnapped from your family under legislative threats of imprisonment and violence.

You'll be herded into militaristic institutions upheld by a thinly veiled illusion of mind expansion and patriotic goodness because without the most thorough and rapid brainwashing your inquisitive little minds would easily see through all of their dirty tricks. Yes son, legalized mind-rape for 13 years - 6 to 8 hours a day, 5 days a week. Like a caged animal you'll be taught to follow orders unquestionably, fear disobedience, sit still, keep quiet, require permission to drink, eat, piss, shit – all the quintessential knowledge appropriated for excellent productivity in the future corporate interest.

Think you'll outdo it? HAH!! The media will squash your attention span into the proto-human mold. No matter what they might have you believe, you're a docile consumer drone in waiting. You're conception of a free thinking, liberated existence will be deluded by radios, televisions, computer screens, professional sports, McDonald's, Walt Disney, organized religion and mental inactivity of boundless varieties.

When a politician calls for 'more education' what they really mean is a higher degree of crowd control. You can rock the vote all you want, but it won't change a goddamn thing. The popular vote means nothing; it only exists for good P.R. Every election is rigged because the Electoral College has already been bought off. There's only one political entity and it's called the 'Corporate-ocracy.'

By the time you're an adult a handful of men will control the entire economic being of the world system. One corporation to inevitably trademark the structure of human DNA itself. Good luck trying to find a meal untouched by genetic altering. Transmutation is the next step of evolution. You'll watch the complete collapse of Gaia. Biotechnology, nano-technology — scary, ain't it?

In middle school the police will fabricate lies and terrorize you into complacency. You'll be subverted with horrific tales of convicts and prison and anal rape. And drugs – my god the drugs. The smart ones are the ones who fuck themselves up. The more substances you abuse the closer you come to the truth. It's a little known fact.

And just so you know the vast majority of police are not our friends. Behind all law and order lies an animal with a gun – an animal playing god that's always right no matter what the circumstance shielded by widespread corruption to do whatever it wants at any given time without the slightest consequence of its actions. It's really that simple.

You'll get into music during those years. While you'll think you're being rebellious you'll be nothing more than a demographic. Corporations like Clear Channel have it all laid out for you. The revolution is a fairy tale they sell to you through posters at Meijers. It's all advertising and image, the greedy conjurings of Harvard trained marketing executives. You're fucked son – it's important to learn this now.

Oh yah, and that whole God thing – he doesn't exist. God's like Santa Clause or the Tooth Fairy or the Easter Bunny except adults never let go. Religion is only here to calm and stabilize us, to look after death for paradise and not dramatically alter the hell we've created. When you die it will be just like before you were born. Try and remember that. Ha Ha! It's funny, really, it is. All perspective son, remember that...

If I had the ability to travel through time I would hunt your pregnant mother down, roof her and get to work with a rusty old coat hanger. I'd like to lie to myself and pretend this misery comes as a result from my own actions but it's really all your fault.

Shit, I had it all going before you came along. My band was all set to head to Los Angeles but then my idiot ass fucked a fat groupie in the rehearsal space. Ozzy was on the boom box. I cummed during Randy Rhodes' Crazy Train solo. I only spoke three sentences to her that day. She was just one of those one night stands that looks great after a case of High Life and you throw away just as easy as the condom afterwards. But I slipped up. I tried so hard for her to go to the clinic but she wouldn't budge. Too much Christ in the veins. We would've been huge too...

Now look at me. I'm married to a fugly stranger, breaking my back day in and day out at a shitty dead end job, sleeping on the couch and a receding hairline. I had it all, now I'm nothing. And it's all because of you. So remember this – dream of it for years to come. This is my Remington. This is the barrel. This is my chin. And this is the trigger. Goodbye son. You were the worst thing that ever happened to me. (Click)."

I look up, having choked out the venue with misanthropy. 15 people left standing, all with mortified reactions, dropped jaws, ghostly complexions. I'd cleared a room of 300 people in 10 minutes. I see the future clearly, that blazing writing. But as I scan those disoriented faces, there Neil P is, way in the back, with a shit-eatin' grin & wide eyes, doing the dramatic slow clap...

I head over to the Jam Rag office, which is the dank basement at Miss Loveless' house. Dodging the neon pantyhose dangling from water pipes, I sit down & read some concept writing that is to be part of a new political column – "The War On Terrorism Chronicles," aka "The T.W.A.T. Chronicles."

I'm hot on the trail of Lana, and inquire about the loopy guy with the Jason mask. Steffie tells me: *"Oh that's Stanley, he's a strange one. He's been doing photos for us for a really long time now. He's kind of a musician, but I don't really know what to make of his stuff. It's all Casio keyboards with that built-in drum machine.*

"Kind of like Wesley Willis or something?"

"Sort of, but not like schizophrenic ill – just eccentric. The lyrics are totally bizarre. You just kind of gotta hear it. Hold on – I'll get you his number..."

Stanley Pluto meets me at Coney Island. He's in his early 40's, short brown hair disheveled & messy with a 5 o'clock shadow. Tall guy, wearing a tweed suit coat without a dress shirt or tie to accompany it.

He's got one-step-from-legally-blind bifocals and a crazy grin. He also has sound proof plastic ear muffs he's always wearing, like the ones construction workers wear when operating machinery because loud noises cripple him & he has debilitating ear aches.

Stanley Pluto takes me for a ride in his beat up old dodge, and he drives all over the road weaving in & out of lanes. His backseat is loaded with weird bits of electronic equipment, toys & odd trinkets he either trash picked or discovered at Value World.

He keeps referring to Lana as "Leeloo," tells me she ditched the nutty boyfriend. Tells me they hang out driving around to the *Dawn Of The Dead* soundtrack, picking trash as their magical stash...

Stanley Pluto drops Leeloo off at my apartment. We go eat, and she's just as I remembered her – eyes like vortex periscopes from another galaxy. She's happy. She's funny. She's laughing – and I am too.

She's a model now, getting paid $200 an hour. Big Detroit art scene paintings and hot shot photographers selling their work for ten grand a pop. Says EMINEM is all over her, keeps asking about her...

We go back home and watch *Troll* on VHS. I don't ruin anything. She falls asleep next to me, and I spoon her. When I awake she's not in the bed. I stumble to the window, and she's hopping into Stanley's beat up Dodge below...

She comes back a few days later, having blown off EMINEM for me. I tell her I saw this movie that reminded me of her, and together we watch *Eternal Sunshine On The Spotless Mind*.

When it's over, she explains that she was in the mental asylum this year. Tells me she tried to make them give her brain electrolysis, just so she could erase me.

Night of the Presidential election, Bush vs. Kerry. All day Moses & I have been awaiting the downfall of W. Exit polls in both Pennsylvania & Florida say that Kerry is up 60, maybe 70%. The Death Star is exploding, raining chunks unto Endor.

Suddenly, the election results turn grim. The actual tallies coming off the DieBold funded/created/installed touch screen voting machines are drastically different then the earlier exit polls in FL and PA. Nearly 30% different – the only time news network exit polls have been wrong more then a margin error of 2%. Like a highway cop allowing a shit-face drunk back on the freeway, America might leave Bush at the wheel.

Lana knocks on the door & Moses takes leave. She and I are now alone. She walks slowly to the bathtub & flips on the hot water. That same hopelessly romantic 1930's bathtub surrounded by all the hand glued floor tiles like a luxury spread.

Lana comes back through the living room, makes sure I see her, then floats down the hallway removing her clothes. She slips inside the bathroom and splashes in.

I smile wide, knowing I'm about to get my wife back. The debut novel is about to come out. I quit smoking, I'm the editor of a new magazine. FILTHPIMP is inching closer to our debut and Slayer's former tour manager is interested in the record...

Frankie is going to open a nationwide restaurant chain. The original editor from Real Detroit came back and fired the indie rock schemers, offering me free reign. Tomorrow I might wake up and George W. Bush will no longer be president. I am 24 years old, and I will finally have a date for Valentines.

I head down the hallway unloosening my belt, grinning. I turn the corner & try to find her eyes, but they are staring up at the ceiling. From the vortex, those periscopes broadcast shame.

Like a religious icon, like a surrealist portrait, she floats naked in the bathtub like a wilted flower, hair flowing through the still water. Heroin trackmarks climb up & down her arms like spider webs, purple veins colliding in gruesome harmony.

I get on my knees, slowly, slowly. I speak soft. I ask what she has done to herself. She doesn't reply, just looks as if she is bleeding to weep but feels nothing. This dramatic manner, this all-or-nothing blitzkrieg of grimness. I pour some purple liquid into the tub, hoping some bubbles might mask the hideousness. Gently, I stroke her face with a rag...

I see the camera lens pull back, somber & fluid. I witness myself on the floor, crouched on a bent knee, rubbing this lost girls face. And then I remember why I threw her away. It wasn't because of calling random people in my phone book.

It wasn't because she killed our child with pain pills. It was because one early morning, as we were stretched out on my bed with all my defenses down, she told me that she loved me. The first time she said it. The only time she said it. And in that moment, I had no defenses, merely a stomach full of bleach...

And like a monster, like a fool, I threw away the love of my life all because the very power of that love had dismantled me. And now, from miles behind, watching myself as if in a gruesome scene of some awful movie you want to change the channel on but cannot, I rub her face ever so gently, so that her eyes don't burn from bubble suds. I keep telling her, *"It's ok Harley. It's ok..."*

It is the next morning and we are driving south on Gratiot, past strings of buildings with barred windows and barb wire enclosures. The radio informs us that George W. Bush will be president 4 more years. The Patriot Act is forever law, and Iraq will never end. Bush is still president, and I am escorting Lana to methadone. I am taking Leeloo to a place of concrete & barb wire with buzzers on the doors and... ***You can stop now...*

It is the night of my book release party; Saturday, January 5ᵗʰ 2005. *Before Thanksgiving, Lana went to Court.* Tonight is my grand triumph, and I will sit behind a desk in an uncomfortable chair jerking my upper torso around as to avoid the nerve damage firebomb throughout my spine.

I will sign my autograph into every copy that is purchased with a personalized message to my fans, just like all those big writers who looked so fulfilled in victory.

Lana had gotten in trouble. She was walking down the street in Royal Oak and this guy kept following her, asking if she had a Vicodin he could buy. She said, "No, leave me alone," and he kept following her, bothering her for three blocks until she was so fed up that she just said "Fuck it, here, just give me $2 and leave me alone." That's when the undercover cop detained her, and the squad cars rolled up.

I take the lint brush to my tie and iron my suit for once, because I want to look good for this. *Although it was Lana's first offense, they tried to put her in prison for 10 years. She would've received the full sentence had her father not re-mortgaged their house to pay $50,000 in lawyer & court fees.*

I climb into the car and speed off to the venue to spend my last night as Mr. Media Golden Boy, the night before they actually read the contents of the book. At the venue I take my seat & watch faces pick through the pages. Some of them point out the incorrect grammar or misspelled words, while others' eyes grow chaotically wide or recoil in frantic repulsion.

Despite being a first offense, the judge sentences Lana to 8 months in prison & another two years of reporting probation with hundreds of hours of community service as well as drug rehab classes she somehow has to pay $50 dollars per visit to attend. If she does not have the money, they will lock her up for another year in violation of her release terms.

I sit in the chair flanked by my bible of hatred, this gospel of contempt with it's grainy low-res pumpkin orange cover that showcases the evil clown of madness which is now an acute mirror. There I am, right there on the book – the scourge of HellCity, the Mayor of Freaktown, the Clown Prince of Grime.

Somewhere in a concrete cell Harley is detoxing from heroin, vomiting into a toilet. She's wondering just how much longer it'll take for me & Two-Face & Penguin & Frost & Ivy to come bust her out of Arkham...

I feel that tingle, and I know she's in the room. I gaze up from the hell of my own creation, ignoring some guy that wants an autograph so that I can wander to the side of the staircase.

I'm bathed in shadows, lurking behind her. She slips into the crowd looking lost, frightened by the loud noise of the bands. I slip behind her like a ninja & gently tap her on the shoulder. Zelda turns around, and we lock eyes once again.

Two days later, and we're on my bed. I ask what she wants to do, since it's the first we've hung since she ran to Tennessee. Then her tiny body floats atop mine like a gliding feather.

She clasps her arm around my body squeezing tight, absorbing me. Zelda lets loose a giant grin that is pressed against my chest, ear tuning into my heart just to gauge the rhythm. I don't want to interrupt it for anything.

She opens her eyes a little, climbs up my shirt with gentle grasps and kisses me. The earth grows quiet. We make out slowly, passionately. She starts to pull up my shirt, I lift off hers... The sun is rising, and we've been at it for 6 hours.

We both laugh, realizing the eclipse of time. I head to the toilet, for once not noticing the bath tub. I try to urinate but so much serotonin has weakened my knees. Dizzy, I timber in front of the toilet and begin vomiting from profound joy. I am free.

Acropolis Now

The textbook definition of disaster is a calamitous event, especially one occurring suddenly & causing great loss of life, damage, or hardship – such as an earthquake, airplane crash, or oil spill of unprecedented caliber...

As is what's happening right now, in The Gulf, in 2010. Mistress Maam and I have been living at The Acropolis Hotel, charting the ecological terror _not_ broadcast on CNN, FOX, MSNBC, DrudgeReport, InfoWars, MichealMoore or even PeterWerbe.com. There are a number of reasons for this, of which I will soon begin.

Under Obama's authorization, the United States Coast Guard *(& British Petroleum)* have dumped nearly 50 million gallons of the untested, experimental dispersent Corexit 9500 *(& the far more lethal 9527)* into the ocean, creating an ecological monstrosity buttressed by 500 to 900 million gallons of crude oil. No one is quite sure the actual figure.

Even by the lowest of estimates, Deepwater Horizon now equals 3 dozen Exxon/Valdez's – previously the worst oil spill ever sustained – and which in aftermath left the majority of cleanup workers dead from toxicity levels.

All of those deceased grunts, it should be noted, never had to contend with Corexit – a chemical 4 times more toxic then crude in itself. Corexit's function is to literally eat the oil, obliterating it into minuscule particles. In theory, these particles are biodegradable & mix into the ocean currents like loose grains of sand.

In reality, Corexit had never actually been used on anything larger then 1000 barrels of oil – which is why all of these globules have accumulated into a massive jelly blob roughly the size of Rhode Island.

Furthermore, the chemical immediately releases the most deadly, latent properties of crude, causing the surrounding water to soak up 3,500% more of the toxic properties then it would in its natural state.

This aquatic Corexit landmass – this oxygen-deprived, toxic vacuum – has already killed hundreds of thousands of fish, altering the ecosystem for decades and permanently mutating the genetics of all ensnared life forms.

As The Blob heads towards Southern Florida, smaller chunks continue to wash ashore in Louisiana, Georgia, Mississippi, Florida, etc. At a microscopic level, it's been continually ingested through skin contact of any & all swimming those same beaches.

Having never been tested at length on human subjects and banned in the UK, all emerging research now comes from the epidemically ill Southern population & rapidly dying mass of cleanup workers. This past week an investigation determined Corexit 9500 to be a a confirmed carcinogen – *in all probability worse then Agent Orange…*

This brings us to a multitude of barbaric realities. Foremost, all of that Corexit, crude oil & methane gas has for some time been evaporating and, in turn, raining down upon the region, the East Coast, the Midwest – all the way into Canada. This precipitation, in turn, is now eating through plant life as an acidic pesticide would.

One search on YouTube will bring forth hundreds of amateur videos of this, as well as testimonials from people dizzy & vomiting after heavy rains, passing out, sick for days – their homes covered in oily residue & the streets slicked with *"rainbow film."*

There's been a 65% increase in people seeking emergency care for respiratory problems all over the South. Even an official CDC survey in Alabama found that 50% of all questioned claimed newly emerged respiratory problems.

In Louisiana especially, as well as Florida, it is reported that entire communities are now vomiting blood.

A recent study has also found that this mix of rain, oil & Corexit has altered sediments natural ability to cleanse arsenic from the water supply. 16 private wells outside Tampa were found to be of nearly fatal, poisonous levels.

Dozens of studies have also confirmed the unspeakable contamination of waters – oil up to 220 PPM (parts per million); in some areas of Mississippi 620 PPM. Even beach sand is testing around 200 PPM. There should be none.

And then the air quality. On May 3rd a Russian television crew confirmed that the air in Venice, Louisiana was so filthy the camera operators should have been wearing contamination suits. The EPA claims that 5-10 PPB (parts per billion) or Hydrogen Sulfide is acceptable. The news crew had clocked 1192 PPB.

The VOC count (Volatile Organic Compounds) clocked in at similarly hideous ranges. The State of Louisiana says 3.76 PPB is acceptable for Benzene, Methylene Chloride 61.25 PPB. On May 2nd, the air quality registered 3,416 PPB combined VOC's.

Likewise, in September, a team from Bio-Cascade (*an air-pollution specialist team from New Jersey*) visited Alabama and found 110 PPM of VOC's in the air.

Unmarked Coast Guard planes have been continuously spraying Corexit over civilian populations, over shallow waters & beaches in a frantic effort to annihilate the aforementioned aquatic jelly blob before it reaches shore.

One couple, living in their boathouse, woke up soaking from said airplane spray and immediately started puking blood. Their skin is now covered in sores, like lepers – same as the other hundreds of individuals now coming forward.

There are dozens of families that went to the beach for a scenic Sunday, coming home covered in blisters, bleeding from their eyes. These people are generally rushed to ER and the doctors are clueless how to combat these symptoms – all toxicology reports indicate a poisoning by unknown neurotoxins. Emerging blood tests show staggeringly high amounts of ehtylbenzene, hexane, xylene, isooctane, and both 2 & 3-methylpentane.

There are many other frightening examples of the above predicament and even more unanswered questions regarding the following. Ever heard of Vibrio Vulnificus, a rare waterborne illness originating from oyster beds? V.V. claims a small number of deaths worldwide, yet last month six deaths were attributed to V.V.

One of them – a 12 year old named John Lopez –walked on a Florida shore barefoot and was eaten alive within 24 hours. There is distinct evidence that this strain may have been a mutation, which an ongoing study at Louisiana State.

Beyond all this, the true horror emerging is the negligence of the EPA, whom <u>refuse to test the seafood</u> emerging from The Gulf – *which means, quite frankly, that a staggering amount of individuals have been ingesting Corexit daily, literally eating it for months on end, at a global scale so criminal it cannot be fathomed…*

Millions of people are going to die.
And no one knows – no one except for me & Mistress Maam.

No one, that is, until The Blob actually touches shore in a definite, unavoidable, in-your-face kind of way. And then America will catch on in a definite, unavoidable, in-your-face kind of way. And then things will grow exceptionally grim, exceptionally fast. And then The Great Panic will begin, which is the major reason this is not being reported.

The Federal Government has failed so abysmally in such a cataclysmic, catastrophic way that not only is it an embarrassment to their prestige, but the lineage aftereffects I've entailed are so hideous, so murderous, the only way to solve the problem is to pretend it simply isn't happening.

The straight answer would have been immediate evacuation, which was stalled through fear of economic/political backlash. The NAVY had already evacuated by July 2nd under the guise of fighting a drug cartel, having relocated 46 warships to Costa Rica capable of carrying 200 helicopters & warplanes, plus 7,000 U.S. Marines *"who may circulate the country in uniform without any restrictions"* for *"anti-narcotics operations & humanitarian missions between 1st July 2010 until 31st December 2010."*

And also by July 4th NATO's Chairman of the Military Committee Admiral Giampaolo Di Paola ordered 2,400 Canadian Military Forces to prepare for deployment to the Coast to assist FEMA, simultaneously moving all critical NATO assets 100 miles from shore. Much movement & tactical placement has occurred, though much of it secretly and unable for definite confirmation.

The real fear it seems is not the deadly chemical, but the rupturing of the seafloor itself. At the moment it is "plugged" – but all data indicates a rupturing for miles beneath the surface, oil still seeping through the ocean floor kilometers around.

If the seabed gives way, this would equal an instant tsunami so massive and violent in its force that it would cover Florida within minutes, wiping out millions in one stroke.

But even that seems child's play compared to the possibility of an oil hurricane. Just what happens, pray tell, when a Class 5 ripper just barrels through Texas leaving a trail of toxic, cancer-causing, brain hemorrhaging, methane suffocating death?

What does "evil commie nigger" look like then, when he sends National Guard to forcefully remove Grandma Bush-throttler by gunpoint? Or what happens when he simply does nothing and the Texas Tea hurricane comes anyway – when all those people are proxy butchered by this callous breach of human dignity?

There was no contingency plan from the outset. And the only way out is to keep burying, keep blacking it out. The entire Washington elite allowed this to happen – and now their asses are on the line at such an appalling, historic level that no previous tragedy in American heritage remotely compares.

And still, no one knows. You can grab a man on the street, scream at him, shake him by the lapels, explain point for point what I just elaborated, but not a thread of it sinks in. All they can envision are petroleum dolphins, beached whales & pelicans shitting oil. Their ignorance is manifold, engulfing, complete. Here, in The Dead City where The Acropolis is center of the filth-ridden maze.

Whereas previously Barack had floundered, struggling against unsparing criticism & distortion, he has failed unspeakably & decisively. Since inauguration he waded through an avalanche empirical attack stunting the smallest progression – the slightest shove to the GOP & a firestorm in return.

He lost the propaganda war early, decisively. They swarmed in and tore his flesh, Jackals devouring his entrails from the floor. The greed kingpins subdued & suffocated, sucking the very marrow from his bones. It was already over. Long before Deepwater H.

Which is the reason why Obama – via executive order – made it a $40,000 fine & felony with a max 15 years for filming the oil spill or "cleanup" without "official authorization."

Barack brings his own family to Florida for economic gear-greasing, poll strengthening, panic-diverting propaganda. Has his kids jog shoreline in swimsuits. Has his wife smile & wave-lure the hesitant, signaling all to doom while clenching pearly whites...

The idiots are at the gates, swarming. Every issue the 1960's dodged now spasms in a completely reversed spectrum. Instead of social revolution, we get the digital revolution. Instead of minority rights, we confront gay rights. The atheist/agnostic movement is coming out of the closet, and the 9/11 Truth Movement is entering mainstream consciousness.

Instead of Nixon, we have Obama. Instead of MLK, we have Sarah Palin – the first major anti-feminist female marching endless scores of mullet evangelicals...

The GOP hijacked "Tea Party" – how does one even begin to describe these mouth breathing lunatics? Where does one start, assuming this explanation is the only one which may be handed to future generations?

It's kind of simple really – after they leveled the World Trade Center, they unsheathed their finely tuned, years-in-the-making culture of fear, then ran the Orwellian illusion stark-weasel wild. In one blinding shock & awe campaign against all civil liberties & human decency, they dropped this thing called The Patriot Act on us.

Then they trotted out an apparatus called "Homeland Security," an "Axis of Evil" to eternally fight, two illegal wars & dozens of secret ones, and yet one more stolen election in which both candidates were blood related Skull & Bones members.

Then they signed a variety of permanent no-bid war contracts, slashed endless social programs, then further moved us towards a total surveillance society augmented by the largest domestic militarization campaign this country has ever seen. Terror, terror everywhere – reinforced daily, endlessly...

The man at the bottom of this pyramid has never been abused more voraciously. In his economic hardship, this unwitting stooge blames all the wrong people. He salutes the flag unflinchingly, then sends his children to be blown into mutilated chunks in obscure deserts, because an idiot criminal duped him into suicidal sacrifice. Hand in hand they follow, goose-stepping into oblivion...

And then comes Obama. After 8 years of fascism he somehow, by fluke, becomes president. Not feeling the need to continue this insane march towards the doom of our species – *or trying to stop it as much as his puppet presidency will allow* – the constantly reinforced propaganda immediately dissipates. And just like Stockholm Syndrome, the slaves shout at the TV upset they are no longer being fed endless doses of terror... *The message of hope has already failed; the entire country is about to crumble...*

I never wanted to move to Portland, and it was because of her that I prematurely aborted Seattle. All I wanted to do was go home, ever since Florida, where I met her. I have been trying to get rid of Mistress Maam ever since. Every time we break up she mutates into another of my ex-girlfriends that I am forced to both court and sever ties with once again.

Mistress Maam is a psychic chameleon; her uncanny ability is to burn her green eyes through me then speak entire lines of dialogue pulled from the compartmentalized memory banks of all my ex girlfriends. She spits them out word for word, these vocal echoes burned deep in memory.

The black magic beast knows that I am her prey, such as a hapless gnat in the mesh of a great web. Her chameleon eyes augment from sharp green to the partial color of whoever she's channeling. She absorbs everyone, consciously or unconsciously, like a skin-walker on auto-pilot spaced from one too many vials of liquid acid. More often then not the bad parts and unruly edges.

I am her protector; if she were to be left alone, monsters would eat her. I am the rusted Golem which she drags through Oz. It is for her that I will eventually be put in prison for covering up some heinous crime that she will no doubt commit.

I need Mistress Maam to thieve my computer when primed for monumental trance-writing because I'm not paying enough attention to her. I need her to leave physical threats on my voicemail like digital land-mines of an internal Normandy, or to send text messages declaring she'd set all of my belongings on fire while obliviously at work.

I need this total psychopath prone to violent rages & frivolous tantrums to physically throw people out of the car while driving 30 mph over the Burnside Bridge.

I need this pear-shaped lunatic to not let me sleep because she compulsively ate heavy duty ecstasy and is now wandering Downtown lost with blurry vision can't read any signs because the words are ping-pong trails smacked between two wooden paddles.

I need my adorable nuisance to go on insincere dates with other guys then text me about it while cooking through a dinner rush so she can propel a 3am near future of angry choke-out karate sex.

It is her that I need to spontaneously demand I drive to the middle of the forest under the full moon so she can ritualistically burn all of her clothing and items pertaining to a former life. I need this BDSM fiend to shout & throw things & make a big scene inside the fine-dining restaurant because I won't slice her up with razors.

I need my vial girl to appear at the back door of my work sobbing because she snapped an hour earlier and intentionally began weaving through hi-speed freeway lanes at 80mph trying to kill herself and anyone she could take with her. I need Poison Ivy and her sleep terror demons & hallucinogenic worm beasts sliming through the walls...

It hurts me to hurt her. Even if the woman she takes the form of had been cruel to me, I stop myself. I realize it is not really her, she's just freeing haunted memories from locked sarcophagus. Mistress Maam is all of them combined, all the nasty vibrations of former truncated love. I know it is so, because I created her such as Serpentor with an unruly black magick trumpet aimed at the heavens. I know it is so, and now I must defeat the worst qualities of all of my ex-girlfriends.

But when she slaps on that makeup, when I see the contours of her lipstick lesbian face, she instantly becomes [][][] – she moves like her, talks like her. I am again that little worm on a big fucking hook, and I hate it. I feel the humiliation all over again.

Portland begins looking like Detroit, and I am called out. I am the phantom without escape.

I have this notion that once I've defeated every last one of these ex-girlfriends, the real Mistress Maam will stand before me. Just like peeling paint from a wall thats been done over 40 times I will see the concrete for it's natural shade. She will cease chasing me down the streets calling me a motherfucker & throwing rocks. Undiluted, I just may glimpse the love of my life...

Linda was putting me on a blind date. She knew something had to be done following the Detroit women who were set to visit me but were railroaded. Linda also wanted me to stay in Florida, and thought a woman would act as a paperweight on my drifter existence.

I was at the dinner table, curling up tiny shreds up of paper on Valentines day after the Vietnamese lady had stood me up. 29 years, and not a date for Valentines. Linda mentioned her co-worker, Mistress Maam, whose real name was the same as so many of the past majors: *"Really Ryan, she's cute. Real cute – and she likes all this Polish death metal crap. She's from Michigan, like us, trying to start a new life. You know how when I'm looking for something, just searching for an item & you'll say 'I ate it?' She does that all the time – ALL the time. You both say so many same things it's eerie..."*

"You can leave if you want, just go back to Seattle. But we're all going to a metal show on Friday, this dive outside Tampa. I told her about you already. And it's the only thing going on Friday – it's been months since you've been to a gig. So you can sit here and be depressed, or you can tag along. Choice is yours."

Sometimes you know you're stepping into a rat trap but you're so hungry that nasty piece of cheese is worth the spinal trauma. I knew that if I was ever to go home, it was best to stay put. _But_... Parabellum was playing, whose doomy stoner record was the last album I reviewed before leaving Detroit forever. It was apropos.

I wasn't knocked out by Mistress Maam. She reeked black magick juju the way a witchy woman always does, and her burning eyes were trying to crawl through my head. I pretended not to notice or care – don't try to pull Anne Rice shit on me honey, I deflect you.

She had this gothy *"night out on the town"* get-up with black leather boots, black dress & trenchcoat. *Black, black, black, Number One*, you know? Said she'd dreamt of me last week, that there was a man with a shaved head & a book in his hands. She likened me to Mr. Rabbit from *Alice In Wonderland*, checking my stopwatch, rushing about in need of the rabbit hole.

I acted uninterested, proceeding with my usual pacing around business rant – the: *"I do this blah blah I do that blah blah I need to move ASAP I need to go back to Seattle nothing's gonna stop me..."*

She came to visit the next night, showing up in a ratty Grateful Dead tye-dye & denim shorts. Listening to the woman banter on about banal gibberish I wanted to dig up Garcia's corpse and fed-ex her the excrement-caked remains...

The next day, I go to her pre-birthday party out of boredom. There are a bunch of us riding in an SUV and the stereo is jamming Opeth.

Mistress Maam lets her tomboy out and is headbanging & screaming lyrics in the car, being viciously metal & so so drunk.

We hit up a string of bars around Treasure Island where idyllic white sands & turquoise blue water reconnects us with the randazzle of our tropical victory existence. Back home, in Michigan, it is 20 degrees. We are still young and any direction is possible.

I turn to Linda, who just appeared with her boyfriend, and smile. Finally feeling it after all these years, slightly inebriated, I comment: *"George Bush isn't the President anymore."*

It's dark outside, a crazy purple/blue powered by Zmoon reflecting off vast ocean waters. We're sucking face outside a bar, she's against the concrete of the wall. Both of us taste like whiskey...

Next day it's her birthday. She is bright & sunny – she does not know the monster that I am. I feel like I am lying to her, even though I fabricate nothing.

We go to a shopping center, searching for socks. She makes sleazy BDSM comments that catch my attention and soon we're actually communicating. She starts talking about Tool & A Perfect Circle. Starts talking tarot & divination & all that mumbo jumbo hippy dippy too much faith in the universe bullshit.

She takes me out to sushi. It has the air of an absurd job interview in which I have no interest of employment. Two hours later & *dirty, dirty, dirty girl*...

A few days later I'm on the curb with all my stuff in duffel bags. The moon is full, it's deja vu. Mistress Maam pulls up and takes me home, has me move in with her...

Loneliness, that's why. Under a blackened spell and living without the touch of another. Loneliness is why we hatch the plan to move to Seattle together, to just drive all the way from Florida. Just blow this pop-stand on my birthday.

So far as I can tell, she's another one of those girls that go city to city. She'd been to the Bible Belt, lived in San Diego & come to Treasure Island by chance...

Even if I don't want to be with her long term, she deserves the Northwest. Kick and scream as she may, curse me as she will, in the end she will thank me, for I am not only Mr. Rabbit but I am the Ferryman on the River Styx, thousands of kilometers from port...

Within a few days, the disturbances start. The paranormal stuff, I mean, that became the unhealthy glue of our relationship. It started long, long ago, and is another story entirely. But it had been quiet.

See, there's this baggage I carry. This baggage, see, is baggage I don't want to find me. I leave it at the house before I get on the airplane, so to speak, and I travel to avoid my luggage. I like having no clothes. It's important to just be naked for as long as I can.

But this baggage always finds me, like a pyramid of duffel bags snuck into my house by reverse burglars. Then I go to the next spot, just to stay naked. I pick up more clothing, so to speak, before the inverse thieves just pile a duffel avalanche onto my carpet.

And again I go, dirty socks stay put. Stay where you should. Mentally, to bury this concealed aphorism, I keep buying fresh new socks. In real world, that is – black ones, always the same. Always fresh. New feet, new steps. It's clean again – it is quiet.

It is 1am, the world is asleep, I am at the table, at one with black java. Through YouTube I exhume the wealth of ghost, alien, cryptid & conspiracy footage littering the internet. I push past the silly hoax videos about the human sacrifice Owl statue Illuminati camp and stumble onto the possessed voice of Anneliese Michel recordings layered over grisly photographs of her late-stage transformation. *There is a reason she received 67 exorcism rites...*

Playing that voice – those voices within voices – it makes every hair crawl. But it also made strange noises, strange presences in the house. The dog began freaking out, the cat. Windows start making weird clinks where nothing should be hitting them.

I hit stop. I felt something bad be summoned. Not because of the video, but because I kicked into that part of my radar. Drugs are cool. They keep it quiet. I wanted quiet. Avoid the dirty sock pile that just appeared in the living room.

Back to my central confrontation, that pesky 9/11 thing. Beforehand, I just assumed they knew what would happen, but let it happen as an excuse to justify everything they soon achieved. I had a naive belief that perhaps they assumed the people/airliners/authorities would foil the plot – but if a little blood needed be shed, so be it.

But now I knew the physics, the science, the blatant & systematic use of thermal explosives. I understood what it would really take to bring down a building that won the Nobel Prize for architecture 'cause it could withstand 15 Boeing 747's flying into it.

And The Pentagon, of course, where the remains of the plane & black box just vanished with all passenger bodies 'cause it was so hot it just burned them into vapor, leaving a 16 foot hole in the wall.

The next hole was 12 feet wide, and went right into the Pentagon Wing that was emptied and under major construction, where Rumsfeld had just relocated information pertaining to $6,000,000,000 missing dollars. And to prove to us there was no foul play they confiscated all video camera footage within a 100 mile radius at gunpoint by black suit spooks without warrants. <u>Haha</u>.

And then Building 7 just exploded for no reason, you know. And the camera man who worked for FEMA, who was positioned with FEMA operatives on September 10th around the World Trade Center with dump trucks and tactical crew. He filmed FEMA setting thermal charges before quite realizing what this was, and soon as the planes began crashing he immediately fled.

Right over the Mexican border with his family, and they made it to Argentina. He now lives there under political asylum, in hiding. The evidence he possesses is what he believes keeps him and his family alive. Coincidentally he's on the most wanted terrorist list of the USA government, and bin Laden isn't. Haha.

Enough about that. We're getting around to dirty socks. A rock slide of them, pouring like a waterfall. Within a week, it sounds like there is a pacing army encircling the house with foliage rattling as if we're in the tame eye of a hurricane even though there is no wind. Lights turn themselves on, cupboards open.

White candle flame blows without a source of wind to propel it. The things in the walls are ripping their phantasmal claws from behind the concrete, and a shadow lurker stalks Mistress Maam about the house. Every night we are woke to it standing outside our bedroom door breathing heavy, pacing the living room & vanishing.

Mistress Maam was taking a shower and it began beating on the door from the other side. To protect my Mistress Maam. I must vanquish again the Fruit of the Loom.

We must go, the both of us, for if I abandon her now, The Goblin King will snatch her up. Stolen by transparent gypsies; heisted by celestial criminality. She will be an unsolved footnote in the newsprint, a made for TV psychic detective movie in waiting. I must rescue Mistress Maam from all which goes bump in the night...

We were on the road nearly a week before reaching Kluck. I hadn't dealt with him in over a year and a half. He was the central linchpin in the collapse of San Deigo. The ugly scene that went down was a result of 15 of the most extreme people in America living under the same roof – but his presence set the tone.

I really wanted something to happen, and he wouldn't let it happen. None would. It is only now that the tragedy has settled. I have a new monster by my side, and I don't need him around.

Kluck was trapped in Texas, needing to skip out on shoplifting charges. He was going to do time somewhere outside Dallas and begged me for a life raft. I didn't want to be responsible for him. I told him I would consider it, but I did not want to live with him and he would go no further then Portland.

Seattle was to be mine, Oregon his – carving up the landscape like Tito and Stalin so neither bombs the other. And then when he was all set up we could possibly be like exchange students – provided he got off dope. He claimed to be clean & living with his father in some trailer park.

Kluck had the only remaining copy of my secret book that was physically printed. I was obsessed with only having one copy exist, one perfect version where no one could ever pervert it with special editions of early text I long ditched.

This old version was crap compared to what I now had after years of addition and editing. Kluck refused to give it up. He likened it to Kafka wanting all his old work burned after his death. I had to go there and get it. I had to torch that thing myself.

We evacuated from Largo soon as Mistress Maam was fired from her job. All she needed was one last weekend as a waitress. She came out crying, knowing she lacked gas money to get us there, knowing she would have to rely on me, crying because she thought I might leave her behind.

A table of rich yuppies lied to the management and said she dropped the f-bomb, when she accidentally said "*shit*" when dropping the guy's credit card. They acted like it was nothing and laughed it off, then they turned their smiling Floridian upper class faces to the management and got her fired for the explicative.

We gathered our belongings and fled, heading up through Tallahassee into Pensacola, onward through Mobile, Alabama and Gulfport, Louisiana, riding high above New Orleans and through Baton Rouge, up to Shreveport & into Dallas.

Every mile in Texas might as well be 4 or 5, because you're always on edge waiting for some fucked up bulldog of a steroid pig to pull you over so he can pull down your pants and wedge his badge up broken spokes.

We got to Kluck's dead-end trailer late at night, insect noises on full-blast country setting. I snuck up to his window where he was staring blankly into the glowing TV where I could feel a slow eruption of an aura of 8 months of *Yee-Haw* reruns, police harassment, zero job prospects & way too much porn – a whole new caliber of wasted time and slothful effort.

I rap-tap-tapped the window, and he gave a blank stare. Then something stirred. He struggled to escape his nest of doom, put on pants, and then make it to the door. Soon as I saw him, I snapped out of it. Mistress Maam seemed absurd, and I felt terrible. I wasn't quite sure what I was doing.

We dug out the bonfire pit & Kluck cringed as I burned that murky manuscript he deemed so holy. He was going to sell that thing on Ebay for $30,000 one day – it was his retirement plan.

The 3 of us left the next morning. Before we headed out I shook him down, and caught him with a hypodermic needle. He threw it out the window symbolically, but I had no faith in him.

But at least I could dump him off in San Fran or Portland where he could be a happy junkie. At least he could catch some good gigs during his spiral of self destruction. Kluck was static as always, jabbering riffs on his unending deviant sex comedy nightlife. He was the trailer park raider of cougar community.

We drove through Texas avoiding funnels as always, and crossed over into Oklahoma. We went straight for Norman, where the ruins of Fortress Andromeda were boarded up by the local authorities. The crust cluster I'd met on Downtown Brown tours were still in town, and we spent 2 days around campus and crashing in dirty dog houses, drinking wine on top of apartment buildings and overlooking the dust blown streets with bulbous street lights.

I'd my last glimpse of Athena, who had gone in another direction entirely. The girl I crushed on had changed dramatically within months. She'd returned to college, shacked up with a new mate, and moved on quick.

It was somewhere in the desert, in New Mexico, when we began having radiator trouble. Mistress Maam, she was a real grease monkey. Ultra tomboy when she gutted those motors, grubbily splotched in oil. She could handle it with a few tools. Wasn't shit to her, this leaking.

We stopped on the side of the road to check it out, and as I went for smokes, another car rolled up. They were small talking for a few minutes and she had brought up my book. This guys' friend had downloaded it from the internet, spent $30 to print it at Kinko's, and was telling everyone who would listen to do the same.

I was more floored to meet someone that put me on their upcoming reading list then he was to meet me in person, randomly, in the desert. He gave us the coordinates of a secret party that was membership only.

We patched up the car and made elite gathering by 10pm. It was at a historic building, like a log cabin fortress built into a tree and stationed on a weird slant. It was full of every counterculture slice you can think of – hippies were dancing to the goth industrial DJ, and metalheads were drinking whiskey with the ravers at the bar.

This gothed out obese woman got a crush on Kluck, and we peddled him like unsavory pimps. He took one for the team and agreed to cuddle those flabby arms so we'd have a place to sleep.

As Mistress Maam and I slept soundly on the carpeted floor, she pounced in secret. Kluck said it was the first time he couldn't hold an erection, and all he could see when closing his eyes was a moist & sticky waterbed made of flesh.

We blew right through Las Vegas without stopping – Barstow, Bakersfield, up the I-5 and into the I-101. We soon made our way into the steel Goliath that is San Francisco and landed our shuttle outside Golden Gate Park.

Finally, back to the United States only acid-head reservation. The Natives have them, but this one spot – this patch of sacred land in LSD folklore – this is the only spot where you can run around naked on hallucinogens and it is totally legal. So long as you're not playing with yourself.

Golden Gate is crawling with drug dealers, street kids, train-hoppers, scumfucks. You name it and it's there, like a cauldron. It is the grody forest of eccentric enchantment. Mistress Maam spotted the scumfuck tribe, splitting 40's in the distance. Innocently, she asked: *"Where do they live?"* Kluck chuckled: *"Under that tree."*

I wandered up and broke their circle. I was back, and these blood-puking alcoholics were the ones that really toughened me up for street world. I never really fell through the cracks in that *"west coast street crazy"* way until I rolled with their mob, soon growing accustomed to their lice-ridden, scabbed up, bruised n' battered gutter punk traditions. Every time you check in with these guys, another two have died.

As Kluck went off across town for a mission he didn't want to discuss, most likely gay sex for money or the Craigslist seduction of a tranny, Mistress Maam and I wandered around the Castro District, down Mission, through complexes of bars.

We snagged Kluck from Height/Ashbury, both of us relieved he wasn't nodding off from dope. We headed up to West Oakland to sleep in the car, and it was chilly & raining hard when we awoke.

We dropped by my writer friends apartment, this girl I knew from MI. She cooked us bacon & eggs while describing her zombie romance book *The Loving Dead*, which had just come out in print.

We proceeded up the 101 for the nature. At some point in the mountains, battling the road so the car doesn't spin like a sled off the cliff, I find a voice message from Lana. Her mother had just died of AIDS, and the sad girl is calling me because she doesn't want me to die. Don't die Ryan. Don't die... I can't call her back becuse Lana is the past. Lana is gone, Lana is phantasm, and there is no other alternative but forward motion.

We roll into Portland & it's crisply cold – bright blue skies. Everyone rushing to work as we cruise downtown streets. I'd only been here once, with Jeremy, when we got stuck on that Greyhound for 6 days. But that was a limited excursion in Chinatown.

Here I saw a Portland I never knew. Here I saw the future, with it's cluster-fuck of time eras & architectural lineage, it's octopus steel bridges & endless tavern spawning.

We met up with a local metalhead who'd emailed me back in Florida, that had read *The Big Shiny Shiny Prison*. I was hoping to dump Kluck on him, or at least push him in the right direction. Guy comes out the house in a GG t-shirt, and soon confirms we discovered Kluck's long lost cousin.

He was another who'd kicked the habit, who invested his energies into making deranged art & editing a scumbag zine about heroin culture. He was into misanthropic black metal and was a professional porn henchman. I handed Kluck $60 and left him with metal dude, hoping he'd get it right this time. If not, I was absolved.

Mistress Maam and I rolled into Seattle. As the freeway lines blurred by our speed she was jumpy with joy, yet all I felt was betrayed by its stark outline. I had violated her, and I knew it. All my fanciful visions of Seattle broke apart – the saga of 2009 was a fabrication in my head pieced together by absurd logic. All I wanted was sleep.

We swung up to the university district and dropped by the punk divebar where I'd spent so many nights. Tonight it was bleak – just some grisly alcoholic punk guys with elitist train-hopper attitudes. Fellows I didn't want to associate with, and they pretended not to know me anyway.

Miss Monster soon called, and said she was unavailable for the week due to family stuff. Throughout my winter misadventure I'd nursed this fantasy where I'd return & her kids would run up joyful to see me, hug my legs, that sort of thing. Uncle Bartek was back around, and the little girl would draw crayon pictures with me as the boy chatted up *Spiderman* comics. It was an illusion and not my life.

I burned through the rest of my phone numbers, reaching only dead ends. I had no clear idea where to go with this human baggage I now possessed; I was stuck with Mistress Maam.

Holly Doom met us at Cal Anderson Park, in tight leather pants. She looked terrific, and was clearly waiting for me. The weight around my neck fumed in veiled jealousy. *Holly, Holly, Holly Doom...* I wanted to ditch the complaining, difficult girl.

We walked up the park slope so I could reclaim my earthen pinnacle – the mound at the north end of the park, where at night the luminescent skyline of Seattle stretched out beyond the The Pyramid of floating water inside the odd cylindrical reservoir lake.

That sight once invigorated me, filled me with hope & promise. Yet tonight, even the grass is uncomfortable. And the police were now stationing their squad cars inside Cal Anderson park, acting like rigid security and kicking everyone out by 11pm.

Holly goes home sad 'cause I'm not going with her, and the disgruntled woman & I sleep in the car. Next night, again in the car. 3rd night still no one's called – we again sleep in the car.

4th night, after hours of MM's verbal assailing, I get a motel. Always that same room which finds you at the end of the line – nowhere left to go but that cracked-wall cubicle with ants & cold showers, bulletholes in the walls, cracked out methy hookers shuffling outside the window & parking lot like ghoulish zombies.

Phone on non-stop & no returned calls. Craigslist hustle full on with dozens of emails raged out & still left in the cold. Nothing. Nada. Zip. Any sympathetics are clearly avoiding the potentially nutty broad I'm dragging along, or they are plainly avoiding me.

Worse yet, all my key people were gone that were transplants from other cities. No one could hold out against this fang-bared, every-man-for-himself economy that emerged after Wall Street collapsed barely 8 months ago.

Every person I wanted to seek out were attributes of an absurd impulse, because I knew them through "people watching." I was acquainted with half the city, yet no one knew my face.

What am I supposed to say? "*Excuse me, but I've seen you wandering this city over the past year. I've gotten to know you quite intimately through visually stalking you for longer then I care to admit – and often on one too many psychedelic drugs. Would you care for some awkward Free Therapy?*"

I cursed my anti-social 2008 version for not doing what needed to be done – *shoulda, woulda, coulda*. I let myself get sloppy, thinking I could fuck around for a year & get back to band life. Now I was a stranger in a strange land without a solid bedrock on which to rely, and I'd rubbed too many people the wrong way.

I laid out on that hooker motel bed looking at the bullet scars in the wall. Mistress Maam was exasperated, berating me. Saying my friends were worthless, that Seattle was a joke. I didn't want to explain that she was the buzzkill, that no one wanted to play hot potato with our doomed coupling.

I also still felt horrible for the scene on our second day here. Our message of distress was picked up by Bianca, Dr. Jeremy's ex-girlfriend. Throughout 2009 he had lived at her family's home and she'd been quite involved in our Food Not Bombs laboring.

Furthermore, Jeremy had cautioned Bianca was a volatile nut. I wasn't interested in making my life hers, but Mistress Maam & I were in need of a place to stay. No harm in a night.

Bianca had mutated from Dr. Jeremy's coveted ideal of the dread-headed vegan anarchist girl into what appeared to be a New Age, tarot-reading, crystal-collecting, short-haired yoga lesbian. For the past year, she'd told me to skip out on Seattle, to head to Portland – that she'd tried repeatedly to no avail.

As we were about to hop the freeway & give Portland a second look, she made clear that Portland was no longer the place to go. I was needed in Seattle – the battle had yet to conclude and I was to stay at her home. She seemed overly friendly, having been shaky with me previously & jealous for Doc's attention. She was all smiles, and I knew something was up.

Bianca had us stash our belongings in her room, and said we could just live in the basement for a few weeks. Mistress Maam exited our presence and I sat on the bed. Bianca prettied herself up in the dresser mirror.

She was coating on the heavy eyeliner, asking questions – slightly dirty, slightly concealed. She made some sleazy comments, vaguely hinting that we were beginning some bereft three way tryst with MM. I realized the trap I was getting into. She wasn't interested in my girlfriend though, not one bit.

Mistress Maam came back in, fiddling with her belt. I asked if it was broke, and she said: "*Nah, I just have to nigger-rig it.*" I felt a cold blast from Bianca as she paused her makeup smearing. "*Man oh man oh man,*" thought I.

In Detroit, everyone says it. Through Ohio, Indiana, Illinois & beyond. "Nigger-rigging" is a term used by everyone – *and mainly by black folk*. It doesn't imply crude racism, but rather ghetto ingenuity. It's a self-empowering exclamation used when a terminally impoverished person figures out how to super-glue their leaking radiator or fasten the engine in place with coat hangers.

It is proudly stated, because the victor had defeated the white mans' trap of having to pay a mechanic $500 to fix a problem the car company had relied on from the beginning.

In Detroit, for instance, you pull up to a car parts store with a sunroof crafted from a chunk of wood laying in your backyard, and a random black dude is in the parking lot with a wide smile. He loudly shows it off to the other bystanders: *"He done nigger-rig his car!!"* laughing hysterically in that solid way which is on your side. And then the other black dudes in the parking lot notice your hackjob, and all stand around marveling at your supreme *"nigger-rigging."*

But the Northwest is another creature. The left-leaning progressive bubble has manufactured an often joyless political correctness & somewhat sterile version of America in which no comparable ghettos exist.

See, when you erase poverty and ignorance in a way that most America cannot, elitist standards begin to create strange grids. People can become focused on problems other then the street level communications at the lowest rungs.

Every fucking everybody used the term *"nigger-rig"* in Detroit. And in Detroit, people used the word *"nigger"* to describe any piece of shit regardless of their color. But I know what doesn't fly out here, and I was careful to augment my speech since.

But Mistress Maam, she is a newbie. She just let it slip, fumbling with a belt buckle & trying to knife in a new notch: *"Nah, I just have to nigger-rig it."*

It is at the bar, after hours of wandering Capitol Hill with the girls holding hands & grabbing at my ass when this ramshackle scenario is going to crumble. I have been totally uncomfortable with this the entire time, and stupidly allowed myself to drink.

Bianca is drunk, sees MM lean into me, and flares with jealousy. Her eyes turn cold and evil, and I see everything Jeremy warned me about. She starts screaming *"NIGGER RIG NIGGER RIG NIGGER RIG!!"* midst this haughty-taughty, too expensive martini bar on Broadway. She grabs her coat, then storms out.

I give it a few minutes hoping she'll calm down, but then she starts texting me. Says she's taking the bus home, and she's going to burn all our shit and destroy the computers. Mistress Maam flips out.

We find Bianca outside and she starts swinging punches. But she is the only key to getting our belongings back. I'm not sure what to do. MM will kill this stupid girl if she lets loose. She is holding back, even as I become the totem center of a cat fight which I'm steadily moving to the car like one difficult, violent organism.

After fighting each other for 5 minutes, and Mistress Maam looks like she is going to cry, and with this scene breaking my heart completely, Jeremy's skeezy ex-girlfriend gets into the back of the car. She demands a ride home.

She's in the back seat behind Mistress Maam, and once we get on the freeway she starts kicking the back of her chair as hard as she could. Repeatedly, while we're going 70mph on the freeway.

The evil, psychotic loon rolls down the window & hangs out the side of it, screaming for people to call the cops and pull us over because we're drunk, trying to flag down cop cars as we drive. I'd never come so close to punching a woman in the face.

We get to Bianca's house and she runs inside. We wait, and wait, and wait. Her mother drifts out & tells me to get our stuff. I creep upstairs and Bianca is crying on her bed, weeping like a 12 year old girl. I never wanted to see this fucked up poo-bah again.

We rendezvoused with Jack at another bar on Capitol Hill. He showed up with his cultured lesbian girlfriend, and they asked why this scene occurred. It was like this fly under a microscope, trying to explain the use of "nigger rig" & all the candle-lit tavern hipster people turning around and scolding her. Jack just slipped me that look: *"You seriously going to ruin our plans over this chick?"*

We lingered around Seattle a few more days. Craigslist yielded nothing, and I felt unwanted. I was cast out, like a leper. We left the hooker motel and Mistress Maam found an ad for a room in Portland. It said it was a goth-industrial house, and that anyone who wanted to live there would have to deal with loud music all the time, but that the room was $200 a month. It said just show up in person.

Bruised & battered, I swung by Lesbian Dan's to pick up my guitar & book stash. We stayed the night and he flipped us a bag of grass for our drive. Long ago, when starting my new life in Seattle with3, I declared that Seattle would only end in: *"death, imprisonment, or forced exile."* I never foresaw *"silent exile"*…

We drove up to the goth house on a pot-hole laden street filled with redneck homes that had meth vibes. An overweight hillbilly woman answered the door as several dogs barked explosively: *"Ah don't know nothin' bout no goth house – yer the 5ᵗʰ person that's come by tah-day!!"*

We'd been pranked! Whoever posted that ad was most likely peering out an upstairs window a few houses down, getting incredible kicks out of the self-created, ridiculous situation.

We redirected to a nearby coffee shop and erupted into a shouting match. I regained my cool as she sipped coffee angrily, then called Kluck. Maybe he'd made magic happen & been adopted by a house of freaks blaring Polish death metal.

Instead, he was again in Texas. He lasted 4 days before flaking out and willingly returning to a trailer park in the middle of nowhere in which he was hunted by the police. Rather then just hustle with a cardboard sign, he simply had his father wire a plane ticket to Dallas.

He had joined a shelter, but they wanted him to complete a 6 month program. He got into a scuffle with a vagrant and ran away before the police showed up. They had his info and assumed he'd be arrested. He just caved, the moment I needed him.

Unsure what to do, we headed downtown and got stuck in traffic. Once the auto-cluster broke loose, Mistress Maam caught a weird psychic impulse. She turned to me and said: "*My grandmother just died.*" Her phone rings, and it's family telling her exactly that. She hangs up and I turn on the radio to AM news. The Deepwater Horizon refinery had just exploded, and untold gallons of oil were saturating The Gulf.

Slumped in the passenger seat, sober & exhausted – with Mistress Maam about to bawl her eyes out – the phone rings. A mystery man responds to our emergency rent ad and offers us a place to stay in Beaverton for only $100 a week, up to 2 months if needed. Says he's about to leave town for days & if we are serious to come over immediately.

We pull up to an apartment complex in Beaverton, a suburb of Portland. A Hispanic man in his late 20's lets us in. His name is Ricardo – a community organizer also studying to be lawyer. He's in post-grad school and working as a tutor, and won't be around much because his girlfriend absorbs the remainder of his time.

He leads us through the swanky, fully-furnished apartment with its large screen HD TV, leather sofa, prime kitchen appliances, slick balcony and master bedroom with king-size space-age NASA fabric mattress that instantly molds itself to your spine.

No roaches or bugs, no broken toilet, no shouting domestic violence neighbors to keep us up at night. I slip Ricardo a $100 bucks, he writes down our driver license numbers and simply leaves us there with a smile. For better or worse, we now live in Portland.

Beaverton, I soon learn, is where Portland ends & the pan-American grid begins all over. Those well-lit identical streets with corporate neon logos adorning franchise after franchise.

The only difference between Beaverton & any city with a population of the same size in Illinois is in accordance to the foggy morning & mountainous surroundings. Here we feel the primal aura of the rain forest, even if subdued by concrete.

Close to the apartment is The MAX, the crown jewel of PDX. It's an above-ground subway modeled after the Metro systems of Europe, stretching for hundreds of miles. Combined with the Trimet bus fleet, they cover over 570 square miles.

No other city in the United States compares to the fluidity Trimet offers in terms of accuracy, it's late night/early morning schedules, or it's bare-bones price of $85 a month for endless rides. Within the borders of Downtown, The MAX is free.

I hop on with little more then a handful of resumes which vastly overestimate my kitchen work experience. I need to find a job immediately, and the clock is ticking. The MAX stop within walking distance is a futuristic looking transit center with architecturally pointed peaks. I descend the cement staircase onto the platform, and the train arrives.

With a black shirt & tie & a pin-striped black fedora I hop on feeling & looking like another lost soul of the Great Depression grasping at straws to stay afloat.

The MAX whizzes to the first stop, a gigantic park named Washington. The next is the Oregon Zoo. The next the soccer/baseball stadium, the next creeping into the realms of western Downtown. We cruise through the heart of Pioneer Square and a few stops later I hop out, walking into the first restaurant that could conceivably hire me. I chat with the chef who I quickly learn is a major rivethead. After a few Ministry references, I walk out Club 242 as the freshly hired prep cook.

My eyes grow wide as the flame of consciousness grows. Effortlessly, I have secured a full time kitchen gig and fully furnished apartment. Gears turn, tangles unknot, Rubik's unscramble. I creep through the numbered avenues of Downtown Portland.

The cityscape is a weird hodge-podge of 1950's apartment complexes and mid 20th century business building high-rises flanked by postmodern green-buildings sustaining their energy through solar paneled glass windows. It is a mix of Detroit's Jefferson Ave. waterfront, Chicago & Lower East Manhattan + Seattle.

I made my way to the waterfront along the Willamette River, where the map divides the greater Portland area by East/West. It was their version of Golden Gate park, stretching two miles along Naito Parkway. Dozens of pow-wow huddles of rock n' roll stoners plotted themselves across the long grass stretch, passing pipes and blunts.

I turned down 2nd Avenue, heading north to Burnside which is the Portland equivalent of 8 Mile in Detroit. Like our famed blvd, Burnside determines the base line between North & South Portland, just as the river configures East/West.

At Burnside Bridge, I spotted the rough tribalism of the desperate homeless. It was clear the city had pushed their negligible population into that tidy, dark corner which reeked like piss.

I passed through the vagrant apex and approached the Chinatown entryway, with its golden dragon statues & Hong Kong flavor. Dirty, haunted streets with bad psychic vibes beneath the clusters of drunks clogging this area.

Beneath were the infamous Shanghai Tunnels, where Chinese slavers would capture drunk sailors and imprison them in makeshift cells before selling them off. Poor bastards would be hammered at the wrong bar stool & a trap door would open, dumping them into an underground maze patrolled by Yakuza. These roads felt built upon a minor Auschwitz...

Ricardo returned the following Sunday with a bottle of wine, inviting us to his girlfriends home. He was chipper as I, and our two happy couples would share a feast. She lived close to the apartment in a rustic house with a slight cabin feel.

Arranged about the long table with veggies galore were an array of seafood, oysters, shrimp – anything aquatic we could devour before the oil spill would render this future option moot.

The women got along fancifully as Ricardo and I chatted about Obama. My central dilemma was that here we had a classic capitalist politician, even if marginally sleazy in the greater context.

But something about Barack Obama resonated that he wouldn't cross into total darkside territory. Perhaps he might actually take a stand. Perhaps he might expose whatever shadow government was really operating the show.

Maybe when that top secret meeting of military brass came, Obama would strike down their unjust designs for another profiteering war. He would deny the weapons contractors primed to make billions, he would slap the red stamp on a brewing False Flag. Maybe, just maybe, he was the enemy of Halliburton.

Unless the aliens just replaced him with a clone or a shapeshifter moments after swearing into office, soon as he was out of sight from the world. Ricardo laughed, and I smiled. If there's any one thing I learned, it's that if you talk about aliens in a joking tone you're usually covered; you have a back door to weasel out.

I'm not really convinced aliens are running the show, but at the same time I really wouldn't be surprised.

In any instance, Ricardo & I both felt Obama was the final belch of perceived hope through an American presidency. If this man failed the change he promised, would there be another? Ricardo added that the man was a total enigma to even his own party, and was near impossible to predict. He was Harvey Dent incarnate.

One hour later & two bottles of wine down, Ricardo's girlfriend – leering at me with squinted eyes & Merlot breath – muttered something about "*The Roman.*" I didn't quite catch what she meant, this attribute of Ricardo. She kind of chuckled then said: "*You know, The Roman – like fucking guys from behind and not getting fucked himself... I think he's got an eye for you.*"

Maybe the pin-striped hat was a wrong signal; maybe this cat didn't know I just dig wearing ties. It sobered me up.

Ricardo burst from the bathroom, eyes glazed from a fat rail. We all arise sloppily drunk & head back to the apartment in the jeep. We acquire more booze, and park outside his place.

They take whiskey shots in the jeep, as does Mistress Maam – they're buttering us up for swinger action, definitely, and what that really means is we'll be living in our car again by tomorrow night. SHIT. We exit the vehicle & return to the apartment; Ricardo busts out the shot glasses & flips out a fat sack of ganja.

The night grows dark, and everybody is hammered. Ricardo keeps going into the bathroom, then emerging more frantic as I take shallow sips of booze. I keep chucking the shots off the balcony, covertly ditching the whiskey I keep being handed. This is no time to lose it, lest I desperately wake up in serious need of Preparation H.

I nab MM by the arm and take her inside the bedroom. I start to explain the gravity of the situation, and then we hear shouting outside. Somehow the other two are now out front in a serious shouting match. The girlfriend is drunk in her car with the engine going, and Ricardo is arguing at the top of his lungs. Both of them are hammered, and they keep getting louder.

I turn to Mistress Maam as if to say "*the cops are coming,*" and we hear the girlfriend screaming "*Fuck you, fuck you you fucking fuck!*" & squealing tires.

Two metallic objects smash together, and the building shakes. I pop my head out to view Ricardo running away, then I head down the staircase.

The girlfriend drove into the wall of the apartment, then backed out with a mashed upfront bumper. She's angry, shouting that Ricardo just punched her in the face, like cold-cocked her, even though she has no marks. She slams the gas and drives off in a rage, presumably to run him over.

Moments later, Ricardo – who was hiding in the bushes – runs back into the apartment, wide-eyed & doing that "too much cocaine" pee-pee dance. He grabs some clothing and says *see you guys next week* before running off into the night. The girlfriend comes back, parking in the same spot with her wrecked front.

Mistress Maam & I kill the lights, then hide in the bedroom. We peer out folded blinds like a noir film as cops zoom up with blue & red flashing lights that illuminate the whole complex. The officers give her a drunk test, having her walk in a straight line. She sobs pathetically, making a hammy show with crocodile tears. They cuff and transport her, and a tow truck comes for the jeep…

The next day, Sunday, almost 2 weeks into the part-time cook gig at Club 242. Even though extremely rusty, I've been able to cloak my inexperience. I've been hesitant to jump behind a flame broiled grill 'cause my burn lines are shaky & spotting meat temps my weak point... but it's going ok. I'm feeling... Weirdly safe, for once...

As is why Mistress Maam calls near the end of my shift – flipping out, like an angry dragon.

Soon as Ricardo came back, he got her drunk and dropped a bag of cocaine on the table. They started getting ripped, and he wouldn't keep his hands off her. I was trying to screw her in the bedroom, and she wasn't having it.

He kept following her ultra-pushy, then shoved his hands down her pants & started fingering her in the kitchen. She pushed him off and stormed out the apartment. He freaked out just as the night before, grabbed a duffelbag of clothes, then again ran out the door, hauling ass across the parking lot.

We couldn't stay there any more – I just couldn't look the other way on it, because it was a direct soiling on the established respect between two men.

A guy like Ricardo doesn't see a woman but instead a vagina, but when he sees a man he sees a man. And when he shits on that premise, it shows the all around character at every angle. We could not ignore such a devil in our midst...

Thanks to an emergency ad on Craigslist, we had a new place in 20 minutes – again in Beaverton. It was an older lady, a Dead-Head, trying to build a communal house.

She was friendly, but had a goofy vibe. Her daughter stayed there, as well as a suicidal lady with a head injury is in the back room. The upstairs had been rented to a slightly cracked 18 year old guy, and we were given the haunted moldy basement.

It stinks down there, and even though we pop a tent and hide inside it, this situation is uncomfortable. MM had nightmares about a house like this – and in the busted up backyard a creepy water well.

At work I'm called into the office – all the prep has been done so I get the night off. They cut me an early paycheck, and we all know what that means. I take a walk downtown and the sous chef calls, saying I'm shit out of luck.

At least with this check I'd paid our expenses since coming to Portland. If there were a time to go back to Seattle, this would be it. But I'd become enamored – this was the sort of place I always wanted to live but thought impossible to exist.

I begin ghostwriting a book for a guy in Seattle – a dystopian tale where money was erased as part of a one-world government, and the central character was thrown into a connected plot where authorities had framed him for the murder of his wife. He was escaping through the desert & barren landscapes in a bid for revenge. The author floated me $300, and again "The Street" was postponed.

I walked every inch of Downtown Portland applying at any business which might hire me. I sent at least 300 resumes through Craigslist. When none of that worked, I kept going farther into the suburbs. I circled around Beaverton, took buses in random directions hoping to stumble onto anything – temp agencies & job assistance programs. I'd a 3 week window to stone broke poverty.

Had I the stomach for it, I would just turn to crime. But what is the use of becoming a drug dealer when you have no clients? Mistress Maam was just as desperate as I. Anywhere she'd lived, she had a waitress gig within a day. Here, it was vicious. Portland was a new level of "*who you know,*" and we didn't know *anyone*.

After applying as a janitor for the college, I walked past a series of high-rise buildings with heavy security. Maybe that was the answer – be a security guard. I head up polished marble stairs into the spacious lobby and approach the gun-clad lesbian at the desk.

She buzzed an intercom and sent me up one of the several elevators, into the main office of an independent security contracting firm. I ask for paperwork, and they instead put me in the office of the VP that allocates personal.

The guy is a total ham. He unveils his employment opportunities to me from behind his desk – a smiling, jovial reenactment of the play-acting from countless corporate training videos he'd no doubt seen.

My age, my background, my spotless criminal record – that I was young, white, and had all my teeth – I could advance far into the field, should I choose. I just needed to take and pass this extremely detailed background check with 1000 questions for personality profile and run through FBI and DHS databases to afterwards be saved by both organizations.

There were comfy health benefits, pension plans, company vehicles, paid vacations. I would be transferred from facility to facility, ignored for hours and left to a stack of books while huddled around the monitors of dull warehouses & chemical plants.

Day shifts were available – relocation to other cities, perhaps other countries. I could even possibly be transferred to Europe, and the company was so legit, so backed by the FBI and Homeland Security it pulled all the right strings to obtain a work and residence permit in Germany, Holland, France.

Then he gets up, and paces to the drawn blinds with his hands behind his back. Dramatically, he looks down from his corporate perch to the ant people below. Says: *"Your assignment, Ryan, if you can handle it [while smirking & assuming I'm a Reaganite scumbag like him] – see those punk rock kids down there? The ones hustling for change. The ones annoying our customers, butting into decent folks' lives?"*

"Your job will be right here, at this very building. Your function is to go down there and chase them off – intimidate them, whatever works. Try not use force but, heck, if it's necessary, you have the right; the cops have your back."

"And then when you scrape those parasites off this block, we'll move you to other buildings around town to do the same. So long as those punk bums are around, you got plenty of overtime."

Turning back to lock eyes with me, grinning like a prison warden, he says *"Think you can handle that?"* I nod, just to hear what this monster is going to say next. He turns back to the blinds, serious like Clint Eastwood. Tells me, with epic hamminess – *"I need an answer by sundown tomorrow."*

I left the office and returned to the street, consciously avoiding the crusty kids. With the future self-incriminating psychological profile FBI dossier in hand, as well as the stack of unnecessarily long application forms, I headed to Pioneer Square and sat upon the column steps.

This really was that moment I knew would eventually come, when there is no fog of perception and you see clearly that you are an adult male of a Great Depression. That you truly are about to fall through the cracks, and it isn't because of laziness or refusal of employment, but because no such opportunity exists. Where the nation is absolutely ruined, and the economy has been transferred to Chinese Sweatshops & Unicor slavery. Where you look about streets overflowing with fresh homeless gripping college degrees.

It is here, at this stark moment, when society hands me this last opportunity to buy my way back in. To just become another one of the assholes, keep my head down & shut up. To vent my stifled life-force at street kids like a sold out chump in shiny black boots and swat team gear, trying so hard to look tough. To become authority. For money.

With great sadness I rise up, make my way to the public trash can & throw the heap of documents into the plastic pit. If this is the end, so be it. If I am to fall through the cracks, so be it. If my entire winter of busting my ass to save money just to come home was a farce, then I accept its boot to the face.

They can write whatever they wish on my tombstone, but the insignificant legacy of Ryan Bartek will never be tarnished by mutation into some asshat with swat gear and a crew-cut. This cat makes his stand with the street, shares dumpsters & splits rollies – he ain't 'fraid to lose half his teeth...

Back at the DeadHeads house, Mistress Maam and I have a pow-wow inside the tent we are living in. It is one of those days where the visage I have created around her crumbles, and we are just normal people again. She does not seem so scary, just a sad girl that wants to be loved. I pop off, woefully explaining that this is not the life for us.

It is my fault having brought us to this ridiculous end. All of our clothing smells like mold and the rain will just not stop. It seeps through window panes supplanted decades ago and rolls into floor drains that barely function. It is cold, it is dark, and we sit around a burning white candle to ward off terrible haunted energy.

The DeadHeads house has brought a wretched set of circumstances. The 17 year old kid she let move upstairs is now relentlessly hitting on MM, trying to hook up with her while I am out searching for employment.

The old woman's daughter is begrudgingly living their now as well, having been kicked out of her other house for being a meth addict and starting fist fights with her freshly ex-boyfriend. In between screaming matches with her mother she lurks upstairs, stealing from the younger kid.

Yesterday she jacked half his video games and pawned them for crystal while the Old Woman hides in denial. She redirects this sadness with "chore sheets" that she wants everyone to participate in or be thrown out.

The other room upstairs has been rented by a suicidal middle aged woman a little slow from a head injury, whose boyfriend had left her after 17 years. Her own children won't speak to her, she cannot find a job, and sits silently hating her life trying to muster the willpower to off herself.

Everything about this place is a monstrosity, and it needs to end. Whatever it takes, I will free us of this limbo. The protective white candle burns out and we sleep deep and soundly in between fits of coughing from the unfiltered air, clasping to each other like lost souls on an aimlessly drifting ghost ship. She wakes throughout the night in sleep terrors, and I keep holding on, bringing her back.

The next day I am again wandering with job resumes in hand when I get a phone call. It is the last place I would intend to work, the restaurant forever on Craigslist that for whatever reason cannot find anyone to stay. Maybe because it is a gay bar and people are weird about it, or maybe the management are freaks or just shady with their employees. Who knows?

After all most straight men cringe at the thought, and most flamboyantly gay men don't want to get dirty and covered in food scraps and burning oil.

Only a dirty dog can really stomach being a line cook. Only the right sort of mind can handle throwing hunks of dead animal on a burning grill all night and running around like a spazz while guzzling endless red bulls.

I wandered into Grimmson's half expecting it would be one of those creepy queer hangouts where 1970's highway rest-stop fucking is heralded like a golden era.

Like the one in Raleigh I stopped at briefly, where defunct urinals were fastened to the walls inside the restaurant and mint candies filled the piss drains. No matter how pleasant the message of free love there is always grotesque bedrock – a casual amalgam of shame & dirtiness prettied with a big pink bow.

Grimmson's was a normal restaurant by all appearances. It was clean, respectable. They were trying to provide a 5 Star dining environment to the wealthy older gay guy crowd and the drag queen circuit. It looked like the kind of place Liberace would hang out when he wanted a Madeira Flat Iron.

The owner, Mr. Grimmson, was a balding older man with a neatly trimmed Hitler mustache. The look wasn't intentionally fascist, but of overdoing his neatness.

His accountant handed me the menu – this ludicrous wave of text with 70+ items. I felt like I was reading the intro to *Star Wars*. Everything was a pain in the ass, and all expectations were on par with the fancy cuisine of a Parisian diner.

This hole in the wall didn't know how to operate – amateurs pushing a ridiculous menu with little profitability. They had a chef for years that ran the place, but he was fired for stealing absurd amounts of product. The guy was ordering boxes of high-grade steak, chicken wings, poultry breast, roast beef, etc that he was just packing his car with and taking home.

They kept the menu and demanded anyone hired off the street memorize it. No sane business would throw this at some newbie, let alone a revolving door of Craigslist bottom feeders.

For whatever reason, Grimmson kept doling out the unemployment checks rather then simplify the menu so any Joe Blow could learn it in 2 days. He didn't seem to care if we were throwing out everything and he wasn't making a buck.

Despite being the fancy 5 star world famous gay restaurant of Portland, no one in the gay scene even seemed to know it existed. They had zero promotion, no outreach, and they scared off the younger crowd by refusing to have a drink less then $4 bucks. Woo-ha – $5 french fries & the bargain beer's $5 after tip. And a buncha whiny old sagged-ass queeny guys to contend with.

It was a wreck of an operation hatched by a bunch of servers that worked for the fancy-pants gay restaurant downtown & said *"let's just start our own business."* So the Island of Misfit Cooks hired me, because I had all my teeth.

Even though I hadn't been a real line cook since the mafia restaurant of Detroit lore, I knew enough to struggle my way through it. I needed fresh experience to solidify my skills. I would make this work like a second hand ramshackle culinary institute. I knew that in doing so it was my only shot at raising the money to travel Europe...

2 weeks passed as I learned the shamelessness of gay men. Anytime I sat

down to have my shift drink, I felt trapped in an elevator with a half-dozen bears hitting on me. If only women were so direct.

Most my life had been spent in self-deprecation, thinking that no woman would ever want to be with me. I was always beat up in Middle School and told I was ugly, stupid, not good enough. But here I was, with tons of muscle (and flab) pining after me like hounds released from 12 years imprisonment.

Was I missing something? What was it about myself that made women ignore me yet make men lurch after me like flesh-starved zombies? I could only imagine the hideousness that every attractive woman goes through, being surrounded at all times by cat calls & hungry eyes, and knowing that all these beasts want to do is slap their balls on gooey membrane and then leave at 3am.

The DeadHead amped up her presence as an unruly high school principal, following us around with her chore list. We played ball awhile, knowing the old hag was using MM for her car with ceaseless errands. Eventually she snapped: *"We fucking pay you rent! God damn BITCH!"* and stormed off into the basement, leaving the perplexed mob of gray permed hair looking shocked at the outrage she had fermented.

We scored a room to sublet for one month only in the hipster heart of SE Portland, and were secretly in the process of vacating.

Thus, we decided to ditch out on the leech-like hippy immediately. Like gremlins cackling over a malicious prank we slid open the basement window and Mistress Maam crawled out. One by one I pushed our belongings through the opening and she quickly & silently filled up the car. I slithered out the window like a ninja and we quietly approached the car doors.

It was then that Mistress Maam had realized she locked her keys inside, and did not have a spare. The world stood still as we stared at each other in mute panic.

We began to hear a buzzing sound, then both slowly turned our heads to see an obese retarded man joystick riding an electronic wheelchair. He looked lumpy and misshapen, such as Sloth in the Goonies. He turned his head to us, and gurgle-drooled *"huh-hey-aaaaaauuuuhhhh"* in the most ludicrous of ways you could imagine such a character doing.

It was beyond *Ren & Stimpy* – & mid-way through the driveway, his wheelchair dies. He starts gurgling.

We are stuck between a locked vehicle and an unfortunate specimen of botched evolution – and we cannot leave! All is lost... until

Mistress Maam realizes they are hanging out the trunk lock! We get in, but the mechanized retarded man can't get it started! The DeadHead sees us from the upstairs window. She's getting ready to come out at us, probably waving around graph paper!

We fire the engine, the retards wheelchair kicks up, he rolls out the way and we hammer on reverse! We spin backwards in the street then blast off onto the freeway where in moments we reach a traffic jam. A massive pine tree had timbered into the lanes, crushed a few cars, and slowed all east bound vehicles.

It would be another 45 minutes of waiting on a near empty gas tank before we got off the highway and exhaust-puttered to the nearest ARCO...

We had officially cracked the mythical Portlandia. I now lived and worked in SE PDX where the Dream of the 90's lurched forevermore. Slackerville, where everyone rode bikes and cops didn't arrest kids for skateboarding. Where you could wander the streets openly smoking weed and not one person would telephone the police or bat an eye.

Where every other front porch was full of people jamming acoustic guitars, partying, discussing all the tenants of innumerable subcultures. There were house venues, urban farms, artist co-ops, media collectives. We had it all, even if I, like almost all transplants, had to work a night job and waste away in the summertime simply to stay afloat. But we could breathe. *At least for a month.*

It was a big house near Division and 25th, close enough to work where I could walk home in 25 minutes. The roommates were the hacky sack & banjo jamming variety, and they were a chill bunch consistently blazing ganja. Things had been going just fine at Grimmson's, even though our secret kitchen motto was: *"Welcome to Grimmson's, don't eat anything with butter."*

The head chef was a runaway from New Orleans, and he took me under his wing to mentor the true schematics of culinary work. He loved ranting about the aliens as we boomed dubstep through our shifts. He was a master of improvisation ever since the owner demanded that if anyone brought in a dish to make, we would simply have to make it. The menu had no gravity. We had people bring in live lobsters, ham hocks...

I felt I was making real progress in life, while Mistress Maam sharpened her talons. She was stir crazy & deprecating. She'd found a part time job at a coffee shop but it wouldn't last long. Constantly nagging at me, moaning I was too busy promoting my projects online. I was busy, I had work to do, and she was obnoxiously opposed to my lack of interest in her. I wanted it to be done with.

We kept moving forward together, even if I knew it was Stockholm Syndrome. My willpower to sever myself from this woman after we shared an entire reality of integration into this new Portlandic world was simply not strong enough.

I felt like we were begrudging astronauts that had arrived on the same ship, and that we would have to work together to complete our mission. At some point, we would have to zoom off in the shuttle. But that was in my head. I was guilt-tripped & stuck, hooked to bad noise. I continued to push for a break up, trying to wrest my way out of it, but she held me captive in one form or another.

We went for a drive up to Bagby Springs, a spot for thermal baths in Mount Hood. The legends are that it's one of the most refreshing spots in all of Cascadia. We could never find it though, and MM was brought to frustrated tears. She had tried so very hard to make this happen but we gave up after multiple false directions.

We started back towards the city. Through word of mouth, we heard of this raunchy club were Ron Jeremy had a BDSM party open to the public once every Thursday.

It was fairly new in Portland, and all the hipsters flirted with the idea of showing up but never quite mustered the courage. But we were both perverts. For the past few months, Mistress Maam had been reading *The 120 Days of Sodom*. It was her new bible. It instilled a lunatic gleam in her eye.

The club was swanky and blaring Rammstein. Everything was black or red; gothy types and cougars galore were rocking black leather. Folks in suits, some Sci-Fi con types and renascence festival people and lots of desperate fatties. The hot women were hookers or indefinable baggage of supernatural proportions.

Plenty of married couples out for a swinging thrill as well. Cheap drinks, porn cinema projected on canvas, bed bars arranged so people could drink around a bunch of people fucking. There was an endless free taco bar, unisex showers and torture racks in the front room next to the dance floor.

Upstairs was a small labyrinth of private rooms with the option of pulled or closed curtains. What began as a slow, chill vibe soon turned into an onslaught of buggery.

The crowd was calm until the booze set in, and by 11pm the swingers were in full swing. People were whipping each other in the dungeon lair while others were screwed by jellyfist extensions on a jackhammer. People were bountifully bound and gagged.

Then there was the couples room – the curtained, dimmed pad of an epicenter with 12 beds & writhing bodies everywhere. She pounced me and demanded I make her star of that show, that instant, the deranged moment. For once, it felt like she really was my girl.

The cracked 17 year old from the DeadHead house calls from a new number and says he just got out the mental institution. He had decided to now becoming a Buddhist monk and apologized to me for shamelessly trying to bang my girlfriend.

The authorities had found him wandering outside on the freeway naked whacked on acid and picked him up. Said they locked him in a rubber room and couldn't stop laughing for days.

Kluck calls, having stolen a truck. He has sliced open his dick with a hunting knife and is driving around with a gun somewhere in Texas, absolutely suicidal.

But I've heard it all before. I'm not phased by it. He is blabbering and not making sense. So I tell him that GG Allin would call this a pussy ending, because he has yet to reach his peak. I tell him that Manowar would never approve. I just kind of blow him off, talk like Harvey Keitel as The Wolf and tell him to return the car, patch up his dick, then sleep this ghastly nightmare off.

Not long after my friend from Michigan contacts me. The one whose been in therapy ever since we were in Florida and she said: "*I just need to go back this one last time.*"

She had testified against the man who attacked them in court. He was going away for a long time. She was totally wrecked from the awful spectacle and now ended up in Oregon, dating her cousin. Yes, dating her cousin. She had asked us to come over.

It was a strange thing stumbling into this situation. At first, I didn't know how bizarre this would turn out. I hadn't spoken to her since the transgression. I didn't quite bring up the whole inbreeding thing to Mistress Maam.

I mean, she was a weird chick. But you know, I am too. And I had no opinion on the subject except it just wasn't for me.

But there she was, and there he was, and they were an item. They seemed totally happy too, and in sane minds. They had apparently always felt this way about each other and just went with it. Their families disowned them for it. It was tough, and it was crazy, but it was true love. I couldn't judge.

Unfortunately her cousin was deep in druggy raver realms & she spiraled. He began calling me, trying to use me as a buffer. When I begrudgingly did so, he tried to get with MM – texting her all smooshy while trying to dump my "never ex" off on me.

We'd all gone up the snowy heights an hour outside Portland for an outdoor rave with camping. I hadn't been to an actual rave party since 2002, and I missed it.

With the cousins nothing came from that weekend except awkwardness. It was going downhill for them fast – she was crying all the time in PTSD. Avoiding the couple, MM had met Krissy – a hula hoopin' clowny girl with a jester's grin who'd did fire poi.

Back in SE Portland the lease was running out & the heat blazin. It'd be July, and we were uncertain where to move. Craigslist was again our savior, and oh so apropos: *The Acropolis Hotel was open for monthly rental.* Located near the soccer stadium, and a 10 minute walk from Downtown, it was a jackpot of a furnished room at only $400 a month with no lease or utilities. What better a place to finish a book called *Acropolis Now*?

I contacted the landlord – if we got there next day, seemed respectable, had $$$ & could pass a background check, we'd be in.

I had just enough to make it work. So long as I worked a full time job & stay put, the math equated a guaranteed escape to Europe.

Grimmson's would hold out since the only way to get fired was to show up drunk. Opportunities like this rarely present themselves – PDX was red-hot for Americans attempting to escape their mundane lives & Acropolis Hotel was a blessing.

Mistress Maam had been learning fire poi – the art of spinning two metal balls hooked to chains while soaked in kerosene. It's a trend among the circus-obsessed subcultures of clown & raver tribes.

Before an initiate begins lighting up her instruments, she is to practice with the metal balls to master the weight and movement. It takes months of training. It will deform the ungraceful.

This particular night, Mistress Maam was preparing to try fire for the first time. She was balancing her normal swings when BAM – she takes a metal sphere straight to the eyeball. It cracks her face so hard it rips the skin off her eyeball.

When I find her she is at our house in severe pain, completely freaked out and holding an ice pack to her face. She looks mutilated. It's bad. All the while she refuses to go to a doctor, convincing herself it will be fine. She will not listen to me.

The next morning she is in agony and I have to take her to the Emergency Room. Her face is swollen and her eye is black, and the hospital staff grimaces at me as if I was an abusive partner.

They give her ointment, an eye-patch, and enough Vicadin to knock out a hippo. But we have to pick it up and when we arrive they want $200. Because she doesn't have insurance. Because that's what the name brand goes for.

After a tug-of-wear with the hospital to get approved for generics since the doctor had left for the day, we finally get scripts and head off to meet the management of The Acropolis.

As we sit at The Captain's big desk, with his pictures of sail boats on the wall and his sailboat Captain's hat, The Captain chews on a cigar. He's trying to feel me out.

This is a guy that deals with derelicts on a regular basis. This guy has probably had so many fuck ups and drug addicts rent out these rooms in the past 20 years its unbelievable.

Well there I sit, and there rests Mistress Maam. She is drooling, nodding off, and her face is black and bruised, and it looks like I just socked her in the face as hard as I could. It just looks like I beat the living shit out of her.

I, on the other hand, am smiling a big grin, wearing a pinstripe hat, and rocking a dress shirt and tie.

His old man's eyes seem to question if I'm some kind of weird pimp. But then I talk about Michigan, and working for Ford's. He used to live in Michigan too, lots of family there. Thought I reminded him of someone so-and-so. I knew I had it, even as Mistress Maam fell asleep propped up in her chair.

I cannot remember our first night there, but I remember waking up and always thinking I'd been there. Everyday the sun would rise in the distance outside our window, giving a soft glow over the wooden desk I now typed at every morning & night.

It was cozy, 1950's. I felt inspired as if in a minor Manhattan. I celebrated July 4th by releasing my discography for free download, and again had some of the biggest metal news feeds on the internet run the press release. A.K.A. MABUS was vindicated.

I took my usual walk, this time avoiding Powell's Books which had become an inescapable black hole every time I tried to venture out and make friends. If anything, the gravitational pull of the greatest book store in America was preventing my growth in this new environment.

But could you imagine a guy like me easily saying no to every book ever written, just sitting in one pile and begging to be read only a short 5 minute walk from my house? A trap it was, and well set. I felt myself yearning to overdose on literature, just so the impulse would cease to dog me in the future.

But back to the walk. I made it down 6th ave, past the food carts and into Pioneer Square. And as I sit on those steps of "Portland's Living Room" I get a much needed phone call – *the one and only Dr. Jeremy Sullivan.*

I wait on the corner and the Max Train passes, revealing the wide-eyed, sponge-like consciousness that is Doc. He walks up to me ghost-like, never blinking.

We head off for a stroll, two kingpins catching up like wayward mafia dons. He tells me that Corexit is killing the gulf, that it is raining down clouds of neuro-toxic poison throughout the Southern USA and across the East Coast.

He tells me that the situation is beyond insane, but despite everything, Free Therapy is blossoming. For one year now, Dr. Jeremy Sullivan has been eating LSD nearly every day – just straight drinking the backwash of entire jars.

He has successfully climbed aboard the railways of the US as a train-hopper and is uniting Food Not Bombs tribes across the nation. He has rigged squats and communes to no end.

Most importantly, he has aggressively germinated the seeds of the Free Therapy movement. What we started in Seattle has grown, and it is now being exported across the nation by our initiates. He asks me if I am ready. If I'm down to hop trains. He wants me to go all out and help him lead the mish-mash resistance.

When a guy like that pulls a Great Gatsby, and invites you to share the hobo triumph, it is best that one takes it. In a perfect world, I would love to run off with Doc for a mad mission.

Health is a factor, and age. If all you get is one shot, what option do you take? Tackle Europe calculated? Or follow madman Peter Pan into American oblivion?

I had seen America, and it was over. Portland was the edge of that world and I had it all right here. As I left Jeremy with an undecided yes or no, I headed back to The Acropolis.

The phone rang, and it was my tragic friend. Both she and her cousin had shot crystal meth as if it were heroin. She was out of her mind. It was like death calling you directly from the vortex.

I pictured the sweet, awkward girl I knew from high school. She was from a strange broken home, and was one of many kids in our group that sought a sense of family. Even if I never quite registered it, she had looked to me as something of a brother figure. She never had much of anything in terms of family, just a very conflicted mother.

She was hyperventilating; it sounded as if her head would explode before her heart. *"I've never done anything like this, this is fuckin crazy this is fuckin' crazy this is fuckin"* on and on and on. Her screaming at her cousin, the both of them in some maniac frenzy of hate and anguish and absolute tweaked out intensity.

I just hung up the phone, knowing she was gone. Within days, she had moved back to Detroit. Anywhere in the world, and she went there, like a captive slave made learned to love its master.

I went home, flicked on the computer, and began researching the Gulf Oil Spill. Everything Jeremy said was true. I sapped into a state of shocked depression. Poison was coursing through the nation, and people in Florida and Louisiana bleeding through their eyes. I wanted to do something, I wanted to help.

"All of the conspiracies in the world and you have to tackle this one?" Mistress Maam is jealous for my attention. She hates my computer. She is sick of hearing about The Gulf and I'm driving her insane with paranoia.

However, the public must know they are eating poison which makes their brains bleed. They must stop consuming fish immediately. Discontinue use – this is my mission.

In the alternative news response is Sal Petero, a longtime resident of New Orleans. One of many covering the BP oil spill, Sal has been broadcasting YouTube updates from his home. It felt like an unfurling disaster movie – I began to communicate & sent a mighty list of email contacts for legit news outlets. He gave a shout-out to the anonymous donor on his channel & I felt accomplished.

MM, again: *"Why don't you go after something that means something, that camp where they are worshiping Moloch the Owl God and doing black magick rituals and having gay sex orgies and mock human sacrifices? If you want shit to change, just freak America out with that shit. None of those people would ever be voted in office again – they'll be ruined."*

"Because it doesn't exist."

"Oh yes it does."

"No that's just some loopy bullshit Jeremy was trying to pass off on me – this wacko bullshit about voodoo redwoods and...."

In one fluid, forceful movement, she batted me away from the keyboard as if I was clutter in the way. She went to YouTube, click-click-clicked, & hit enter. *"There"* she said curtly.

The hidden camera video magically transported me to an awful spectacle in the middle of the redwoods where the entire gamut of the

American Right Wing Power Elite and various members of world governments and monarchies were in wooden bleachers to watch their fellow corporate power-mongers participate in some bizarre *Fantasia*-like scene where they dress up in KKK-like hoods and burn a coffin that symbolizes "care" in a secretive ceremony called "The Cremation Of Care" with torches over a bottomless pit covered in moss & surrounded by a pentagram while on top is a human effigy as a metal skeleton that is revealed burned inside the coffin – all underneath a 40 foot owl chiseled out of stone & covered in moss like a Sumerian demigod as the altar beneath it holds yet another pentagram & genies lamp rigged as an eternal flame. This kicks off a massive gay orgy & two weeks of secret meetings by top-tier bastards in all aspects of politics & economy...

Bohemian Grove was real. Surely there was a rational explanation, no matter how freakish – *but it was real.*

This was the George W. Bush hootenanny. It was the deranged finale at the end of the rainbow, the hideous truth of all these snake-oil frauds who rewrote our history, lulled us into fake war and Federal Reserve slavery.

This ensemble of incorporated puppeteers – they had their own freakish private version of a Burning Man. And if Jeremy was right, they were plotting world domination. Marching, marching onward – for the The Owl God... *Please – anything but "Moloch"...*

My life was ruined. I was a serious political journalist, or had tried to be. How could any journalist in America ignore this weird, creepy shit? How could this successfully be hidden for so long? Not one reference in a movie?

I wanted answers, I needed the truth; it was just too fucked up and bizarre. I could never again look at any of these politicians except as an interlocked mob of cultish vultures...

When President Obama promised change, no one assumed it meant altering federal law so anyone caught filming the oil spill "clean up effort" (*without official permission*) would receive a 15 year prison sentence in forced labor camps with a bonus $40,000 fine. Yet here we were, and CNN had been shut down live on international TV.

The president had done pissed off Mistress Maam and there was just no stopping her. She quickly made plans to go state by state gathering henchmen as to storm the beaches with hundreds of anarchists gripping cameras in a staged mass arrest so brazen, so earth-shattering in its tantrum that the entire country would have no choice but to pay heed to the scream.

Plus she wanted my attention. If she couldn't get my head unglued from the laptop screen, then she would simply crawl inside my computer so I would have no choice but to watch. She and Krissy were both spinning fire poi and busking. And both wanted to travel (*plus MM had the hots for her*)...

The two bounced out of Portland hitchhiking and soon attempted to train-hop. In Idaho they were arrested for trespassing. Mistress Maam came back with a $300 ticket for lurking a rail-yard. They lingered a few days then head back out, hitchhiking far as they could then took a Greyhound to New Orleans. Jeremy was waiting for them in Florida, but Sal was in Nola and excited to meet my export of a journalist team.

I feverishly awaited the next video by Sal. This was epic teamwork, and the villainous Obama would soon get a proverbial boot up his ass. Instead of confronting the oil spill, Sal posted creepy old man videos where he followed the girls around talking about how they were lesbians. He was just trying to get them to make out.

I called MM. They were lounging around the guys apartment in Nola. She had told me the upsetting tale, about how big a joke this guy was. In the past day, he had been crafting YouTube video uploads on his opposition to gay marriage. To be an idiot male is one thing, but a closet queer attacking fags is another. He'd a live-in boyfriend – a twink who was mentally challenged.

I wrote a fiery letter to Sal and he wrote volumes of apologies. I'd been had by an absolute loser. The videos were taken down & the girls headed to Florida where they met with Jeremy. Doc fell for Krissy, and Mistress Maam turned stubborn girl.

Mistress Maam began refusing to talk & kept sulking by the side of the road so no one could successfully hitchhike. Krissy and Jeremy abandoned her with another one of these YouTube journalists as they went to visit J's parents in Jacksonville.

The alt media guy soon tried to bang my girlfriend as well. Qnnoyed, MM burned all the footage & killed their documentary.

The 3 of them were alone again, reaching the worst beach they had encountered. Sprawling red waters & vile black sand stretched the coast while Mistress Maam sat like an angry lump. Krissy gave up, and Jeremy wandered around the mutilated beach. He found a blackened lump of Corexit 9500 that washed ashore.

To make light of the situation, he rubbed a streak on his beard trying to get the warring gals to lighten up. From that moment onward, the hair he streaked would never grow back. He was left with a bare line forever etched on his left cheek, smooth as the buttocks of a newborn...

Netherworld Imperium

Click, click, click went the keys of the scorched maestro as the totality of sunlight rescinded through gray overcast. The grace of Ra had again retreated, silently abandoning the terrain. Now there was only the growing darkness of a still kitchen, its cold tiled floors sending shivers up the absurd mans bare feet.

On this blackened day, vast escapism had not procured its intended effect. The deranged architect knew it was indicative of a death centered squarely as the internal rings of a great oak. The past was finished and the future unraveled, sliver by sliver, a series of grim hurdles.

Click, click, click went the keyboard in stark realization. Perhaps it was the settling darkness that had driven him into the clutches of infernal tornado. Somewhere midst the rocky cliff hang, he'd been deceived by his own cunning instinct. Contrived paths lead to formidable complexes, unending corridors, truncated avenues…

Click, click, click went the sovereign nation unto himself, 51 cards stacked in a deck of black diamonds & crimson clovers. Lurching forth in conquistador hypnosis, the once-grinning assaulter joylessly extended his digital influence, launching continuous emails like a baseball slugger swinging at leather-bound mirages...

As so many other freakish lone wolves, he'd waited since the dawn of America Online for a unified social platform. AOL pioneered the mass market with a user friendly interface; within a few years, a hive-mind birthed a minority segment of the population.

As the adults of the 90's remained ignorant to the ground swell, the digital age quietly solidified their Hive Mind like invisible armies. A new order was forming in lieu of humanities technology mutation. The 90's were primer, and the adapted minds who'd weathered 28k modems the successors.

The 90's & early 00's were a build-up to internet social networking, but every keen wit recognized lightning fast communication would eventually hit – and the freaks would recognize their strength in numbers with a frenzy of shared ideas so monolithic an interpersonal world evolution would dawn.

Enter MySpace – 1 year after public launch & 90 million users. Every artist had superseded the need for a label or external management. The ease of travel, job seeking, home rental, squatting – the game changed entirely. The fanatic could now classify personalities like a filing cabinet or renegade NSA department. Spread before him like tarot cards were the profiles of MySpace, each tiny digital box a reality which he could inflame or manipulate; powers vaguely dreamed by men like Constantine or Caesar…

Yet on this darkened day, the hanging fool felt less a bolt-throwing Olympian then he did the puppet Mussolini typing empty orders at the heart of the RSI. Having never known the grace of true love, this depraved incinerator merely understood acting out of malevolence.

Festering inside was the same steely misanthropy that had led nations to war; like the wayward sons whom blot the course of mankind's development with anger & chaos, he'd become a machine attempting to destroy the world and remodel it in his own image – yet it was little more then purification by fire. He had no end game, no strategy for peace – just the echoes of mad laughter haunting a scorched & burning world. A slave to the flame he was, and fire is an element with no master.

Upon catching wind he'd released a book, the blood family on his mother's side ordered it. There was now a deep silence & divide he could feel at his most primal. Even if they had little communication, being the loopy black sheep of the clan that he was, still he felt they were there in the wings, able to be touched.

Yet that feeling was now Siberian. He could only imagine their faces reading the intro – how he'd nearly blown off his head with a shotgun, and continued life to enact revenge. He desired to ruin it for everyone by using that evil book as a megalith neutron bomb against every trace of the victimization that created him.

His mother was now emailing him cautiously, grimly, in the calm fashion a police negotiator utilizes against a hostage taker. She admitted battling skin cancer; he felt ravaged making her sustain this horrific literature. She blamed herself for everything.

It was that moment when The Victim Tyrant finally snapped out of it. Realizing that another Valentine's spent lone had come and gone, like a man stumbling from sleepwalk he again resumed control of his body. The Mutilated Soul gazed at the half-dying computer monitor with its flickering screen as snow began to fall outdoors.

It was 3 months since he'd released this great book of hate, and the ammo it unleashed was met with return fire. He was released from Jam Rag. His wings were clipped at Real Detroit to limit his influence, and the editorial departments of all Detroit newspapers had banded in agreement to prevent him from spreading.

This was not paranoia, but a direct tip-off from staffers. The message was clear: *"Look what EMINEM did to our kids with poop lyrics – you think we're gonna push this insane shit on them? Think we're willingly gonna build you into some urban monster of Grimm's magnitude? Down in flames you go, Psycho-Boy."*

Click, click, click went emails to band after band who now refused to deal with him. Zelda was gone, already. It happened so fast he couldn't remember why. She simply rebounded her unresolved emotion & went back to the voice on the other end of the phone in a happy world of family & pets & goldfish & a silly little brother jumping up & down on the bed.

Lana too was gone, imprisoned, writing letters in crayon like a deranged child. All the old flames had vanished, leaving dripping candles & burnt sulfur. And Lisa, perhaps the darkest splotch on his memory, would remain in her coffin. There she would stay, and here he would rot a living death.

The tears welled up & his body trembled. He again felt the distant echo of Lisa. Hers was a love that needed no sexuality to justify it – it was motherly innocence. Lisa had a way with him; she could reach him unlike no other at a vital time of growth. Yet in the end she was distant, and he was a ghost of a brighter past...

Lisa committed suicide, yet all she had to do was call him. It was his fault that she did not, based upon his negligent maelstrom. Had he stayed alongside her, despite everything, she would've called. She had designated him her protector, and he'd failed. He'd ruptured their good standing with his behavior and pushed her far away. But that was Lisa – never a fake. There was no cried river for attention. She set the noose and dove right in. She got the job done.

Which is why, on this bitterly cold day, the Depraved Man finally cracked. Like a water balloon erupting behind the flesh of his face, the salty monsoon seeped through every pore.

In death there is no growth, and in life no greater evolution of soul then the healthy adult prime. *"She was only 18,"* he sobbed, over and over: *"Only 18."* Yet there she would stay buried in frost-laden soil, and here he would remain the anvil of sorrow.

Had he written the book now undoing him as a means to prevent any future Lisa's? Or had he, like a sadistic maniac, unleashed this beast to accelerate the dark impulses of such youth? Was he a catalyst of doom meant to cripple the wider world, or was he trying to set them free through spiritual purging?

The wounded man found the strength to leave, but the destination unclear. Into his vehicle that lacked heat he climbed, driving off as his breath frosted the windows. It was the blackest of Detroit nights where ice coats the road & heavy winds chill sub-zero.

The streets were clear at every turn – so profound in their vacuous appearance that the casual observer, given no frame of reference, would assume this was footage from a post-apocalypse film and here was the last man on earth cruising fruitlessly through dead wreckage.

He kept making turns instinctively, pushing his vehicle into the most dangerous corridors of Warzone Detroit. Perhaps subconsciously he wanted a crack-house sniper to put a bullet in him, some gang member seeking to hide their felonious operation with violent paranoia. His tires crunched on broken glass, their rubber blazing over rusted nails and the potholes of deformed asphalt. He wanted Grendel to swallow him.

He then cruised through his old neighborhoods in Dearborn. Years ago he could stop at one of many houses and find 10 or more peers ruminating about life. Yet house by house the Human Ghost drifted by, lights off & interiors solemn. He knew not where to go. At barely 24, he was already scourging the junkyard of his youth.

The Collapsed Colossus veered through icy roads into the depths of Southwest Detroit where the frayed ends of Dearborn's vicinity break down into industrial stacks & poisonous yellow steam. He drove by his former workplace as a Ford auto-parts delivery man, again confronting the grim future once in store for him.

Deeper he zoomed down cracked streets, past the flame-shooting industrial stacks and by the Slag Plant which pumped a pungent, asphalt-like odor. Just beyond it lay the stark and barren cemetery where Lisa was buried – a grave-lined field he used to regularly drive past at his Ford job.

In 1999, he would have Déjà Vu that some day Lisa would be there. Like all such feelings, he shrugged them off as crazy. But at the basest reach of his internal compass, he knew it would occur.

The Marionette parked his vehicle on the shoulder and sealed himself in his leather trench to brace the howling winds. Like an incarcerated prisoner allowed to roam the Corrections yard, he clasped his hands on the icy graveyard fencing.

Perhaps it was destitute karma which offered the sick impulse that if he were to find her, dig her up, she would be alive and well under that mound of soil. Perhaps he would break her free like a prisoner, and she'd hug him warmly. He would drape a blanket over her shivering body, and they'd stumble back to his icy vehicle.

They would fill the gas tank and zoom far away from the world that had both killed them. All would be forgiven. Within 48 hours of highway they would reach Florida. They would abandon the car and approach a sunset warmly glazing the finest white sands Madeira Beach had to offer...

Yet it was done. There she would remain an anonymous collection of bones arranged in the form of a human, and here he would remain a penance of his actions, scalding tears thickening icicles on his drought face...

In the crowd he saw her face. Her eyes were always the first he noticed – bulbous & round, yet snake-like. Like the eyes of a giant shrunken to a scale smaller then her face intended. Like blazing marbles they shined.

Despite the sweaty crowd pressed to tthe stage, there seemed no other human present. Again she shined as when they first met – those thick lips grinning a playful, dangerous smile. And her skin...

(Still pretending she's a black girl are you?)

Pale – clown white. Consumed by tattoos that wrapped around her unique physique. She had the curves of a black woman; one gorgeous Negro seed tossed into the DNA blender of a 100,000 tough-as-nails Eastern European women. She could easily be a Russian assassin out to snuff James Bond...

Yet [][][]'s body was almost baby-like; soft, with puffy cheeks that flowered with her deranged smile. Her hands were almost spherical, and the length of her fingers seemed too short   wide and nub-like, like little cigar-knives. Her arms seemed a few inches too short of her frame; she was one of a kind, and hypnotic. Everything this woman was drove him utterly insane.

The crowd hollered in satisfaction. FILTHPIMP was here, and their debut pummeling. Like Sisyphus, he'd inched this thing along for years to little avail – and now was the hard-earned launch that he refused to let end a sunk Titanic.

The stage they were playing had been constructed over the last several months, and a half year of his booking gigs turned this once ignored club into the hottest new venue on Woodward Ave.

Until now, there'd been nothing like it in the area. Ferndale was mainly a tiny gay neighborhood between 8 & 9 Mile, wedged between ghetto Detroit & the more amicable Royal Oak Township. He'd recreated this place into a blustering enterprise, and tonight was the official re-launch of the venue with a new sound system.

Even the station manager of WRIF – the largest FM rock station in Detroit – had brought him on air for a live interview to promote the gig. That was something that just never happened for a guy like him or the scene from which he came.

But even as he wailed on the guitar to the pumping fists in the crowd, he knew instinctively things would go wrong. The bar owner & his other business partner hung in the back watching FILTHPIMP play with backstabbing daggers in their eyes. The owner wanted to make this place a Creed cover band hangout, and her smiling buddy-buddy henchmen couldn't wait to be rid of him.

All the metalheads, freaks & punks that resuscitated this dying dive would have to go. The owners' 7 local drunk customers just didn't like the abrasive noise. They wanted Godsmack & Nickelback covers – band members with faded barb wire tattoos.

Thus, they cut The Strange Man from the picture, as if the audience he culminated would continue to show up. As if by taking down the incredulous Bartek in a silent coup they would retain the good fortune he'd brought upon them.

The Nervous One turned his gaze away from the conspirators & back to the crowd, but again she was all he could see – he imagined her a Mayan Empress-Sorceress upon an altar of sacrifice, blood soaked & cackling, covered in jewels & gold bracelets, like a Renegade Cleopatra created by forgotten Gods, mountains of dead bodies from defeated empires littering the jungle floor...

Despite his vocalists pleas to avoid [][][] at all costs – that he should simply hook up with the bombshell redhead instead – The Distorted Man opened his car door to her such as a gentlemen fashions.

He hooked her with all the lame charms of attraction he'd fashioned – the black leather trench, the blue mohawk slicked back with spider web hairs dangling, the jet-black '95 Ford Thunderbird with the Judas Priest decal & the built in, hot-wired switch to shoot the thing up to 120mph & the bumping, monster stereo slamming Wumpscut & KMFDM & the lit, dangling Marlboro & the New World Order rants & crude Darwinian ambivalence...

She ate it up 'cause she looked the part too & together they were a gruesome two-some. Their functioning prisms were impossibly negotiable though; disaster was coming – a drastic, squalid upheaval that would train-wreck everything the band had fought for if these two egomaniac psychos seriously gelled.

Bobby knew the severe loneliness which gripped his guitarist, and did all he could to dissuade him – these were not arms for sanctuary but rather writhing, venomous snakes. Bartek sealed his fate regardless, and with the Rivethead Empress drove off into the frozen Detroit night, grinning like Daryl Van Horne.

The doomed couple soon made it back to [][][]'s apartment, where everything screamed his aesthetic – the black leather furniture, leopard-print bedspread, zebra-striped rug; the touch-turn lighting, horror posters & circular table ideal for Euchre.

It wasn't long before the two were in her room, the spider beckoning its prey. To his left he noticed her night stand – on it a copy of *The Silent Burning,* already beat up & loose from re-reading. He turned a few pages – passages were notated, sections underlined.

It had been out for 3 months, and it looked as if this copy had gone through 40 years of re-sale shops. She'd barely read a book since dropping out of high school, yet she knew chunks by heart.

He swooped into her like a diving hawk. She smiled; the switch flicked & she turned a hundred miles of frozen concrete instantly. He could feel her brain flare spastic electronic, and inside she morphed into a black winged beauty. In her soul, laughing, laughing – like a cat-eyed Medusa with hyenas for snake heads.

She kicked him off like a pro wrestler & sent him across the bedspread. Despite all his play-acted toughness & know-it-all blow-harding, he didn't know quite what to do. She was a demon and desired another demon to play her dark mind games. She intimidated him unlike any woman he'd known – he was hers, undoubtedly, forever & ever. And then she made him sleep on the couch...

Time passed. [][][] again hooked up with her ex-boyfriend, and in loneliness some quick flings had come for Mr. Bartek. One was a preschool teacher that'd shove meat hooks through her back & be suspended for the endorphins. They had zero in common except the industrial club, and he mostly liked the idea of being some nightmare reality behind the happy-land classroom with its rainbow painted walls & push toys...

There was another he picked up at the same club, in her 30's with 3 kids & a MUTANTS tattoo, one of his favorite punk bands (**real name withheld – not San Fran's Mutants from the late 70's*). She was the ex-girlfriend of MUTANTS guitarist, and for whatever reason, she lunged at our anti-hero with incredible lust & infatuation.

She was definitely hanging off the cliff of some personal edge. She had a psycho threatening ex-husband to avoid, and was already talking to Bartek as if he'd be the new poppa of her kids. She was raging horny for a hot sex motel vacation across a number of states alongside a mad cocaine binge.

He finally called back, knowing he was to be thrown into a cauldron of trouble. Yet the voice explained she was now in the nut-house after a super-coke binge & suicide attempt & (*if Narrator's memory is correct*) some kind of knife attack on the kids' father…

It was out of practicality that he turned to The Redhead – a friend of FILTHPIMP's drummer. There was zero chemistry, yet on paper she was a marvel. Cast her as Jean Grey & she'd rock the X-leather. She was busty, gorgeous – daughter of wealthy Irish immigrants.

As an architect, the father had built one of the many grid-like modern "communities" emerging in stereotype America – a sub-division of identical white homes with brown roofing, tucked away in a semi-rural town. Our protagonist was always mentally allergic to such properties, because they were static, designed for upper white class families who lived by rule of Walmart tribalism.

With an aristocratic feel, the Irishman had owned the largest home in the sub-division. It was unique and appeared square-center in the grid, like a stone-brick castle. There was a massive fireplace, spacious living arrangements, a backyard of open acres.

Her bedroom was luxurious with a large window giving view to the open territory behind the home, perfectly arranged so the moonlight would pour into her bedroom. Daddy's little princess pricey oak furniture & posters of Jim Morrison everywhere.

Our Shuffling Fool had been invited to stay the night, though he'd definitely be sleeping on the couch. Anything involving larger family functions petrified him, because he'd emerged an only child from a single-parent household where feelings towards a significant other were often degraded, or forcefully subverted.

His mother, another red-haired Irish woman, was controlling. She'd been extremely disparaging to any female that came around, made it near impossible for him to open up – and her memory alone crippled the thought of closeness to any Redhead.

She was branded to his soul – a degrading, depressive cat-lady that made sure he knew every girl he'd fancied were nothing but whores, floozies & liars.

So here The Wreck found himself – a wealthy, healthy variation of what may have been his own life. But the years had deranged him, and the blushing Redhead was too well-pedigreed. She wore perfume & dresses, had an expensive sports car. She never picked through a trash can or been assaulted for wearing a heavy metal t-shirt. Without a foundation of violence, he couldn't connect.

The father apparently liked him, shaking his hand with a *"good ol' Irish boy 'eh?"* But even though our Protagonist Failure was on the Celtic edge, the Irish association always annoyed him. He was American, and heritage was shit. Druids were cool, but he could give a fuck all 'bout the Blarney Stone or wearing green. If anything, he assumed the Hungarian/Maltese background, feeling a Mediterranean impulse. He talked with his hands like an Italian.

Still, to this Irishman he acted as if he wanted to be there, even if drifting through a relationship he only felt he'd had to. Because the Redhead really wanted it – and Bobby kept pushing it.

Bartek wasn't sure if depression was blinding it all – that he'd loosen up & notice her soon enough. He cruised along, on auto-pilot, secretly wishing [][][] would eat him alive like a spiritual cannibal. He yearned for her stiletto in the base of his skull...

It was now early May & her parents were out of town. It was just them & the castle house, bright moonlight pouring into her bedroom. Any casual spectator could plainly see that sex was on the horizon.

Yes, they'd already consummated sometime ago – awkwardly, quickly, drunkenly – but this was to be that ice-breaker night where they could go buck wild, for hours and hours, in this modern Gaelic fairy tale room with the moon-beaming window. Even though he disliked wine 'cause it gave him heartburn (*and didn't enjoy drunkenness if no loud band was performing*), still he played along. She brought it on heavier, but he couldn't concentrate.

All he wanted to do was pace around smoking Marlboro's, 'cause his mind was locked into the status of FILTHPIMP and the horrible scenario he found himself – *that every Neo-Nazi in Michigan (and the wider extreme metal Nazi underground) now wanted to kick his ass, cause trouble for his band, or just politically curse him forever in the international metal underground.*

Earlier that week, a local Detroit thrash band had forced their way uninvited onto a concert he'd set up. It was essentially a private show, booked for his band and their friends only.

Without asking, this thrash band told the bookie that Bartek was cool with it. They wanted to be buddy-buddy with metal journalist guy, and they thought they were doing a favor lending their scene cred.

Problem was their leader was a rednecky skinhead with a gigantic Nazi swastika tattooed on his back. While this thrash band was his "non political" metal band, his side project (*which he wrote all the music &*

lyrics for) was literally one of the biggest, most influential Neo-Nazi metal bands on the face of the planet.

The apolitical thrash band contacted Bartek the previous year when he'd refused to do a CD review, explaining: *"that's just his side thing & we don't agree with it, he isn't us."* To avert a scene war where Nazi skins would stalk his FILTHPIMP shows, he told them he'd get in trouble if the mag caught wind of the background.

Even if this was the "clean" band, it was still on the "not racist" subdivision of the white power label his main band was on. Furthermore, the "clean" album was dedicated to the ringleader behind the largest Neo-Nazi metal label in the world.

And so, believing the issue had blown over, the Nazi guy forced his band onto the show and was incensed when Bartek kicked them off. He was sent an email from the angry NS warrior – *CC'd with 1000+ email addresses of every Nazi label, zine, musician, promoter, etc in their underground.*

He was calling him out & making sure every hammer-skin pack leader knew the treachery of the man called Dr. Ryan Bartek. This was *"his one chance"* at redemption – to apologize or clearly state if it was because he thought the thrash band "sucked." If so, he was challenged to a public "riff off."

Having received this after attending the German film *Downfall*, Bartek held back best he could. He returned a cautious exchange explaining he didn't want to mix crowds because conflict was inevitable. This man was free to hold his own opinions, but he wasn't obliged to accept them.

When the Nazi came back more venomous, threatening & insane, Bartek responded with the fury of several million WWII vets. He'd rather hang out with Michael Jackson because at least all he does is rape children, not throw them in ovens. He made it clear that every Nazi was his bitter enemy, that the white power underworld could insert his erect penis into their drooling, inbred mouths. And he CC'd every email as to "flip the bird" at every head honcho...

So there he was, listlessly wandering the big Irish home, realizing he'd likely made it impossible for his band to play locally again without receiving the "Napalm Death Detroit Treatment." Perhaps even now it was impossible to tour without mobs of HammerSkins attacking. He'd also, by law of gravity, made the Redhead a target.

As the Irish beauty lit candles & romantically primed her room, Bartek slumped into a Lazy Boy. There she found him, a wreck of nerves, staring blankly at the TV broadcasting black & white footage of Hitler's advance through Europe. She was already more so history then the documentary itself.

He could not hear her over The Fuhrer's frenzied speech – when she finally broke him of the dead maniac's spell, he gave a haunted gaze. Bartek made some lame excuse, then abruptly left.

The next day she called his house, and he provided her circular, nonsensical banter. He avoided verbal confrontation regarding anything they were supposed to be. And finally, after months of trying to get his attention, this stunning beauty that sighed exhaustively & hung up the phone, never to contact him again.

FILTHPIMP was the priority. The bassist had just been let go for a "no call no show" & the drummer had been a serious problem. He was a little dopey, and probably half-insane from black mold. The only time the members went to his home they discovered it had a large in-door swimming pool – uncleaned & undrained for untold years. The water surface was covered in thick moss, as if a swamp, and the walls had borderline black mold crawling up them...

6 months in he could barely remember the songs. He admitted taking a baseball bat to the head in a street fight – serious brain damage affected his memory.

The drummer took Bobby to his car for whiskey shots. The drummer was proud of his fresh vehicle, having just wrapped the car Bartek sold him around a telephone poll high on pain pills. Bartek could've gotten at least $500 more for the Mercury Sable but wanted to ensure that the band would continue unabated.

As Bartek strung his guitar, Bobby ran inside smelling like freshly pounded gut-rot: *"Unless this guy goes immediately, I quit!!"* Bobby glanced to make sure the drummer was still outside. *"That guy is gonna get us all killed!! He's a snitch for the DA's office!!! This guy – he got caught with a load of pain-pills & been sent out as a rat snitching out coke dealers!! He totaled that car & now he's gotta rat a dozen more out or they're puttin' him away 15 years!!!"*

If there was anything Bartek hated more then the police, it was a snitch. And now his home, his band was violated by incognito scum. FILTHPIMP needed to record while they had him. The last 2 shows were booked – one at The Tavern, the other at a UAW Hall (*which would be canceled from Nazi drama*).

They hurriedly recorded a 4 song demo & played their last show with tech-metal giants Signs of Collapse & Relapse Records' Dysrhythmia at the dingy, dark Tavern downtown. They ditched the stool pigeon & began searching for a new drummer.

As always, most peers were stuck in the nu-metal 90's, had never heard of Relapse Records or listened to any European Metal. Detroit was 10 years behind – just infinite Korn clones, sleepy Pantera's, 8th rate Slayers & knuckle-dragging Hatebreeders...

The Tower

Bartek received a late night voice-mail from the Woodward bar owner – all his shows were canceled 'cause *they weren't making any money.*" No lie had ever been more profound – their attendance sky-rocketed from 7 people a night to 50 or more. He'd turned it around financially and in reputation, and had been back-stabbed in favor of Creed cover bands.

With a string of shows still booked, he turned to his buddy Jason Lockwood – vocalist of hard-rocking punk band The Whiskey Diaries. He was neck-deep in the anarchist circuit and a DIY fanatic, booking gigs all over town. They'd become acquainted through Idle Kids, the collective space that had just fallen.

Both he & Bartek were already sentimental for it, as the "new" Idle Kids had just reopened – and been over-run by cocky younger kids, way too "in-your-face-anarchist" for their own good. They also claimed way more influence then they were marginally due, as if they'd established Idle Kids originally.

Nobody wanted to play shows there anymore, and the original crew had taken the zine library & P.A. Equipment with them. All it'd become was 6 kids sitting around debating Goldman.

Lockwood had assumed control of the The Tavern, a dingy little bar in the center of Detroit, straight across from Comerica Park where The Tigers played. The bar was painted black; at its center a flight of stairs that led to the basement from *Fight Club*. The walls were black & moldy; its corridors a defunct kitchen with broken deep fryers.

When not rigging shows downstairs, they'd use the main room adjacent to the bar. With a midget stage & red curtains, it looked the sort of place a ventriloquist would perform.

The venue was extremely haunted and had terrible energy. Everyone was looking over their shoulders, listening for whispers or expecting inanimate objects to slide across the floor.

That the building was plagued by freaky ghost energy was no secret to anyone with such a radar for it; paranormal activity made a half-dozen quit. Simply hanging out in the place you could *feel* the building. No one ever wanted to be there alone.

Bartek asked Lockwood if there was anything else to see in the tiny place, any corridors to stash equipment during gigs. Jason gave a funny eye: *"Go out the front door and look up."*

Bartek did so, and could not believe his eyes. When approaching The Tavern by car, the monorail track obscured its view. The forever empty train running from vacant parking lots to nearby sporting events was suspended 12 feet from the ground and made The Tavern appear a tiny patch of glass windows wedged underneath – people would never be able to find it. And either could Bartek on his first try.

Thus, when he finally stepped out & looked up at the marvel he and his acolytes had inherited, he simply couldn't believe it. The Tavern was the base floor of a 34 story skyscraper – a colossus of broken windows, topped by a Beaux-Arts/Neo-Classical crown. Reaching a peak of 369 feet, the side had a gigantic hand-painted whale leaping out the ocean towards the sky.

Bartek cringed from the omen – whales were a constant in his worst nightmares. Too often he'd dream of being stranded in pitch black ocean, with huge aquatic dragons & whales rubbing against his bare feet as he frighteningly tread water.

They had absolute control of the building, access to all levels for anything they wanted – *including rave parties*. They could even live there for free, just as their security guard had been.

The Tower was abandoned in 1980 – purchased for $50,000 by 10 investors. One was running for Mayor, and another was owner of the goth-industrial City Club. He was notorious as one of Detroit's biggest slumlords, obsessed with gobbling up the once-supreme landmarks of the city. He'd been on a warpath of slum empire since the early 80's and was rumored to be acquiring all the freaky, haunted buildings for weird occult reasons.

He'd started buying property in middle school, just signing on the dotted line & sending in deeds by mail and lying about his age. By 2005, he'd owned large swathes of the city which sat rotting. Bartek had only once glimpsed him at The City Club, in a suit and tie with a steel-tipped cane.

Like most of Detroit's architectural triumphs, by the late 70's The Tower had become a sparsely utilized business plaza. It was launched in 1928 as Detroit's answer to the Empire State Building; it was "the talk" of The World's Fair and appeared on front page news worldwide. Every floor was rented out like a high-rise, and the wealthy had come from across the world to roost there.

But it was haunted in a way reserved for abandoned mental institutions & brutal prisons. The turn-over rate was heavy and businesses among lower levels kept leaving. By the late 70's it was near vacant – two floors for insurance agencies & accounting firms. Since 1980 its been a silent, unoccupied tomb.

They'd hosted a rave party weeks prior, on the 3rd & 4th floors – but people kept leaving ghost-white, unsettled from "presences." People kept seeing apparitions walk through walls. Security would yell at party kids to get out of an unpermitted area – they'd follow them but they'd just vanish. One security guard quit over it.

The *Fight Club* looking basement was the same story – punks would walk downstairs, feel its creepy vibe, then turn around & just go home, looking ghost-white. Meanwhile, in the stage room, every night something would delicately peel taped posters from the window and set them on the table as if a phantom wanted to sit at it's favorite table and peer into the street without visual hampering.

Bartek entered a hallway hidden by curtains – the elevator room. The ceilings were painted in murals, the shafts painted gold. Wall edges were gold-trimmed; a faux-diamond chandelier hung up top. At its end were imposing staircases. Standing there, it felt like an airport terminal – as if thousands of travelers rushed past hurriedly, paying no mind to the man simply standing.

Bartek was then led upstairs on a tour through the aforementioned rave area – rooms crumbling & spider-webbed, floors covered with ripped paper & broken glass. An old Dentists chair was turned over in the hallway; graffiti slopped over everything. The place didn't look as if it had simply shut down, it looked a Chernobyl hospital left to radioactively rot.

He was led down a long flight of stairs to the basement levels, 4 of which were totally submerged by black water. The storm drain shattered years ago and an underground lake filled the subterranean levels. In order to legally sell food, a scuba diving team would have to clear the pipe – for $500,000! The building was, however, cleared of asbestos, which made it so valuable.

Lockwood mentioned something about phantasm fires, but stopped himself. He gave a sly look: "*Don't worry 'bout that – let's just get some hard drinkin' metal bands in here...*"

Lockwood, Bartek & Co. would remain in control so long as their go-to man stayed on the development board. He was a short gay man who was often bartender – he never wanted to be there, alone or even with people, since he was sensitive to its haunted nature.

That patch of land where The Tower stood was apparently the epicenter of Detroit's origin. It was claimed the building was erected on a Native American burial ground – one of the most important of such and exceptionally sacred, since it was in such close proximity to the Detroit River; holy land & holy waters.

It was the Ground Zero compass point for the invasion of the French, where they encamped & entrenched the white man's culture. It is a site where legends say they executed many natives, then intentionally defecated upon their memory building their structures on the disrespected dead. As the flourishing nexus of white civilization come to reap their manifest destiny, this haunted chunk of dirt became the blackened heart of Detroit. Myth-wise, it was the reason this metropolis was allegedly cursed.

Bartek was soon back with [][][]; she was cautious, quietly seeing a few men, feeling out the right direction. Bartek didn't care about her peripheries – nor did she question his. They were staring each other down, still – he was perhaps the largest shadow in her orbit.

In the soft darkness she retained that spiritual glow. The closer he got, the more she consumed him. They spent the night talking calmly, having dropped their acts. The contrast was dazzling; the only ones who saw how these two interacted alone were they themselves. They talked about the little girl, how she needed a father. By all means she was still a tattooed metal kid. In midst of her chaos, she'd ended up with a kid. She was terrified...

Quite soon, in a not-so-distant future, it would be difficult to imagine a world without iPhones & Facebooks. MySpace was still so new few could grasp its potential, let alone work it. Bartek didn't even have a cell phone back then, because they were still impossibly expensive & promised years-long, credit-affecting contracts.

Digital cameras were still uncommon. This will be hard to fathom for futuristic readers, but folks once took film to get developed. It could take a week to get prints, but it was standard to receive 2 copies of each photo.

Earlier that day, [][][] been digging through old pics. As you may recall, Bartek had those mischievous friends at The Phallus House who'd launched their prank assault on EMINEM.

Bartek, Jesus and Krooner were a brainy, intimidating triad. Even though it was something of a punk house, very few anarchy kids could debate-battle Jesus/Krooner's Libertarian-leaning, unfashionably pro-capitalist rhetorical onslaughts. They loved to pick a verbal fight & derange the foundations of some victim's reality – it was a bizarre war of conservative logic through the warped lens of a man stalking EMINEM with Twinkies.

Jesus was a shit-talking but Krooner the counterbalance. Both had no mercy for stupidity, yet Krooner was always gentle with the ladies.

Many women looked up him for his non-damning way of speaking. He never "man-splained" anything, per se. He wanted to educate people, not scream "*buffoons!*" at them, such as Jesus.

Often when in discussion with Krooner, Bartek would say something profound that came from nowhere. It wasn't so much what Bartek said that hit Krooner so hard but rather the viewpoint of logic that had formed it. When catching wind of the strange universe Bartek arranged his thoughts in, Krooner would often ignite his own brainstorm. Brought to silence by some Bartekian "Tree In The Forest" clarity, Krooner would excuse himself to process it with a cigarette & computational solitude on the backyard porch.

Bartek did just this to him one day, and while Krooner excused himself, Ryan gazed at the tacked photos on his bedroom wall. One was his ex girlfriend – it looked as if a mountain range were behind her. She'd a black hoodie on, masking the top of her head except for short reddish/purple died hair that ruffled out. Her eyes closed, she was kissing her baby daughter on the temple.

Kroon had snapped the photo when she wasn't paying attention – just this loving, honest moment. With her eyes closed & head titled, it revealed three-quarters of a face which even in its obscured form was intoxicating.

It made Bartek long for family. The woman in the photo mattered not, 'cause it might as well been a prize winner from *National Geographic*. To assume that in real life he'd ever meet a woman so beautiful – let alone possess the ability to strike her fancy without quickly & pathetically sabotaging himself – this was about as realistic as a 97 year old heavyweight boxing champion.

Years later, as [][][] flipped through a stack of old photos, lo & behold – *she had the other copy*. She had not only dated Krooner once long ago, but she had in fact been bat-shit crazy about him for many, many years. She looked to him like the epitome of knowledge, attracted to his intelligence above all. She even thought she might end up marrying him, perhaps.

Once the "small world" coincidence was established, and he mentioned Krooner & he debated philosophy & politics constantly – that Krooner often found himself flabbergasted & stumped by Bartek – this struck her visibly, like lightning. Her eyes burned holes through his head, and he felt gloriously entrapped by sharks. One wrong tread of water, they shall sense and devour.

What a gift it is to granted love at first sight – and not once, but twice! And for it to unfurl in this absolutely magickal way? It was beyond coincidence. And no romantic fire-starter could ever compare to Krooner's self-willed long-time no-contact with [][][] telling her Mr. Bartek was, in fact, one of the smartest, coolest dudes he'd met in his long history of Michigan life...

Lucky was he indeed. Metal Maniacs – one of the most important English-language metal magazines on the planet – had given press to his new book. Two world famous metal critics had listed it in their monthly playlists as to what thy were reading that month!

As big a victory as that was, he'd also somehow managed to devour *half* of the unsigned band demo section! It was totally unreal, since this section is what metal bands all over the world struggled to be featured in.

In the era before the internet, it was like hitting jackpot. Any band lucky enough to be featured with a good review, or even just a few lines saying they were decent, was destined to acquire label interest of some kind – or at the very least serious networking and promotional opportunities worldwide. It put a band on "The Map," instantly, globally, as if benighted by the Heavy Metal Illuminati.

Thus, a glowing review is one thing – *but to be given an entire half-page article for a book??* They printed the cover of *The Silent Burning* and its grinning, evil clown – below it the first paragraph of its introduction, as if to declare: "*This book is so hardcore & cult classic we don't even need to tell you what it's about, we're just gonna drop the first few lines here...*"

Somehow without even strumming an instrument he thieved this great honor by justifiably earning it – and found himself being promoted as a new breed of writer totally unique & relevant to the strange artistic history of the global metal underworld. Had he paid for ad space that size, it have run $10,000.

Thus, Ryan Bartek once again defied history & smashed impossible odds, carving out the origins of a new path. He'd eventually come to occupy a strange place in the history of heavy metal. Seeing his book printed in Metal Maniacs was a dream come true – and far as he was concerned everyone who ever doubted him could *yadda-yadda yakkity-shmakkity blah-blah-blah*. His misanthropic tome had broken into the underground like a rabid demon clawing its way through the crust of earth.

Miss 3 sat on the bathroom floor, soaping up [][][]'s little girl in the bathtub. Like a 1940's pin-up, 3's hair was pulled back with a hastily knotted bandanna. She looked like a farm wife that had been draping wet sheets over clotheslines in the sun.

She was curvy & young, a year away from exploding into unrelenting hotness. She was certainly a tomboy, and had the capacity to land one mean punch. He had a great affection for 3 – she was loving & sarcastic, slightly home-body & probably quite the handful when drunk.

Her motherly instinct had kicked in since moving in last week. [][] [] was grasping at straws trying to work full time & holding down an apartment. The girls were both from a city bordering Lake Huron; Miss 3 was playing nanny for housing.

Aloof as Bartek often was, he maintained friendship with women over men, and was attuned to their logic. He, like all women, detested pushy, sexually harassing, idiot men. Having been raised by women, he always spoke like a woman that hated men, and this distance from any kind of driving male stereotype is what always had him surrounded by females as if a rule of gravity. He was the guy among strippers, laughing with them at the ways they con money out of the drunken idiots. He worshiped Venus.

He might as well have been a lipstick lesbian with a dick. One step removed, he would speak in a way that women do among themselves. Bartek hated the tacky domination of men; he wanted the goddesses of the world to rise; he supplanted anarcho-feminism & witchcraft propaganda anywhere he could.

They all took a long walk into the muggy June night. They were all horror movie fiends, and had been watching *House Of 1000 Corpses* way too much, which translated into their desire to have one big psycho family. [][][] had an infatuation for Baby, and wasn't a far cry from it. A sadistic wrecking ball, [][][] loved to toy with fool men. As a showgirl, she vamped them dry.

Chatting up the greatness of *Witches of Eastwick*, Bartek summoned a lil' Van Horne charm. Yes, he animatedly fashioned himself a devil of sorts – and yes, he longed to again have a coven of witchy chicks messing with him endlessly. Only thing he missed about high school were the pagan girls who'd do his tarot, read his runes & torture him with affectionate Voodoo doll stabbings. He loved it when gothy occult girls summoned him like a Djinn. He wanted that sort of thing back, childish as it may sound – and he wanted a family. He was determined to adopt these deranged kittens.

They returned & Bobby from FILTHPIMP burst through the door, flanked by drunken metal guys. Spastic & hammered, he told Bartek: *"Hey, guess what? I just knocked up my girlfriend again!!"*

Bartek rolled his eyes – it was the death of FILTHPIMP as a

touring band; the fat lady was singin'. He envisioned being hitched to [][] [], all of them broke but happily cooking BBQ like all the other punk rock adults. The kids would run around the lawn while Uncle Bobby & Poppa Bartek smoked weed behind the garage.

And he was <u>OK</u> with it. He remembered what a co-worker told him about turning 25 – that you look around at your life & that's who you are, that's what you are, and you can accept it or stay miserable. What was soon to arrive was the life of a working man with crazy luck & strange perception – *but with tangible family...*

The shows kept coming – up to 2 concerts a week. Still he was writing for a dozen journalistic outlets & running a PR company & MySpace sites & hammering out material for future books, screenplay notes & promoting his ill-begotten *The Silent Burning*.

In addition to The Tavern, he was working 40 hours a week at the mafia restaurant. He also foolishly embroiled himself into attempting goth/industrial Sundays at The Tower. It was failing abysmally; Bartek would soon give up his industrial DJ ambitions.

Lockwood's crew were aggravated with him 'cause he was booking bands that weren't metal/punk. Those bands didn't draw – and if they were not to go bankrupt, they had to dip into the weirdo rock scenes. The owner agreed with him, and Lockwood was resentful. It's not as if he didn't want to do heavy gigs, or was "selling out" – he was doing what was necessary. Still, unfortunately "the wrong way" they were rubbed – and the cocaine now flowing through the place only added to the aggressive tension.

They planned a full-scale re-launch of the venue on September 1st, with press in local media & a two stage fest to kick it off. The investors were in talks to allow advertising space on the side of the building that would generate a $1 million per year.

There was plans to open the nearby garage for free parking & the entire strip was to be re-launched with new restaurants, a music store, a larger venue. Even for The Tavern they'd a blueprint for a mini movie theater + new stage & sound system. It could be the origin of a new Detroit smack-dab in the middle of the city.

Kluck again was released from prison, having completed 7 months for probation violation & heroin possession. Last year he was only a few weeks shy of being free of the system, and was pulled over & arrested in front of Bartek's apartment – they dug through Kluck's new car, arrested him, called a tow truck & stole his vehicle.

Yet free again he was, and Bartek took him to the Sounds of the

Underground tour where GWAR & Opeth stole the show. Afterwards, they drove to [][][]'s apartment. They walked into the living room as she blared Ministry's "Scarecrow," her favorite song. She was in "Baby" mode, the tough-as-nails destroyer.

It wasn't long before Kluck & Miss 3 were sucking face. They all drank & played cards & jammed metal & had a good night. At the fridge, Bartek went in to kiss [][][]. She ducked away from him, but he gently clasped her wrist: *"How long are we gonna do this?"* She didn't want to get into it.

She was still hung up the last guy, and her actions were rooted in fear for the kid. She didn't think Bartek was serious. [][][] morphed back into her ever malicious self. Kluck & 3 spooned on the couch while Bartek slept alone on the floor.

Bartek rode his bike to 8 Mile and took the inner-city bus downtown. As he approached The Tower, it never ceased to creep him out how each pair of broken windows seemed like eye sockets gazing back – how dirty the limestone was, how photogenic.

He shook off the feeling that The Tower itself was watching and walked through the front door. No one was around, though the co-owner was somewhere – he'd asked Bartek come at 2, and it was now 2:30.

Bartek walked up to the bar & cracked a Pabst Blue Ribbon tall boy; the co-owner strolled through the front door: *"How'd you get in here?"* Bartek explained he'd waltzed right in. The co-owner got the chills: *"Look, I'm positive that door was locked... If you haven't noticed, I refuse to be here alone. Place gives me the fuckin' creeps. I was just hangin' out front waiting in my car for you."*

He told the co-owner that Lockwood admitted The Tower was built on a sacred burial ground. *"Well, there's a lot more."* He nervously looked around, as if being watched...

"There are phantom fires that appear. Like out of thin air, they just appear & vanish. And it's not just this building – its multiple buildings, all in this area. You know how City Club has this same problem? How the upper floors are all burned out? No one could pinpoint where the blaze came from. Even if it was a legitimate fire, the place still has ghost fires..."

This was true, or so rumored. Everyone that hung around City Club knew about the fires that would just appear and vanish, sometimes burning out a room. This is why it only cost $300 to live there in a penthouse suite.

"Last year, about this time, we began working on this place. I went to get something from my car and had this feeling to look up – and I did &

the top floor was on fire. I started to panic – thought this entire place was gonna go up. And then the firetruck got my attention – they were already unloading. We didn't have electricity up there, no fire system that would've alerted them. I went up to the driver and he was spooked – he didn't even wanna step out."

"The driver told me it was known in the fire department just to be here on that date, that same time every year 'cause it'd just happen. A fire would break out on the top floor, sometimes other floors, and then just stop – June 11th, like clockwork, every year."

"In the Fire Dept, they passed knowledge of this from one administrator to the next, doing their best to keep it silent. The mayors of Detroit past & present all knew. The police department knew. Ghost fires raged all over the area, but it was like The Tower was the generator. It was the strongest one, they said, as if it all spiraled from this cursed land."

Bartek didn't believe it, but the tone of his seriousness couldn't be denied: "Look, this place – it's nothing but dark energy. No one ever wanted it. That's why it sat here for 25 years. By the late 70's all the upper floors were empty, and only a few businesses still operated on the lower two. By 1979, it was a gay bar – one of the first big ones in Michigan. But it didn't last long, it was just too damn haunted. This place had a high rate of suicide jumpers too – wealthy people who ran businesses, had wives & kids & nice lives & no history of depression or warnings."

"Last month, on the 11th, we had another ghost fire – Jason took some guys up there. By the time they made the penthouse, the firetrucks showed. And you know how they are in Detroit – cops, paramedics, firemen – sometimes they won't show for hours. But they all knew what was up."

"When Jason finally got up there, just a thin mist was floating in the air – no burn marks, nothing. There were a half dozen of us that saw this fire just standing on the street. The top floor was just blazing away, and then it was gone."

Bartek wasn't buying it, and the co-owner knew it. "Look, that elevator room over there – you feel it right? The whole place you get goosebumps, but that hallway is..."

"Look, I'm not even Christian – I'm gay, you know – but I am superstitious. I think that maybe you can trick energy, or spirits, by whatever it remembers is real. Maybe ghosts get exorcised not from the ritual but by them being Christian in the past and they just remember what it means. And it works 'cause lingering memory."

"So I decided to call a priest. It took awhile, but I finally got *someone to come after bugging them with voicemails for a week straight. He came and had the attitude of a nice old man just trying to comfort a scared person. He took a few steps in that elevator hallway, stood there out of my view for 2 minutes, then came out ghost white. He told me there was nothing he could do for me, and he left. He wouldn't even return my calls..."*

"And then I went right for the Archbishop. He went in there, said some rites, and then tried to cleanse the building. He pulled out this vial of Holy Water and sprinkled it on the floor and... and it just... it fucking bubbled – it bubbled right off the fucking tiling..."

Bartek laughed in his face. If this guy wasn't pulling his leg, then he was totally delusional. Bartek wiped the hysterics away and refocused – *the man was about to cry...*

Jason came in the front door with his crew. Everyone huddled around the bar and like little kids indoctrinating him in their clubhouse, they fleshed out the larger tale.

Yes, it was true that The Tower was built on a Native Burial ground, but it wasn't the first architecture erected on its supernatural compass. In 1803, when the population was about 600, the town whorehouse was established dead center.

It was rife with the chatters of an abominable haunting. For 2 years it was the bane of the religious folk and especially the fundamentalist sheriff.

So on the early morning of June 11th, at around 3am, the sheriff rode up on horseback flanked by henchman. They barricaded the doors & windows then tossed kerosene lanterns inside as the prostitutes slept. They burned them all alive.

The fire went wildly out of control – as the flames jumped it quickly spread throughout the city, creating The Great Fire of 1805. It killed untold scores & it's devastation was later symbolized on the flag of Detroit with the latin motto: *"It will rise from the ashes."*

Official history reads that the blaze began when John Harvey, the local baker, failed to extinguish the ashes of his tobacco pipe. A barn caught fire, and the flames spread quickly.

The myth, or perhaps reality, was that the sheriff had officially changed the story. The surviving townspeople had approved of the lynch mob, and all were guilty. They were damned, and the truth no more be spoken.

Years passed and on its ashes was placed The Grand Circus Hotel, at the center of Detroit's 1800's version of Times Square. At 6 stories with nearly 100 rooms, it was heavily frequented. However, phantom fires would appear & vanish at random. By June 11th, a huge one blossomed and returned to the elements.

The police, the fire department – many of whom had survived The Great Fire – saw to it that every June 11th they would have squad cars & firetrucks in place. This disturbing reality was quietly handed the secession of Fire Chiefs & Police Commissioners from generation to generation. The Grand Circus itself eventually burned down as well, and The Tower was erected on it's ashes.

Bartek didn't know what to say. His co-workers were of the belief that the coming July 11th was the 300 year anniversary – and they were due for a third Great Fire. And across the street that very day the All Star baseball game was scheduled. Camera Crews & sports heroes & baseball fans from around the world would be flocking there. Only, perhaps, to be incinerated by a demonic blaze.

What their little group did not know was that the 300 year anniversary had already come and gone – it was June 11th, not July. And yes, there was a large ghost fire in the penthouse, because everyone present (*except Bartek*) had witnessed it.

It seemed apropos that he would be there for something so inherent to his Detroit myth world. Bartek questioned if they'd like to film that night with night vision cameras, just to see if they'd nab any strange footage. All were psyched.

The group kept a lid on the whole haunted thing, 'cause it'd be bad for business if the music scene found out their cool new venue was Barad-dûr. Still, one thing was certain – The Tower was unlocking itself for Bartek. It was an open armed embrace of Overlook, beckoning him inside with a curling finger of shadow...

Bartek woke up with a call from Coleman, the security guard living at The Tower. He was in a deep hole after a long bender – no car, no money – just Jason & his circle, sleeping on the balcony above the bar. He wasn't happy, but he definitely wasn't suicidal.

Coleman woke in a sleepwalking trance. Like a piloted marionette, he tightened a rope on the balcony overhang, slipped the noose around his neck, then jumped the railing. He woke up mid-fall. The rope snapped – just weak enough to break from his plummeting force.

Coleman landed on the cement, spraining his ankle. He was mortified & felt an army of shadows watching him. He ran out the door & hobbled the empty downtown streets terrified until dawn. He then called Bartek begging to crash a few days.

The man with the noose bruises was a fine edition to the madness that had become the barbershop apartment. Moses had gone over the deep end and Bartek wasn't quite sure what to do with him.

Earlier that year, Moses was beyond frustrated. Bartek said his problems were not severe and all he needed was to get laid. Moses scoffed. Bartek questioned how long it'd been. Mr. Good Guy admitted not having been laid in 3 years – *and he'd just turned 25!*

Bartek, in sympathetic anguish, made an impassioned speech to get back up on that pussy train. Moses sneered: *"Oh that's just you."* In pity, Bartek visited the porn shop to acquire for Moses a stack of lesbian sex DVD's & a huge $1 store tub of generic Vaseline. Moses thought it was endearing that his friend was looking out for his interests, but wanted him to take them back...

Months later and Moses was blowing entire paychecks on dirty movies. The DVD piles were climbing to the ceiling like Jenga puzzles, and emptied tubs of petroleum jelly littered the apartment.

Moses had not only become a living, breathing erection, but he'd learned to somehow to take poppy seeds and mix them with a certain juice that extracted potency, filling empty plastic two-liters with a mushy, blackened green chunk-slime. He was sky high deranged from opium water, leaving discarded soda containers around the apartment with black sludge like rancid coffee grounds.

His hobby was now using a Game Genie on his 8-bit NES & typing in random codes to make the craziest shit appear on screen, playing nonsensical games that were bizarre art experiments.

He'd also met this girl and finally gotten laid; together they were drinking this opium water & eating Ambien pills. They convinced each other they were really aliens, and they had both known each other in a distant interstellar system, and that they were placed in these human vessels to find each other on Earth. And Jesus Christ was of course an alien too, and for whatever reason only they could decode the signs of what he really meant.

Moses had also built an extensive, miniature Christmas village in the front room – a white Styrofoam slab he'd been gluing grass & glitter on. He'd rubber-cemented tiny metal figurines all over it. He led Bartek through their intended effigies: *"And this is you, and this is Flannigan, and this guy's Neil P., and..."*

When 3 related the news, Bartek was shocked – [][][] had picked up some clean-cut, short haired bro in Bartek's absence. Sure, she was still feeling out options – *but a clubby sports guy?!?*

They were googly eyed, talking about god together – a made for

TV movie where the heroic, square-jawed jock gets the goth to drop her black for a pom-poms. Bartek was enraged – only a traitor would date a Christian. How could someone even have sex with one of those things?

Bartek realized he only needed to materialize one great night that could not go wrong, and all it'd take was maybe $100. *But he was broke.* A bright thought "dinged" a luminous bulb – he'd cash in all those savings bonds his dead grandparents once sent for Christmas. He thought of those estranged ones, and his grandfather's voice boomed in his head: *"No problem Ryan, ha ha ha ha..."*

After cashing the bonds, en route to [][][]'s apartment swarms of mayflies had unseasonably hatched – like locusts they buzzed over dry territory that didn't make sense. Resembling giant flying cockroach/centipede hybrids, they were mating & spawning in grotesque clumps. They hung from telephone polls, covered street lamps, splatted on windshields like ugly paintballs.

Defiant of nature as it was, the oddly supernatural eeriness should be noted. Bartek had serious nightmares involving these things as a child – horrendous, lucid dreams crawling with them.

He had been in this area once, at 7, when a rednecky town had a celebration to commemorate this mate-spawn-die cycle. He always remembered the big floppy red shoes of a clown battalion marching in the city parade, crushing gnarly clumps of flying mosquito-grasshopper creatures.

Bartek was taking the girls to a metal concert – one of [][][]'s favorite bands whose female singer she looked up to for empowerment. Bartek bought the booze & tickets, but [][][] was in a foul mood. He stood next to her in pit, intimidated as always yet trying to act cool. But he had to say something, anything.

[][][] mentioned something about the band onstage, and he popped back with the first thing in his mind. Of all the sentences that could be strung together, he somehow chose this magic combination images & emotions: *"So, um, uh... Do lobsters freak you out?"* She looked at him like a buffoon and quietly walked away.

After the gig, Bartek, 3, Kluck & [][][] drove back her apartment. The mood lightened up with a 24 pack of beer cans. As they settled in for what was to be a chill night, a knock rapped the door. [][][] let the Christian Jocko guy in, and kissed him right in front of everyone. He didn't even look at Kluck or Bartek, just wandered into [][][]'s room. Miss 3 & Kluck's eyes bugged; [][][] sat down at the kitchen table as if nothing was odd.

She asked what they wanted to do. Bartek stood up & scratched his freshly shaved head: *"If you'll pardon me, I have to go home and shampoo my hair."* [][][] eyes twitched in a dumbfounded glare, fixing her retinas at the table top as if a scolded child. 3 was electrified; Bartek & Kluck abruptly bounced...

Overworked & stretched too thin, Bartek was not taking to the summer heat. Whenever mid-Summer hit, the manic in his depression would soar. With the dark spell his book had cast and ever freakish nightmares of The Tower, this was an intense mania.

His relationship with [][][] was crumbling – at one angle a jock seducing the soul he was attempting to fuse with; at the other an abusive psychopath that wanted him to "play along" but was such a brutal fox that he was utterly unequipped. Bad boy had bitten off more then he could chew, and Mean Momma had 'em grappled.

Bartek wrote her a big, pissed off letter, because he never leaned his lesson. Even short, pissed-off letters don't help – let alone the amount of words this gifted writer could push out. Even ifmolded by humor & sarcastic ribs, he'd still done broiled himself on a big ol' grill of stupid.

When she refused to respond, the mania pounded. He'd fix the problem by writing an even bigger, more stupid letter and physically mail it to her. When he heard nothing back for 4 days, he wrote an even bigger, infinitely more stupid letter. He stomped to the mailbox & slid it in, cursing her forever – returning home to find his mailbox containing the even bigger, more stupid letter marked *"Undeliverable – Return To Sender."*

Which made him think the infinitely more stupid letter would bounce back too, and it had been a lucky blessing. Yet the next day, [][][] did indeed receive the 2nd letter which if read alone was totally out of context & filled with condemning hate. And she made sure he knew she received it, giving no more info then that, leaving him in the dark and at merciless onslaught of his fever pitch mania.

Bartek could barely sleep. He woke up early on his only day off. Forced to send emails & book gigs instead of simply live, he wanted to formally resign from this self-willed machine-man catastrophe he'd entombed himself with.

A hard reality – it was certainly over with [][][]. He typed from morning on through the roasting afternoon, took a bike ride, then returned before sundown. He switched on the computer and the screen went haywire – strange text & scrambled lines. He reset it & still digital dementia. He called a tech who said to bring it into shop.

Bartek hung up & smelled something funny, like sulphur. There was a small fire on the kitchen table – inside an open copy of Pit Magazine, turned to the page of his CD review for the California black metal band Sol Evil.

Somehow the CD review was smoldering & flaming – he killed the flame & examined it, stoned & confused as he was. The only thing that made sense was an ember from the joint he'd just smoked must've fallen off while moving around the kitchen. It felt creepy though, and deeply wrong.

Bartek disassembled the computer tower and hauled it to his car. When he turned the ignition, it wouldn't start. There was battery charge but not the click of an alternator. He tried again – nothing. From inside the apartment, Moses began screaming: "*AAAAAAAAHHHHH!!!*" Bartek thought he'd slipped down the stairs & broke his leg maybe – but the panic was from inside Moses' bedroom. Was it a night terror from Opium Sludge?

Bartek rushed inside – tiny red ants were eating his gerbils alive! Their corpses writhed with them, internally swarming, as if the carcass of a dead calf bloated with maggots. They'd never seen these ants before – they simply were not anywhere else in the house, not in the past or in the future. There was no trail of where they would've come from either. An hour ago, those gerbils were happy & well fed.

Were Bartek's witchy gruesome-twosome "going to town" with their little spell-casting playbook? He couldn't help but feel like 3 & [][][] were taking turns stabbing his voodoo doll with 8 inch pins inside a circle of burning candles. Bartek went outside to shake off the eerie malfunctioning & devourment of devil bugs. He tried the car again – this time it started as normal…

Hours later; nothing had been wrong with the computer. He set it back up and dove into internet land – the first email he received was a dispatch from the wife of Lord Morder, the first man in America ever tried & convicted as a black metal terrorist.

In drive-by style – not meaning to harm anyone but rather "send a message" – his crew had popped off gunshots outside a Christian rehab center his drummer was at after going Born Again Christian & renouncing his occult past & black metal in particular. Morder was now doing a 10 year sentence for his part.

Morder's wife had gotten a copy of *The Silent Burning* and printed it out, mailing it chunk by chunk to his prison cell. It was a letter to Bartek by Morder himself via her, explaining that this was now one of his favorite books of all time and that he'd read it multiple times over. He wanted to interview Bartek for his satanist prison magazine. The band he came from was <u>Sol Evil</u> – *the same band from the CD review seemingly ablaze without reason!*

[][][] invites him over. Everything is calm – she ditched the Christian Jocko guy. Kluck shows up. Everyone is happy – music & movies, fun & games. The crazy kids get all tuckered out from the slumber party. *And then she made him sleep on the couch...*

The co-owner from The Tower called – they'd been illegally removed! Japanese businessmen were paying a fortune to rent the skyscraper as to have their own personal view of the All Star Game at Comerica Park across the street. Bartek imagined them all running from waves of phantom flames as if Godzilla's atomic fire-breath.

 The development board had tons of cash waved in their face and simply evicted their venue/bar without any warning. To avoid litigation, they allowed them free access to a nearby venue – a little bar wedged into the side of a large brick building. Bartek was demoralized; he'd finish out his remaining shows & be done with it.

 2 weeks later the co-owner they worked for sold his stake in the 10 person corporation for a massive turnover. The man they'd so diligently worked for fled to London overnight with all the pay-off cash. No one saw a dime. Bartek got shafted, but Lockwood was screwed out of 3 grand.

 The largest real estate developer in Michigan was now revamping The Tower as the centerpiece of Detroit's renewal – $10 million dollars worth of updates. But unbeknownst to them, all those moguls were really doing was forcing any screw-loose future inhabitant Jack to be a dull boy with all work and no play.

Bartek was free of a great weight; the path was clear for a family, a home, a united future. Bartek decided he'd formally ask [][][] to go steady with him. Save The Vegetables was coming up, this time at The Theatre Bizarre. Every band at the fest were brothers-in-arms; every positive connection in his life would be culminated on the one patch of magickal land he considered his spiritual homebase.

 Theatre Bizarre had played a major part in their early fling. She'd never heard of it & he'd taken her there for a "Stolen Media Festival" on the stage with the giant zombie clown head. Clips of short movies & cartoons projected on a makeshift screen with 60 of his friends hanging out at that carnival fortress art-squat.

 After the program, they walked the twisted fairgrounds. A

doorway that stood on its own, ripped from an old house & painted so it looked like the open mouth of a demonic clown with burning red eyes. She leaned against it, her body language like a date hanging out her door for a kiss before slipping inside.

[][][] got on the subject of her daughter – she needed a father, and [][][] herself was desperately seeking family. Bartek flinched. He barely knew her, and all Bobby did was discourage it. And so Bartek told her in a snake-like tone *"Don't ask too much from me."* It's not that she was pushing things hard, she was just direct. There was no point of even involving herself if that wasn't an option.

Nearly a year later and Bartek was driving to her apartment to finish that conversation. He would bring she & her daughter to Save The Vegetables at Theatre Bizarre, and he'd ask her to go steady. Even with festivities, it was still a family affair. Punk rock parents would bring their kids and =children would paint themselves up & run around the grounds. He wanted her little girl to be one of those happy kids, lounging with them on a picnic blanket.

He was happy, truly happy on that drive. He parked the car and ran up to her apartment glowing. He knocked at the door, ready to surprise her. Miss 3 answered the door with an awkward, fearful look. *"She's really pissed at you, you might not want to be here right now – she's coming back any minute."*

Bartek didn't understand why. 3 said they'd gone out to eat with the little girl. They asked what she talked about when alone with Bartek. The kid said HE said [][][] was *"evil."*

Whoa whoa whoa whoa whoa... he knew what she was getting at, but it was totally out of context. The daughter would often talk with him when alone, and [][][] had encouraged it. But the kid was always at odds with the mother. [][][] was a whirlwind, and so was the kid. Her sloppy, tough love parenting was at times heavy handed. But the child's growing resentment towards her was not something she was willing to confront or deal with.

Thus, one day the kid was near Bartek while he was getting ready for work. The kid kept saying "I *don't want you to go, don't leave me with her, she's evil."*

It was some harsh phrasing, but he knew what she meant: *"Ah don't worry, all mom's can be a little evil sometimes. She just loves you and has a lot of stuff going on and she doesn't always know how to show her feelings. You know, I think people were a little mean to her as a kid, other kids maybe, and they teased her a lot, and she's a little defensive don't always show her true feelings. It's ok, everything will be ok."*

That was it – he meant no harm. But when the phrase *"evil"* got around to [][][], her switch flipped. And then the kid asked *"Why are those people being mean to you?"*

Bartek lightened up, 3 as well. He explained, and she understood. It was nothing. Bartek sat on the couch while 3 watched TV. Soon, [][][] came in with groceries. She noticed Bartek and her eyes flickered. She sat down at the kitchen table and stared at its tabletop as the magma slowly rose to the chakra crown.

Convinced that Bartek was brainwashing her child to hate her, the volcano exploded in a dazzling eruption. Shouting and feral, she would not listen. She pushed him out of the apartment with vicious strength and slammed the door with all she had. In a cold, clammy stupor, he spoke calmly & slowly. She howled it was over and unless he left she'd call the cops.

With the lumbering fluidity of a mummy he returned to his car & drove off. He was ice cold, empty-eyed, cruising along the freeway with his heart torn out. He kept muttering: *"...but I was really real. I was really, really real..."*

He attempted to flip the turbo switch of his Ford Thunderbird, but the transmission began jerking – bad sounds were emanating on under the hood. With the car sputtering & grinding, Bartek barely made it home. He tried to call her but she picked up the phone & slammed it. He sat blankly at his desk until dawn.

Save The Vegetables came and went – yet all the smiling faces couldn't help but notice something had died in him. The Thunderbird was screwed – the engine & transmission weren't compatible! It'd cost $1000 to fix, totally bankrupting him. The cumulative bill of his life expenses hit at once – he needed 2 full time jobs if he were to save his credit & make rent. *Back to bussing tables & 80+ hours...*

Bartek was sleeping 4 or 5 hours a night, running on all cylinders. With the miserable string of chiropractic adjustments, he'd no willpower to learn yoga or healthily re-tune. He lived on scraps from his jobs, and ate the worst fast food. He turned to pain-pills ever more frequently, developing an unhealthy dependency...

September was approaching; Moses & Bartek let the apartment go. Bartek was offered a room at Stoner Joe's for $300 a month. He was sick of stressing; it didn't matter if it was a trailer park – it was freeway-near & straight downtown in 25 minutes.

Bartek got his troubled car back – *but then within days its electrical grid shorted out! The car would stall mid-driving!* The near heart-attack inducing physical work of the summer meant nothing! He'd be broke again in a week with no car, riding his bike even further out everyday – and all public buses ceasing at 9pm!

He got word that [][][] lost her job 'cause she couldn't locate a babysitter and had swiftly been evicted, checking herself into a home for battered women 'cause they were the only ones who'd help.

Bartek coldly drove to Stoner Joe's. The once unstoppable drag-racing Ford Thunderbird Beast sputtered, then abruptly died – right in front of the trailer park where he now lived.

Bartek bought a '92 Dodge Daytona from Lockwood for $292. He drove his new wheels to the city where Miss 3 & [][][] came from. When he arrived, it all returned to him – he'd been there as a child.

In his dreams all of Detroit was an interconnected blob – this place was at the end of his dreamscape. The bridges, the lighthouse over the water all hit him like a ton of bricks. Like a great painting, the place had its rustling leaves & fishing village architecture.

3 was in Detroit that weekend, so Bartek visited their mutual friend. Yet within an hour, [][][] called up that mutual buddy at random. She made Bartek get on the phone. With an enthusiastic tone she said come over. When he got to the apartment she was cautious. She was awaiting her new boyfriend, who she'd just met last week. Bartek's evil clown book was on the coffee room table, and she'd been imploring people to read it.

They hung out that night like a meeting between prison glass. Before he left, she burned her Medusa eyes through him: "*You should've played along.*" Her new boyfriend walked in the door; she looked her new lover squarely in the eyes before they kissed with effortless resistance. As Bartek left, he pondered if she meant a statement of their relationship? Or a "calling out" of ineptitude?

Back at the trailer park, notified by email, Bartek learned he was being removed from his position at Real Detroit Weekly and replaced by a fiery young clone. He was unhinged, and they wanted him gone. His reputation had been destroyed by his evil book. Bartek wrote his final column and sent it in to great relief. He could finally be something else now – not the tired journalist routine.

He went online to find his MySpace hacked & defaced. Someone trounced his profile & rewritten it. He knew it was [][][] – he'd forgotten to log out at her house. She claimed not to have done it, but there was no other culprit. They started getting more heated and the word war escalated;

she was a Goliath of shit talk. He told her he wanted nothing to do with her, then abruptly _deleted_ her – a viciously symbolic act in this futuristic digital war of the sexes...

Back at Bobby's, our forlorn Bartek saw some old video cam footage – a precious moment with [][][]. She was in a field, chuckling with her mouth shut. Then she stuck out her tongue – it had a live mayfly on it, insect legs writhing around. She was laughing, happy, then spit it out. The mayflies were like locusts swirling around her.

Bartek would always remember that. Like the wrapping of a mummy, he coated it around the remains of what they'd been. Buried in the same sarcophagus was the vast humiliation of his own ineptitude, stupidity & drama.

The Locust Queen had rocked on with her bad self, and Bartek was left to lick the wounds. If anything saved him, it was always art. He was a writer at core, and no literature was ever more profound then the kind of writing birthed from the anguish of romance. This sort of human pain told the most extravagant truths, most often of which the world is unprepared. By years end, [][][] was pregnant and engaged.

Ze Occupied States Ov Mabusvania

Just as when losing himself in Batman cartoons as a child – imagining himself the administrator of the asylum & presiding over his unique psychological specimens – Bartek again began a thorough acquaintance with all the villains of cinema which inspired him. When all else failed, a celluloid maniac would never let him down.

He'd lived a roller coaster & been excruciatingly spit out. His car was dead, and he'd broken his ankle drunkenly hopping a fence. He was sky high on pain-pills with no health insurance, hoping it wouldn't heal funny or he'd be fired from missing too much time at the mafia kitchen.

FILTHPIMP was to start again in November, once Bobby dug himself out of debt enough to quit his 4th job. Bartek felt it was the final act of his journalism shtick & his Detroit life at large. He wanted to go out on top, make one bad-ass album, and play a ton of shows – get raw & gritty, punk & slamming.

No one knew that he could shred. They grumbled 'cause a "writer" and not a "musician" was giving their albums a bad review. He would change all that and come swinging at Detroit with his lethal new band, pouncing & bludgeoning with sonic fists.

He was going to teach the punks what punk rock really meant and crush the metal kids with grinding death weirdo rock. He would rebel by doing it all, mushing all subcultures into one weird blob.

It made sense that he should go back to his roots. He needed to reexamine himself, ideas and influences that shaped him. Thus, he began constructing harsh experimental/industrial using a primitive string of programs, such as Cool Edit Pro & Fruity Loops. Nothing pro could come from it, yet hunkered down he was – extracting sound clips from VHS tapes that promised raging EQ levels with no sonic ability to coalesce with his out-dated untz-untz-untz software.

Even as Bartek promoted this experiment as Echelon Prime, the dark impulse underlying it was to examine the great enemies of the world, ingesting them all into his DNA. He imagined himself as a supervillain at the round-table of the Injustice League, unveiling a great catastrophic plot.

With his Lex Luthor-like genius, he'd unleash a mad plan that would crash through the plot-lines of every comic on the stands. Just as when Marvel introduces a new galaxy-spanning baddie, he'd disrupt not only the Detroit music scene but the worldwide underground with a band that's message had to be much more then simply a conduit of strange sounds. It had to pierce reality & shake it up directly; it needed a message to warp imaginations of its converts.

Bartek recalled the *Antichrist Superstar* Marilyn Manson, and his great prank that made every parent, cop, teacher & priest in America detest them with savage repugnance.

The brilliance of Manson's lost message was that while even dressed up in the most disturbing facades, the message was still inherently the truth – and utterly positive while appearing wholly negative. More importantly, it pushed every youth bound by its spell to run amuck in an essential religion-destroying temper tantrum.

Bartek devoured the essential foundations of many cinematic baddies those first 2 months at Stoner Joe's – Gabriel in *The Prophecy*, John Milton in *The Devils Advocate*, Unicron in *Transformers*, Frank in *King of New York* – all the Batman villains.

Having isolated himself to a grim work cubicle in a trailer park, there was no one left to whom he could turn. There was no one there to shield the darkness choking him. This new "research" wasn't so much at getting to the bottom of something, but a sickness that demanded fuel.

It was Adolf Hitler, more then any other villain in world history, that had driven him over the brink. With his depressive obsession promising nothing but an ever-darkening spiral, the worst possible book to end up in his hands actually did – *Mein Kampf.*

It was when he decided to actually sit down and read the thing that the hellish vertigo swallowed him. Having watched *Downfall* again, having read about the occult Hitler, he fell into that horrible thing quickly. It's sheer awfulness captivated him; he read it not as a crude, appalling essay of pure horrible, but rather as a highly-configured black magick spell.

Mein Kampf was the ultimate black magick grimoire, and had forever been promoted by the victors of history as merely a political tract of utter propaganda.

For whatever Hitler may have been, he was a to-the-bone black sorcerer. To dismiss the Pagan War background of Hitler is not only grossly negligent but defeats the lesson we must learn – he was the creation of men & women of the occult world as to literally install their half-baked Antichrist concept to dominance.

They knew what they were doing, they succeeded in not only fooling the public but brainwashing Hitler further with his madness – they put him in power, and he killed them all for silence & secrecy.

Magick is the art of using meditative willpower & the imagination itself to manifest something into reality. The sentence by sentence, paragraph by paragraph formation of *Mein Kampf* represented the most masterful psychological programming Bartek had ever seen – it was an almost mathematical code. Hitler was the DaVinci of Propaganda. That he mixed it with his stadium concerts made him the first rock star of sickest approach.

The Fuhrer Prinzig, where Hitler had in fact gotten his name, was an ancient black magick rite of the highest caliber. When one man is in absolute control of the masses, when they think he is god and convinced of it, when the blood is pure Aryan, that man becomes a direct conduit for WOTAN – the Viking Satan. Homeboy was shitballs insane, and utterly terrifying – sacrificing himself for Satan & trying to become immortal in the process.

The freshly unemployed Bartek now all the time in the world to drink whiskey, snort cocaine, and transcribe handwritten notes as he consumed the psychological evil that was *Mein Kampf,* and a Encyclopedia Britannica reprint of the Nazi handbook which described the foundations of social fabric. The reprint was filled with commemoratively drawn pictures of all the different uniform designs & graphic representations. It was bizarrely 50's. The text was what had been handed in Germany to newly wed couples & communities.

It taught openly how to re-construct reality so that National Socialism started at home. How house by house, block by block, this New Order is formed and the militant functions of each fanatic block, with volunteer community watches like prison guards tapped in through local councils basically led by Nazi Land Barons.

The web of horror these people were seduced into had no equal. And Bartek, more then anything, sought a way to make every house in the world an *antifascist house.* How could he render the panoramic photo negative?

Which led into *The Life And Death Of Adolf Hitler,* the fine biography from Robert Payne. It was a low point for Bartek. Here he found so many parallels to his own life he felt sick to his stomach – he understood quite painfully the cold, machine-like train of constructive logic that, if nurtured negatively, could grow to horror.

He understood the painful sequence of events which created Hitler. That over and over, it seemed as if Hitler tried to kill himself but forces beyond our world somehow kept him alive just to mold him into something monstrous.

After everything Bartek endured, no amount of black irony could prevent the sinking, horrible reality that the man he most resembled was this "prototype machine man" that Hitler embodied.

Even if Bartek was anti-fascist in every way, he was still living the life of the fanatic. Materialistically threadbare, a weird blackshirt to some fanatic impossible cause, sealing himself up in a room every night to type & type & type & create his little designs & only stumble into public to give a speech or play the part, then retreating again & again to the vortex of creation.

Bartek understood now more then ever the urgency to never let something like this happen again. He saw in Hitler's design a way that fascism could be used against itself. He saw a ripe opportunity to emulate his primary influences in a purely American way, mutated into a surreal discordian religion.

Sparks flew in his head, influences grinding into a slow-churning brilliant explosion – NSK vs. Subgenius vs. Nostradamus vs. Metal/punk Mayhem. Tongue in cheek, but dangerous ideas nonetheless. He would overthrow reality or die trying...

Bartek did not want to be Tyler Durden; what he sought was a "Project Mayhem" expressly created to destroy the Tyler Durdens' of the world. His Pan-Tribal Conspiracy was aimed at convincing every man to recognize his own physical body as the territory of a state, and for every such man to become his own anti-fascist dictator.

The surreal, bizarre message that Bartek propagated is best described by this analogy: instead of creating charismatic men to spellbind nations like Pied Pipers in jackboots, he wanted exactly the opposite – for those spellbound victims of the crowd to instead over-run the theoretical Nuremberg stage in a stampede, trampling and killing Hitler in the process.

With the entire crowd now populating the stage, and not a soul left in the audience, each of the former spectator puppets would rip off their clothes and approach the microphone absolutely naked and wholly exposed to the elements.

Having disowned the flags of every nation – and replacing the need of nationalism with a patriotism of the soul – these newly crowned emperors of will-power and self-determination would begin, one by one, to recite the text of their own personal anti-fascist *Mein Kampf* expertly crafted to destroy all facets of negative control.

Shouting their fanatic designs to an empty stadium, the microphone reverberations would bounce off emptied concrete, because no one would be left to hear it.

One by one, the Anti-Mussolini's would froth at the mouth with impassioned rhetoric, passionately screaming towards invisible crowds that no man should ever convert to their frenzied & fanatic message, because what is right for them is not right for everyone else, and that every man should be free to think for himself, to follow his hearts desires, and that through mutual understanding and compassion they be united in their quest of peaceful individuality, open communication, and respectful intercommunalism.

That absurd scenario was the core of Dr. Bartek's message, and by all means it sounds lovely on paper. But one cannot gloss over the fact that an intense xenophobia was still at the heart of it . Just like Fascism, it presented a specific vision which could only be attained by the destruction of specific elements.

What if, for instance, a Hitler arose whose message was not the extermination of the Jews but the extermination of the Nazis themselves? Would it then be considered Fascism? Was any ideology that specifically targeted something for elimination trapped under this banner?

However to be true fascism it would have to be calculated by violence and a physical state and authoritarianism. If something is against the elimination of an idea and at the core remains the principle that no violence shall ever be enacted on its behalf, then it eclipses the orbit of being determined fascist because it has no bureaucratic structure or physical form of political appendages.

So we must examine the basic foundations of Bartek's "Pan-Tribal" revolution, and if it could – even with its fanciful notions of anarchic liberty – be considered a bizarre form of "reverse fascism."

In order for any ideology to exist it must take root in opposition to something. Even the most liberal democracy has at its core a distinct repudiation of key items and themes.

If a modern society bans & burns *Mein Kampf*, is it equivalent to the Nazi book burning of the 1930's? If a country condemns the Neo-Nazi minority & demands obligatory prison sentences for anyone promoting this specific "hate speech," is there any distinction between Nazis who imprisoned political opponents?

Well yes, indeed there is. It is very much the difference between acting out of love and acting out of hate – or rather, out of "preemptive protection."

So here Bartek was, with the manifesto of an anti-state – one that was amoebic & center-less, existing in the mind as opposed to a literal political appendage. And like all ideologies – especially radical ones – it had to pick concepts to oppose.

Thus, to defeat any notion that this was a weird, surreal form of fascism, Bartek knew very well that any inclination of violence to those opposed to these ideas would have zero tolerance.

It is physical violence that gives fascism its demented character; fascism is created when the line is crossed by physical attacks against those in opposition to its ideas.

But when an ideology selects specific *IDEAS* as the enemy instead of flesh and blood humans, it eclipses the anatomy of fascism – especially when the ideology explicitly condemns the use of violence to achieve its objectives.

So here we are, the bottom line of what Bartek's "Pan-Tribal" revolution concerned itself with. Even if he refused to admit it, his worldview was hard-line anarchist (*although most serious anarchists would it appalling, simply in the way its written*).

He was promoting a sort of exclusive anarchism for specific mindsets inherently meant to aggressively absorb vast blocks of the counterculture into its framework (*whether anyone liked it or not*). Truth be told, it was funnier when they didn't.

It's exclusivity concerned itself mainly with the music scenes he felt attacked a larger "herd mentality." In other words, he was gunning specifically for the metal and punk scenes, the industrial world, the drug culture & rock n' roll freak majesty. He wanted to resurrect Abbie Hoffman's vision of a *Woodstock Nation*. But he certainly was still out to annihilate most religions, and people were just not very happy or comfortable with such venomous intent.

Thus, the puzzled pieces aligned fluidly. The FILTHPIMP album was to be named "*a.k.a Mabus*" as if the band itself were Nostradamus' Third Antichrist. So why not go full-tilt ludicrous and rename the band A.K.A. MABUS & simply claim that they literally were indeed The Third Antichrist "MABUS?"

In Nostradamus' writings, MABUS suddenly appears then dies, sparking some wave of global change which soon gives way to "ALUS," The Fourth And Final Beast. ALUS is represented as a conglomerate of all factors embodying the end of times – backed by this new ideology that, having gone horribly wrong, becomes vastly more disastrous to human kind then Marxism or National Socialism.

Why not make an American version of NSK that was centered around the concept MABUS, backed by shredding music of all metal/punk/rock/weirdo/EDM subcultures, and accompany it with a discordian religion based on MABUS? Why not disseminate this propaganda magick attack to educate, confuse & disturb? Why not have a fan club be a tongue-in-cheek doomsday cult?

Why not masquerade Bartek's insane manifesto as the feared

ideology of which Nostradamus warned, and declare whatever non-spacial territory they occupied (*as in the minds of their audience*) "The ALUS Republic?"

As Bartek was consumed by his dark research, he let go of the search for female companionship. He let go of people entirely. In any event, no woman sensing his nervous energy would touch him.

Brandon & Onyx had both left for California, taking with them the punk rock kids who looked up to Bartek. Loopy as he was, Onyx was an important part to Bartek's stability. He might as well have been his psychologist. But they too were gone and relocated in sunny California, inviting him to stay out there forever.

On November 5th, Kwame Kilpatrick stole the mayoral Detroit race, and he felt more politically doomed then ever – Kwame as mayor, Bush as president. What a low point.

The next day at work Bartek waltzed into the walk-in. All the frustration building inside him welled up with a single tear. He walked to the line and told the sous chef he was quitting. There was only 30 minutes left of his shift. While his boss was in shock, Bartek went back into the walk-in and – angry because of the missing hours on his check – stole a giant vacuum-wrapped log of uncut Swiss cheese before running out the back.

From thereon, no job prevented his thorough examination of propaganda & WWII at large. He devoured book after book as he slugged whiskey, reliving the entire war in a month. Like a man in the trenches, he sent handwritten letters to friends. By December 5th, Lana was sentenced to 8 months in jail. She began writing him letters in crayon again, like a little girl...

It was New Years Eve headed into 2006, and A.K.A. MABUS debuted at Smalls. What should have been a legendary start was derailed by humiliation.

Bartek had forced his way onto an already packed bill not of wanting to use up his scene points in a slimy way, but because he thought the bands on the show would be receptive. He had, after all, attended their gigs for years and helped with their press.

When he handed out his joke Jehovah's Witness-like fliers about MABUS as a ridiculous religion, one of the punks crumbled it into a little ball, chewed it up, then spit it out on the floor.

When they finally played everyone filtered out the room except a few. One guy up front was a thrash metal guy, with patches all over his vest. He and his metal friend got MABUS and ate it up completely. Bartek took off the black admiral's coat and showed off the t-shirt he made – a green shirt with the phrase FUCK RYAN BARTEK huge on it from messy white-out scrawls. The thrasher guy lit up and started laughing, head-banging, going nuts.

After they were done playing, he knelt down to talk to the guy. He said "*Yeah, fuck that guy!*" and Bartek said: "*yeah, fuck him totally!*" and they talked about how much they hated Ryan Bartek for 10 minutes. Then Bartek said, "*Come on man – I'll buy shots*."

He went to the bar with the smiling thrasher, the audience grimming him. He said his band was a punk rock band, which they were. Bartek's style of punk rock – punk and metal intertwined. Its music, you do whatever the fuck you want with it.

With the eyes of the scene police policing his every move, he hung out with the thrasher for 10 minutes, buying the rounds. Then he asked "*Hey man what's your name?*" "I'm Armand, who are you? "*I'm Ryan Bartek.*" The thrashers face went blank. Bartek said: "*No its cool man, its cool – drink up, drink up.*" Armand walked away in a sort of shock. For the next year, he would come to every single A.K.A. MABUS gig.

It was clear how the punk scene felt about him & what he was doing. *They didn't get it, and simply were not having it.* They were trained to immediately reject propaganda at first mention – something ironically culminated by the propaganda of the records they listened to.

They did not understand that propaganda did not immediately mean something bad or wrongfully manipulative. They didn't see it as some magickal power technique they could easily wield themselves for noble purposes – they only understood it in its obvious military, government or advertising sense. They believed it was something solely used by controlling systems to try and make them submissive and sheepish.

Furthermore, he was a "sell out" because of Real Detroit Weekly, the newspaper with the strip club & cigarette ads. Furthermore, they didn't need to kiss his ass anymore for press. When trying to move the band forward, he found mostly brick walls.

"*Are you sure you want to do this? I'm nothing but trouble.*" 3 looked to him from beside the Daytona, her duffelbag packed next to its dulled wheels. Just as the Déjà Vu had been consistent through his life, this moment rang like a bell.

It reminded him of the finale of so many of the zombie movies he'd watched obsessively through his life. Here the two survivors were, next to their escape shuttle which in normal film terms would be a helicopter. Even if they survived the horror of the first film, the sunset they rode off into would only promise more undead cannibals to chew the gristle from their bones.

He wouldn't let the zombies get her. 3 had been such an honest-hearted character in his struggles that he would have done anything for her. Whenever he'd take his leave from [][][]'s apartment, she'd fight for him. [][][] would live out her chaotic sprees, and 3 would be the bedrock whom managed the situation.

With [][][]'s abrasive style of parenting, the child always looked to 3 and Bartek as the time-out. 3 wanted [][][] to seriously be with Bartek – and she understood his serious longing for family.

Both Miss 3 and Bartek had felt like they lost their sense of family, even though the child was never their responsibility. [][][] had kicked her out the apartment not long after shunning Bartek.

After, it was just she and the kid – impossible for her to manage. She soon lost her job and apartment...

It was over though now, and the two survivors were aside the road. 3 waited for his reply, gazing at him with those expressive and emotional eyes. *"You're not trouble – I'm trouble. I'm fucking Satan – you're a sweetheart."* 3 gave a slight smile: *"Or so you think."*

Perhaps it was a bad idea, but at that point he couldn't care less. Beyond lonely, beyond the magnetism he felt towards the situation they both lived, above all he wanted to help her. He wasn't going to let 3 go to prison over a marijuana roach.

She had fucked up bad, and it would still be years before Michigan joined the medical pot states. In 2005, Michigan was plagued by ganja inquisitions. Parents would have their kids taken if caught smoking, children thrown into juvenile prisons...

Even in Detroit or its suburbs, to be caught with a gram meant up to $10,000 in fines, dozens of drug classes and a possible electronic tether. And if probation was crossed in any way – if classes missed or fines paid late – it could mean (*and usually meant*) an automatic 6 months to a year.

3 had gotten the shaft. The prior year she was pulled over and searched – they found a roach in her ashtray. *They tried to give her 2 years in prison!* While this might sound extreme, understand that only a few counties north of Detroit the laws get more severe. This is where 3 got caught – by bible-thumping redneck cops who get paid more by the amount of tickets they wrote & convictions made.

She had been on probation nearly 2 years, and was very close to being off the hook. They'd call her in to take a random piss test. She'd been drinking some vodka the night before and a little came up in her stream. Since she was 20, they were giving her 8 months for her first offense plus underage drinking.

The cops had might as well killed Lana, but 3 would not be permitted the same fate. She had no option except go to Florida where there were no extradition laws. So long as she never came back to Michigan, no one would send her to stand trial. There was a guy there she liked, and they both had severe crushes. Bartek wanted to give the happy ending she deserved, and promised to buy her a Greyhound ticket with the money he'd soon get from taxes.

He didn't mind seeing her go, even though they'd had sex all weekend. It had been so long Bartek couldn't recall the last he'd been with a woman. She was a consolation prize and couldn't get too wrapped up into it – she gave to him all the pent-up love she watched him struggle so pathetically to achieve with [][][].

What was supposed to last days became 2 months. He'd just started a kitchen job, but was stuck with 20 hours at half-pay training for 2 weeks! His tax refund fared no better – the government demanded he pay $600! In America, vampires suck blood from rocks.

Bartek was additionally screwed from his '95 Thunderbird. He sold it back to the kid he'd bought it from for $300. He never registered it & left it on the side of the rode once it died! The cops mailed him a surprise towing bill for $300!

And if he didn't pay it, he'd have a warrant! He emptied the last of his savings to the bloodsuckers & signed legal paper declaring the car was now property of the state, so he'd have no further legal responsibility.

They, of course, lied – and sent a bill for $750. They made him pay $1000 to keep it in the police lot before going up for auction. It only went for $250, so he owed the rest – or his license would be suspended, or eventually arrested on bench warrant! Locked up for months, lest someone show up and pay it off! Then they'd let him go, free to work & roam, but on probation with a time frame to pay that money, and if all debt wasn't erased they'd arrest & jail him again and double the fine, endlessly repeating the process.

$1000 he had paid for that bullshit Thunderbird, and yet another $1000 to fix the transmission once it soon died, & yet another $200 bucks to solve the electrical problems, which simply did not work, and another looming $900 if he were to fix it!

After a summer battling creditors, the phone company attacked – $600 with growing interest! A video store with a rental he'd definitely returned was demanding he pay $100 or be targeted for a credit-nuking lawyer blitz! And everyday unpaid, another $30 cumulative fee attached! The irony in harassing a psychologically unstable man for a copy of *A Beautiful Mind*, with Russel Crowe!

Financial woes had brought Bartek to nervous collapse. It was a new year now, but he was still traumatized & neurotic from the stint of cruel bankruptcy scammed at every opportunity, with this forlorn woman sleeping in his bed that had no way out but wait on that big check that would come early February.

In the meantime, the purgatory was inviting. 3 put up no real fight against what was going on. She was scared to even venture out of the house, because the cops might run her name & arrest her for the court date she skipped out on. In a sense, he'd inherited [][][]'s housewife. In the winter darkness, they grew closer & closer. Horror movies spread across the floor and stacks of books from the library entertained, Bartek found himself quite happy.

3 was everything he'd really searched for in a woman and they had an interplay that was absolutely calm. They spoke at great length about any subject under the sun, and he never once felt dejected. She never judged him. Since this was a moment outside of time, the war of the sexes was discarded. They were wounded survivors of the Zombie Apocalypse calculating their next moves.

3 had a way of delivering lines – she was always spewing them out. She knew exactly how to work him. She didn't need to play in a band or be on magazine covers – the spectacle of the show was something someone else did, she was purely audience. She wanted to feel home, and she wanted to be loved.

On Bartek's part, he wanted that – the easy shit. He wanted some pretty 20 year old to write his name in the middle of a heart on her notebook, some sweetheart with thighs built to shit kids. The chemical response to her pheromones owned him totally – she was so sexy and just screamed baby-making.

She had a way with him that no one had had since Lisa in his youth. She was a rugged tomboy with a big heart, physically pulling him around whether he liked it or not, never realizing he wasn't this way with anyone else. He never really let people touch him, and she could play with him like clay. It was basic and took him out of his head. And the scar above her eye making her appear vixen assassin...

But what would Kluck say? Surely he would flip out. If he wanted someone, even if he didn't deserve them or even really care about them, he could get really weird and jealous.

In reality, this was just some chick that he made out with on a couch a few times. He wasn't concerned about her and they hadn't even spoken in months. Even when she was trying to get him to visit her he wouldn't budge. Even when she was close by he made no attempt to get to her.

Bartek had pushed Kluck on 3, and 3 had pushed [][][] on Bartek. When neither party showcased any seriousness, they became totally burned out from the prospect. What was left was 3 and Bartek, and they were both staring each other down.

Kluck had his chance, and simply did not care. Bartek also knew it was best if he never brought up this last-minute romance, lest Kluck make a gigantic stink and it rupture their rocky friendship. Kluck was a heroin addict & cutting open Fentanyl patches & sucking the gel out of them. He shouldn't even have been alive.

As Bartek readied himself for a long work shift, he received a call explaining that Kluck was on life support at the hospital – his kidneys had died from heroin abuse, and he was being kept live by machines. In all likelihood, it would soon be over.

Bartek and 3 pulled into the hospital parking lot and looked to each other. What would their excuse be to be seen together like this? They decided to say she was visiting her fictional aunt in nearby Sterling Heights, and he'd swooped her up on the way.

At the front desk the nurses looked to each other with darkness. The couple were coming to see the doomed and dying man who had no chance of recovery. At some point they would need to remove the machines and he would not last much longer.

Kluck was excited hearing Bartek's voice – he was happy, though looking like a corpse; pasty white & delirious. He never asked what the two were doing together, he just wanted us there.

Kluck went to say something real. Bartek kept repeating: *"This is not a death for a metal warrior – Manowar would not approve of this."* Kluck stared at the ceiling in frustration: *"Can't you just drop it Ryan, just for once? Can't you just knock it off?"*

Bartek left the room to let 3 and Kluck speak their likely last goodbye. Bartek snuck him a handful of cigarettes, since he was not allowed to have any 'cause the drugs & increased blood pressure & etc. But Bartek passed these last smokes to a man such as one waiting to be executed.

They left after 20 minutes of speaking what they'd do in the future once he healed. 3 was upset, but masked it. They were convinced it would be the last time they'd see him alive. They left the hospital and went to Bartek's hometown of Dearborn where they ate a pleasant Chinese dinner with his mother, then across town to visit some of his old school teenage friends.

The couple returned to Stoner Joe's with a half gallon of Black Velvet whiskey. Bartek unplugged his land-line phone and retreated to the world where there was nothing but 3 and hard liquor, where they consoled each other of the looming death of Kluck. They would remain drunk a few nights, blast off from the world and only return to it when ready to accept his funeral.

Before they shut out the world he called his friend Simon, who was also tight with Kluck. He told him he better take the day off work and go see him, because Kluck wasn't making it out of this on alive. It was a dark night indeed, and he held 3 as she wept in his arms. They always talked as if they were survivors in a zombie film, and now they were another man down. Nothing outside the windows but snapping jaws.

When Bartek gathered the strength to call Simon, he didn't find an empathetic tone. Simon was on the phone, yelling because Kluck *didn't* die and Bartek made him take a day off of work. Bartek was shocked to hear he was still breathing, but even more so by Simon's attitude. What it meant to him was that even if he himself were dying, this little shit wouldn't go visit him.

It was so self-serving that Bartek slammed down the phone and refused to speak to him for a long time. After so many years of looking at Simon like a younger brother, there was not much point.

Kluck bounced back and the nurses deemed it a miraculous recovery. Kluck described what he thought would be his mortal end. With the catheter shoved into his penis – and electronic monitors running tubes into his skin to keep his kidneys moving – he lifted himself from the bed with what little strength he had.

No one noticed when, dragging the heart monitors and equipment with him, he'd managed to get in the elevator and go down a few floors to smoke out the side door.

Then – thinking it was his last chance – he walked into the chapel of the hospital. It was a mini-church with a stand holding an opened bible, created to sooth the dying patients. Kluck sluggishly moved to the center of the stage, pulled the catheter needle out of his dick, then shouted a mighty *"Fuck Jesus Christ!!"* and pissed all over the rug, the podium, the bible.

He sauntered back out, up the elevator, and back into his deathbed where he closed his eyes, expecting it to be over any minute. But the end never came.

Kluck wanted to hang out soon as possible, and he was asking the whereabouts of 3. He wanted to see her once more, because his deathbed had made him reconsider how he felt about her. After all, she was the only one that came to visit his final hour.

The jig was up – 3 was restless, and Bartek would finally be getting one big fat paycheck. In those last few days, 3 questioned if prison was really the only scenario. Could she fight it out in court, just pay fines? She looked at Bartek with loving eyes and did not really want to leave him.

Yes, she wanted more then some dead end trailer full of stoners, but this could be the nucleus from which they sprang. With a heavy heart, Bartek told her what she needed to hear – Michigan was tombstone, and she was better off just going.

Personally, he didn't think the punishment would be that severe and yes, he would've waited for her to get out if she were to be sentenced. Yet escape is what she deserved. Bartek booked her bus ticket that Valentine's morning, then drove his vacating love down to the cold, windy freeways and parked on the hellish concrete corner the Detroit Greyhound depot lay upon.

With darkness spreading like a cancer, he led her to the gate. She turned around and gave a warm peck of a kiss. Her eyes were filled with light & hope; Miss 3 went out the loading doors without so much as looking back, and Bartek went back into the frozen Detroit daytime to his rapidly disintegrating Dodge Daytona. Black Valentine's was here, and he was again alone.

Like a luminous savant, he now saw the world in terms of propaganda. All the puzzle pieces of his life came under its open ended understanding. He saw the key to defeat the control which secretly guided the misery of lives caught in the mesh. And he could be found at Applebee's, feverishly scribbling phrases such as *"the elimination of all the basic deficiencies in the collective body."*

By night he was a microwave cook, piecing together sandwiches. By early day and late into the dawn, he was a cold machine of profuse whiskey-driven typing or relentlessly devouring book after book on Mussolini, Stalin, Pol Pot, Goebbels, Franco, Tito, Himmler, Mengele, Vlad Tepes & Carlos The Jackyl.

He'd also let himself be consumed by The Wall. He was mutating into the Fascist Pink, and the pulpit of A.K.A. MABUS allowed him the realization of his dark fantasy. On 6.6.06, in whatever form it took after months of creation, he'd release to the worldwide underground his guerrilla manifesto of unrepentant propaganda war.

Following the messy upstart on New Years, A.K.A. MABUS had played a number of well-received shows, but never quite by the crowd they sought approval from. They were instead building their own rag-tag world of the open-minded. In addition, their debut album had already been recorded.

How rare was it a band could only be together 6 months and have a 15 track album? Dubbed *"Lord of the Black Sheep,"* the title was a reference to a question once asked. "I don't get it," the friend said, *"Why is Satan always a goat?"* To which Bartek replied: *"Because he's the Lord of The Black Sheep."* Thus, their album "SATAN" was in the can, waiting for a proper release that fall.

He'd begun talking to 3 again via MySpace. She had signaled things weren't quite so well in Florida. She'd stay there, but he could visit. She may or may not be getting her own place, and she may or may not be single again. Bartek was thrown a life raft.

He wrote her some big, stupid letters that while cautious were obvious as they come. But nothing could ever be stupider then sending her his secret autobiography which if leaked would destroy his life. It would certainly be his undoing in the wrong hands, but he wanted to be understood.

He knew that if bared his soul – if he could make her see only but a fraction of the world he saw – he could win her heart devoid of physical presence. He could win the entire bloody war without firing a single shot.

What he really wanted was away from another grueling Detroit winter. He wanted to live out the rest of his 20's on a beach with a hot momma metal wife playing extreme metal. That wasn't such a bad deal, right? Touring Florida playing gigs with legendary old school death metal bands of the region? A.K.A. MABUS was the band he always wanted – but the "Detroit Scene" would never accept it as would the West Coast. Maybe just play death metal in Florida?

And so, sending the biggest, stupidest letter he could ever send woman – 220 pages of absolute, awful mistake – he Fed-Ex'd her a compendium letter handwritten by depressive candle light. In 2 days, she'd read the entire thing. Bartek stepped outside for the call. With the cell ringing, it was just like the dream he had years ago.

3 had a trembling voice and was at her friends home having run away from the abusive boyfriend. He'd urinated all over Bartek's

manuscript and set it on fire. He threw her against the wall and said if he ever came to Florida Bartek was a dead man. And she couldn't respond, she just had to go. And then she hung up.

He went to the library and wrote her on MySpace but she wasn't responding. He hung around that computer room all day – no response. He went home awful and barely slept, just waiting for the library to reopen. The next morning it was bleak, rainy & wet with patches of snow still grappling the grass like miniature white islands.

He checked MySpace and she *deleted him* – with a message from the boyfriend saying the most dreadful of things. That she hated him, that she thought he was a monster. And if Bartek should ever come to Florida, he'd break every last limb.

Bartek pulled off his reading glasses with a shaky hand, weakly arose from his chair and stumbled out the library a zombie just like all the other zombies wandering the parking lot, driving rainy roads with blank eyes.

His rotting corpse managed to steer the rusting scrap heap to the mausoleum trailer, and then with flesh melting from his bones he entered his room with all belongings packed into cardboard, ready to evacuate. And then the lumbering, undead creature sat on the floor and read a book about Hitler.

The A.K.A. MABUS guys were paranoid he'd flee. He admitted that he was at the end of the rope, and needed a 2 week vacation. All parties backed down fearing to lose him. He admitted to Bobby that he nearly ran away with 3, but made it clear he was staying put to do the band. For Bartek, there was no other objective.

…but then Metal Maniacs accepted his query. He would return the favor for the incarcerated Lord Morder, the "black metal terrorist" in California who'd promoted Bartek's book in his uber-satanic prison magazine.

Morder deserved the press not only because he was serious, but because it showed how the prison system can drag the metal scene's extremity into sentencing. It was a classic Boogeyman trial, and could happen to anyone attached to the satanic metal world.

That accomplished, Bartek wanted to make journalism fun again. He was over boring CD reviews. He no longer wished to be a tireless scene workhorse – it was joyless. People could write about his band for once. He'd done his job, so let the next firebrand carry it on. Yet he had the idea of doing a story on California, interviewing metal bands from San Diego in person while there.

Get back to what inspired him in the first place – the crazy traveling Hunter S. Thompson gonzo thing. He had a major magazine backing him, so why not play it up?

The editor of Metal Maniacs approved his story concept, and he promised substance. He would go back to the roots and craft his own form of extreme journalism. He had a mission again, not stacks of CD's to machine-review 'cause if not they'd stop sending stuff.

Onyx, Brandon and Skinner had ended up in San Diego after fleeing. They had a house locked down, and a strong crew. They'd spread Bartek's urban legend and kept telling people *"Bartek is coming."* Brandon and he had spoke of revolution constantly when growing up; Brandon & Onyx were true believers.

The problem was they bloated it, and then people in San D. started calling them "The Bartek Family," as if he were a shadowy cult leader. He was Groucho Marx if anything, but they all wanted their own private Project Mayhem – and lots of crazy, fucked up adventures. This he could do.

Bartek settled on San Diego for his brief retreat & purchased the bus ticket for June 7th, 2006. The night beforehand was A.K.A. MABUS at the Theatre Bizarre's ultra-secret 666 Party (6/6/06). On the bill were also Downtown Brown which presented a milestone – Bartek and Neil P. finally on the same stage! And he'd finally unleashed the notorious "Pan-Tribal Manifesto" earlier that day.

Even though Bobby choked on the heavy fog machines, and the monitors were too low so the band played a little sloppy, it was still magick. Bartek came out in a white-collared priest get up with a white luchador mask. The rusted carnival rides were working, scantily clad women were dancing with giant snakes, men with flame throwers shot fire over the crowd.

As he perused the identities of the crowd members, he kept expecting to see Lana. It is rare the symbolism is ever so ironic that she would be set for release by the corrections institute on 6.6.06. But that was Harley. She had been writing him ever increasing letters in crayon… and was released a week early.

Even in the depths of loneliness that he trudged through like a swamp he knew it'd be bad news to get back with her. She'd just served another 7 months, give or take, due to probation violation. She'd done over a year & a ½ over a noise complaint & 2 Vicadins.

When he'd last seen her, she was trying to get a job at the mafia kitchen. She looked pretty drugged out. She was trying to get a job where he worked, using him as a reference, even though they never spoke. He was prepping food and one of the servers said "*Hey Deb – there's a hooker looking for a job*." Bartek took a glance, and began laughing hard. He said it was his ex wife.

Now Lana was cleanly out of jail and going at him like a missile. The day of her early release, some of her friends had thrown her a surprise party while Bartek was busy at scrubbing the floor at Applebee's. He wasn't even supposed to be there that day. Lana wanted to go straight to him but she'd been ambushed by a candle-lit cake. They made plans to meet the next day.

Lana came to the trailer park, chaperoned by Stanley Pluto. She was a twitchy wreck, nodding out from methadone, her eyes just bouncing around her head. She was stammering her words, obviously still in love with him but driven half-mad. Stanley was playing the middle man, trying to guide her.

With her long hair draped over her face and the slow silence of prison still ringing like an echo, he saw how much of her soul they had taken away. She looked to him like a blond, dried version of the ghost girl from *The Ring*.

It was this image of her that would stay with him, haunting his dreams. She would appear to him always out of touch, face blurry & soul empty like some observing corpse. They took their leave. It was not Lana anymore; she was gone…

It was the Greyhound itself more so then the destination that captivated him. Miss 3 had also impressed bizarre and sad dreams, and he would often see the bus driving her way.

He remembered distinctly how he awoke Black Valentines, dreaming he was chasing on foot the Greyhound carrying her away. He awoke in a terrible jump, and realized that he'd destroyed what could've been true love.

When he took full account of his situation, he realized she was still sleeping and still had hours before she was to leave forever. Despite knowing the great sorrow that would overcome him in her absence, he knew it was the right thing to do. To keep her in Detroit promised an inherently dark future. He had to let her go, and there he had to remain for one last extreme metal attack on the Detroit music scene. It was his life's mission, even if belated & forced.

Bartek would dream of that Greyhound bus, its motor running, that rumbling steed of mechanized hum. He knew that if he just kept riding it, kept going, somehow he'd discover all the pieces of himself he'd lost.

Perhaps his soul could be stitched back slice by slice like a self-tailored Frankenstein. Or maybe he'd earn a new soul in the process. He knew it was the right thing for him. For once he'd live totally for himself and not the fanatic belief in some revolution or metal brotherhood or political uprising or literature art quest or whatever. It was about him.

San Diego was perhaps the finest city he could've chosen. He'd never been further west then Oklahoma, and simply passing through the Denver Mountains subconsciously rocked him. He liked that he could step off the bus at any time, in any city, and just live a completely new life. San Diego had potential.

He spent a week ingesting California and its completely estranged nature from the Midwest. He took a trip to Temecula, went to the furthest outskirts of San Diego County, spent glorious time on Ocean Beach. They lived at a small one story two-bedroom home that he renamed The Villa Winona, in tribute to Henry Miller. They were a non-cannibal lunatic family without chainsaws.

He never wanted the adventure to end. He was like a freak Mafia Don; everyone looked to him for instruction & approval. Contrasted with the bickering nature of A.K.A. MABUS, the dead end Applebee's position, and the looming frozen death trap of a trailer park, Bartek had all but made his decision.

Bartek returned like a man on fire. He belted out a 15 page free-form article he dubbed *"The Big Shiny Prison: A West Coast Escape Attempt"* about his interactions with a handful of metal bands, life at The Villa Winona & having been brought into a Scientology brainwashing chamber to watch L. Ron Hubbard videos.

It was some of his best work to date and redefined what metal journalism could be. The editor from Manics loved it, but it was too gigantic to release in the mag. Though he was now given a green-light to travel abroad and make condensed 1000 word versions of his travel journalism. Bartek devised a plan to perhaps do this by living on Greyhounds. It was fanatic & far-fetched – he dug it...

Upon returning, Bartek found the Detroit scene and his wider network baffled & repulsed by his propaganda manifesto. NSK was not well known, and they thought he was some weird fascist. What he was saying flew over their heads entirely, was bizarrely unnerving or simply in bad taste.

Bartek found himself being dodged by bookies & bands alike. Bartek and his few remaining acolytes were resigned to trot off like black sheep into the midst of the crappy local metal circuit, filled with bands doing the 10th rate Pantera thing or kind-of-OK bands that were into

Lamb of God and just now discovering European metal. The old death metal world avoided them and the punk scene had serious bugs up their asses.

Divorced from scenester bars and the anarcho-punk house venue world, the outer circles became their new stomping grounds – the dead end bars spread across Detroit. Still, every time they played, people thought A.K.A. MABUS were on tour. One by one they made their converts. Bands that were previously lackluster started aping them, singers started copying Bobby's chemistry. But it was working, one gig at a time...

Zelda emerged from her lost orbit at one of these sparsely populated shows. They ate dinner after & she went back to the trailer park with him. They walked on the play-set for kids. It was under a bright silver moon that they kissed softly, passionately. She stayed the night, but only in cuddle-ness.

He'd last seen her when he'd booked her at The Tavern. She did a harsh gabba set. With fairy wings & glitter, Zelda ran around The Tavern like a fruit loop. What did it matter anyway? His attempts of a Sunday night industrial bar weren't working.

Booking Zelda was a last ditch effort before he hung up his hat on the industrial DJ business. His shows were striking out; a nightmare of parking meters & cops kept ticketing everyone.

When Zelda mentioned she had a fling with Irish, Bartek snapped. He and Irish spoke at great length about Déjà Vu, and Bartek just knew. Irish had just read Bartek's secret book and possessed the only printed copy. Bartek asked he do two things – burn the book & do not hook up with Zelda.

Irish said he didn't even know her, but Bartek explained the dream where they were at war over her. He didn't want it to happen – and he made it clear that Zelda hated organized religion, and she wouldn't ever touch him for this reason.

Irish swore on his life he would do both things asked – *but he did neither*. That dude fucked Zelda senseless & never once spoke up against her infinite trash-talk on The Trinity. Bartek wanted him to be the the truest of the true. In Bartek's weird dictator-brained world, Irish was like an Albert Speer. Irish believed in "The Vision" & was integral to it; Bartek considered him a 5 star general....

When Zelda found out that Irish was a hardcore Christian, she almost vomited. She was cartoony, happy, fairy-like, but she'd talk about assassinating Jesus Christ all day long. Bartek told key people he didn't want to see Irish around anymore and when he showed up trying to talk calm, Ryan bounced his head off the wall & threw him out of the trailer. Charming behavior, indeed, but this wasn't about him being religious – it was about selling Bartek out.

Only one obstacle remained between his old flame Zelda – *Sir Lancelot*. She was working the renascence festival circuit and was lost that summer to being a weird elf girl. She had a thing for Lancelot, and they'd recently hooked up. Bartek of course was The Black Wizard, and could not stand losing to such a symbol.

Bartek invited Zelda to a street fair in Detroit where many of his friends were. It was a glorious set-up in prime summer and they were going to share it together magnificently. It was so totally a date, and he was quite excited to belittle Camelot. Bartek waited at the street fair for her to come, realizing what a glorious day it would be.

He got a phone call from a shaken Zelda – on the freeway her car spun out at 70 mph, crashed into the rail, hit other vehicles & destroyed itself. Defying death, Zelda took it as an omen to just go home. It was a sign from the universe to leave Bartek to history. She hung up on the heartbroken one, and off to Camelot she went.

On the day Lana was first released from jail, their reunion was prevented due to her surprise party. At that party was a guy she'd been seeing a month before imprisonment. She was horny & couldn't say no... *and got knocked up that day.* Two months later, after another noise complaint, they incarcerated the pregnant Harley for another 8 months. *The pigs demanded she give birth in prison...*

The final months of Bartek's existence were plagued. Yet what was the exact second his tolerance snapped such as a brittle twig? The answer is manifold. Either way it was over – to do the band further would be a 2 year commitment if it were to be done seriously.

The only prospect for romance was a blind date always trying to be set up by the guy with the fishies – the California hippy guy that worked at the pet store & rented a room at the trailer. He was 23, had braces, and was really into *Magic: The Gathering*. He was always pushing this blind date, saying he just wanted to see what happened when they were put in the same room together. All Bartek could envision was a chubby girl tapping mana.

Curtailed by too many depressing stories then this Narrator has the time for, it should be correct to safely observe that the writing was now blazing on the wall. By November all rational hope for victory was long extinguished.

By December he was sleeping 12 hours a day, staring at the ceiling from his broken mattress, lost in torrents of the slowest, most punishing doom metal in existence.

The more he shut out the world, the more the PR people came at him. He could travel to New York or LA for invite-only record release parties. He could tour with bands he worshiped in his youth writing lengthy stories about his experiences for Metal Maniacs, PIT Magazine, Hails & Horns, AMP, or any of the zines he now wrote for. Yet he simply would not pick up his phone, haunted and jaded by the world that had once ignited his passion.

Bartek – whom many of his inner circle now believed frankly mad – declared he'd wage the Detroit war to its apocalyptic *Gotterdammerung*. While he paced around frothing in a tirade of such rhetoric, he inwardly obsessed over escape.

Bolstered by a fling with a waitress before she moved to LA, she invited him to lounge her apartment in Hollywood as her punk rock plaything. It wasn't true love, but boy did she have curves.

Thus, the tarnished Golden Boy swallowed his pride and faced the A.K.A. MABUS firing squad. Their peers deleted him from MySpace as a flaky traitor, and the man once cursed or acclaimed as one of the most important counterculture journalists in Detroit's history was little more then a mere bundle of tired flesh.

For within a single year he'd gone from prominent figure in a multi-million redevelopment deal that would have saved Detroit to none other than haggard trailer trash – a desperate, powerless Sawdust Caesar handicapped by poverty; drowning in booze, curtailed by highs, grimly watching his life's dream irrefutably crumble into nothingness.

There was no *Clausewitz* in this Propagandist's end – just the banal last moments that failed tyrants have endured and have deserved to endure down the ages. Bartek had long outlived an aspiration to greatness, and a friable Pan-Tribal Socialism – exhausted of credible meaning or social purpose – had long since crumpled into nothingness.

At the end, cornered as he is by history, his view of things is consistent, and in a strange, inverted way, correct – *invariably, what is right for him is wrong for Detroit*. Ignominiously forced in his professional career to work as a microwave cook for Applebee's, he acknowledges that Detroit's rebirth will come only after total defeat, anticipating a new era well into the future. *The divorce between Bartek and his beloved underground had truly been complete…*

And finally, the sinister adventure ends. One December night, a lone figure pulled himself silently onto a bus, the fire at last gone out. The great prank ended in tragedy and no reincarnations or returns are to be expected. Ruined and sobered, R. Bartek set out to find himself...

…yet everything that was Hyde within refused to compromise. Those deep-seated psychological forces grabbed the forlorn old ham, tossed him back on the road, and went right to creating the nucleus of a freshly constituted "*Pan-Tribal*" web. With tendrils coursing through the magazine racks of 125 countries, he was now the Hunter S. Thompson of the biggest Heavy Metal Magazine in The World. They could all kiss his white ass. The era of MABUS had eclipsed.

CROATOAN

anticlimax leviathan // volume two

1. *9inth Life Assassination*

2. *A Weather Vane Without Compass*

3. *Cascadian Dermabrasion*

4. *Waiting For Clownbaby*

5. *Somewhere Over The Rainbow*

6. *Stone Golem Babycakes*

7. *Singulare Monstrum*

8. *Anticlimax Leviathan*

9. *Loose Ends*

10. *Free Therapy*

11. *The Ballad of Don Juan Quixxxote*

12. *KlownFührer*

13. *We Are All Anonymous Now*

9inth Life Assassination

The contents of his spirit had so dramatically changed following that intense year of travel that but an echo of his former incarnation had remained. The "extreme journalism" experiment had been a success – but his growth as an individual much more so.

No memory spoke louder to him then when on a Greyhound headed to Albuquerque in March 2007. Riding on the return ticket to Detroit from San Diego was his secret way out if he'd flaked on his mission. Yet here he was, hopping off in New Mexico and discarding the continued ride "home" in the nearest trash can.

It was then, at 3am in the desert – with the headlights illuminating a whizzing mountainous region & his eyes focused on the sharply colored rocks & foothills – that the reality of his ultimate escape hit him, and tears began to well. He began laughing softly, with wet joy, muttering under his breath: "*I don't have to go back, I never have to go back*" while summoning visions of the oily bus refueling post he'd once been employed.

That feeling of freedom stayed with him as he traveled that year sleeping in parks, in alleyways, crashing at squat houses & band rehearsal complexes. Even as he rummaged through trashcans for food the smile never left his face. In one year he'd rode nearly 670 hours on Greyhounds – from Detroit to San Diego to Hollywood to Albuquerque to Denver; back to SD and LA before San Fran when – forced to the streets the first real time – he'd been gratefully reborn.

From those same SF streets he was captured by Downtown Brown and brought on a USA tour before a return visit to Detroit. Without struggle he freely left again, heading to Alabama. Then again to Detroit before NYC, then Detroit, San Diego, LA, Seattle and in the end Detroit before another 6 week, full-scale USA tour with Downtown Brown. They hit nearly every major USA city he'd yet to cruise through.

Here was a man that, having given up the ghost, better understood humanity. Here was an individual that, having discarded his shameful egomania, sought rebirth through ebb and flow. Here was a fresh soul assuming humility, communicating with an open heart and listening ear. Here was a living repudiation of the nihilistic, hateful grimness that had previously defined him. Though disowning pride, he'd become a proud example of growth. Ryan Bartek had changed, and he wanted the world to change with him.

The irony was that he had to return to the volatile nexus he'd created in San Diego. Still, the past meant nothing in terms of restriction –

if someone just uprooted themselves to an unknown habitat where none had previous contact, they could just fabricate a completely new life. They could just be whatever they wanted to be.

He was still in hardcore travel mode and had essentially just completely stopped in the middle of his greatest journey. It was as if he was planting definitive roots while ironically remaining on a highway with his thumb out, trying to hitch a ride.

He'd lingered in Detroit longer then needed, having a short-lived romance with a girl named Clownbaby. They barely knew each other but both felt as if they'd known each other somehow, like a separate reality going on side by side with this one.

Perhaps in alternative quantum realities, they'd actually had a blooming romance. True, she took him home the night they met, and there he stayed a week.

He had told her *"You are like the great consolation gift of my life. It's like the universe showing me what could have been, or what should have been, and this is our only dance because somehow we missed it."* She agreed, as they both fell into an undisturbed peace. In ditching the war of the sexes, they'd formed a pleasant ying-yang.

Bartek selected Seattle as his next port; getting his extended family of California runaways up there the next priority. Fall was rapidly engulfing; it was growing cold & time was short. What else was left but to go it alone? Thus, he left Clownbaby behind.

Once he actually did get to Seattle, he wasn't quite sure what to do or where to go. He'd made friends in the metal/punk scenes during his *Big Shiny Prison* experiment, and one of the punks offered a couch. Guy even led him to a hardware store hiring employees ASAP. It was all right there for the taking.

In his gut, Bartek knew Miss 3 would return. This was why he made no fuss regarding Clownbaby. It didn't matter how intense their imagined romance might've been in an alternate reality – his willpower to escape Detroit was stronger then it was to atrophy.

It was still 3 he wanted. During his long voyage, she was the Adrienne to his Rocky. He'd envision her egging him along – push harder, never give up. That *"we"* did it – *"we"* beat them...

3 always talked about running away to Seattle, and he just knew in his bones she was to come. They'd have their day; he could be a normal person, never again be stuck in a whiskey hole in a trailer park reading about dictators secretly wishing self-euthanasia.

If he wanted it flawless, he had to make Seattle work. But he was also down to $200, and the non-stop Seattle rain would continue for 7 months. He had no equipment, no music gear, no computer. He had to write his book, but all he had was paper and a pen. His friends were in San Diego where it was warm & dry; all he needed was a few months & several paychecks & a galvanized crew...

One last hurdle – Kelly, his first real girlfriend, from way back in high school. They weren't together long because he wasn't quite ready for it. Later on, Kelly became like Mother Goose of the gothy witchy girls, and Bartek was the Trenchcoat Mafia wunderkind.

It was always going on between them, though they never crossed that line again. Sometime after graduation they began hanging out again & he developed feelings for her. Then one day, as he showed up unannounced to break this silence, she'd run away to Seattle without telling anyone.

She began writing him, speaking of the glorious freak kingdom. That he should just jump on a Greyhound and run away with her. But he wasn't ready; they were so fresh out of high school he still felt inclined to finish the larger plot-lines of his youth.

Within months it had led to darkness. He was on the brink when his girlfriend of the time, a Mexican girl from ghetto Detroit, was nearly murdered by her father after discovering he was white. Padre been molesting her for years.

Just days before New Years 1999, in paranoia about Y2K, he'd gone to a cabin in Northern Michigan with some of his trusted friends. The Y2K mission was largely a front – he had intended to shoot himself. All he could imagine were the purple fingerprints on her throat every time he closed her eyes.

He had written one friend about his intentions, and she'd contacted Kelly who discovered the motel they were staying at. Kelly talked him down, and said all you need to do is come back & we'll run off to Seattle. He did – but when he returned to her family home (*she was on vacation*) – when he was ready to profess his undying love for her – she'd just left on an airplane for Washington. Again he was alone & surrounded by drug addicts of the Rave scene.

He continued to speak with Kelly for months, saving money, but once spring came she'd drifted. By all means he wanted out, but he had to finish loose ends. Maybe she would be there when he eventually came. Time passed, he wrote his first book, and then was soon hired by Real Detroit Weekly. He was handed every opportunity he ever sought on a golden plate. He couldn't say no.

Now that he was finally in Seattle, Kelly took him out to dinner. There was no reason to run – her apartment was a large studio near hipster bars & concert venues. They were laying in bed, watching TV. Confidence overtook him. He laid his fingers on her arm: *"How long have we been doing this for?"* They quickly went at it...

The next morning, she again tried talking sense into him. He was tying his boot laces – had to go to San Diego and get his crew. She kept asking: *"Why do you feel responsible for these people? Why can't you just stop?"* He tried to summon some lines from his Pan-Tribal Manifesto, but they seemed ludicrous.

Tenderly, she looked him in the eyes: *"Just stay here – with me. We'll have finally won."* She gathered her belongings for work while he bowed his head in shame. He knew he couldn't stop. And he was hopelessly in love with the ghost of 3.

But he knew right then, right there, he could have stopped. He could have dropped it all & just lived his life. Yet not willing to stop or being strong enough to stop, that night he simply vanished on the next Greyhound, skipping out on his lost high school love.

Since arriving in San Diego, the little house dubbed "The Villa Winona" had been amplified in its voltage due to Bartek's presence. The ludicrous crew had lain in wait for his arrival, expecting he waltz in and summon the thunder of his glorious revolution.

They never quite understood his vision, but they were well aware of their own – what they wanted was to play *Project Mayhem*.

True, Bartek had penned "The Pan-Tribal Manifesto." True, he'd picked a litany of misfits off the proverbial ground and gave to them a sense of togetherness and unity. True, he repeated this culmination of fringe lunatics into clusters in cities nationwide, even if they were unaware of his covert design. True, he did have a plan – but the denizens of The Villa Winona didn't quite understand it.

Bartek did not want to be Tyler Durden; what he sought was a "Project Mayhem" expressly created to destroy the Tyler Durden's of the world. His Pan-Tribal Conspiracy was aimed at convincing every man to recognize his own physical body as the territory of a state, and for every such man to become his own anti-fascist dictator.

What Bartek promoted was something between tribal, xenophobic anarchism & individualist LaVeyian satanism, though he did not describe himself as such. To use the term "Satanism" was defeatist, because it had so many skewed connotations in its wider global perception. He likewise refused to claim himself an anarchist, because he didn't quite understand what that really meant at the time.

What he had produced was a network of "autonomous cells" independent of "central leadership" because there was no implication of a "central command" in the design.

The goal was not to be the dictator, but to establish a willing mental segregation that included as many freaks into its web as possible. What he wanted, in the end, was a family. And the only way to get it was by play-acting the part. Even if he believed totally in the concept, a ham he still was.

Walking away from Kelly didn't bother him, because whatever chemistry they had changed with age. She was no longer the gothy industrial queen of the 90's.

Unlike the wiry Bartek who could still pass for 23, she looked like a fully-figured adult in her 30s. She was into the indie rock, had her TV shows, went to themed pub crawls. Bartek on the other hand was still that quintessential punk rock bad boy, still doing psychedelics and moshing around at metal concerts. He was a dog incapable of neo-tricks.

Walking away from Clownbaby though...

She was the love of a life that never was, but that life had indeed ended. But by all means, there was a chemistry there that would have soared and blossomed in a proper context. She was his age and even though she assumed the bar-crawling, favorite TV show sort of vibe that Kelly had, it completely gelled with him.

In so many ways, they were at the beginning of a lifelong friendship so long as he didn't fuck it up. He didn't want to lose her, and often "crossing the line" is what shatters things. Because once a couple establishes that connection, it's a permanent subconscious basis even if marginalized to 1% impact of remembrance.

But there was Miss 3, the unfinished mega-crush (*slash*) traumatic-dead end. Unfinished love was this Don Juan Quixxxote's worst enemy as he foolishly stumbled half-blind. His romantic steps were senile to a point beyond that of a Mr. Magoo.

Weeks passed at The Villa Winona – 15 people now living at the cockroach-infested home. Major characters such as Bartek's brother-from-another Brandon, his psychologist Onyx The Urban Priest, aspiring band mate Mr. Skinner.

Both he and Skinner had planned to do a band once he returned, so naturally Skinner wanted to dive right in; Bartek needed time to adjust & write some of his book before another band.

Patience needed – yet Skinner just wanted to get it done. He was one of the punk kids from the trailer park in Michigan; he hopped on the Brandon/Onyx escape pod in 2005. He was supposed to have been the bassist of FILTHPIMP, but never had equipment.

Skinner was a nightmare to work with. When trying to write songs, he wouldn't take instruction – just thrash one riff in a trance and when anyone tried to stop him as to learn the next part, he'd start making puffy-cheeked Harpo Marx faces. Or he'd jerk away the guitar and keep playing like an angry child.

He became bitter when Bartek refused to hire the drummer he'd tapped, because he was excitedly talking about how many people he punched & kicked in "the pit" the night before. He was a bully in a Tiger Army shirt that couldn't work a double bass pedal.

Bartek wanted grindcore, and Skinner a Rancid vs. Nekromantix thing. He had some good riffs, but no structures. He had no long-term vision except that Bartek manages. He could not take the initiative to hire musicians, schedule rehearsals, or keep a job to pay for a practice space.

He grimaced when looking at a computer screen, had no knowledge of how to promote online. Bartek was "the famous guy" to "make it happen." Skinner was a slacker to his own fanaticism. Lazy musicians are hardly an endangered species.

Skinner had to be the center of attention at all times. He had girls all over him being the handsome, pierced, tattooed, alpha male type at 21. But he was still a kid, and tried way too hard to show how weird he was. That's how it generally is with an egomaniac cartoon – but Skinner was way over the top. His obnoxiously oogle *"look at me-me-me-me-me-me"* bullshit didn't fly with anyone past 23.

They grew more annoyed by each other, more fang-bared. Bartek had made the mistake of getting him a job at the same pizza store, and now he was stuck with him 24-7.

Bartek couldn't get any work done on his book because Skinner would keep popping up at his window, intentionally interrupting him. He had turned from trusted companion to a gremlin of severe nuisance. It wasn't that Bartek disliked him – Skinner was just a goofy kid and needed to turn it down several notches.

They finally broke the ice. Bartek admitted to being desperately lonely, and if Skinner was to get him *"hauling ass"* on a band, then help him find a good woman.

Bartek was popular with the younger punk girls 'cause Skinner built him up as an urban legend. But Bartek couldn't mix with them – he was too old, too experienced for 19 year old drunk punks. Why "cross the line" and ruin anything with anyone unless substance? Better to have a friend then alienated, abortive lover.

Lana called, once again free of jail. Bartek had talked to everyone in the house about it, and those present remembered her well. They'd always looked at Lana as his eternal girl. They always felt that was what was right for him, and all parties supported her visitation. If all was harmonious, she could stay no problem. They egged him on to do it. They wanted their fearless leader happy, and anyone who remembered her actually missed this Harley quite thoroughly.

Even though wary of the prospect, he decided to let it happen. He was going through the motions again, but Clownbaby would never travel to California or live in some roach infested punk rock shithole. Lana, however, would befriend the insects.

Bartek dialed her cell phone and uneasily prepared himself to say something like: "*Yes baby, come home, we win – me and you and ocean beach and Hollywood and making horror movies like we wanted and etc etc.*"

As the phone went ring ring ring, nervousness was replaced by a wave of joy which wholly overtook him. Something just clicked – he envisioned her healthy and free, laughing and running about the sunny pristine Ocean Beach with all his friends as they cooked BBQ and splashed about the waters in the glorious raging sun.

Lana answered the phone, and she was sobbing like mad. He thought she was breaking down in romantic explosion, that this was a scene straight out of tear-jerker cinema: "*Ryan, Ryan... they're putting me away again. I'm in the backseat being taken to prison right now. Back for another 8 months... They are taking my son from me... I can't do it again... I'm done, I'm done, my mind is gone... I love you, I love you so much. I wish you were here, I wish you...*"

Harley broke off into a trail of sobs, and Bartek flung the cellphone to the ground in shock. He began to twitch. With a vacant look of spirit horror he gazed at the wall with the eyes of a dead man; tiny cockroaches crawled over satanic death metal posters masking-taped to the wall. He began to snicker, like the slow crackling sound of hiking boots stepping on patches of dried twigs: "*heh... heh heh... heh heh hee hee heh heh heh... tee hee hee ho... ha heh heh heh... hahahahahahahahahahahahahahaHAhaHAHAhahaHahahahaAHHahahHA HAHAHhahahahHAHAHHhahahahahhahaaaaaaaHahahahaHAHahaHa hahaHAHAHAHAHAHAHAHAHAHAHAHAHA!!!!*"

The nights grew cold & it was nearing December; he & Skinner were rampantly feuding – every person connected to Villa Winona were out of their minds.

Kluck tried to move there, but flaked out causing Bartek to cover an extra $300 in rent, bankrupting him. Bartek refused to live with his dark energy anymore – Kluck was a hopeless heroin addict. When he ignominiously bailed, Bartek was no longer obligated to carry his dead weight. Furthermore he was "sure" that 3 was coming back. If Kluck were there he would throw a jealous fit & ruin it...

Bartek pondered his 9 lives, and imagined dangling from the cliff with his final incarnation.

Of his 9 lives, the 1st was at the age of 2. He had lunged himself at a plate glass window and smashed through it, dangling over a massive shard of glass peak stuck into his belly button. It held him off the ground as he swung back & forth like a pendulum. He should have been an impaled, yet had not a scratch.

The 2nd life was at 3, when in a car wreck at a stop light. He was in a baby seat in the back, and a car smashed 40pmh into it. In the trunk were oxygen tanks of his dying grandmother, and even though punctured, none exploded as they should've.

The 3rd life was when he had put a razor to his wrist and came close to taking himself out at 13, but instead collapsed & gave in to the delusions & hallucinations that drove the young man mad.

The 4th is when he overdosed from a stomach full of Prozac – not out of suicide, but 'cause he had abused them when given free bottles by a crazy teen that had dismissed them. He was pushing it hard for weeks, gobbling 5 or 6 times a normal dosage every day.

Finally he collapsed in a bathroom. His heart stopped as he lay on the cold cement, just staring at a tiny ant crawling against linoleum & studying how intricate & amazing its physiology was. Soon as the heart began pumping again, he vomited so hard he popped a blood blister in his eye & was sick for days.

The 5th was at a rave party when the building started on fire. Everyone was locked in the main room with a steel door clamped shut, and 2000 thought they were going to burn alive – all of them on acid. They were clawing at the cement walls like frenzied animals, crying in absolute terror.

With the music cut, all those people could hear was Bartek's insane laughter as he stood on stage waiting to burn to death at 19. Steroid men ripped the door from their hinges & the panicked ravers escaped into the night like a stampede of cattle while dozens of riot cops tackled & beat anyone they could grab.

The 6th was a spin-out at 70mph from black ice on a freeway. The car turned a perfect 360 in seeming slow motion, and as the view of the windshield flipped in the other direction 8 semi-trucks were headed his way. The car gently glided to the snowbank on the side & stopped before a fleet of Mack semi-trucks whizzed by, blazing their horns.

The 7th life was at his landscaping job – the warehouse where they kept equipment. Each autonomous crew had their own fenced area to keep leaf blowers, hedge trimmers, so forth. He'd slammed the fencing shut & within centimeters of his eye came a jagged 8 inch nail. Had he stepped one inch closer, it may have penetrated his brain, or simply an eye patch for life.

The 8th life was the taxi accident which completely mangled his spine. The ever-constant pain added to endless stress of his life.

He was most likely a man of 30+ lives when rationally thinking about it – certainly in the twilight of his lucky stars...

Bartek shook off these visions of multiple near-deaths and went into Onyx's squalid bedroom to check his email. Onyx grinned: *"Hey, I got a surprise for you – Space Monkey is coming!"* *"Shit."* thought The Doomed One.

It was Onyx pet name for Kluck. He'd gone around me and sweet talked Onyx into letting him move to San Diego, but Onyx had one specific condition – that he be his personal Space Monkey. Or, better put – slave to the revolutionary training/non-sexual BDSM whims of a schizophrenic man on an absolutist power trip. Kluck agreed, and was already on a Greyhound there.

Bartek was not happy & made it known, and a tone of impending doom rolled across The Villa Winona. A week into Kluck's arrival, and he was just not gelling with the situation.

Bartek had gone full blown into traveler world with its squats & crusties, street crazies & anarchist etiquette; Kluck showed up a fossil from a bygone era. They were a pyrate horde and he was the bereft stowaway. Onyx was also making him do insane tasks, and it wasn't long before Kluck was nodding off from dope again.

Another friend had lost it with crystal meth & was facing felony charges in another state for a sheathed katana in public. Dr. Santiago had the showpiece sword strapped to his side. The cops didn't like the look of him, arrested him, and held him for weeks.

He was formally charged a felony guaranteeing 2 years of prison and was set to appear in court in months. Just some harmless 20 year old punk rock kid with peace tattooed on his arm. Well, at this point, he was living in the backyard eating leaves & trying to ingest the sun for nourishment. He could live off the sun 'cause it was all mind-frame – mysterious Tibetan people did it, you know?

There came a grueling night when – not knowing how to proceed but wanting to drop the tenseness – everyone laid down "their guns." Sailor Jerry roared through the kitchen & Villa was packed with singing, drunken, loudly ranting freaks.

Brandon was in the bathroom, blacked out on whiskey. He had serious anger issues towards a woman that had erroneously put him on the sex offender list & ruined his life. These violent feelings focused his rage on a black velvet painting. He thrashed it to bits: *"fuckin' cunt – I'll fucking kill you!!"* between drunken, lost sobs. They let the nightmare in the toilet play out as they made pancakes.

Cops burst through the front door – 4 of them, hands on guns. Responding to what the neighbors thought was a domestic violence call, they walked right into the front room conversation of the 10 punks drinking booze. Bartek had a joint in his mouth & continued smoking it – openly passing it to Skinner who blew a lungful of in the cops direction. When they opened the bathroom door, Brandon threw his hands over his head: *"I give up, I give up, I give up!!!"*

Brandon had done so much time he was institutionalized and mechanical about it. He was trained to the fear. The cops realized there was no one savagely bludgeoned, and then looking about at one another – realizing there was no warrant and they hadn't knocked or followed procedure – abruptly apologized & walked out.

The police raid was so swift it was as if it never happened – no one even got that allergic adrenaline of authoritarian paranoia.

The next day in hungover aftermath, among MySpace friend requests was <u>Miss 3</u>. He was soon awaiting her call. The cell rang & Bartek walked off into the night with her voice, ducked into the alley & propped himself against a garage hidden by palm trees.

They spoke for 2 hours. To great relief, she did not think him a monster. She had read the entire secret *"Zug Island"* book – it only caused her affection to grow. He'd upset the balance of Florida and it tore up her heart.

Her boyfriend was thrown into a rage & became controlling & violent: she'd gotten tangled up with a control freak that made her MySpace delete all her male friends – *even her cousins!* So it was no surprise that he'd urinated all over Bartek's book & set it on fire.

She'd gotten out & moved elsewhere in Florida. She was mortified that perhaps Bartek had despised her all along –that it was too painful a backlash to withstand if she established contact and he flipped out. Bartek asked her out for ice cream – and 24 hours later, she was boarding a 4 day Greyhound for San Diego.

When Bartek broke the news to Villa Winona, the reaction was horrible. Miss 3 was a bane & curse even before arriving. Kluck had, in a jealous maelstrom, made her out to be The Antichrist.

Secondly, Bobby from A.K.A. MABUS heard about it & felt inclined to stab one last dagger in the back. Bobby talked an awful lot of shit to Kluck which he'd no business repeating to all the punk kids at Winona who were massive A.K.A. MABUS fans, so they were taking the side of the screaming voice they'd never met.

Skinner was even more jealous it seemed then Kluck, because he thought it'd ruin the band they were attempting. Skinner rigged the situation for failure – it didn't matter who was coming, she was a threat. And if the band fell through & Bartek left, Skinner's girlfriend Panda (*now pregnant*) thought she'd lose Skinner as well.

Even the larger cast of that house which have gone unnamed – each person had some vendetta, each a domino in a long line about to be clicked. Bartek would not let anyone take this from him, and everyone in his street family were dead-set on annihilating the "Evil Bitch" they hadn't even met. They'd pack her bags for her.

Bartek was in a position of checkmate at the end of his known world, and the trembling fingers of his imagined 9th life that still gripped on to the side of that proverbial cliff loosened. It wouldn't take much disturbance to slip, grip, plummet, ker-plunk.

The clock in the Greyhound station crept its way to 6pm. It felt more like home then anywhere since Michigan. Unless he was on the go with a well-defined mission, he didn't quite know what to do. He permanently lived in that between-world stasis of the bus ride.

Or maybe it was just the taxi driver in him, who once operated professionally in that transit purgatory. Maybe he felt primarily centered while at work and was secretly reliving the squalid public bus job, deluding himself that Lana was still at home in their apartment. Perhaps all this bus madness really reflected his subliminal wish to return to Year Zero.

5:53pm, and Bartek had a last feeling of Clownbaby as she faded away in some other time continuum. They had been talking on the phone before Miss 3 emerged from hiding.

Bartek had saved $1200 cash and had his pick of many female

admirers he'd met while traveling. It would have been so easy to seduce any of them with an all expenses paid vacation in sunny California. But Clownbaby was the first time he'd felt anything since Miss 3. It was sick to think he'd gone 2 years isolated from love...

Clownbaby had a positive effect on him – she'd really pushed him to complete his acoustic album Bartek as a modern "satanic Johnny Cash" – The REAL Man In Black. He would counterbalance tour dates by spoken word/comedy shows.

After the Downtown Brown tours, he had gained the confidence to take his act to LA. He was going to slime through the comedy circuit. Clownbaby was like a generator of humor for him – the synergy she provided coagulated in his brain & he'd dissect it for days after, coming up with a litany of jokes. She was a powerhouse of dialogue; he'd remember everything and pick through it later like chopsticks in noodle wok.

He'd simply met Clownbaby too late. 3 would be back in his corner, the Adrienne to his Rocky. There was something instinctual, overpowering – 3 made him feel like a man. Not a 20 something searcher, but a grown adult. She inspired him to rebuild his health; he was sick of being a chain-smoking, druggy, skinny bag of bones.

Above all he wanted a family, and now he was pushing 27. It was getting late, but not too late. He could do what he set out to do with music and art and live it up and still be Poppa Bear by 33 or 34. Even if Clownbaby was gone, 3 would be in his corner laughing her head off at the comedy gigs. She inspired humor in him too.

3 was keen on being the photographer of his journalist endeavors, and they could travel abroad in Europe and The Americas being an underground metal journalist duo. Over & over he'd seen this pairing; always some zine guy and his fishnet-legged girlfriend snapping photos. It seemed surreal that it never happened for him – he was, after all, the quasi-gonzo champ of extreme metal journalism. Why was he still doing this alone? How could it be?

The clock struck 6. Through the gates she walked, grinning and expressing a wide spectrum of undefined emotions through her body language that flew towards him like a ballistic missile.

She grew close and looked him in the eyes. This was not the 3 he recalled – her entire aura had mutated. Through the influence of the past (*and a long stretch of miserable, abusive entrapment*) her soul had been rearranged. *She was now a genetic splice of [][][] and Bartek combined.* Their influence had thoroughly molded her.

Throughout those 4 days of inherent sleep deprivation, she must have intentionally been summoning the essence of [][][], like a well-disciplined harnessing of dark Chi.

Bartek hated her instantly on sight. It was clear that she wanted to play-act the girl she thought he'd always wanted, and mirrored her new presentation out of mad love for the Old Bartek – the dead man comprehensively detailed in his secret autobiography. The same man who Bartek just traveled a year to internally murder.

Perhaps she had not understood that the *Zug Island* book was a confession aimed at hell-bent catharsis. The most dead-end, repulsive incarnation of Bartek was the man she so loved and sought to marry. Her heart was enthralled by a rotten, crude, bullying, violent, egomaniac gangster.

Before she approached him for an awkward peck of a kiss, she grinned with terrible mischief. In her hands she gripped a present – one that he could never touch and would always be in her purse, her backpack, always at her disposal.

There Bartek was – a *voodoo doll* with dozens of pins jammed into the effigy of his discarded, vile persona. The Old him stared back with black button eyes, screaming for eternity. Covering its hemp-sewn chest was a tiny green t-shirt and a phrase scrawled in white-out: "FUCK RYAN BARTEK."

It was a quiet bus ride up El Cajon. The two doomed lovers stared out at the whizzing scenery with distanced faces such as convicts freshly released from prison or soldiers jammed into a 'Nam evacuation chopper over scorched rice paddy fields following a major incursion. They rented a motel in prostitute alley.

It was again that same motel room at the end of the line, hookers & tweekers lurching outside like zombies, the scars of bullet-holes infesting white, cracked walls.   They were already speaking to each other like a married couple, and she questioned how long it would be until he knocked her up. The tone of her voice confirmed it was the undeniable future, and that it was ready and waiting whenever he so felt like it.

Dominant as she was, she was still totally submissive in terms of classic gender roles. They spoke to each other in a deprecating yet playful way, like Peg & Al Bundy. She was careful to say that they shouldn't rush the inevitable, but was already curious where their children would go to school, what names were options.

On his part, he went through the motions. He play-acted toughness and confidence, and – at least for once – was amazingly gifted at not saying the wrong thing. He could not and would not allow himself to ruin this, even as he remembered the vicious children back at home.

He bit his tongue no matter the sentence she spoke. Even when speaking up the glorious, squatting, anarcho crust world he now operated in, all he could envision was Skinner's fuming eyes, scraping his blade against the water stone.

She emerged from the shower with dangling wet hair, then straddled him on the mattress. She looked deep into his eyes; he'd forgotten how inviting they were, and how unbearably sexy he found the straight-line scar above her left eye. She put one headphone of her Walkman in his ear while the other ear-bud remained in hers.

Things began getting hot to Faith No More. She kept teasing him with her eyes and her lips, her dangling wet hair gracing his skin like welcomed tickles. Then she leaned in, and planted a juicy kiss on his lips. 600+ hours of Greyhound purgatory vanished from his soul. There was nothing in life but that moment alone.

It wasn't long before they were totally naked, and she was laid back on the bed awaiting the missionary. Like a 40,000 horsepower engine, he was on all cylinders.

It was hard to think that a drop of blood remained anywhere in his body except for that one throbbing central nerve. He pulled out the handcuffs and her eyes grew wide. He pulled her hands behind her back and CLICK went the right wrist. "*Ryan...*"

The little worm on the big hook squirmed before the leviathan's devourment. He reached for the other unsecured cuff, and grabbed her left wrist: "*Ryan...*"

Over the two years of displaced anguish, he'd must have jacked off in anticipation of this moment at least 400 times. He looked into her savage eyes, and saw his queen. Her trembling, lust-filled voice boomed through every contour of the bullet-scarred dead-end motel: "*I want your baby... I want The Antichrist.*" CLICK.

* * *

3 had fallen into a deep sleep, her body fighting off the vicious, shivering sickness that made her cold to the touch. With her newly shaved mohawk bringing out the intensity of her wily tattoos, she could have passed for Christie Mack's stunt double. To Bartek, she was the most beautiful woman in the world.

Dr. Santiago was hunched over the desk in the motel room corner, his head resting in folded arms, deep in an exhausted slumber. He'd finally come down off a long crystal meth binge, and earlier was having a trance-like moment of clarity.

Whatever was left of him spoke at great length with Bartek about the events that had led to this terrible moment. Bartek lay next to his sleeping beauty, staring zombie-like at the bullet-scarred walls of the exact same motel room they'd consummated in 3 weeks ago.

Bartek was cold to the touch same as his embattled love, but his physical suffering was of monolithic despair. Dark and quiet, he could barely hear the muffled promulgation of junkie prostitutes on El Cajon Blvd. Again he'd returned to that same motel forever at the end of the road which encapsulates personal Armageddon. Both his lover and his good friend voted out of The Villa Winona by an inquisition formed purely of his street family.

True, 3 had acted a fool and had humiliated him – but she was just a kid. They all were, save for Brandon and Onyx. It was karma and he knew it well; he'd pushed his own inquisitions through time, drumming rat-finks & soft-cores & Jesus-baiters out of dozens of groups. Now he was getting a lethal dose of his own medicine.

Still, this was brutal in its callousness. He certainly had reaped what he had sown, but for once he was truly acting out of love. Even if he'd changed for the better, he still couldn't erase years of experience with these alienated misfits who looked up to him like a Big Brother, if not The Leader. They were beholden to and acting upon his rotten play-book.

It didn't matter who walked in the door – they were on a warpath to drum them out. When she finally did, there was nothing but distrust & anxiety. Bartek followed her inside and witnessed a sea of eyes like flaming organic lanterns. 17 unfriendly nuts as a motley welcoming. He could not see furniture, walls, bodies – just hot eyes like incendiary coals sniper-scoped at her position.

For days Skinner had amped up his paranoid doom-sowing. One by one, he pulled The Villa denizens aside for secretive conversations, conspiring to nuke Miss 3 by setting the rancid tone like expertly-placed C-4 charges in the elevator shafts of the World Trade Center: *"Everything is about to end, don't you feel it guys? Everything is going to shatter. This girl, she's the start of the apocalypse. She's going to show up and the whole operation is going to explode. You know it in your gut, don't you? I don't trust her, none of us should. She's gotta go, we can't let her ruin us..."*

He had made it impossible for her to exist, and knew exactly what he was fermenting. Thus, like spurned children attempting to ruin the relationship of a single parent to a new lover because they feared that parent would throw them away too, they came at her like a rumor-milled gremlin jihad.

The Villa Winona became a closed-walled paranoia farm.

Whenever separated from her, they would make it a point to humiliate Bartek Any story they had in their bad ammunition to try and make him look weak or stupid. Anything said to make them go at each others throats; anything to bust them up and make mockery of their relationship.

Finally, Skinner told him: "*That bitch told my girlfriend she only came here to fuck Kluck, and she was using you to make it happen.*" Skinner swore up and down 3 had put in almost exactly those words. Bartek had been in a massive fight with her the night before, and was in a prime position to exploit. He was so humiliated by the entire situation he really just wanted it to end.

The depression had grown so bad he could barely function; every night slumping over the kitchen table drawing pictures as his child soldiers bickered with his child wife. In two weeks they had wedged an unbelievable distance between he and 3, notwithstanding the wedge she herself aggravated with her [][][] play-acting. It was so well orchestrated Bartek appeared a flailing, helpless man.

Bartek believed Skinner's line of bullshit, and its harshness snapped him from the haze that devoured him. Bartek felt himself again – in control through well-refined anger. He marched off leaving a worried looking Skinner behind, because no Skinner knew that he pushed a Big Red Button that as not quite a wise prospect.

Bartek swooped into Walgreen's and bought everything he needed for his escape. He rushed to The Villa and approached Skinner's girlfriend Panda, looking her square in the eyes. She really was someone he wanted to trust. "*Did she tell you she only came here to be with Kluck? In those exact words, did she say exactly that? What was the quote, word for word? Tell me now, right now, and do not fucking lie to me.*"

Panda looked terrified by his intensity; she finally caught a glimpse of the inherent violence of his soul. And Panda blinked. She hesitated. She froze. He knew then she was lying, but wanted it all to be over. And Panda, playing into the scheme Skinner probably hatched, nodded her head in faked honesty. "*Yes,*" she said, "*word for word.*" Panda iterated: "*I'm in love with Kluck. I came here to get with him, and Bartek was the bus ticket.*"

Miss 3 walked up the front door having just taken a walk with Dr. Santiago. She was laughing, smiling, finally looking as if she'd settled in. It was a new day, a new dawn. She approached him and locked eyes – it was the woman he'd remembered all along.

Like King Othello having gone mad with paranoia, Bartek zoomed towards her like a black nebulous. He pierced those loving eyes with his own emanating searing hatred. All he wanted to do was hurt her, break her soul. He wanted those deceptive eyes snuffed out for eternity. He shouted that he wanted nothing to do with her, that this was over, and to get the fuck out.

The impulse of *Gotterdamerung* evaporated when he saw the love for him dim & fade, rescinding to blackness. He had just killed her. Miss 3's play-acted Godzilla-stomping she-devil crust punk Ma Beagle badass bitch routine all but crumbled to ruin.

He shattered her heart & she burst into tears. Skinner rushed up having just got off work. Like a rabid dog Skinner got right in her face, shouting she was a cunt and to & never come back...

Things had grown calm. Bartek was like a dead man, simply nodding and reciting whatever anyone wanted to say like a lobotomized patient.

All of his friends, family – they were sitting him down like a condemned man in front a panel of judges. They were voting as a group, as a democracy like he'd shown them. And they were all united in voting her out. The verdict was given, and she was exiled. Bartek, like an emptied vessel, stared at the ground.

3 returned, having took a long walk on the beach. She'd returned with a conciliatory tone, having dropped the act. She and Bartek were speaking softly, the way couples always do following an explosive fight. They were just people again. Skinner flew out the door like an enraged pit bull. He began shouting, calling her a cunt, saying to get the fuck out.

Bartek stood there limply, in shock that it was happening. Skinner was an attack dog barking away, and Bartek a solemn scarecrow. Brandon dragged Skinner back inside as Miss 3 slumped on the grass defeated, bawling tears. Skinner continued shouting from inside the house: "*Come on Bartek – let's go!!! Leave that fucking cunt there, lets just fucking go man – LET'S GO!!!!!!!*"

Bartek snapped from his standing coma and like a medic on a battlefield knelt down and lifted her up. They limped off down the street like two blood-caked survivors of a horror film and headed back for the motel where it all began. Brandon soon met him halfway down the block with their backpacks and some clothes.

Miss 3 was a corpse on the bed, all her stupid tricks discarded. Again they were just as they were in Michigan – naked to each other and the rest of the world a distant concept. The sad girl moved her head into his lap, and he gently stroked her hair. It was over in so many ways, but they dared not confront the repercussions or what comes next. What they needed was rest.

Santiago wanted to meet before he left to Ohio. The group had voted him out. He couldn't live there anymore, so long as he was actively using meth. He just wouldn't stop & banishing him was the only punishment they thought would make him sober up.

Santiago predictably flipped out, cursing everyone as traitors. And here he was in that same dead end motel forever at the end of the line. After, Santiago wandered off into mystery.

Bartek awoke to 3's packing. She was moving fast & needed a shower. She stripped naked, and went under the hot spicket. She summoned the clammy bag of bones for pity sex. He pumped away like a corpse, reaching out for her soul like a shadow Chernabog yet finding no grip to maintain her.

The closer he got, the further she'd tug her spirit away; she would never again allow him control. He climaxed & she reached down & felt the gooey mass of white cells. Don Juan Quixxxote had done a terrible thing.

They walked back to the Villa for her belongings. Outside, they awaited her ride back to the Greyhound. Just like Black Valentine's, and only a month shy of its 2 year anniversary, he was again sending her to Florida. The tickets to and from + the vacation in total amassed over $900 dollars. Bartek was near broke again after months of sacrifice, sleeping on a roach infested floor.

The car pulled up and 3 turned to him, after having stood silently like a cross armed, icy Goliath: "*If I'm pregnant you're paying child support.*"

Her cold, dark side noticed the car pulling up behind her, and she flinched when catching it from the corner of her eye. In one flash he saw the last dying embers of what could've been. She bubbled in tears. She couldn't talk, couldn't. She climbed in and off they sped.

Bartek thumped onto the ground, watching the vehicle go. He was a cadaver at an open-air wake for view of the sun alone. The Self-Immolated One, with his army boots & SWAT pants & navy blue work coat with the Agoraphobic Nosebleed patch dental-flossed on back & his Coroner work shirt & slicked back mohawk & half-cracked Cool Hand Luke aviator glasses. He was a tragic cartoon.

What could not happen had happened – his family, his wife had assassinated his 9th life. San Diego was over, Los Angeles too.

Bartek stumbled inside & slid down a dresser, propping his back against it & looking at a ticking clock nearly same as Greyhound. Everyone waited for him to speak. Brandon eventually approached. "*I'm a total failure.*" Brandon chose carefully: "*How are you a failure?*" Bartek replied: "*Because they don't understand.*"

Bartek drew pictures at the kitchen table as the house let him be. Skinner arrived – payday, and he'd nabbed an 8-ball. In Skinner's room, they cut up lines on a plate. Bartek was a corpse. He looked at Kluck & Skinner, a gruesome two-some that both lived and worked at the same place as him & whom he had no life outside of & represented everything terrible about his former life.

Skinner snorted his 3rd rail of cocaine, then threw a stack of lyrics at Bartek. Now that "*The Bitch*" was gone, the band was back on track. Yet the fact was he'd tossed them in a callous, power tripping way that screamed: "*You're my prison bitch.*"

Ryan left & found Panda: "*What exactly did she say to you, just so I don't have to think about this anymore. I need to move on.*" Panda replied: "*Oh, you know, she just – um, you know – she said that she, uh, had some unresolved feelings for Kluck.*"

The next day, Bartek cashed his paycheck & went home early. He'd done the unthinkable – booked a Greyhound for Detroit. He'd needed quick recoup & had already found a couch in Seattle.

As he rummaged through his belongings, the scene was tense. Skinner hid with Panda & Kluck. Brandon lingered, putting up a lax resistance. Bartek stormed out with a backpack, duffelbag & luggage case. With his Cowboy hat & *Cool Hand Luke* aviators, he looked tougher then the sunuvabitch who named that boy Sue – *and headed straight for Clownbaby like a nuclear warhead…*

A Weather Vane Without Compass

And Don Juan Quixxxote – *crucified* – began his descent. Spiraling downwards did he, brittle bones gnawing against the curvature of rock. Down, down into the catacombs of the earth where the mind retracts upon itself, trapping the soul in shackles of lye...

En route he'd twice passed out from sickness & fatigue. The 103 degree fever in Las Vegas carried savagely into the Rocky Mountains where the mighty land bison broke down, its mainframe giving way flickering lights & fading exhaust. Shaking beneath blankets & pouring sweat, Quixxxote found himself inextricably linked to the 55 people lassoed by the blackest of night, cringing sharply at an altitude where every movement pops eardrums with aerial crunch...

48 painful hours he stumbled from the bus. Accursed Detroit, the hollow tomb – frozen chill powerfully assailing, concrete & ice one solid mixture on every inch of territory.

As he waited in Detroit's station for his coming ride, he described his train-wreck fable to another Greyhound journalist from New Orleans – a seeker who stumbled onto the same GhostNomad game & was 6 months into his journey. The boy cocky with sponge-like perception, the karmic torchbearer duly listened to his tale taking heed lest he one day walk these same ragged shoes.

Quixxxote arrived again in the suburbs, to the peaceful sanctity of Lisa's couch. He slumbered beneath blankets for 2 days of raging fever & seasick hallucination. Soon his mother would arrive; the truck pulled to the curb, spreading slush like shrapnel. Quixxxote trekked back into the Detroit winter, steps struggling through half melted snow. He climbed into her vehicle, and off they sped into the drizzling ice rain cloaking the deformed asphalt.

Quixxxote stared away from her positioning at the wheel, peeking through the windshield to observe the barren branches of leafless trees which blurred incoherent visuals in the hallucinogenic night. Again, just as in his youth, he was assailed by her ancient refrain of cowardice. Her same gut-wrenching speech, her tired old chorus of hydra incarnations. Quixxxote could barely withhold the tears, struggling to grind them back into their arctic sarcophagus.

Bartek had forged his life's work in an attempt to embolden those stultified in their defeatism; to renew with vigor those casualties unable to redress life's promise or overcome parasitic stigma. To combat and replace their repugnant Gods, broken time, unjust death & horrid disease, Ryan had long ago assumed the fools mission of rendering himself Atlas. Like all the self-conquered wretches preceding him, Quixxxote bore the weight of slaves on broken shoulders until their sheer weight collapsed his spine...

Don Juan had wore his cartilage to the bone, trampled thousands of miles, dived deep into the pool of fanatic imagination desperately seeking the key to change everything.

He ingested all the truth he could withstand, attempting to conjoin it like a pressed diamond. One day, this glowing orb of self-tailored light could be used to annihilate the darkness engulfing all.

This glaring truth of learned struggle he now possessed, its tap overflowing like the screaming wheeze of the kettle. All those white pages, all that empty space – a new bible for starving, virgin eyes was envisioned; a fresh sustenance from the void, a Genesis black-smithed from the nether regions of forbidden exploration...

Yet try as he did ever so zealously, his search ended fruitlessly on that cold February night. His valiant, supernaut efforts could not reverse the process of spiritual assassination which darkened his history.

Quixxxote was uselessly unequipped to promote in any clear language the nova of truth which he'd ingested. The wisdom of 10,000 luminous lives were compacted into one glowing orb which he readily extended, yet all within earshot had grown deaf...

Quixxxote looked upon his mother and outstretched his hands, palms filled with radiant light that's wealth showered like golden coins. Whereas she could only see a burned out husk, the reality is Quixxxote's being had collapsed from the gravity of unrelenting beauty. He knew too much, he had seen too much, but the words fell from his mouth like invisible spiders.

Quixxxote grew silent, knowing that not a word could disturb her ensnarement. He turned to the window, staring silently with tired eyes and traced the frozen beads of rain galloping across the pane...

His mother, driving quietly with no sound but that of rubber tires sloshing through banks of dead leaves, appeared utterly disgusted. To her Quixxxote's long spiritual quest was nothing but a useless parlay into disreputable vagabondage. She declared it another stunt in a long line of unsavory stunts, all of which summed up her son's gutter character.

For her, Quixxxote's life was a sprawling, multi-faceted in-joke played on her. That his voyage towards illumination maintained no motivation but to bring shame upon their family and corrode her standing in the eyes of The Lord...

Quixxxote's mother then turned to him. She said, in words bearing no exaggeration: "*My cat is dead. My husband is nuts. And you are the way you are. I'm old, and it's too late. I'll work 5 more years, get my pension, and that's that. My cat will be cremated and when I go my remains will be buried with it. And so long as I'm alive, you'll keep on with your act. And you will never change. The joke will never end, and its not funny, and it never was. You are the way you are, and its pathetic. My husband is insane, and you will never change. And now I'm just waiting around to die. I should have had other children when I had the chance. Now all I have is you.*"

Quixxxote, poor Quixxxote, whose epic quest was of no value to the greatest of authority...

They parked outside the condo of doomed marriage and dragged up the stairs. He walked as a zombie into the white-walled cubicle and saw the broken adults fully bloomed in their ghastly routine – laughing forcefully on cue with every per-programmed laugh-track burst of that glowing television.

Strung out on Vicadin, hypnotized with Ambien, The Old Man yelled at Fox News that the Drug War wasn't enough. Both of them, doped up, nodding calmly to Bill O' Reilly, mutually biting their lips as not to scream NIGGER so openly when images of the President flashed upon the screen.

Unable to fight back the tears any longer, excused himself. He declared he would enjoy a stroll through the snow blanketed night. This request they found odd, ill placed – they couldn't understand why he would want to be in nature, in the frostbitten cold. There were hundreds of stations to choose from...

Quixxxote sluggishly entered the elevator, descended through the complex, and soon made it to the waterfront. This river, once so beautiful, was so polluted from the steel refineries that to swim in it would mean to die of contagion within a matter of days.

He sat upon a bench, a lonesome figure beneath the glow of the ice caked lamppost, and began to cry. He wept as if he now mourned 1000 funerals. In between sobs of ultimate defeat, all he could do was summon visuals of the home in which he was raised, the room that was his refuge until his flight from the distorted nest...

He thought of the girl in high school at the center of it all. How every day he'd rush home, as would she, and they would could call one another at exactly 3:30pm. Everyday – Monday through Friday on the dot – at least two hours of conversation. Perhaps the best friend he ever had in youth, gone to the ravages of time...

Surprisingly, he did not think of Number 3. He held onto her, yes, but he knew all too well that he'd been humiliated by insincerity. He thought of Natasha, little Natasha, whom walked beside him hand in hand 9 years before along this same toxic riverbank, only a few days before her father tried to kill her because he was white. He thought of the abuse, the rape.

It flared up dormant thoughts of poor Lisa, in the back of Quixxxote's mind still dangling from a cat collar in a closet as if no one had ever bothered to cut her down, her blood-drained face white as a porcelain doll...

He pictured Clownbaby, the love of a life that never was, that he'd so foolishly walked out on only a few months prior. Quixxxote gave it all for his family, as he had to, and found himself sold out at the edge of the world. He reached behind and felt his shoulder blade seeking to remove any one of the many invisible daggers dug deep into the muscle tissue...

And Quixxxote – the hard-boiled legend existing only in his own mind; the iron-willed juggernaut of stealth & unrepentant adventure – exploded in anguish. He slumped over on the bench, face in his hands, and wept uncontrollably: *"I just wanna go home,"* he said, to an audience of cold winter chill. *"I just wanna go home,"* he muttered, on and on and on. *"I just wanna go home"* – sobbing, sobbing, sobbing... *"I just wanna go home"*...

But home there was not. Kaitlin was someone else now. 3 had made a fool of him, Natasha was married, and Zelda might as well have been. Lana was in prison, and Lisa was dead. He reached out to figments, lusting the warm embrace from any of them, just to know he wasn't alone. And there was nothing he could do to change any of it... All went quiet, save for the deadly river slapping its watery poison against the dock, muffling the funeral pyre…

Cascadian Dermabrasion

The descending nova was a sharp, squinty eye of the Northwest, barely melting the snowy remnants of a winter soil that still clung to the red of autumn. The trees hurtled by such as the pavement below, the Greyhound's spinning wheels hypnotizing Quixxxote as his inner compass bore council. Since his earliest he'd felt guided by forces beyond his control – assuredly, a product of his imagination.

To be forthright, there was nothing supernatural about it; he simply knew the world would change dramatically during his lifetime – yet deep down, he felt he'd somehow minor domino a larger sequence of events. It was never in the cards to become a savior of mankind, some historical figure. Rather, he felt a helpless, hapless pawn in a monolithic design of impossible comprehension.

In this, he often felt a sense of protection. Imagination, perhaps – yet many times, it seemed as if some unknown force had allowed him for years to get away with his mad mission. That this unseen hand was nevertheless pushing him to a future position he did not want to accept. And that with every action he made attempting to escape it, that action would in fact continue the inevitable. More often then not, he felt a delusional marionette.

Soon his long road would end, and in climax, The Emerald City. His haggard attempt at mating had been hideously thieved. Even though much too late, Miss 3 would be in Tacoma, an hour's bus ride south of Seattle. There she was enrolling in school and living with a friend & her family. It seemed a stacking of cards in his favor. How could it be chance? The woman he was intent on winning was at periphery of his Great Gatsby scheme.

She'd fall in love with Seattle; they'd find jobs & comfort. Quixxxote would no longer wake up to cold bed sheets, haunted by the laughter of fictional children. In 26 years, true love had never been reciprocated. Anything close was clunky, the robotic movements of a young man directed by examples of others. A true merging of souls as one inseparable organism was foreign.

And so he addressed *"The Voice"* as if a puppet-master from which he sought liberation: *"All I want is the girl & to be normal, without seemingly magikcal properties. I want to seal my fate to the randomness of earth – I want out and to know peace."*

Bartek's self-willed specter taunted: *"Are you sure?"*

"Yes" he reiterated, wanting free of this contract with unknown devils: *"Just leave me be – I want nothing, I want silence. I want to be*

totally Anonymous." Bartek felt the rumble of an invisible belly laugh from the darkest pits of cosmic nihilism, as if this were now Loki he chatted with. "*I just want the girl, please.*"

With the universe mocking his decision, this communion a hidden god of Jesters receded to it's realm beyond the echoes. Again it was Quixxxote who'd read one too many comic books, amidst the blur of pine trees and disorientation of sleeplessness.

R. Bartek was broken from his trance at the last stop before Seattle, a gas station north of Olympia. Another passenger asked to bum a smoke – Winston was his name, looking harmless in a puffy white coat covered in tiny light-brown teddy bears. He looked a silly, gentle raver with a quiet mean-streak.

Having never been to Seattle, he besieged our ragged protagonist with questions then promised to smoke him out once they entered the city. Upon arrival, outside the station, smack-dab Downtown – Winston sat down his travel bag (*his only bag)* then pulled a large sack of marijuana from his teddy coat. "*Here smell this*" he grinned, handing over the over-sized Ziploc bag. Bartek took a pleasant, eyes-closed whiff to savor its freshness…

…then noticed the unzipped gym-bag below, where a fancy water bong sat atop a *GIGANTIC pile of guns* – *revolvers, Uzi's, half-assembled AK-47's & grenades.* Winston quickly began stuffing the massive bong chamber with stinky green. He lit it up in plain view of the street, in front of people leaving the station, in front of cars and taxis passing by in traffic. Takes a giant rip and then exhales it like a fog machine which drifts in all directions – towards pedestrians, towards Greyhound security hanging in the doorway.

He gave the enormous smoking bong to Bartek: "*Take a blast, dude.*" Quixxxote, jolted by paranoia, felt he should run – but feared disrupting Winston's calm demeanor.

Bartek hit it & tried to hand it back quickly. Winston refused, being courteous: "*Go ahead bro, no worries – smoke the whole thing yourself. I need to find a pay-phone.*" Then without further instruction, Winston ran around the corner & vanished – leaving Quixxxote with a smoking bong & a gigantic bag full of guns.

Bartek panicked – *was he being set up?* Was Winston a mass murderer trying to dump his cache on a lone traveler? *Was he calling the cops right now with an anonymous tip???* Was he a lunatic assassin? He had traveled cross-country with no clothing, food or water – *only automatic weapons, grenades & weed???*

Pot paranoia raging, Bartek questioned if there were even cameras inside the bus station. Would the driver, as a judicial witness, remember these passengers in court??

Ryan's ride would arrive any minute – he couldn't just leave all those guns on the street, and he certainly couldn't take them. *Were there even serial numbers??* What if he left them there & someone else stole them – and then have a hit on his head from a teddy-bear psychopath in the *first 5 minutes* of his dream relocation to the Northwest?? *What the fuck was this?!?*

15 minutes alone with this hellish fun house of terrible options... What would he say when his friend pulled to the curb? He can't just shout: *"HEY, JUST LEAVE THE MOTOR RUNNING ONE SEC DUDE, THERE'S THIS GIANT BAG FULL OF GUNS!"* He could envision his buddy motioning for him to come to the car, to drive off to a new life, and he'd nonsensically have to shake his head "NO", act funny, weirdly insult the guy by outlandish interaction so he just drives off & refuses to answer his phone – *instant homeless!!*

Or what if he gets so freaked out he doesn't allow him a couch to crash, believing this was all some interlaced plot and Bartek isn't fessing up to horrific, silent crimes? Or what if he thinks this situation will somehow lead back to him, like a "They" will come for him too, and he himself will end up dead or in prison?

The bong-rip blasted its fuzzy peak. At any moment, sirens & flashing lights could lurk. Suddenly, Winston whisked back: *"Hey, thanks man – here, I got us some smokes."* He slipped Quixxxote a Camel – just as the metalhead pulled up. Bartek, having avoided life imprisonment, then went home & watched *Escape From New York*.

Arriving with $555 & a naïve belief that being into metal & punk would easily find you somewhere to live in this silently xenophobic-to-invaders climate, Bartek set out to find community – just find dudes with Bathory t-shirts & explain the situation. Metal Brotherhood goes a long way, and it works everywhere else.

But Seattle was Freak City – sprawling as New York & jam-packed with "Big Fish" from every "Small Pond" one could imagine. And in small town USA, the weirdos band together naturally while in "The Big Leagues" of Seattle, PDX, SF – it was tough shit, dive in & swim – and passive/aggressive to the core.

The hometown inhabitants discounted outsiders; they wanted to prevent the in-flow of aberrant settlers & stray artists. Unfortunately for them, Bartek's fanatic mission was specifically to raise the black flag, propagandize this new world, and entice thousands (*if not millions*) to relocate here, Portland, and the Northwest at large. He looked at the Seattle underground as if real estate to devour, like an inverse vulture capitalist.

He quickly found these ideas soundly rejected. He'd expected to be thrust into a town of artists with inclusive, wild synergy. Instead Seattle was cold & clenched, unsmiling & inconvenient – its skies gray & its fall/winter/spring a melancholy, moderate drab. Angry, competitive egomania drove many nasty.

In Detroit, the winters are brutal – they keep you on your toes. In Seattle its a slow, leech-like glumness. Always in the 30's, with drizzle showers & rarely any snow – just eternal November & occasional January. It burrows into the character of the populous and their doom-sowing amplified malaise.

Seattle was flooded with heroin & anxiety-riddled loners & lost souls. The atmosphere wept black coffee. It was a place to always be reading a book hungover. Bartek dismissed this farty drabness, still eyeing potential. As he wrote to 3: "*Seattle will only end in death, imprisonment, or forced exile.*"

The months that followed were a slow motion catastrophe – a burdensome leech that drank his plasma to the dregs. The first 2 weeks were establishing contact with the personalities he'd met previously. Yet as he bounced from meeting to meeting in mind-numbing March, everyone was in a form of hibernation. The maps & intel he'd procured in building a tour network was met with a resounding "*meh.*" People were sleepy, and drinking off the cold.

He scored a job as a prep cook at Pike Place Market, the tourist trap along the harbor. All day, heavy crowds of tourists & street people with their con shtick & outstretched hats.

There was a sanity in being an everyday part of the city pulse. Mornings he'd arrive to quiet downtown streets, steaming sewers & pigeons fluttering off cobblestone. He'd walk down the old alleyways to the back door of his job, past the famous wall of bubblegum. He'd listen to thrash metal all day with his co-worker.

But the moment he clocked out, with no long-term friends or people telling him what to do – *he was lost*. The metal guys he stayed with were cool, but they came home late & slept. He didn't want to overkill his presence there, nor could he spend money. Most free time was walking rainy terrain alone, pondering depressing items. He had to save every dime, 'cause he had to move out in May.

Thus, he continued editing his road book before seeking a publisher, catching up on missed books & films, checking the internet at the library across the street. He'd scour Craigslist looking for a better job or somewhere to move, or to have vacant conversations with his wannabe wife in Tacoma.

Here they were in Seattle, the city they always fascinated – *yet he could not get her to step on a bus and just go there*. She pretended to be scared of riding it, and somehow never had the money. If she was broke he'd repay her, but she didn't have the gall to borrow $5 – and she'd never lower herself to bumming a buck at a transit station like "*some homeless person.*"

Like a teen sleepover, she was living by curfew of her friends' parents & asking permission to do things! Constantly repeating she was serious about being with him, she just would not budge. He was dumbfounded, hacking up bloody stomach lining from a growing ulcer, so desperately alone with cold sweat sweeps. His San Diego people would appear like a bad dream in his head, degrading him, saying he'd sold them out for a liar. No – *they were just kids & so was she...*

Early on, 3 met him in Tacoma. It took weeks for her to appear in person. They met at Waterfront Park – another jigsaw of Déjà Vu. She unveiled her new tattoo – a dead, rotting baby. He looked into her cold eyes – yes, it very much directly relating to him.

They walked the quaint, boring town awkwardly and had sleepy teriyaki chicken. He felt as if an uncle meeting a niece who'd enrolled in college.

He was mortified to learn the infected tooth from back in Michigan was never dealt with – her cheeks would puff up like a squirrel & green pus oozed out the infected lump! When it flared up, which was often, she could not stand or walk!! The infection was paralyzing her!! She'd be laid out for days – *because she feared dentists!!! She lives with borderline blood poisoning 2 years!!!!!*

Bartek was fucking flabbergasted: "*If that was me, I'd sit outside the dentist begging for money until I got it pulled. I wouldn't even leave that fuckin' parking lot – I'd occupy it with a tent.*"

She was annoyed by his "*crazy talk*" – she'd do it the American way – *by working for it!!* It could kill her any second, and she was scrambling to raise a thousand dollars so that her *furniture* could be shipped from Florida to Washington!! *Furniture!!!*

Quixxxote pleaded with her that this was suicidal. Why not spend $50 bucks at Salvation Army and get a bed frame, night stand, chair & desk? *"I'm not doing that poor person shit – I'm getting new stuff. I'm not like you – I'm not gonna live on a couch with all my shit stashed in trash bags like a moat."* She talked smack on Stoner Joe's, how I should've been ashamed for living in a trailer.

Then she mentioned where she was working, and it sounded like a strip club. He didn't want to know – after all, who wants to admit their fiancée is a visual prostitute with green pus seeping out her gums? She parted with a cold peck of a kiss.

He went back to work, weeks without seeing her. It was now April 4th, Bartek's birthday, and all he wanted was to see her. By now, his friends thought she was a delusion, this ghost woman believing Tacoma was like a marvelous Disney World.

3 promised they would hang out on his birthday, and he'd swore that if she ditched him it would be the end. There is no way ending it now could ever reach the misery of Black Valentine's II. *What tragic irony!* He sends his love away on Valentine's 2006, mopes over her ghost on V-Day 2007, and then after reuniting in glorious romance she's cruelly taken away again on V-Day 2008!!

She would only write every few days, which enraged him. He was jealous thinking she was with someone else and lying to him. But she assured him, after a lapse, that she would be at that same Waterfront Park on his birthday at the requested time.

He got on the bus, walked to the quiet, cold park on the harbor, and waited for her to arrive. And waited. *And waited, waited, waited.* With tears in his eyes, he caught the last bus & spent his birthday alone on a couch surrounded by his moat of trash bags.

The next day she apologized – her tooth acted up & she passed out from pain. He agreed to meet her again that weekend. Same scene – wandering & talking college for photography.

Bartek repeatedly stressed that he wrote for 2 of the biggest metal magazines in the world, and she was now his personal photographer – that his editors had *already approved* this, and she was now literally a famous photo journalist getting paid for her work – and they could travel the world doing this, starting tomorrow.

He offered her immediately what 8 years of hard schooling wouldn't accomplish – *but she just would not listen!* She simply wouldn't believe him! She had to do the "right thing" – which was signing onto a $100k student debt loan and then likely stripping her way to the $1000 needed for bed-frame & dresser shipments!!

He rented a motel room so they could have peace. It wasn't about sex, but being close. She rolled her eyes as if obligated to fuck him but did so anyway, after venomously complaining he shouldn't be blowing his cash on some dead end motel – and she wouldn't stay the night, either. She had a house curfew – *at age 23!!*

Back to Seattle he went, thinking of his love life as a balding, twig-like, 40 year old with a tiny dick & black socks trying to hump some walrus to regain his manhood.

After 5 weeks, Miss 3 and her roomie *finally* came to Seattle, being difficult & giggly the whole duration. On the bus they were loudly making fun of the cross-dresser, then talked smack on trans people as they walked to the apartment where they quietly mocked his friends to each other, calling them "*Metalocalypse.*"

She moaned about *Cloverfield, the film they were wastching,* how it was total garbage. Afterward, she cornered him in the bathroom to kiss him unemotionally. She looked him in the eyes & told him that she loved him, but they spoke only lies.

Her friend left early, leaving the cursed love birds downtown. It felt, at least for 1 hour, that the rough drama had passed. She again wore a smile.

In conversation the election came up – Obama & Clinton were still duking it out over the nomination. Bartek spoke of Obama, about how this really needs to happen for a variety of sound reasons. 3 scowled: "*I ain't votin' for no god damn nigger.*"

<u>WHOA</u>! *Where did that come from?!?* Bartek nearly tripped & fell on his face. Yes, he remembered getting a little Archie Bunker towards the end of Detroit – after being captain PC for so long, he started throwing around the n-bomb to shock people. But that was depression talking – Black Lava coprolalia. He wasn't racist, just in a whiskey hole – *and he'd hated Honky Ass Crackers above all!*

He wondered if he'd made a grievous impression on her. He remembered them both loathing g-thug gangsta crap, but he never would take it to that level. Bartek was bewildered that he never caught it. He wanted her gone just as she was finally smiling.

As he stifled through small talk, that dramatic n-bomb flew 'round his head. She kept saying how her attitude on Seattle changed. That she'd stay the night every weekend once he got his new place. The future was theirs. She kissed him warmly, the first since San Diego, and got onto the bus. He waved her goodbye as she smiled & waved back. The bus went off. "*Good riddance,*" he thought.

The next day he wrote her, as delicate as possible. This isn't going to work for reasons A) and B) and let's be friends, etc. She was heart broken, writing panicked letters. She finally admitted to him that the reason she had been avoiding him was because *she was pregnant*. 3 months without a period, freaking out the entire time.

Bartek predictably freaked out. Here she was, his pregnant wife, drinking & smoking weed with him – *and a life-threatening tooth infection!!* If she was going to have his kid, it would not be retarded from drugs & alcohol. Everything had to change.

Bartek demanded she take a pregnancy test, and she floundered claiming no money. She just didn't have the ability to raise $10 – *he'd just have to wait 2 weeks until she got paid!*

He came at her like a battering ram until she made it happen. It was a long night of waiting, an even longer day at work and an infinite bus ride before he was able to check his email. He smoked a cigarette before learning his fate, then – *not pregnant!!!*

He'd never been so relieved. No matter what life would throw at him, at least he wouldn't be hitched to her miserable caboose. He launched the breakup letter – he was free of her. 3's MySpace pic was changed to pitch black, and they did not speak for weeks.

Bartek moved into a small ant-infested basement room in the U-District filled with college kids begrudgingly together. 3 began writing, scrambling to save their dead relationship. She didn't understand how he could be so swift in ditching her.

It was the first week of May, a fresh start – that's what she kept emphasizing. She begged him to stay. So he gave her one last chance – meet at this time, on this day. And like always he waited, and waited, and waited. Just over two years ago she'd told him that she was "*nothing but trouble.*" Well, she was right.

The Narrator must note that the oddest part in this odyssey involving both [][][] and 3 was the most magickal. His early 2005 reunion with [][][] and into the summer – their presence coincided with one band in particular: Devotchka, the Latin-flavored band.

He had two albums, and each song lyrically related to key moments of the past 2 years. They were random CDs he thought were obscure world music albums sent for review. "*How It Ends*" was the first disc he slipped into that Thunderbird's stereo.

And so, after falling in love with these women to Devotchka's soundtrack & their accompaniment along all those lonesome Greyhound rides – when he walked off from being stood up he did not know where he was going, just kept following whatever magnetic pulse swayed his direction. The ice-soul zombie of GhostNomad kept drifting, hoping to mute the cataclysm.

Pulled by submission to ebb & flow, he made his way up the Pike Street incline to Capitol Hill. There was a street festival and the mystery headliner was about to play – Devotchka burst on stage!! An utter surprise, thinking they were not popular but some obscure South American band!! When Nick Urta came on stage to blazing horns, there could be no more a fitting end to Miss 3…

…except for the real end, which is fuzzy to your humble narrator. The life of Don Jun Quixxxote was forever hampered by shock, and this end would be incongruent to his history if it were not accompanied by a brutal twist. As it turned out Miss 3 *really was pregnant* – and because of his sharp refusal to deal with her, due to the stress it put on her, she miscarried, or so it seems, or so it was implied, or so it vaguely focuses in the memory of this narrator... A tragic end indeed – his home gone, his family broken, his wife estranged, their child dead. *And he'd done it all for love...*

Waiting For Clownbaby

In the threadbare room he lay, picking ants off his skin. The discarded, stained mattress of the previous denizen poked into his wrecked spine with wily springs that were somehow nurturing and seemed to align the sore vertebrates into their normal position.

No one mentioned the insect problem before he shelled out $900 to take the room for summer. It was supposed to be month-to-month until the landlord found out last minute. He would've bailed, but he'd nowhere to go – and still didn't understand exploiting Craigslist. It was only now that he'd been shipped a laptop from his parents that he got this business in order.

For all their right wing contempt, despite the heckling things they'd say about his views or character, they still wanted to help. They were always trying to give him money, which he routinely refused. It was important that he did it on his own.

He felt they only pretended to love him because they were following the protocols of what decent parents were supposed to do. They at least wanted to live up to that, even if they rejected everything he was and chose to blind themselves. Many years ago he stopped telling them anything beyond a PG-13 version of his life.

He could have been anything and they still would theoretically love him – a mass murderer, a dope dealer, a cannibal – just anything, please god *anything* but a faggot. That part was crystal clear. They would joke about it at the family gatherings with warm merriment – get them queers out of society & away from children.

All his ugly views had come from them – his mother & stepfather, as opposed to his real father, who was a dark, unknown, shadowy figure that his mom had built up as if The Antichrist – a womanizing, alcoholic, pathological liar. She made him hate his father so much that he attempted to nearly murder him twice.

As a child, he tried to puncture his tire so the car would flip; at 18 he had discovered the address of his aunt & uncle on the Bartek side, and visited unannounced.

The next day, thoughts of his father rampaged through his head. Driving the deep ghetto apocalypse of Detroit as Ford parts delivery man, he glimpsed a prostitute get stabbed in the stomach. It put him in a dark trance, and after work he just snapped – he headed to his fathers new home to bash him with a crowbar.

In the middle of his explosion he received an emergency call from Irish who was hiding in a park, hunted by police who were going to lock him up in the asylum.

Yet his father – who now as an adult he could blame little – was of no significance. If anything, he hated his dad 'cause he'd left him alone to the whims of his mother, an often shrewd, berating woman. Combined with his stepfather, they made an Irish Catholic military/cop backdrop – showering him with appalling views.

Bartek had never been racist, had never recalled his mother being venomous except the low-key *"welfare swindling"* ghetto mentality. Bartek was never a fan of *"money & bitches"* talk & rejected "The Game" – it was an attitude he abhorred.

But once his mom united with his eventual stepfather her latent poison streamed out. He found himself besieged by dead-end conservatism and "Diet Westboro" vengeance of god views.

Thus, at 12 – pushed to laser-point his hatred towards some despicable target – he began spewing the most awful sorts of fascistic "problem solving." He believed that people with HIV/AIDS should be rounded up & exterminated – and for the good of humanity against plague they should willingly accept it.

Somehow, through his twisted, abominable, pre-teen logic, he wanted all the neo-Nazis to experience the same fate. He wanted to gas the Nazis just like they did the Jews – in the chamber next to the bodies of the AIDS corpses awaiting cremation. He even, at times, claimed that all children should be removed from gay custody, and constitutional amendments preventing same sex marriage.

These terrible ideas seemed to bother his mother *just a little*. She could sympathize with them to a degree, but ultimately ignored them assuming he'd grow out of it. This was just some senseless crap her angry young son in a Danzig t-shirt was saying. But the fact was that she was not truly appalled or concerned.

With Bartek, it ran deeper. He had an inner darkness that could come unhinged & manifest itself in violence; a pyromaniac sadism suspended in hushed silence. He exhibited great precaution in self control, channeling this destruction through creativity. Without a pen and paper, who knows what he might've become.

Bartek didn't have split personalities, per se – what he had was a volatile, uncontrollable emotion of destruction that – when pushed to his limit – he simply would become, as if in a trance. He'd slip off into a rage-filled auto-pilot and his awful thing would take over, like a genie loosened of its lamp. A huge part of his isolation came from this – the fear of losing self-control.

There were times that he narrowly missed breaking someone's jaw by accident of sleep terror. Even as a kid at slumber parties, he would wake up savagely pummeling some sleeping child because in a nightmare he got into a fight on the playground. It was among the myriad reasons the children of his elementary hated, feared and mocked him.

There were times where later in life he'd terrified his girlfriends from waking suddenly and punching a wall or flailing thrashing limbs. He never physically hurt any of them, but always feared he may somehow unconsciously swing in his sleep.

In school he was the freak of all. He so drastically wanted away from them he used violence as a means to secure it. During lunch the kids ate at the fold out tables, and if one kid was bad that day, the staff would make them sit alone across from the other kids & eat by himself. Bartek realized this tactic would suit him.

He spotted the nice girl that he had what might be considered a crush on. She was the most angelic of the lot, which meant his punishment would be severe. He began attacking her, punching her, pulling at her hair. They made him sit alone, then the next day told him to go back to the kids. He attacked her again, and they segregated him. He just kept attacking her every day until they made him sit on the other side of the lunch room permanently.

And there he remained, all the way until middle school, called a freak, called a faggot, having food thrown at him and insults hurled from the mobs of other children, all as he smiled and ate his lunch alone, dining with The Black Lava.

For him this repression of violent impulse was always a struggle. He would do everything he could to bury it, shove it away until something just pushed him over the edge.

This serpentine function of his psyche was like losing control of the steering wheel. Physically, he wasn't that intimidating – he wasn't a big guy, just wiry & fast with an average build & height. But when that surge came it was like a maniac rush of endorphins.

Destroying things would be like a drug, especially bad people, and had a serious problem where in blind rage he'd use any nearby object as a weapon. For most his life these potentially catastrophic episodes were prevented either by intimidated aggressors or others physically stopping him. It was the product of a lifetime of bottled rage compressed into an unstable force constantly swept back under the rug.

In his high school teenage years, around 14, he stopped trembling at this violent force inside him. He grew twisted, feeding this hateful blob like a cancer.

In the Dark Era 1990's – with bands like NIN & Marilyn Manson reigning over the minds of deranged teenage outsiders – he went about undetected. He really wanted to push the entire nation over the edge. He wanted every kid to drop out & run away & turn to insane *Lord Of The Flies* tribalism. He wanted every bible & Quran & Torah thrown into a pile and burned. He wanted to incinerate all money & put all cops in straight jackets.

For years he got away with both promoting and enacting this supreme extremism under the "weird kid smokescreen," because no one took him seriously.

But in his heart there was a serious derangement. He was a danger to himself and all those surrounding him, because it was that hypnotic Black Lava which essentially drove him.

So what was it that changed him? When did that schism erupt that made him fear himself, that demanded the cessation of feeding this Black Lava? There were three big moments, actually. The first was a fistfight in high school, in which he squared off with a jock while 250 kids surrounded him chanting *"Kill the freak! Freak faggot!"*

He exploded, unsurprisingly, and took it out on the jocks face with fists. It was growing gnarly, like a mixed martial arts ring fight gone too far when an unconscious opponent keeps taking the heaviest blows to the skull possible. He had been physically speared off and dragged from the fight.

Afterwards, much of it escaped him – though he started looking for fights to engage in, working the boxing bag every day until his knuckles bled. It felt better to mangle flesh then ever before. And he was getting worse.

Next came the bad acid trip at barely 18 which ruined him. It had climaxed with a blackout , but he knew well where he went – just 30 hits of dirty acid and that Black Lava void. He was fried from it, and it launched him on a dark, suicidal, drug-fueled path.

If anything killed the demon, it was love. Zelda had appeared to him at the age of 19. She was the drugged-out wayward child of a heroin-addled home. To him, she was the innocent, warped angel of the Detroit Rave Scene.

Lost to his own PTSD in the depths of Detroit winter, it was she that held him together. It was she that was his saving grace. He would protect her, and this was cause enough to climb out of the pit. She became the daily gentle voice on the other end of the telephone. As long as she existed, he was prevented from slipping off into destructive psychosis.

Eventually, after years of refusal, he finally broke down and ate a tab of ecstasy. And no one can describe the way "The Wall" falls that first time. All it took was one fat pill to erase so much pent up hatred. Never mind "Blue Monday," or "Tedious Tuesday," or "Wallowing Wednesday" – MDMA saved his soul, and he was smart enough to not go hog wild. While his friends were rolling 5 days a week or more for nearly 2 years, still he stayed removed…

The remembrance of these monstrous views struck him hardest as he now tried to regenerate in Seattle. Though he'd long ceased feeding the Black Lava, he was cursed by The Demon it created.

He wondered how long he could live here quietly before he was called out. Would this new world reject him if they found out this terrible history? Would they ever believe that it no longer mattered, such as a Nazi skin gone SHARP?

For the first time ever he was truly cut off from the world that preceded him; he was a grown man with the inalienable rights granted to every civilian. It was all on his back, and there was no one *on his back* to do anything.

He had now spent 7 months in total darkness – a period where he needed to strike, physically at his peak, when he could not afford to collapse to depression. Yet the situational nature had dismantled him. With this fresh start, he refocused. He'd come to build a new base, a new family; to play music and tour. And all of that would come – *after summer*.

As he sat gazing up at the bright orange light pouring through the window he felt euphoric hope. The desire for true love now propelled him. He didn't want to mercilessly throw himself into a band because he needed to feel out his soul.

He was content to spread his prior albums & writing around the Seattle art and music scene to sow seeds. He wanted to meet everyone he could connect with to network something fierce.

He wanted to read every book he never had the chance, watch every movie he missed, listen to all albums he glossed over, see all the great local bands that never toured. He wanted to ingest the life of the young man in The Emerald City of 2008 to its fullest.

His job was going fairly well as a prep cook inside the Pike Place Market tourist trap. He'd be off by 3pm & given a complimentary 6-pack from their micro brewery everyday. And the marijuana was pristine. He was OK with relaxing, reading inebriated in the sun. But he knew it was limbo, and it was running thin…

Lana & Zelda were no more then pleasant memories infected by a sea of rust, and 3's severance had absolved any attachment to the world of [][][]. In his wounded retreat from San Diego, he'd grasped for open arms – finding only cold, separated distance from the woman he sought to love. Marginalized, ignored & tormented by false promises, he had become the voodoo doll she'd clutched.

He was destitute for love; a man who'd somehow been buried alive in a watery grave that only by grace of the ocean was loosened and flushed unto the deserted sands of a forgotten isle. He was malnourished and weak, literally spitting blood from an ulcerous stomach. His entire history had perished, and he felt utterly alone.

He knew all the right people, had every connection for success – but he did not _know_ them. And even they uncomfortably saw his brutal, obvious depression.

Bartek felt like the monarch of a great, empty castle. Seattle was an enormous labyrinth of opportunity; his eyes set upon it like his distant relatives The New World on that 2nd wave of ships after the Mayflower. He felt the genetic memory of his ancestor pilgrims embedded within alongside a deranged irony that just as they had, he'd traveled endlessly to establish a colony in total repudiation of all the pilgrims had stood for.

Our tragic anti-hero was now sincere in dropping his machine-man war to share the world with someone. Though he met women while traveling the country, none had the right chemistry or shared his end game agenda.

Even if those components were in alignment, none had what it took to tackle Europe. The ultimate plan was a lengthy, grueling, backpacking/hitching exploration of Europe – and a hard boiled determination to stay there. He was determined not to do it alone.

Still, loneliness screamed beneath him. The new _Batman_ film would be coming out in July, and he was going to bring an ultimate date to the movie. There was such a huge buzz following the death of Heath Ledger that the American movie public were in a state of teased cinemagasm. It would be a romantic night for the ages.

Prone to impulsive, irrational attempts at love, Bartek was at the same time never smitten at first sight. It took him days, weeks, months to build up a true affection – in some cases years. Because of his voyeuristic, guarded distance, it was often much too late when he would decide to strike.

Clownbaby was one of a very small number who owned him immediately. At first eye contact she saw through him. Her beady eyes claimed him like a hapless insect mummified in webbing. In all, she was a high-voltage spontaneous flash amid his restless movement through the country.

Without questioning it, without conflict, they merged naturally as a healthy, co-dependent organism. This symbiosis perhaps came from the clarity of distance amplified because they knew they'd soon part. This was a pleasant bubble in time, soon to end, and there was no need for games or drama.

But they both clearly realized that this harmony would be present regardless of how they met. They came from the same social circles, populated the same areas, bars, venues – yet somehow missed each other 6 years.

They connected in a way that was profound, and again, when ready to leave Michigan once and for all (Attempt #2), he could very well have just stopped. He probably would've been happy for many years. But the Greyhound pulled up and off he went to Seattle in the rainy fall, homeless with $250 in his pocket and a zealous intent to make it happen on little more then his snake-man charm & invisible scene points. Like a used car salesman, he'd talk 'em silly.

It is dangerous to throw oneself mercilessly at a shadow in the suffocation of utter heartbreak. He knew this was true, but he also knew his feelings were legitimate. Clownbaby had been a crazy voice in his ear ever since he left, calling at random times, texting strange word battles. Through the saga of 3 – all the times Bartek would depressingly go to the library to check MySpace for any message from this woman that was supposedly borderline engaged to him and hearing only crickets, Clownbaby would always be there. Ever since they met, she was right with him the whole time.

As is why when riding home from work on the bus, strangled by the reality that he might just check his messages and find out that 3 was indeed pregnant, that he would be stuck with her for the rest of his life – Bartek reached a moment of clarity. If he got out of this one, he would move mountains to bring Clownbaby here.

If he was spared this gruesome fate of 3 for life, he would snag Clownbaby right up & give her the date of a lifetime. Nothing mattered – not his band, his books or tours. Thus, on that long ride he texted to ask if she would be his date for the new Batman film. She said yes, instantly. He said he would fly her out if he had to.

Bartek smoked a nervous cigarette, then confronted his possible doom. Pregnant she was not – *and free he now was*. He ended it right there with as non-venomous a missive as he could, then left the library into the sunny day. He climbed the stairs to the heavy metal apartment and nestled up in his little garbage bag corner behind the couch. He kept muttering to himself "*Clownbaby's comin', Clownbaby's comin...*" in exhausted relief, just as he would repeatedly over the next few months as if meditating...

In October 2007, immediately after his *Big Shiny Prison* book tour, when Downtown Brown dropped him off at the curb, he knew not to go in public in Detroit, lest something like this happen.

There was too much riding on getting out quick & silent. Yet he negated his karmic paranoia and went to a mysterious local dive bar to have a drink with a friend near midnight on a sleepy Sunday.

His pal was late to show, and he crept along the tavern avoiding people. Soon he got that psychic tingle of being watched and mentally dissected. He turned to lock vision with the tiny, beady eyes at the bar stool pulling him in like tractor beams.

He kept trying to look away, and she kept swinging her head around, knowing that he couldn't say no. Her pupils were like a slow, curling finger beckoning him towards her.

He approached her and she immediately began playing with his hair, and he could feel her psychedelic-whacked spirit through her fingertips. They melted like butter. "*I wanna paint you like a clown.*" He kept trying to escape from her, acting as if he was in a rush to go somewhere. But she just smiled that mad grin, and knew he was lying. He didn't have a choice.

As they exchanged numbers, Linda – who had for so long played his relationship grief counselor & listened to his woes of lonesomeness & dating chaos for so many years – walked up behind them for that late night drink. "*Ah Clownbaby! Good to see you! Been a long time since you guys got to hang out huh?*"

The budding couple both looked to her with question marked stares. Bartek said, "*Um... we just met.*" Linda's eyes went wide in disbelief, then amusement, then to an undefined mystery, and finally a very sad, somewhat ashamed look.

Shakily, with perked eyebrows of amazement, she sat down and had a beer with the two. Clownbaby and Bartek ranted at each other for a high-voltage hour while Linda remained silent, casually drinking her beer and watching them as if a nature photographer spotting a rare coupling.

They were communicating in that razor sharp way where they were forever finishing each others sentences no matter how totally disjointed and seemingly impossible. She would pull a random absurd topic from the whole of civilization and he would be right on it, and she the same with him. They made plans to hang out before he left town, and Bartek took off with Linda.

On the drive back, Linda was in disbelief, if not shock. She was in a sense his protector, the big momma bird of maternal instinct that was like a den mother not only to him but the larger group they hung out with – particularly the stoner, disc golf playing, *South Park* consuming quasi-hippie clan that were ever-present at Stoner Joe's trailer and the many houses that wide-spanning crew would travel through. She was the analytic psychologist date-matcher who'd also take care of the larger group with strong maternal instincts.

As is why she looked ready to cry as she steered her car through the night: "*Oh god, oh god... I'm sorry Ryan, I'm really sorry.*" Bartek knew what she meant, because it was now clear that at any point in multiple years of listening to both his and Clownbaby's lonely dialogues she could have just stuck them in a room together & they might very well have lived happily ever after.

"*No, no, no – you knew Clownbaby, there's just no way you never met.*" Bartek shook his head, "*I think I saw her at that diner on Rochester Road once or twice, maybe a party or two, but we never talked.*" Linda knew he was doomed to experience an unfinished "what if?" of mega-proportions.

They continued their conversation at her dinner table. Linda kept rubbing her brow in exasperation. Even though she refused to state it, he could read her body language – "*don't call her; just get out.*" She had worked him through some cataclysmic relationship collapses and always understood that no matter how nuts he was about a girl, these were not end-all-be-all couplings.

Like most dating in the 20's, the women he coupled with were all living symbols of eras he was experiencing; they represented facets of his emotional growth at the time, or what he aspired to be. But they too were experiencing the same, and Bartek was always a fling novelty for most of them. They liked him until he talked, and if they liked him more once he spoke he would eventually say something too extreme.

And if not, they would eventually confront The Black Lava. The only one that ever made "*the goal line*" was Lana, and she burned up in his orbit like a cosmonaut reaching the sun.

Linda explained it quite directly – Bartek had a bizarre fun-house mirror reflection of a female quasi-clone, and her name was Clownbaby. Somehow, from 2000-2006, they hung out with the same people in the same circles at the same places. And whenever he would leave, she would show up. Whenever she would drive off, he would walk right in the door.

Somehow they missed each other repeatedly for 6 years, and no one ever bothered to bring them up to each other because everyone just assumed that these two hung out all the time. Many, upon asking, thought these two were somehow connected at the hip just out of view from them.

In the days that followed, when asking various people from this larger clique about Clownbaby, every person was shocked to find they never met. None thought it possible.

Bartek scurried through his memories, knowing at some point he must have met her. As he concentrated on her face, he was able to place her in a few different scenes. Once in 2001 at a diner at 3am in the booth across from them. He remembered thinking this was one of the most gorgeous women he'd ever seen, but she was with her boyfriend straight out of a rave, googly-eyed from ecstasy.

He recalled her at another diner when he was 19, around 3am again. She was looking semi-gothy with a dark-appareled friend (*probably after leaving City Club*) and he had injected himself at their booth, ranting a hyperactive spiel as the two looked intimidated yet hypnotically enticed by him.

He'd do that in those days – just jump into someone's world, unload a ton of info, then vanish. At that point, she didn't say a word, just smiled crazily. But that night passed and she never came back.

He remembered her at two different house parties, looking grim and antisocial, but moderately dressed, if not slightly preppy. Just sitting on a couch and checking her phone texts as if she was in some sluggish relationship breakup both times.

Isolated from her surroundings, she said nothing and took off with the air of a cold Eastern European man-eater. There must have been another time though, because her eyes were so familiar.

Clownbaby took him home; there they stay cut off the world for days. She lived in a condo that her controlling mother had purchased, and in her isolation it had become a sort of madness womb – like the habitat of a crazy cat lady witchy woman gone OCD in her collections of charming rubbish, broken toys, newspaper clippings, half-operable musical instruments & odd porcelain dolls.

She was a long term problem child in that she was an embarrassment to her family. Not that she had done anything wrong – to them Clownbaby, by virtue of her character, was a freak – a strange, crazy person shoved into her strange little world because they just didn't know what to do with her.

She was constantly degraded by her mother, because she was what she was and could not pretend to be anything else. The mom and stepfather were "normal people" and had big money. They wore fancy silk and shopped at Nordstroms and had new cars and a big old house in the northern suburbs.

Clownbaby was the roach who crawled onto the icing of their wedding cake. Not only did it not "fit the bill" to have such a weird daughter with an obvious history of mental and drug problems – but she was also very, very gay and talked like a character from a 1970's John Waters movie.

She was the only child of a failed marriage which ended abruptly when her father decided to become a full-fledged transsexual. The parents divorced, and soon Clownbaby had two moms. The natural mother would see that Clownbaby be wholly segregated from that world. It didn't work.

She was tiny, fragile and androgynous; she was like an alien that could shift between either gender with a change of clothes. She was an utter chameleon and could pose as anything. Even though she wrote like a child, her linguistics were acrobatic. In casual conversation, her word swarms flew aerodynamically.

The connectors between ideas and her staggering ability to link random impressions into flowing coherency was a skill Bartek had not seen in anyone. She had dozens of accents she would sift through; they would curl out from her throat like a Pazuzu dialect.

With her screamingly obvious alpha-pixie lipstick lesbian neo-circus vibe, her physical immersion into any environment would come with it a sexuality that was so heavy everyone present, be it man or woman, took a look.

And that's why they hated her – she set off that queer impulse and everyone was uncomfortable. She lobbed a flash grenade at the center of everyone's gaydar. And she was often just as uncomfortable, because no one ever just wanted to be her friend. She was a magnet of sexual unrest.

Her aura was enigmatic as if occupied in a thousand directions. She was adorable, self-deprecating – Bartek saw in her a wounded, precious animal he wanted so desperately to breath life back into. Above all she was the very zenith of that certain kind of Madness he was attracted above all else; the depths of her acid-laced craziness was like a fine wine aged since the 16th century.

There she was – impossible to recreate & immediately, by force of nature, growth, chance & evolution – synced to the bottom of Bartek's rabbit hole. His adoration of her only increased when perusing through shelves of odd collectibles; she too, in his mind, was one of the weird porcelain dolls.

Bartek was instinctively a bizarre hoarder as well, though he'd relinquished the impulse. Her den reflected the basement of his youth, filled with broken hunks of trash he'd befriended and brought home, weird electrical motors and such. Now, as a young man, he collected weird characters. She was the most charming, precious addition to that collection in years.

Clownbaby was a powerhouse muse, one of a kind, and even though he had to move on he'd still spoil her from afar, forever and ever, because he simply liked her that much as a person.

There was a pause, and both of them acknowledged the feeling that in so many different incarnations of what may or may not have been, as in parallel dimensions running side by side, they already knew each other. They were key players to existences they'd never know. And perhaps this was the one reality that, for whatever reason, they never made contact 'til now.

And thus she'd speak openly & frankly about any topic under the sun. The hold-ups weren't there – it was thoroughly healthy symbiosis. She spoke of how she ate peyote at 13 and wandered off to who know where for 3 days while cops were searching. If anything was the start of her, that's the grand clue.

She also spoke frankly about sexual abuse, things she'd lived through, and the disgusting nature of unspecific parties response to its revelation. In a calm, matter of fact way, Bartek said: *"Maybe it's a good thing I didn't know you back then."*

"Why?" she asked.

"Because I would have killed him."

Silence. Then, moments after, Clownbaby rustled like a delicate volcano. She emoted her phrase with a shaky delivery that ended with a razor-sharp pointedness, a tone that he was sympathetic with as no other living creature before, and one that pierced through him like a lance: *"WHERE WERE YOU?!?"*

Bartek left for Seattle the following week. He had parlayed his departure, dragging it out with her trying to indulge the moment before the window slammed shut. They both knew he had to move on. They made pleasant goodbyes. He had texted her declaring she was *"the love of a life that never was."* She reciprocated: xOxOxO...

They would be tight for life, so long as he never botched it. Clownbaby to him was like the ultimate consolation prize of 6 years of

Detroit loneliness. Suddenly, his often haunting memories no longer felt alone but with a spectator viewing them alongside him in his remembrances. No one had ever done that.

As has been said, Bartek went to Seattle with $200 in his pocket. Though he could have fought like a devil to stay put, he went back to San Diego to gather his crew on a pointed mission to emigrate to Washington en masse.

What began well soon began to erode; the struggles with Skinner began, when Kluck arrived undeclared against Bartek's wishes. Thus setting the stage for 3's return.

He had been communicating with Clownbaby regularly the entire time, and she had shown interest in visiting California. It was another moment where Bartek realized he could just stop right there... but he knew 3 would pop back up.

Which, of course, she did – with one phone call, she immediately moved to California. After he bought 3's ticket, Bartek wrote to Clownbaby & explained it was quite serious. He knew she was probably hurt, but wasn't strong enough to stop what was to happen. He had cornered himself by the way he lived his life & the explosive characters he surrounded himself.

When he finally walked out on The Villa Winona, not telling anyone where he was going or his end game agenda, one of them again asked: *"Where are you going Bartek? Tell us something!"* While marching down that sidewalk dragging roller luggage with his big brimmed black cowboy hat on like some anti-hero cowpoke riding off into the sunset: *"I'm going to get Clownbaby."*

On his washed up, flu-strangled arrival in Detroit 3 days later, he was bruised and battered To the core of his DNA he had animally mated for life, began a family, then had it all cruelly revoked in humiliatingly cold indecency.

It took several days to nurture his health from the nasty flu virus, running side-by-side with the worst kind of emotional painful he'd suffered. His life had collapsed, and his dream destroyed.

After awhile, Clownbaby picked him back up. She was dating some other guy now who didn't seem quite interested in her. Bartek got on the subject of people they knew – he wanted to uncover just how intricate their missed presences really were.

She had big binders of photo-books. As he flipped through them, the photo's were a lengthy documentation of her chameleon shape-shifting. She was so successful at manipulating her wardrobe that she her physical look would warp as well. Her face was like a clean slate of smooth skin that could contort into any rubbery emotion. She was a Frankenstein monster of stitched personages.

As is why Bartek was dumbfounded when each turned page revealed another incarnation of Clownbaby. Yes, he had indeed met her repeatedly in passing. Bartek had the attention of women in his early 20's – but he rarely reciprocated advances because he knew these women were not like him and would never really accept him. They had nothing to offer except eventual estrangement.

Still, he would now and again bump into candidates and share a strong glance. There were quite a few strong losses on this end, ones that bothered him long after because he was too timid to say something, too frightened of rejection to be direct.

Clownbaby was at least 30 such encounters over 6 years. In starkly different outfits, hair colors, settings. He remembered her from drug stores, gas stations, restaurants.

In the final dark year of his Michigan life, he'd constantly go to the $1 movie theater alone at Dequindre & 12 Mile. It was the Megaplex Cinema at the half-closed shopping mall with 20 movies screening – all close to being on home video on their final buck-squeezing run. In those dark aisles he would theater hop, always running into strange girls. More often then not, it was Clownbaby.

A lost remembrance struck him mightily. The day he moved into his first apartment in Troy, MI (*in 2000*) he'd transported half his belongings. Taking a break, he stopped at Coney Island in Royal Oak, on 12th & Main. It was an emotional moment for him, and he impulsively committed the experience to paper.

As he was writing, a table of girls interrupted: "*Hey you – writer guy.*" Bartek looked up. "*She wants your number.*" The friend pointed to the 6 years younger Clownbaby, whose eyes pierced through him like molten daggers. Her hair was silver, dyed sharp and strong; it was as if her aura exploded and dimmed the lights to a soft red and black. And at the center were those haunting, icy eyes.

He was awkwardly thrown into it direct from a trance, and even more awkward in his response when inhaling those frozen turquoise eyes eating him alive.

He nervously said something about finishing his sentence, then went to use the bathroom. He splashed cold water on his face to snap out of it, looked at himself in the mirror with a sigh, then went to confront the hottest woman on earth.

In those 5 minutes the table emptied. She must've been embarrassed, and they split. It was nothing new – another epic loser fail.

He kept his eye out, often eating at that restaurant. Over the next 6 years, it became one of his favorite spots to write & dine. Her ghost was always at that table.

Bartek asked if there was a picture in her book from that time period where she had silver hair. She flipped right to it. He asked her if she remembered the Coney Island scene. And sensing that dull ache, she recalled it from her own fog. Her pupils dilated a little. She remembered him clearly, and was always looking for his ghost.

They spent a good amount of time together in that final week. She kept dodging her "boyfriend" to be around him, and he knew he could probably stop.

But Detroit was history and if he and Clownbaby were to have a real relationship, it would have to take place on the West Coast – even if he was still robotically maintaining the ashes of 3. In the back of his mind he knew it was over with 3, and maybe...

And so Bartek went to Seattle and had his dragged out end with 3. He sluggishly crawled from her maelstrom as a stranger in an even stranger land. He moved to the U-District, his job was stable, and he had every tool at his disposal for the striking iron.

All he had to do was stay put – all he had to do was wait. And wait & wait & wait, right there, just waiting for Clownbaby.

Somewhere Over The Rainbow

The optic illusion, through his optic nerve – *or hallucination, as some may deem* – was that of an elliptic pyramid eternally rising from the depths of shallow water.

It appeared to him as a fragment of sunken city R'lyeh that somehow, from its pole of inaccessibility, had slid through abstruse subterranean pathways to rise before him like a monolith. The air grew still as the humidity embraced him; he felt a beloved fetus adored by the glow of the sun, its shine unconditional in its embrace.

In the world apart from fungus, at the heart of Cal Anderson park, the rocky pyramid was the cheery craft of a modern architect – a curvature of chiseled rock placed at the center of an inches-deep wade pool. This rectangular pool was connected to an even lengthier, skinnier one, which then led to a stone building that was part of Seattle's former water reservoir system. This structure, created in 1889, was a quarter mile fountain – "The Lincoln Reservoir."

Cal Anderson park is where much of Seattle would gravitate in moments of leisure and social flirtation, such as Central Park in NYC. Mothers would walk sons up and down the length of the massive fountain, and the park benches among its encircling gravel path would play host to the origins of many romantic beginnings and flirtatious encounters. Down the hill were dodge ball, basketball and baseball courts – disc golfers, Frisbee throwers, book readers...

Bartek felt at home as he did at any major park, and dreamily foresaw a future where all misfits of society would banish their drab lives. Cal Anderson made him a believer in a fantasy where he could build a new family based on "Park World' – where Seattle's finest would choose its pasture over tavern dreariness, assailed by picnics, political discussions, bands & mobile info-shops. He'd pushed all summer for his friends to make it their stomping grounds with zero results & was preparing to make flyers as to lure bodies.

He lusted for freaks of all stripes to join this park revolution that perhaps would grow so profound they'd simply take it by storm, plant tents & refuse to leave.

They'd dig in like trenches of World War I & hack off the tendrils of society. And the only thing that could get them to leave was mortar upon mortar of tear gas. And even then they'd come back screaming: *"You'll never take us alive!"*

Yet vision vs. the doldrums of adulthood. He was 27 now, and rioting against a way of life he could not manipulate. Still, crawling atop the small mound at western edge of park, he found his compass. To him that minor hill was the center of his universe & all points of direction derived from that magical patch of land.

Today was the first occasion he'd ever devoured magic mushrooms and demanded that "Park World" take him. Like a priest submitting his services to the deity of a great altar, Bartek bowed to the Mayan Temple now rising from the inch-deep waters below. From its top bubbled down a thin stream of water constantly flowing so it looked coated by a thin layer of living ice, forever rising upwards to the heavens.

From the inanimate glare of its stone intensity came the innervation that "Park World" would somehow come to roost. That alongside the noble onlooking sun & the breathing grass & the candied wind – all of which were assiduously preparing this great shift of world consciousness – the watery monolith iterated that to make this enormous change he'd have to graft the city to his soul.

He had to absorb the whole of its organic verdancy and crisp architecture; he had to ingest the pulse of the city and absorb the wealth of its humanity. Then, somehow, he would be at the epicenter of a new creation, an *au courant* sentinel of manifestation.

The strain of mushroom which inflated his cosmos was the product of another drug dealer entirely, since his previous go-to man had stopped selling to him, fearing for his mental health. It was a shame being cut-off from the most delightful chocolate-caramel concoctions he'd encountered – an extremely rare blend of deep-jungle Amazonian. It was the jungle-borne brain-frenzy which changed the game entirely.

Gazing at the runny temple he had the familiar taste of cow shit nastiness that's nauseating furor makes one vomit. And then the slow Jekyll-to-Hyde transformation – that roughly puking, seas-sick, bowel-emptying, topsy-turvy primordial confusion which gives way to total clarity and wide-awake immersion into the dream realms.

His mind and body would fight it every step of the way – often with dread and fear – but once it fully gave way to the opposite side of the mirror, he was wholly in his element.

"*When in doubt, burn it all away*" – there was no more systematic an approach to leveling the past then the mental acceleration of psychedelia. This pursuit had launched in an innocent fashion, with a sackful of chocolate-caramels & punk rock friends.

Like children they went into the night, creeping through a vast local park. A brush of trees became "Witches Cove," a stone garden the "Faeries Lair," the stone chair in the wall that of the powerful wizard dwelling peaceful, mystic lands.

As the trip ended, the group were laughing incoherently at the threat of SKYNET. They realized when lurking the streets that SKYNET was as big an enemy as ever, and jaywalking blatantly just to defy SKYNET's demands of crosswalk stop and go.

And they also realized through weird, convoluted logic, that the vegan liberal politically correct elite were hinged upon the very existence of SKYNET, like human embryos used as batteries by the nefarious robot legions of *The Matrix*. It all made sense.

The next day he awoke with boisterous visions of the world following T-Minus Clownbaby. Bartek envisioned their mug shots on telephone polls, she joining his grindcore band Sasquatch Agnostic as a 2nd vocalist and performing on a flatbed truck for the public through Capitol Hill, U-District & beyond. Clownbaby was coming, and her anthem was "*Mars, The Bringer of War.*"

The same group tripped again in mass, yet afterwards the consensus was they were on drugs and not some titanic spiritual quest. They grew concerned with Bartek's obsession to "psychedelically fight" Seattle block by block.

As with any mushroom trip, consolidating a definite plan is difficult because simply walking from one block to the next is like battling a litany of unseen forces. Every few paces conceals its own "mini boss," like a stooge villain ramping up to the larger baddie in a video game. Real or imaginary, Bartek wanted to clear them all.

As is why Quixxxote broke away from this new punk rocker family and started tripping alone. Following his last freak-out with the group, the overall impression left upon him was that he was a journalist. He was mentally spit out with neurons rearranged into a sharp, cunning direction – he was still a reporter, and more then ever solidified in his quest to unveil the greater truth.

He could have stopped right there, but the mad scientist in him couldn't refuse the magick potion of derangement. He'd allowed himself to tumble down the slippery slope of incorrigible habit…

The first time he headed out alone on these bohemian expeditions of mini-boss combat he stuck to his research. Even if the drug was unpredictable, he knew his standard responses.

What better a way to ease into the Amazonian grip then going to the movies? He could entrap himself in the theater, where no police would come 'cause he was a consumer & paid to be there. It was the best way to avoid police while tripping – so long as you were shopping, you were doing what you were "supposed to do."

Still, he never tried to sit through a movie at a multiplex cinema. His pick was the freshly released *Iron Man.* Perhaps he'd come out feeling like a superhero, melded together through alchemical magicianry of both Stark's machinery and Black Sabbath's enigmatic figure of elusive depression and revenge. He purchased his ticket in advance, ate the goods, then went for a stroll.

Bartek eased into his psychedelic people watching from a city bench. As the workers left their employment for the long trek home, he felt cleansed in that he did not lead their lives. Would they all jump in his heavy boots of lead if given the chance?

He envisioned himself as janitor of the nearby skyscraper. He lost himself in his fabricated work schedule, donating specific hours to carpet scrubbing, floor mopping, trash can bleaching. He caught himself rising from the bench to apply for the job, because he more then anyone could wax those floors with perfection. With 3 steps forward he caught what he was doing, then roared with laughter.

Pedestrians looked at him strangely, as did some cops, and Bartek wandered into the streams of humans rushing up the boulevards. He used the toilet of a video arcade which was so heavy with bings & dings & flashing lights he'd thought he was in Vegas. In the gamer room kids dumped endless quarters into machines that sucked their life like smiling mini-bosses of SKYNET.

Our vortexed anti-hero returned to the streets, slipping down a flight of concrete stairs into the underground bus terminal. A huge surrealistic mosaic of indeterminate shapes moved around like blobs of color. In one of them he caught sight of Benito Mussolini's pronounced chin and that shaved block of a head.

Bartek sat upon a subterranean bench and stared at it, imagining a dinner conversation with the ghost of Mussolini. They were exchanging info on the creation and structure of the modern nation state as they ate a fine meal at a lengthy dinner table.

Suddenly, Bartek realized that he had no interest being around this fascist. How did he slink from superhero anticipation to totalitarian dictatorship? As if by magic the vision altered – Bartek was now in the bedroom of his youth, with Musso on the edge of his bed. His mother entered and like a fiery Irish woman scolded her son for his rotten company: *"Why are you hanging out with that loser!"*

She began swiping at Benito's rectangular chin with a broom: *"Get out of here you no-good!"* Mussolini sighed, accepting his eternal damnation. *"Oh well, I guess I'll just go get hung up on hooks and beaten with shoes again."*

The tyrant stood up and opened Bartek's closet which revealed a black & white living news reel – scores of Italians waited to beat him to death – a scene he was cursed to repeat for all eternity. His mom slammed the closet door on the doomed autocrat: *"Bring home any more scumbags like that and you're grounded mister!"*

Bartek erupted with laughter, realizing again he was just staring at the mural. Another splotch of the moving paint looked like the head of a missile, and he began to see all of George W. Bush's cabinet members in its amorphous collision.

He saw the Iraq war in all its ugliness; the buses picking people up were transports to Abu Gharib where they would be raped by nightsticks, handcuffed naked in piles, water-boarded, electrocuted & attacked by dogs. And he again saw himself in the painting, yet at a table with the Bush administration. Bartek recoiled in horror – anything to get away from Rumsfeld, Cheney & Condi!

He zoomed up the steps, leaving scores of Taliban below. He began his trek back to the comic movie which would be starting any moment at the shopping mall.

He questioned that if the Iraq invasion didn't bring about the unrest needed to incite his anarchic "Park World" uprising, what would? How many would die before the masses went to the street?

The picture started, and Bartek had thrown his socks in the trash. For whatever reason, his first impulse was always to ditch them. He was sweating heavy & felt like the middle of an accordion as the walls stretched to & fro. He was so happy to be away from the foul President Bush and his Arab bloodbath.

The silver-screen lit up and Tony Stark was an unlikable egomaniac. Even in his drugged state, Bartek realized this was probably to show a future leap of character development. But after 20 minutes of fast talking, billionaire golden boy BS, he wanted to build a robot suit just to pummel Stark. Still, at least he wasn't in Abu Gharib or consorting with Cheney.

And then Stark flew to Afghanistan to sell high-tech weapons to mercenaries. Was Downey Junior toying with him? *Of any continental point, did he have to choose that opium-riddled desert?*

Suddenly, Stark was captured by Taliban fighters! And held prisoner in a mountain cave & tortured by al Qaeda for the next 30 minutes! Bartek was petrified! *Why this?!? Of all plot lines??* Would he too be black-bagged by Islamo-Fascists?

He watched in empathetic horror as Iron Man replaced his heart with a makeshift magnetic battery in a dank cave to prevent the shrapnel lodged in his heart from killing him. *Woe was him!*

Things of course swung around more positively at the films climax. By end credits, he was so wrapped up in the story he was ready to fly a rocket suit & fight villainy like a champ. But as he re-entered the darkened Seattle streets, he'd no money or robot war suit.

He jumped on the bus and headed home; the Puget glistened with sparkles of the luminous moon. The city looked a mess of steel tendrils, concrete giants & wily vegetation – vines crawling up marble as if the post-apocalyptic New York of *Omega Man*. Never had the metropolis seemed so pulsating, as if an organism.

With the trip winding down, Bartek head for the park where his punk friends tripped only a few weeks prior. He went right for "Witches Cove," but the magic had vanished in lieu of empty potato chip bags and shredded strands of nasty toilet paper where a homeless man must have emptied his bowel.

In the distance he heard mass laughing. In the field lay a basketball court, but it was filled with people. He approached them like Sherlock Holmes, pretending he had a smoking pipe & rubbing a curious finger beneath his chin. There were 30 people huddled on the blacktop, all of them in black spandex with turtlenecks, drinking martinis, gabbing drunkenly, totally ignoring him.

Bartek thought that nihilists from *The Big Lebowski* had sprouted from the blacktop like plants – their legs were attached to the court. He encircled them a number of times as they ignored him.

He returned home, and the trip broke. Those people were not nihilist plant humans, but the symphony of a local Academy having a party after a gig. He tried to organize what had happened over the past few hours, but as with any trip once the drug-induced hypnosis wears off it's as waking from a dream. He was no longer a journalist but a mad scientist. And he'd never hang out with Mussolini again.

He continued to trip by himself over the weeks – wandering the night, muttering *"I want chocolate on mah' face"* devouring M&M's & Reese's Pieces. Cackling, he would laugh at his pathetic cataclysm with Miss 3 & mumble *"T-Minus Clownbaby"* over & over.

Weirder the psilocybin adventures became until one day, in precautionary morality, the Amazonian dealer pretended he was out of stock and would be for the rest of the summer.

He went home begrudged & sat at the kitchen table. It was quiet in the ramshackle house of college students. None of them hung out together, and it seemed a fragile truce.

One of them, a friendly gay man, came up shakily. He too had been eating quite a few shrooms but was pulling back from the psychedelic abyss. *"Here, take this from me – stuff scares the shit out of me."* And he bestowed upon our lunar maniac an overflowing bag of the most potent Salvia Divanorum known to man.

The next day Bartek returned to the punk house where his friends had a pound of marijuana trim. They'd been making cupcakes, cookies, frosted cakes of ganja supremacy – the dining table was stacked; sluggishly they moved about the house in a trance. He unveiled the bag of Salvia – *no one would touch it.*

Bartek began shoving weed cake in his mouth, and it was not long before he floated above the carpet. The group exchanged stories of Divanorum horror. This drug was bad trip central. In the history of science, no one understood how or why it worked. It grew on one mountain in Mexico, and was used by shamans to speak to ghosts.

In the ancient days, it was turned to paste & smothered over the body of the spiritually wounded, producing intense visions like a gnarly peyote. Today it was dried & smoked – something the shamans never thought to do (*or had and banned*). The tripping effect lasted about 30 seconds to a minute of absolute black-out and mental transportation to some other realm.

All the stories were terrifying or utterly bizarre. People would be launched into another dimension or live others lives as if body hopping through the space-time continuum.

One guy they knew had taken a rip, then POOF he was a chubby 11 year old in the early 1980's waking up for breakfast with the family, then driving with them to an amusement park. While standing in line for a rollercoaster the fat kid looked up at the height of the ride, and felt scared. Then the transported one woke up – still in his car, head on the dashboard, drooling on himself.

Another guy went into it cocky as a pit fighter against a twig man. He was immediately surrounded and attacked by red-faced Japanese shogun demons for what seemed an eternity.

Another saw a jester rip off from the wall and do a dance. Another went into the void of a black hole and had to reconstruct himself atom by atom so he could wake back up.

One guy was stuck on a giant typewriter in which he saw on the sheet words he could not read but knew they were codified secrets of the universe – *then a typing prong smacked to crush him.*

Another guy was transported to an alien world of gold, and there he stayed for a million years. The impact was so powerful once he came out of it he began learning guitar, drums & bass to create a double album just to explain – *never having picked up an instrument*.

Even Clownbaby was terrified of them. She had ate LSD hundreds of times, shrooms endlessly, mescaline, peyote even – but Salvia scared the shit out of her. The world turned into rubber, everyone's lips into hot dogs, and the only thing she could say, over & over: "*dip dip Spaulding dip.*"

Bartek sat on a bean bag in front of the TV. The program was about pre-Cambrian life, a Discovery channel segment made in CGI about life evolving from giant water scorpions and submersed mega-cockroaches, monster crocodiles and jellyfish the size of whales.

It was a nasty weird thing to lay as a base level for a trip, but stoned as he was from hash frosting he could care less. He took a Salvia rip from the bong, held it in, and waited for the effect.

Immediately he was sucked back into a cavernous hole, as if the center of a quasar had lassoed him. Like a wormhole ripped in time he was vacuum sucked towards an abyss.

As he lost conception of his own body he felt only one thing – the demonic black hand of Leviathan grabbing at his soul as if Chernabog. There was one prominent phrase *felt* from the demon lurking behind the wall of Salvia: "*We got you now motherfucker!!!*"

Suddenly the spell broke, and the black hole dissipated – it simply was not a large enough toke to take him down the rabbit hole. Bartek opened his eyes wide, back to computer animated insect evolution. He looked to the large bag of dried green and swore it off. Whatever it was that was down there could just stay there forever.

All of these mad trips swirled about his brain as he now walked away from that ascending liquid pyramid at Cal Anderson, having begged "Park World" to devour his soul. He put on headphones and got lost in the new Nine Inch Nails album "Ghosts," letting the music instinctively guide him.

Halfway through Disc One, the music went notably dark – bad trip land started brewing. He ripped the music from his ears and now construction crews were crushing pavement with jackhammers & cement trucks were loudly mixing another slab of Seattle. Like an egg sack, the spinning metal containment unit was like a womb. It seemed like the queen of an ant colony pumping out gray larvae.

Unnerved, Bartek left & approached a large tree which cast a dark shadow. He was relieved thinking this was sister fauna of Witches Cove – and there was a figure lurking beneath its shade. He thought perhaps it was a magical faerie, maybe a helpful ogre.

He walked up to the shadowy silhouette which came into the sunlight. It was instead a very fat black woman, a crackhead with drugged-out eyes, moving strangely as if having a twisted spine.

"*Hey-eee-yaay! You got a dolla for da bus?!?*" Bartek just wanted out – right downtown where everything made sense. "*I'll buy you a ticket, just show me how to get outta here!*" She led him to a shelter, and he defensively got in its corner. As he looked around, he'd stumbled into a hostile black ghetto – bad vibes were all around.

With his scraggly green mohawk, camouflage shorts and army boots, he stuck out like a sore thumb. Angry looking teenagers with cornrows were staring him down, encircling the bus stop. The air was hot and blasting the stench of pollution and car exhaust.

A few pretty young black girls were in the nearby parking lot of a convenience store, and a middle aged black man pulled up his Cadillac and parked it with the motor running in the middle of the lot. He got out like a pedophile and started hitting on them, but all they were saying was *"buh-buh-hub-hub-buh."*

Cars were honking, construction crews hollering. Everything was bad news. In nervousness, not wanting to but knowing he had to, he turned to the cracked out, fat lady who brought him there.

In her spandex pants crinkled from cellulite ripples, and her sweat-stained shirt, she gave him insano crack eyes. She pierced into his soul, doing this weird dancing jig like she was riding an exercise bike in the living room.

With all her chub blubbering with her voice, she said in a loud, black, over-the-top tone: *"If it gets any hotter out here I'm-ma-gonna-get-a-BUTT-NAAAAAAY-KED."*

Bartek wanted to scream. The bus pulled up as the cornrow kids where talking smack, trying to get him to fight them. He climbed aboard & made it downtown where he felt again entrapped by steel tentacles and dwarfed by skyscrapers. He jolted off the bus.

Now he wandered by the Space Needle alone, through the emptied carnival grounds where dead rides sat unused & clown images were giant, plastic grinning heads. Back to the world of Clownbaby – this would assuredly be their stomping grounds.

That they could hang with all their fellow clowns in a bizarre realm that could equally have been a hideout for The Joker when avoiding Batman's wraith. Bartek looked for signs of Skinner or any of their San Diego crew who would have gobbled up this setting, But he was alone, and with no company but Trent Reznor.

After a slow wind-down & blast of Meshuggah, Bartek got home. He cleaned his room & looked in the mirror, attempting to sort out the long run of psychedelic mayhem. He'd left parts of himself behind, but had gained more then he knew how to compute. "Park World" was etched on his soul, and he had his vision.

Stone Golem Babycakes

With the eyes of a Calico & a hurricane of charisma, the hottest woman on earth now sat on his porch ledge. Like a wormhole tearing through the fabric of the universe, the nexus of intoxicating madness was like a summoned Djinn.

With one leg scrunched Indian style and the other's knee pointed upwards to the heavens – with her white & red polka dot dress and mess of scarfs wrapped about her tiny physique – she appeared the Cheshire of the labyrinth.

Since picking her up from the Greyhound, she had prattled on with her hypnotic commentary in the backseat of his friend's car – the intensity of which browbeat him into submission. Bartek struggled to play it cool, to keep the dialogue moving, luckily bolstered by the drivers interjections.

The man at the wheel was one of the punks he'd trip with that summer – same who keeled over in laughter from "T-Minus Clownbaby." He, like the rest, weren't sure if she existed, and had a sharp curiosity to peek the vaporous legend of Bartekian mythology.

They sat in the bus depot waiting room, watching that same big institutional clock tick away to midnight. He was avenging the horrible u-turn of 3, mind jumping between San Diego & now.

This time, there would be no roach-infested house of crusty punks; no dangerous too-soon fusion at an apocalyptic motel or jealous ex-boyfriends sowing discord – no meth zombie swarms or constant flashing sirens, no pin-impaled voodoo doll.

Bartek learned his lessons & devoted unlimited funds to make it smooth; he'd a week-long plan to spoil her senseless – a 3 day hiatus from work, the finest dining, the most amusing club life & best shows. He had his friends on stand-by for any kind of adventure she wanted – and 2 tickets to *The Dark Knight* at IMAX.

He picked up some of the finest weed the Northwest had to offer, $50 sack of glorious mushrooms and 2 pills of the purest, most exquisite MDMA. Not that he'd even touched it in years – he just knew that it would make them talk. Ecstasy was insurance against the extreme intimidation she bestowed. All he had to do was get her to Cal Anderson & kick-start a glorious e-bond into the magick of Capitol Hill. There was no way it could go wrong.

But now that his friend had driven off, the perpetually awkward house of college students was dead quiet. She was eating him alive with her eyes, and he was stumbling. The man who was legendary in juggernaut vocabulary found himself speechless. Like a reverse Medusa, she had frozen him with incomparable hotness.

The haze of 9 months darkness still choked him, and it was through that fog of awfulness that he viewed her. Like the periscope of an adrift submarine that's engines had been damaged in a naval firefight, he had no ability to thrust his rudders forward.

He had to say something – *anything* – not just lurch with muffled eyes. His first instinct was to bust out the marijuana, which he knew she'd appreciate having been on the Greyhound 18 hours. He himself had stayed sober all day, trying to ensure his wits be razor-sharp for this tyrant of fascination.

As he looked upon her, his hands were shaky – in this long void of isolation, all he wanted was to curl up into her arms. To hold onto her & absorb her – to appreciate her as no man ever had. All her stories of mentally abusing losers – these stories only existed 'cause he'd never crossed paths with her.

He took a toke off the weed which was so heavily crystallized it looked like sugar had been scooped into the bag; she she took a puff. He was blasted by it's amnesia – very much the sort of strain he referred to as "retard weed." Instant space cadet, the haziest kind of THC delight that convinces a grown man to stare at an inanimate object for half an hour.

The weed made him an instant dope, yet made her speak quicker & more brilliantly. She spatted off her tale of chatting to an older lesbian lady on the bus, that she said go right for Capitol Hill.

Clownbaby wanted to go right for the gay scene, and Bartek hit a brick wall. He'd always been nervous in that environment, and had only been in a gay bar once or twice. It took years to beat his parental conditioning, and even if he dropped any hostility he was still nervous. Things seemed to take a sharp, unspoken turn wrong.

In the kitchen he poured some fruit juice. He looked her in the eyes, feeling like a mental patient that had been locked in a rubber room alone for months. In a jittery voice he said: "*I've been alone here a long time... I'm sorry... I'm really happy you're here*." And he gave a faint, cracked smile, which made her eyes dim more.

They entered his threadbare, minimalistic room with its single mattress and cardboard boxes holding what little items he had. They sat down, smoked more heavy-duty pot; he killed the lights and they curled up. He made no attempt to overstep any boundaries.

He had drifted his hand from the side of her stomach to the softness of her thigh to show he appreciated her there, even if it was awkward. She grabbed his hand & pulled it to the center of her chest, clasped with tiny hands. She cuddled into him & they drifted off.

With the silver moonlight softening the subterranean room, he knew he could *really sleep* for the first since San Diego. Yet slumber meant nothing as it would only deprive his time with her. The magic muse was present, like a ghost materialized from another realm. For the first time since 2007 perhaps, he understood the ever-slipping intensity of each minute.

So it is with little foresight to understand why he stayed up longer then he should have, just to watch her breath gracefully. He did not want to let her go, and he could not allow himself to take this moment for granted.

In his cinematic mind he could only visualize the robot boy of *A.I.* reunited with his cloned mother. Bartek smiled, finally content, finally having caught up with himself in the mire of Seattle's rugged trajectory. And he soon drifted off as well.

They awoke with a slow rise, both at ease with one another. As she slipped into the shower, he hung over the side of the bedding. He felt a great earth-shattering rant building up inside of him, a growing clarity & sharpness. The sun was pouring in, the summer in full.

Tonight they'd see the new Batman film. At this point it had been in the theaters 3 weeks. Being who he was, it was a staggering feat of discipline he managed denying this cinematic impulse. He had to wait for Clownbaby.

Even as everyone on the street were raving about it, he put his fingers in his ears. Even as it was on every magazine, flickering TV & website banner – he refused to look at one image.

All he knew is that people kept looking at him funny, and telling him he really should go watch what Ledger had done with the character before it essentially drove him mad & led to his early, unfortunate demise.

Since making plans with Clownbaby to see it, he held strong. And that he hid in a basement avoiding every female in Seattle because if he hooked up with anyone Clownbaby would never come giving the greatest "What If?" of his life.

That at 27 years of age Ryan Bartek could ignore this new Batman film, not start his lifelong dream band, refuse to go on tour when he could have gone anywhere, ignore his peak as a world famous metal journalist and go absolutely celibate as not to wreck the one shot he he had with this woman – this only underlines the fanatic extremes he was willing to endure. Bartek was hopelessly, sincerely, madly in love – convinced he'd discovered his one true soul mate of the Detroit labyrinth.

Clownbaby came back and sat down. Everything was peachy, even if he was still stumbling a little with awkward lines. To any other human, he'd speak lightning text. Looking upon her, it was as if a giant entered his room.

They gathered their belongings as to head towards a fanciful lunch, and again turned to the skunky ganja which showered crystals as if a ripped bag of sugar. Within moments its sheer power had again mutated him into a withdrawn dope.

The pair went to eat Chinese food. She kept rambling, yet he found himself frozen. The intense pressure of her beauty stifled him. Inside the restaurant – his favored oriental cuisine where he often daydreamed of dining with her – his engine picked up no steam.

The inherent sleepiness his body was weighty; for days he'd pushed it too hard, nervously anticipating her arrival, only sleeping 4 hours a night of tossing/turning. Last night had deprived him even more horsepower in not wanting to let the moment go. The hot tea & heavy MSG of the meal further enacted the languidness.

As the meal reached its end, and he could barely find words, she kept looking to the side, off into space, as if bored by him and wondering why she was even there. He knew he had to assert himself, but this monolith of personality was binding. After all, she still had spent so little time with him and barely glimpsed his nature.

He began cursing himself – he should've brought her right to his group of friends instead of trying to keep her maintained in isolated coupling. He needed that extra push of confidence that could only come from sympathetic wing-men.

This almost didn't happen. Only a week ago, she had vanished. For months they were negotiating on when she would visit, but when the moment arrived, she was gone. No returns of his emails or texts – she hadn't logged into her MySpace for weeks. He began to crumble.

Clownbaby eventually left a late night drunken message saying she wouldn't be able to make it. Instead of heading to Seattle for vacation, she'd taken an impulsive flight to Long Beach to visit her aunt. Her relative had gone elsewhere, leaving her alone in a beach house, drunk, playing accordion for the crashing waves – and she was considering staying there & never returning to Michigan.

It was a tug of war to get her to budge – he succeeded in what might amount to a low-level semi-guilt trip. He realized afterwards that he felt & perhaps sounded like some angry dad berating his loopy, stubborn child into doing something. Bartek did not like this feeling, and had apologized for it.

After that back-and-forth, the human junk pile of desperation was on edge. Something about this general situation broke him. He still wanted to be with her more then anything, but already their mutual craziness were inherently pushing each others buttons. All he needed to do was get her there and get her to Capitol Hill.

Since it was his only shot at bringing her up, and the ticket needed to be purchased that day, he had to dish out $400 – nearly everything in his "stability fund." He was sacrificing the musical equipment he needed to start his lifelong dream band in Seattle.

For her to take the Greyhound itself was very important, because it was the keystone of his wild plan to entice her into wider travels via bus. To a degree, he wanted to repeat his massive USA travel with her.

As he looked at her in person though, slowly eating stir fry, he knew he should've just flown her out. He should've bought nice bed sheets & cosmetically shielded the reality of his minimalistic existence. He didn't look like someone with any normal living plan – his habitat was that of a thread-bare transient.

Suddenly Clownbaby spoke up and dropped her chop-sticks, sharply & nervously saying with the pointed grace of an acid flashback blast: "*I don't like Chinese food – I feel like I'm eating kitties.*" Bartek had an internal slither of Black Lava, which she sensed. He didn't need to speak up – she just knew it was there.

And as he looked up to her, she was spiritually pulling away from him. She seemed a fragile vessel super-glued together and rising with steam that loosened the cracks.

With a shaky twitch he saw a glimpse of fright, and then both of them simultaneously honed their eyesight & nervous energy at the tea-pot in the middle of the table. And by itself, the tea pot slid across the surface.

Her eyes grew wide and fearful, not believing what she witnessed. Bartek took a slow inhale, then set down his fork. He looked up and calmly questioned: "*Was that me or you?*"

Like a woman who'd just seen the visage of a ghost – with hair on end and goosebumps flared – her soft, cold eyes turned again to his: "*I think that was you.*"

She was frightened of him, as they always were. Clownbaby was a weird witchy woman, or thought herself as such. But while she played those empty games, he himself knew he was cursed.

Looking down at his food and slowly stabbing at it with an emotionless fork, he wistfully muttered: *"It happens... You'll see."* She didn't know what to say, and mechanically began eating her kitty stir fry until the plate was clean.

They returned to his ephemeral home after a silent walk. The pot had tapered off into that drab, lazy slowness that comes at the end of the high. They sat on the bed without saying much of anything, then cat-napped for an hour.

They now waited in the long snake of a line at the cinema. For 3 weeks, *The Dark Knight* had been sold out. The patient crowd were equal parts excited newbies and those who'd already witnessed the spectacle and were rapidly turning the movie into a cultish *Rocky Horror*. After all, Bartek wasn't the only one of his generation eternally blown away by Burton's old school triumph, nor the only young man warped by Nicholson & Hamill.

Sensing the dark creation which would inevitably occur if they were to eat mushrooms as planned, Clownbaby put a stop to his compulsion. She knew he'd already gone to a weird place in his leap of psilocybin that summer, and she didn't want loosen the screw.

She had a romantic infatuation with villains, especially the most psychotic and freakish ones. She very much looked at Bartek as if he were The Joker, and he looked at her as if his skewed, real world version of that Harley character. But Bartek was not The Joker – he thought himself as a different character.

Researching villains & examining their roots, he was a wearer of masks. He loved the magickal will to summon them as totems. Like a human chameleon, he could summon what they represented & live their symbolism.

Like a zany alchemist, he could summon the fast-talking, conscience-warping John Milton, the swagger of Walken's Gabriel, the madness of many antagonists.

Clownbaby herself was a deluge of masks – like Bartek, she was anyone who "came to the door" at any given time. And for every mask she wore, Bartek had a companion. Yet when he would see that mask in her, his would shatter. Stupefied, he'd stare blankly.

Clownbaby loved her masks so much she had a plaster cast of Christopher Walken in *The Prophecy* and would often kiss it goodnight. Gabriel was her handsome angel, protecting her sleep.

She was wise enough to realize the leap into crazy land he'd take if sitting through this Batman flick with a stomach of fungus. She convinced them to wait for afterwards – and he'd ground up two eighths each for easy drinking with orange juice.

The lights went down, and the show went on. And there, up on the screen, was everything he had become. Heath Ledger was not playing The Joker – he was the embodiment of the fiery depths which the mega-Aries descends at the anarchist zenith of a kinghell mushroom peak. He was that place personified, hitting the spike – and wanting to drag everyone there with him by any means necessary as to engulf the whole of civilization.

To his deepest primordial Hyde, the Black Lava was manifested on screen. The actor & he both had the same birthday; physically, they could've been siblings. Even out of makeup, they moved the same. And on mushrooms, they really moved the same.

The same facial ticks, the same watery movement, hatred of authority, money, fathers & schemers; the identical sadist humor, fascination of knives & fanatic infatuation with chaos, and obsessively cutting the tags off all their clothing.

Many call it egomania, but no – it was submission to the purification of mocking flame, and in this depraved fire one no longer possesses an ego for the ego *becomes* the living incineration...

The credits rolled & they left the theater quietly, walking to the bus. The film had blown his mind & when a movie is that good, it transports one to another dimension so entirely that once it ends one is left totally disoriented.

As a cinema junkie, he'd no choice but to slowly untangle & process it all. The fact that Clownbaby was back in normal world so fast proved she'd already seen it. Blindsided by film, he wasn't able to think clearly. He knew he should just take her to Capitol Hill, but that was for tomorrow – and he'd be going all out on it, spoiling her ridiculous. For now, the shrooms were burning a hole in his pocket.

They hopped on a bus and headed to the park of his many summer trips, with it's basketball court of nihilist German bean sprouts & it's magickal terrain with Witches Cove. All the punk rock guys had moved from that nearby house and he didn't know anyone in the area anymore, only because he essentially hid from humanity as not to deflate the visitation now occurring.

He knew he should say something to her on that bus ride, anything, but his mind was in a hundred places. With unfocused eyes he watched the architecture of Seattle's rampant gentrification whiz by from the plate glass window. All he could concentrate on was the inevitable impact of this Joker on pop culture.

It was not the hodge-podge of dangerous psychiatric drugs or totalitarian character acting which killed Heath Ledger – it was submission to The Black Lava. And through it's manifestation in the victim of Ledger the sadistic, hypnotic blob was laughing from the abyss through his tragic casualty.

His performance was doing its bidding from the grave, and would sow its seeds like a curse on celluloid. Because no matter how humanity might evolve, everyone will always love a great film. This one would stick around forever.

With all of this – plus the Joker tattoo on Bartek's arm – he instantly understood in the most profound global sense that no woman would ever fuck him again. From hereon, they'd assume he was a lame CosPlay fools pretending he was Clown Prince of Crime.

For the next 5 years – the physical peak of his adult life – there would be an infinite horde of idiot men horridly acting it out, ruining it all for him. No intelligent woman would dare touch him.

Even if they did, they'd all be fruit-loops wanting to be Harley – the sort of maniacs writing flirtatious letters to Charles Manson in prison, 'cause Manson, like Joker, was total submission to the twisted, brutal realm of dark psychedelia.

"The Joke" was that Joker was constantly trying to kill Harley – she just would never die. Torturing her emotions was part of a punch-line. She was adorable, innocent & depraved, hopelessly in love – but Joker did not care. He didn't need her.

If there was no laugh to be made out of humiliating or degrading her, then he'd just shoot bullets at her, squirt burning corrosive acid or chuck her out a high-rise window. But she'd always dodge the acid, zoom away from the hollow point in the nick of time or land in a dumpster instead of splatting on pavement.

Even though Bartek identified with the inmates of Arkham in their totem symbolism – just as the Greek's humanized their gods on Olympus – he never thought of himself as The Joker. He liked to wear the mask, flash the tattoo to throw people off – but this was not his secret supervillain identity (*because every human who read too many comic books has one, and if they don't, then they're lying*).

Bartek totally had a crush on Harley since 6th grade, but what he really wanted was to thieve her from this brutal psychopath. He wanted to demonstrate that he was the real kingpin of Gotham's underworld, the real boss hog of Arkham – and a way more significant clown by every stretch of the imagination.

Because no matter what he was, he was always foremost a clown. And the joke was that he was after Dr. Harleen Quinzel, the psychologist herself. He sought out the nutty girl who in real life convinced herself she was Harley, and in real life he'd steal her.

Just like the one sitting right next to him, his glorious Clownbaby, perhaps the only woman on Earth who would seriously be with him now that this movie had circulated mass consciousness – thus increasing the all-or-nothing stakes of this shaky date desperately in need of a defibrillator...

They were alone at Meridian Park; everything was dark, quiet, still. She was more at ease, and they smoked some more of the brain-numbing pot he'd acquired before downing the shrooms with OJ. Their moderate trip was more underneath then overpowering as they wandered faintly betwixt the flora.

They sat down on the grass, laid beneath the stars; she stared at him and he at her. She was smiling, happy. She kept speaking happily and he felt like they were talking on the phone, with her crazy voice in his ear as if he was resting on his bed.

He was again intoxicated by her beauty, lost in her facial features as always. He pulled himself up and curled into a Indian style squat, listening to her prattle. He closed his eyes, yet all he could see was Joker's shadowy face, smudged with makeup, in the interrogation room. But it was Ledger looking right at him, smiling from the other side of death, wholly consumed by Black Lava.

But then came the moment where he had to say something, anything. The entire scene wailed him like Déjà Vu – he had dreamt this moment, like the gooey Oreo filling middle of his life – this terrible nightmare of this exact drooping, dripping mushroom-headed park scene. Of being in harmony and then this woman running from him like a monster.

He feared this somehow come next if he said the wrong thing – or perhaps it was the alternate reality of this night side by side, where they had ate 'shrooms before seeing *The Dark Knight* and it had warped him as it may have.

In his forgotten dream of premonition there was an evil Joker on some huge screen that seemed like almost an in-door drive-in [hence the Imax] – that smudged face in the dark that Gordon interrogates. And he knew that this actor had gone mad in real life and died thinking he was The Joker. And he was there with some girl, some date he was extremely nervous with.

But in the dream, the moment where Gordon and Joker are alone in the dark, explaining Dent had been kidnapped – Bartek remembered thinking in intense tripness that any moment Scarecrow or Two-Face would appear – and at this point the girl, lost in some head-trip of her own, would totally freak-out in the theater. She woulds convince herself that he was in fact this evil new Joker, that she had to get away from him at any cost.

And they would end up in Seattle, downtown, and she would think he really was him, and the madness would throw them both over them brink in some awful, hideous, soul-scarring bad trip.

POP – he snapped out of the dark scenario. He was still at Meridian Park, and they were looking at stars. Some awful tragedy had been avoid, but he still had to fix the messiness.

She asked him something direct. Like a man whose soul was spent, he broke off from his illusory death stare with Joker & looked right at her: *"That was a really good movie."*

She again rolled her eyes with a spiritual sigh, and he started to question her about when she came out of the closet. How her family reacted, her friends, the background tale. She talked a bit about it, but with the feeling of a straight guy digging at something possibly sexual or creepy in nature. He couldn't just spit it out.

They went back to the house, and the trip wore off. He was feeling much better, as if the entire brick wall of the past day had melted. She caught this change in him, even though she was hammering away text messages on her cell. He indubitably saw that she was priming her resources in order to make an early exit.

Bartek seized on it, and started showing her all the old books & magazines he collected from free boxes that summer – all of the wacky clippings he intended to make mosaics with alongside her.

He began showing her stuff on the computer, different writings, getting her attention again. The next day was "do or die." They went to sleep soon after, but she did not cuddle into him. She slept apart, and from his inches distance he watched her doze off. Tomorrow everything would be alright – all he needed was sleep.

He awoke the next morning; she'd already showered, had her things packed & was talking on the phone pacing around the backyard (just as he always did, in an identical circle). He knew he had to confront her – it was his last chance.

The strange one, the frightened angel, this fledgling of a new order & verbal truncator of misshapen nouns was ready to flee. Her eyes had returned to their cold, neutral form; she clicked off her cell.

She need not say a word, because he read the expression all too noticeably. It would be that same cut-throat logic that would grow on him – "*if it ain't workin', cut the fuckin' chord & move on.*"

With one shaky hand he reached out for a calm pause, then grew steady. With a quick inhale, he decompressed. He had her full attention. This part of him she understood, because she too often copycatted it: "*Just wait, please... You intimidate the living shit out of me. At any other point in life, I can rant a mile a minute. I've just been really nervous about all this because I wanted it to go right, and we got way too stoned, and I was way too tired. I know you don't think it's possible, but we have so many endless overlapping psychological everything's & quirks & speech patterns & modes of thinking & just everything. Please, it's ok – I don't even care about any kind of romance or sex or anything; I just like you as a person and that's why I brought you out here. If you want to leave, if you really want out, I'm sure there's a bus later tonight. Please just let me take you to Capitol Hill. We can just walk around and look at stuff and eat something other then kitties and sit at the park and no anything weird. That room in there – that's not me. It's just some place. Please just let me take you to Capitol Hill.*"

Her eyes morphed back to affectionate gleam. She kind of looked to the side, looked at her phone. He had her again: "*Remember, I said I had you a present? Here, come...*"

She sat down on the bed. Things were calm. He pulled out the big, fat ecstasy pills & she recoiled in anger and disgust. Truth was he didn't even do MDMA – he just sought the crutch to break the ice. It was the only thing he could think of to overcome this Medusa of hotness. She seemed to be into it, at least he thought.

Clownbaby snapped – incensed he only wanted to do drugs. She coldly declared she'd been a massive heroin addict. This is why they never met – heroin ate her alive, for years.

She had only in the past year recovered. All that time, all those missed opportunities where if he'd been there... He'd failed her in a million "could've-beens," and he'd again failed her now.

The enigmatic human refrain of negative reverse propulsion demanded to leave immediately. All she wanted was to get away from him. Even as he waited in line at the bus with her, trying to calm the situation, she just wanted gone.

She who reverberates a deaf ear & tickles the callous of the broadcast arcane gave a false hug & went through the gates, never looking back. Ironically, paying the fee for early departure had made the tab of this one night Anticlimax Leviathan a solid $420.

Bartek went home, lucid & clear; he flushed the ecstasy tabs down the toilet, and felt the anxiety of The Big Date leave him. He smiled, realizing he could write Clownbaby all about it – *but then it sunk in that girl who just left was actually her*.

Over those 24 hours, he could barely comprehend that it was she in the flesh. His fanaticism towards the anti-social hermit-frenzy he'd enacted as not to fail this future date – Clownbaby had absurdly been the collateral damage of it as well.

Bartek blankly admitted defeat, knowing the reality would sink in tomorrow. He had a secret weapon though – a booby trap of the heart which would annihilate the foolish missteps of this shambling catastrophe. Before she walked out the door, he'd handed her a copy of *The Big Shiny Prison*. Only a handful had read it, and all summer he'd been mailing copies to find a publisher.

He was assured it'd pierce through her wall. As a lover, she sought the ultimate virtuoso – and she'd realize the staggering intensity of his passion. She would recognize the empire of possibilities available, and she would not only fall madly in love but agglutinate his crusade. All he had to do was wait.

For now, he comforted that he was intelligent & young enough to ensure his ability to go in any direction. And then, just for old times sake, he rang up Zelda. And just as they always did years before, he listened to her prattle on & on into the telephone receiver with that peculiar, clowny, happy little angel dialect.

The weeks passed & he heard not a word. His co-workers had grown estranged from him, as with all jobs. No matter where he went to make income, things would start well then he'd eventually be singled out from his inherent darkness. He would play up his faked normality to coalesce but at some point he would stop pretending.

It's not as if he caused a conflict, it was just the silent rage they detected in him and the dream world they didn't understand. They just knew at an instinctual animal level that he was deranged somehow, and this unnerved them unconditionally. They knew even as he played their faux-societal role that his thoughts were alien.

They knew he permanently existed in some separate realm, and his philosophical interjections would often unravel tiny keystones of their stability. Once they learned of his secret lone-wolf mad scientist shroom wanderings, they were completely freaked. These same people, ironically, would talk about all the LSD they gobbled in high school and how it was always so great.

It was the same nervous, disaffected attitude he received from the Seattleites in general, and especially the punk rock scene. He had tried to befriend people, but they always eyeballed him as a lurking stranger. Elements of views rubbed everyone the wrong way, and his quiet conflagration was ever irksome.

He'd drift in and out of bars listening in on conversation that he hoped to inject himself in, but all these people were living illusions he'd smashed, concerned with pop culture and record collecting, empty sex and decadence. In this new world of hope he was impossibly estranged & adrift...

Our longing sad-face turned to books & movies for solace – catching up on every great work that eluded him after a life of working full time. He stormed his way through a 100 books & films that year, fairly much living at the library. It was only after the 300+ page interview with Al Pacino that he decided it needed to stop.

Bartek went for a lonesome walk as the August wind carried a nasty chill. Life was already gearing up for fall, even midst these green trees. He walked by the church where he'd had that private moment of misery, back when living with the metal guys.

It was another one of the endless stormy, freezing, rain-soaked days. He felt so lost in those empty, drizzling street – and wandered inside one of Seattle's oldest churches to warm up. It was empty & medieval looking, with burning candles & stark ambiance. He hadn't been in a church since he was a kid, except when he pissed in a confession booth as a heavy metal teenager.

He sat on an oaken pew & stared at the giant cross above the altar. He remembered again Lisa's suicide, and had a flashback of her wake. Her molester father gave a speech to us all, in front of his dead child, lying through his teeth & crying, repeating over & over that he had no idea why she would have done this.

The immense terribleness of the scene replayed itself in his head, and Bartek sobbed. An old woman walked out a corridor and saw him there, perhaps thinking a resurgent relationship with god. But as she drifted by, she heard him muttering *"fuck you"* over & over to the giant cross on the cold, empty stage.

Now it was August, and Bartek walked by that very church knowing at least he'd abandoned that sadness there. He sat on a bench & felt chilly even under the blazing sun. He again asked himself how it had come to this.

He thought of San Diego, how those kids had worshiped him. He felt as Hallie Selassie must have when trying to dissuade the Rastafarians. Those punk kids had turned him into some legend – they'd literally been calling themselves "The Bartek Family."

True, their intentions were zany and more Adams Family then anything – but it was still unnerving to him. He wielded amazing power over them and ironically they turned on him because he refused to wield that very power. They wanted him to play leader, and he wanted them to lead themselves.

At some point, he just accepted it. He'd head off on adventures & come home to his children who were wide-eyed for the glorious revolution he was generating. It was never about him though – he wanted to empower their own noble revolutions.

But once he had chosen a mate, and their flimsy house of cards would crumble, they annihilated her. They killed his wife, his child, his dream, and they very much killed him.

And now this corpse-man shuffled through his ever-cracking delusion that it was somehow still 1993 in Seattle. And Clownbaby would never become the beating heart of this defunct, coldly gentrifying paradise.

Ryan headed to Scarecrow Video, the last of the VHS rental stores. It was a remnant to a cadaverous era, and this moment was its last belch. Within a few years, these places would be extinct. He wandered the aisles, but he had seen every last film that interested him. There was a satisfaction in this yet also an unconditional initiation as well, because he had no more succinct distractions to continue the frantic flight from himself.

He recalled the one movie that was always on the bucket list to rent since he was 7 years old but had never got around to. The one movie that was always beat out by something else, whether it be some *Road Warrior* knock-off or unwatchable zombie flick. He paid rental & returned to the ant-infested, temperamental college house.

He fired up the DVD player for 1978's Piranha – yet the very terrible-yet-charming epic registered no smile upon his glum face. The affection for such campy garbage had long dissolved.

Ryan picked up the remote & paused the image on a bikini-clad woman getting her legs ripped to shreds by mutant fish. In the still of the room, in the quiet of the night, Bartek nodded his head in acceptance. *He finally confronted the real problem.*

Bartek wrote a cautious few sentences to Clownbaby, as opposed to the mountains of nervous text he would formerly ship to her MySpace. He was scared to look at her profile, as she might have posted a picture with a new boyfriend.

Lo and behold it was her grinning on a toilet seat, holding a book wide open and reading intently. Bartek's heart soared – he took it as a silent nod that she'd been reading *The Big Shiny Prison*.

The next day her MySpace reply was sharp & indignant – she would be the one to contact him, not the other way around. His body quivered. He nervously wrote back an apology to which she softly responded – and then explained she was dating "Charles Manson."

Now, as his been stated, this oddball psychonaut loved her villains – she'd throw masks on people with freakish glee. Like Bartek, she'd listen to Charlie's acoustic records with the same fascination as Johnny Cash. Not that either of them supported Helter Skelter, but both had a special spot for street crazy hypnosis.

Bartek instantly knew exactly who she was talking about. He turned to ice, and his soul filled the room like an explosion of jelly. He at first struggled against it, thinking it too impossible an awful joke – *but it was absolutely true.*

But but but... NO! Bartek was the one with the literal "Family!" He was the one who escaped the grip of psychos wanting him to be a cult leader so he could find true romance with Clownbaby! This irony couldn't be happening!!

But it was true, all of it – she had hooked up with one of Bartek's secret nemesis, one of the fakest tight-pants indie rocker losers in all of Detroit! Like a punch to the face, like a tank treading over his skull, he remembered it all clearly.

And he thought it was his karmic doing – "Charles Manson" was literally in the book he gave her to win her heart!! *Is this where she discovered him!?!* Was this cosmic-comic revenge for peddling insincere schmucks of blow-hard crazy hyperbole on the public?!?

He'd met "Charles Manson" in the desert, randomly at a bar in New Mexico. Bartek was drinking alone, and in came this band on tour from Detroit – and they were playing this random bar not even on the schedule. They all knew who he was and wanted to hang out.

Bartek always used guys who were full of hot air and plugging corny bullshit as a means to expedite his own ideology so that he didn't have to be the one to say it. It was, as he phrased it: "*Barteknomics.*" Just like all those phony bologna extreme metal guys babbling Nietzsche, Occultism, what have you – he knew most were complete frauds. He used these people as a public springboard.

Simple plan – you take a cornball like fake Manson and throw them in the limelight saying all the fraudulent crap they do & then some 14 year old somewhere is gonna read it, turn it around & germinate some anarchist commune or insane activity – propaganda in motion, the journalist as puppet-master, etc.

So our beleaguered protagonist was now in the desert, running around the country setting up his illustrious Pan-Tribal web – which, of course, rooted back to the very real "Bartek Family." And Captain Phony, with his tight pants & ascot, immediately started greasing for press. Bartek told him of the travel book: "Yeah man, I've got a ton of metal bands coming out of the woodwork in every city." Shit Head replied: "*Oh, I fucking HAAAAATE that shit.*"

Bartek felt a blast of Black Lava; he envisioned GWAR piercing this turds innards with gauntlet spikes. Corporal Crap asks to wait a moment, then runs into the bathroom to frantically snort blow. He returns to have a coked out "pee-pee dance" conversation jittery from stardust, then starts apologizing for canceling a gig he'd booked with Bartek in 2005 because he'd fucked the girlfriend of the singer of the other band on the bill's wife and if he'd come to the show the guy would've put him in the hospital.

Bartek let the tape roll and then immediately – coked out of his mind and throwing his face into the recorder – douche-fuck starts this ridiculous rant. About how Manson is god and Manson is everything, his idol, his bands idol – all this silly, insincere gibberish. Fucky Fuckerson is looking like he's about to explode such as a kielbasa 10 minutes in the microwave.

So Doopy McDoodle is babbling on & on, obvious he doesn't know jack shit about Charles Manson. When Bartek grilled him on specifics he was totally aloof, like he got all his info from some cable TV special.

Like seriously, what the fuck does this guy know? He's never even heard the term "slippy" and he's degrading crustpunks, talking smack on communes?

He tried valiantly to convince Bartek that he supported Helter Skelter, then followed it up with: "*Yeah bro, the band started as a White Stripes rip-off band, 'cause we were trying to ride the wave to get big.*" Cause, you know, that's his idea of what rock and roll is, what sparked his passion. Then he talks of being proud of the Motor City, babbling Ford Motor Company awesomeness when he's never worked in one of those shit pits such as Bartek, never felt the hopelessness of what's actually happening.

Then he's like, "*Yeah bro, I run my own vintage clothing store.*" How satirical is that? You run a tight pants thrift shop by ransacking Value Village then selling used .30 cent t-shirts to indie rock scenesters at a 300%-900% mark up? *And you're pimping Charles Manson while you're doing it???*

Lamey MacStinkerson's onstage antics were weak & forced and the audience (*grizzled, punk rock DIY veterans*) were laughing at them, telling them to get the fuck off stage. They were all chuckling and looking at each other like "*who does this guy think he is?*" No one would clap after any song, and the bartenders scowled. Then Fucko starts insulting the crowd cause they don't "get it."

The man was so drastically full of shit he was seeping excrement from his pores. And now this sorry excuse for a toilet sponge was thieving the love of Bartek's life. Bartek wanted to unleash a keyboard frenzy, but he knew it would doom him.

He inhaled and exhaled, then asked what she thought of the book. She hadn't gotten very far; the font was too tiny and she had to squint too hard. Secondly, she'd dropped it accidentally. Since it had no page numbering or stapling, the thing had fallen completely out of order. She ended up just throwing the spaghetti mess away.

Everything was now on the line – if he fucked this up, she could very well be making clownbabies with this extremely lame motherfucker who knew damn well this woman was right for me and had no willpower to explain to her the reality of the heart.

He knew we were twins, and he only cared about sex. It was a fate so cruel in its abasement that it made Bartek want to ritualistically disembowel himself like a failed samurai.

He asked that he be able to write her a larger letter, and that no tension would be showcased. He knew that book would not be the one to "do it" and had something else in mind entirely. Bartek spent the next day writing a mammoth 11 page handwritten letter. He detailed very candidly his realization during *Piranha*.

Despite the intimidation he felt from her, the ironic double-side is that he felt he could tell her anything. She had this characteristic to her back-and-forth that reminded him of his grandmother. When he was a child, his grandma was his only friend. He would sit on her bed for hours talking with her, playing cards. The chats they would have were very open. He never spoke that way to his mother, his friends, anyone.

The problem was that his grandmother was on her deathbed, being eaten alive by cancer. He was 5 and his room was adjacent to hers. He would be kept awake all night by the sound of her screaming. Towards the end she was so bad she was bleeding through her skin, devoured like a still projection of moldy fruit.

He was there in the hospital when she went, and right before she died and they led him out of the room, she gave him one last gruesome look – this twisted, bloody smile. He was in the hospital hallways alone, with its flickering lights and gray floors, as he heard his family weep in the other room. It was the last time he was ever open like that – except for Zelda and Clownbaby. Not even Lana.

Sending his secret autobiography to 3 was what made her fall in love, so Bartek foolishly decided that Clownbaby would be the 8th person to read it. He knew this would be a terrible decision, but as far as he was concerned his life literally depended on it.

He could see no future without Clownbaby as a central character. If they couldn't be romantically inclined, then so be it. He would accept that they could only be friends. He knew the indie rock Charles Manson wouldn't last long. He just wanted her to exist.

It was not his idea to eat mushrooms this time, but rather the punk rock guys that had accompanied him in those intense early summer psychedelic voyages. He was now temporarily living with some of them in South Seattle, near the Georgetown district – just sleeping on the floor of the practice room, curled up next to a drum set.

The place had the air of a squat; they had nicknamed it "The Doghouse" due to the spastic canines of the leaseholder. They were a rowdy bunch of mutts that, like all dogs, would bark at him incessantly as if an enemy.

He never liked dogs for this reason – if they didn't growl and bark then they would act frightened and piss themselves. Also, being lazy stoners, no one had much enthusiasm to pick up the mounds of feces downstairs, and Bartek often stepped in landmines.

This time around, the guys wanted to backtrack. There was a unanimous feeling to reexamine what had kick-started the year for them all – namely the magic of Witches Cove and Meridian Park.

Bartek had a bad feeling about it, and didn't quite fancy the prospect of showing back up to the nocturnal playground where he'd tripped with Clownbaby. It would be bad but perhaps the ardor of his companions would work its magic. Maybe this would truly scrape him away from the void that had absorbed him.

The mushrooms were cubensis, straight pulled off cow shit. Getting them down had been a hassle, and the orange juice just burned away at his stomach.

It wasn't long before they kicked in – everyone was laughing, but ugly thoughts swirled like venom. They wanted to see fireworks from their bizarre friend who they all now thought of as The Joker.

Bartek trailed behind as they laughed like goons, and entered Meridian Park in blackest night. As they headed off in separate directions exploring the grounds like children, Bartek went off by himself – straying until he was alone at edge of the field.

The entire year played itself out, like a full blast snow channel of a rabbit-eared TV. In the fuzz he kept ambulating across the length of the field, zooming around like a frenzied pinball.

Mushrooms tell the brain & soul everything they need to hear – this time, they made him review all old trips, compartmentalizing them lucidly. He felt he had surpassed psilocybin's ability of head-exploding brain orgasms. There was nothing left to be learned, and there was nothing to be confronted by darkness.

At the outskirt of the field, Bartek felt as if he was standing at the precipice of the abyss, gazing into the illimitable gulf of the unknown. It was just he and an ocean of Black Lava – and the horrible, twisted, clown-like face of The Joker staring back.

Terror overcame him. He ran back to one of his friends and asked to be taken home. He made it clear that he was heading into a bad trip, and the only way out was to leave that place at once. His sympathetic friend drove him back, trying to calm him down.

He was dropped off and the friend went back to get the rest – a fact he soon forgot. In his hallucinations, he had convinced himself that he was dead and he was a ghost haunting the house – and outside the home was a vast desert and sand-worms ready to devour him whole. A terrible, unspeakable sadness overtook him.

He began hearing the dogs barking, growling, tearing at the back door – they were trying to get in to attack him. All he knew was he was dead and trapped in a house that's walls were breathing, the barking louder, louder – *vengeful*. He crouched on the floor and got into a ball. Perhaps if he just surrendered in an animal way such as playing dead for a grizzly they wouldn't tear him to shreds. *The clawing got louder, the barking more intense...*

The back door burst open, and he clenched his eyes shut ready to be mauled. Four dogs barreled into the room at him and he prepared himself for extreme pain...

And then with bullet-like stealth the dogs became a mammal tornado which whirled around him. They jumped on him to protect him, they licked his face. They knew he was in hell and came to save him. Then they piled on top of him, defending him from whatever it was that they did not understand.

In 27 years, no canine had treated him in such a way. The fear went away, and he understood– they were just pleasant entities. They really were mans best friend, and they were his as well.

In that act of animal kindness, Bartek absorbed them; it was as if he became some half-human, half-dog thing. The chiens realized he would be OK now, and let him up. Bartek stood & smiled at them, and they barked friendly.

Bartek went on the front porch and sat on the steps. A huge wave of sadness overtook him. The world had disintegrated, and all he wanted to do was talk to Clownbaby.

He began sobbing; in his delirium, it felt good – forcibly thinking of all the horrible things that ever happened & letting it all out. It was as if a monsoon of atrocity came through his face – water & mucus pouring out of him with everything that Seattle had been.

The car pulled up and his friends were back. The porch steps looked like multiple, mucus water balloons had exploded everywhere. They looked fearful for him, but he explained, laughing, that he had to get it all out right then. Al of it. They just patted him on the shoulder and let him be. They didn't know what else to say.

He came down with the typical afterglow, then headed to the practice room. In that hazy ardor, he just kept thinking about Clownbaby, imagining them young again where none of this had happened. Just hanging out, being friends.

He was resolved to call her and just talk – no more of this MySpace email stuff. She just scared him by her power, and he was always frightened to talk. The effects wore off, the earth grew still, and everything was set aright.

He called her the next night. She sounded fed up, annoyed at first – but he made clear what just happened, how he went to hell and back, about how he was done with psychedelic drugs...

"Ryan..."

He said that he knew it might not make sense, but he rambled on the story – he was able to talk finally, to show himself...

"*Ryan...*"

He said in the most positive, honest way he possibly could everything that tore through him the previous night. He wasn't over-bearing or creepy, he wasn't stupid, he wasn't crazy...

"*You don't want this...*"

He told her that it didn't matter any kind of boyfriend-girlfriend anything and he didn't care, he just wanted her to exist. That he respected her as she always should have been respected, and that he would have her back forever...

"*You really don't want this...*"

That if anyone hurt her he would move mountains, that he wanted her to be his best friend, and that the future was bright & hopeful & anything was possible & "*Ryan I'm dying of cancer.*"

Singulare Monstrum

Nearly 70 years after Black Tuesday, the greed of Wall Street had again struck its callous toll. The economy had disintegrated via a scorching domino effect spawned of swine avarice. America was destroyed, and hardships would stretch our protagonist's adult prime.

Just as the dazed masses of 1929 recoiled in certitude of Great Depression, Bartek was similarly disoriented. He knew the United States was bound to collapse from negligent idiosyncrasy, but his initial reaction was still a startled double-take. He re-focused his blurry eyes on the newspaper headline screaming in bold caps: "WORLD STOCK MARKET COLLAPSES."

The severity was clear, as were the consequences. The most striking thing about the event was he'd worked all day & not one fellow employee had so much as mentioned it.

He looked about the busy streets and saw only detached people in personal bubbles, avoiding fellow humans as they rushed about their careers & shopping agendas. It spoke volumes of American decadence – the entire edifice had shattered to nothingness & still the voluminous crowds were too busy suckling the empty tit of excess to notice.

Bartek returned to "The Doghouse" and explained the severity of this event to his roommates hypnotically playing video games. He gave up trying to drive the point then went downstairs to pack his belongings. He'd be moving into his new place soon – a large closet converted into a tiny room in U-District, not far from the college house he'd vacated. It was month-to-month, and only $200.

Quixxxote went for a long walk and explored Georgetown – a less developed section of defunct factories, rail-yards & bars in South Seattle. It was an area cheap to live & steadily being renovated with a growing reputation as "The Spot" for crust punks, artists & squatters with house venues & co-ops. After a short bus ride, he wandered into its drizzly, gray atmosphere.

A thin fog hovered like stringy mist in the still wind, and the setting sun was veiled by clouds permeating soft mercury light. These forgotten neighborhoods reminded him of South Detroit. It was strange to walk an identical atmosphere and not feel in danger, as if Jefferson Street along the Detroit River. The more suburban streets conjured memories of Melvindale & River Rouge – without the toxic stank of industrial plants & sewer treatment centers.

He felt an embrace of natural habitat, and thus more awake then usual. Would all America look like this in a few years? The instantaneous

Neo-Great Depression was assuredly settling in minds now. At some point, probably after the presidential election barely 4 weeks away, the nation would totally freak out.

Untold scores were about to go bankrupt, lose their jobs or be thrown to the streets – tens of millions would barely hang on, crushed by fathomless debt. America would be divided between grassroots builders & cannibal wolves.

Socially, politically – America had its eyes on Obama. His hype was everywhere. The possibilities of a black president and what it would mean were the focus of any political discussion on the street, at work, in transit – one couldn't avoid it.

People were desperate to move on from Bush, and there was no more a security threat to the country then for geezer McCain to heart attack & hand Sarah Palin the steering wheel.

He turned a corner that revealed a line of taverns. It almost resembled an Old West city centre, as if he were supposed to tie up a horse before clomping on in.

He picked one at random, and the interior felt haunted. The ceilings were high, the brick walls crunchy – everything was heavy oak & reeked old age. No doubt this was the watering hole of nearby factories for decades. So much depressing energy saturated the place that it gave a cozy warmth.

He sat at the empty bar & started playing the lame version of pong on his flip phone. The snapping fingers of the bartender broke his trance. When he looked up she was extremely familiar but couldn't place it. There were elements of her physicality that reminded him of Clownbaby, but she was taller, more agile.

She did the usual bartender bit – pretty girl paid to be nice & talk to lonely men. He asked for a more expensive draft as not to sound like a PBR troll. As she poured, he noticed her MUTANTS shirt. She handed him the fizzy brew, and he blurted out he used to date the ex-girlfriend of the guitarist.

The bartender squinted: *"Really?"*

Bartek replied: *"Well, not exactly date, but, we sort of... Um... Actually it never really went far, to be honest. It was... well, just kind of a weird thing."* She gave an oddly placed private investigator look he wasn't quite sure how to register. *"No, go on. What do you mean?"* She really wanted to know.

Already falling into this woman, Bartek was surprisingly smooth. He knew she was doing the paid listener bit, so he had no anxiety for once. The recent mushroom trip had really given him a new wind: *"Well, back in the day I met this chick at this industrial nightclub in Detroit. She had this big, fat MUTANTS tattoo. She was the ex-girlfriend of the guitarist – maybe they were still a thing, I don't know.*" Band guys, you know, anyone that tours a lot – they tend to have open-ended relationships around the country.

"*So when was this?*"

"*Oh, like 2004 or 2005.*"

She gave a weird, sharp look that stuck him like needles. Bartek continued: "*Yeah but I was like 23 and she was 36 and had 3 kids. She just came at me hard out of nowhere and was, like, trying to get me to go on this, you know, cross-country motel vacation. But she had all this freaky energy, and was like warning me about her psycho ex-husband. And I hadn't even done anything yet. Then she calls from a mental asylum after a super-coke binge and – if I remember right – some kind of knife attack on her stalker ex... This is just the sort of shit that happens to me. But, you know, she was cool. And she arranged an interview for me with MUTANTS for a magazine I did, and then later on I met the band, then I hung out with the singer a few years down the road. Cool guy.*"

She stared back at him with a playful smile, and he couldn't help but notice her figure. She intrigued him. She excused herself to the kitchen, and he stared at himself in the mirror ahead. He was still young, and felt it for the first time in a long time.

The lone drinker at the far end of the bar came up: "*Hey buddy, this one's a milestone.*" Bartek looked back blankly.

The man said: "*This chick is the meanest bartender in Seattle – it's like her gimmick. She torments every dude that comes in here. Believe me, it's hilarious. But understand there's tons of guys out there that come to her to be humiliated, like goin' to the dominatrix. No fucking shit – I cannot believe she is being friendly to you. This chick – if smoking were still legal in bars, she'd snatch a lit cig from your fingers & put it out on your face, then demand a bonus tip.*"

The feminine Loki reemerged with a grin & sparky eyes. She nabbed a frosty glass and filled it with drought, placing it in front of him with a sharp clank – "*This one's on the house.*"

As before, Bartek gritted his teeth & wondered how long it'd last. Sadique had thrown the kitchen sink at him, and it was just too good to be true. He felt like pampered royalty, as if she was the daughter of a great monarch that had selected a filthy beggar to be her mate.

Even as she sincerely went about her interaction with him – speaking with absolute certainty their hand-in-hand multi-year goals – she cooked him food, rolled him joints, floated about cheerfully as a middle school girl enacting her first-ever puppy love crush.

This time, he reviewed everything before it came out his mouth. She could very well throw him out the door with 1 stray sentence. Staggeringly, everything he told her seemed to come off as alchemy, turning even the most banal communication into golden nuggets. Things that would make any other woman throw him to the curb only drew her closer. She was all about punk psycho guy.

It was going to be something, he just didn't know what. Even with the giant pile of weed she dumped on the table, the endless free cocaine, the admission she knew all the big promoters in town and could get them into any show free – that she was eyeballing him to move into her big, empty house without worrying about rent – that in her cheery simplicity only wanted to listen to punk rock & collect records & watch cool movies & easy, direct interplay without drama or hassle – he was fully aware this would somehow all explode.

Sadique rode a black stallion in the name of Satan, decapitating Christians in the name of punk rock. She bop-danced to Iron Maiden and terrorized society with totalitarian abnormality. Her buttocks bore the mark of The Beast & her dialogue sputtered the fluency of kilometers. And she sought to one day birth The Antichrist, to procreate cathedrals of pythons...

Bartek realized once he dropped his guard and accepted this was actually happening, he'd fall bat-shit crazy in love. He would be zealous errant of the faith of Sadique.

Their second day together, this punk rock Clownbaby clone dragged him through the house showing him pictures & heirlooms. She had her entire plan figured out, expertly crafted like a paradoxical trap lain by an amour-struck Jigsaw. And this is where *she* would spend *her* honeymoon, and this is where *she* would travel lengthily in Europe, this is where *her* kids would go to school, and this is where *she* would open a tavern, this was a picture of her mother just to show what she'd look like in her 50's, and, and, and...

Everything about them functioned fluidly; they were like autistic half-wits coalescing into a superior organism. He'd be the Big Brain, and she'd be The Action; he The Philosopher, and she The Muse. She the Money Maker, he The Accountant.

They were already starting a band where live it'd be all females dressed in cop uniforms, and they'd wheel him out like Hannibal Lectar on a dolly with a straight-jacket before he picked up the axe to wail punk mightiness. They were already drafting their movements through Europe –

the capitols they'd backpack, the foreign beaches they'd inhabit.

Only problem? She didn't get extreme metal, was lukewarm on horror films, and hated Halloween. These were vital keystones in his whole everything, and if GWAR can't crack a smile on a ladies face, then they had no future together...

And so, in a gesture of good will, she began picking up some of the more classic, rock-based metal albums for her collection. She was a rocker chick – but finally starting to get what Iron Maiden & Judas Priest were all about.

Nothing spoke romance like self-initiated baby-steps into the first four Black Sabbath albums. Still, she was lost on death metal. He'd learned to not fight that one – it was "boy music." So what? He had headphones.

He feared that the bizarre coincidence which glued them together was the only reason she'd thrown herself so aggressively at him. Sadique was the ex-girlfriend of the MUTANTS guitarist – and the other ex-girlfriend of the guitarist that Bartek nearly hooked up with in Detroit was the one he apparently was cheating on Sadique with! He'd stumbled onto cross-country relationship revenge!!!

As is why Bartek flipped his lid to learn that Sadique *literally was* the inspiration & subject matter of one of his favorite MUTANTS songs! A tune about the lyricist's idea of the ultimate punk rock woman – one that Bartek would often listen and wonder where on earth he could find such a deranged lady!! *He was living out a literal romance with one of his fictional punk crushes!!!*

The way she looked at him, how they interacted – he thought perhaps this was his future wife. It was never more apparent then his last night at The Doghouse, smoking that last cigarette on the porch. As he gazed into the pouring rain turned misty under the street light effulgence, a wallop of joy overcame him – *karma!!*

As he pondered Seattle's anticlimactic mess, it made sense. He demanded a normal life from otherworldly forces – *to be totally anonymous*. It was all a set-up so that he could wander in right time & place? He began laughing, sadness unburdening. Life had to beat the shit out of him mercilessly as to prime him for victory!

Bartek quickly made friends with his new roomies – one girl was an acoustic singer, and the couple were stoners & computer builders. With an unclouded brain, he devoured Kerouac's *Some Of The Dharma* & a swell bio on Henry Miller *The Happiest Man Alive*.

These books represented a welcome change. No longer would he feed the Black Lava by tossing it the madness & misdeeds of historical villains; he would nurse the better side of him, the adult which sought peace and tranquility.

He recognized the lighter, more human and freedom-starved side of him in Henry Miller. Beforehand, this writer was a blank – he knew nothing of his wider story, and only small chunks of his more famous books. These disjointed segments impassioned Bartek to write, and their wise vantage helped correlate his own thoughts. But he'd only scratched the surface – Miller so greatly inspired him it was as if acquiring a mystic grandpa to mentor & advise him.

He'd now been with Sadique 2 weeks without argument. He also attended a rare LAIBACH performance so moving he wept. The last band that had done that was Black Sabbath, during "War Pigs." He was still awaiting Clownbaby's response to his letter & secret book, but it no longer bothered him as much.

With Sadique, he questioned if the deep understanding he had with Clownbaby needed to be replicated for romance to be real.

Sadique was not a victim the way Clownbaby was. She and Bartek were both survivors of PTSD, and were both deeply mentally abused. So if Ryan ultimately wanted escape himself, should he not just follow Sadique into her alternate reality? *Was that OK*? Why not urge amnesic fog? Isn't that why people moved cross-country?

The major question was how long he really had before they pulled the chair out from under his ass again. Sadique was still existing, though his faith was short. Would she still act this way, once the shit hit the fan? Would she really take him in if evicted?

That America had crumbled was rapidly sobering up the nation; dread had swept the continent. And there were still those people so conditioned they continued shopping... *like Sadique*.

The jobs were drying up fast – lay-offs by millions. Nationally, the numbers were staggering. And as the cold winds drifted record chills & mortgages began foreclosing & Union's were degraded & budgets crashing & unemployment was trickling out the Seattleites acted as all Americans did, moving in a flanking conspiracy of self-denial, silently cannibalizing each other – growing greedier, more fearful, more desperate.

The normal society people poured onto the streets, transplants everywhere bailing on Seattle for hometown ground where there too was zero opportunity...

Sadique still didn't get what was up – she was into sex, drugs n' rock n' roll, not politics. Yet the collapse was now raging in her face – she'd no more clientèle because they lacked the funds to drink. Somehow the alcoholics were too broke to drink & for once the street people were begging for change to actually to eat something.

On November 4th, America voted their next president. The enthusiasm was high. Bartek pondered how barely a year ago he'd come to Seattle and – when asking for a sign of the future – ran into Barack Obama in the library toilet. It seemed an inevitable landslide.

Even if Obama was still a capitalist, there was no greater a relief then escaping W. Bush. At least there was a marginal chance he'd try and do the right thing. Bartek cracked a fortune cookie: "*Your luck has been completely changed today.*" And that night, the streets exploded with parades of cheer.

Sadique sat upon the beanbag of his closet room, thinking the nook was charming. They'd just returned from the punk bar where they'd met many of his friends.

People thought they were a ridiculously cute couple, and perfect magic. Bartek dug through a stack of papers & stopped mid-shuffle. He looked over to Sadique, and she smiled back. Her grin was so simplistic & uncomplicated that it melted his heart.

This was the moment in which he allowed himself to accept everything now occurring. For weeks he braced for the wrong turn which never came. She wasn't about to go to prison, wasn't suicidal or mentally collapsing. She was well-adjusted & knew what she wanted. So long as he played her game, there'd be no Hiroshima. He finally had everything he ever wanted. In that flash, he fell in love.

Yet in her simplicity, he knew her a hollow trophy. He wondered if he were a novelty, or rather a bulwark against a reality she refused to confront.

Bartek was the first guy her age she'd dated in ages – one of 3. During high school she had a boyfriend, but soon was obsessively wrapped up in MUTANTS guitarist for years – a guy twice her age.

She had a fetish for old punk rock guys with Iggy Pop physiques. Her last boyfriend of her age ended a year ago, and they were an item 2 years. He'd dumped her to move across country and join a huge band Bartek liked. She was considering marriage & family, and he just walked out.

For now though, he didn't mind. After the past year of unrelenting darkness, he felt he'd won the lottery. She was holding his hand in public, kissing him in front of her friends – she really wanted it. No one was ever quite like that with him – it was so foreign he had to fake a mundane response.

Now that it was clear this would continue unabated, Bartek let it wash all over him. He was in love, or close to it.

They got in her car & began driving towards a restaurant. Suddenly her smile deflated; she instantly became the cold, ruthless crusher he knew lurked under that starry-eyed Honeymoon glow: "*So, we have to make things clear, now that I'm no longer ovulating and ragging. I'm going to fuck whoever I want to fuck, you have no control over me, you don't get to tell anyone anywhere at any time that I'm your girlfriend while in public, you don't get to kiss me unless I feel like it, you only get to fuck me if I feel like fucking you. I don't want any of this extreme metal shit on my radio, this this this this this this and that. I'm the boss motherfucker, got it?*"

Black Lava crept up his spine, loosened from its slumber. He felt himself slip away. He begged this Hyde not to take the steering wheel, even as he felt himself dissipate like a phantom. After such great caution, again he was being over-run by the vessel of misanthropy, as if a pilot trapped within a drone that he'd no control.

Sadique, in her simplistic unawareness, had no radar for such a thing. She continued to drive, ranting off a series of belittling comments. From his remote outpost he watched her like a prisoner as the unchained psychotic ran the show. He kept trying to calm this blast, but how does one reason with an angry, starved grizzly?

"*Please don't do this,*" he thought to his materialized hate, "*I really like this one. It's just a game, you know it, you know it. Please, I beg you, stop – don't. Just for me, please...*" but the icy compartmentalized rage was now dictating events.

The doomed couple seated at the restaurant – a hipster filled spot on Capitol Hill, packed with a sea of bodies all trying so hard to live the rock n' roll lifestyle. Lots of ugly, useless people talking themselves up, talking about their labels, lame indie rock bands & what it really means to be punk rock, etc. There was not a face among the 50 or so people which he did not despise. All he saw was decadence & vanity, two of the things he hated most.

Sadique started pointing to the various people in the restaurant, all of which he found repulsive: "*I would totally fuck that guy, and that guy, and – well not her, because I'm not a lesbian, and...*" Bartek pleaded with his inherent monster: "*Please don't do this, please don't, please...*"

Sadique kept pointing around, selecting all the cock in the room as the humiliated one battled his kraken. Sadique coaxed him to play along with one of their usual little games. She'd say "*I'm so glad I'm not X, Y or Z*" to which he would compete by adding on another vile noun.

Sadique, not registering the darkness, began pushing its buttons.

She loudly stated: *"I'm soooo glad I'm not a Christian."*

Bartek, remembering the violent war of his teenage years, one-upped her: *"I'm soooo glad I'm not a Muslim."* The residual intimidation and fear of being jumped by al Qaeda children erupted the Black Magma further. It was a scalding iron ready to strike.

Sadique continued: *"I'm soooo glad I'm not a Jew."*

Bartek had flashes of Israeli bombs dropped on Palestinian children, and tried to shift to another part of the world: *"I'm soooo glad I'm not a Hindu."*

And he began to have flashes of moving to Seattle again, the darkness of those first three months and the spiral of madness which led to the bottom of the mushroom-infected rabbit hole; the pitiful scene of weeping anguish at the church pew, the bad-trip monsoon bursting through his tear ducts on The Dogfarm's porch steps – and most of all the racist stupidity of Miss 3 and what she'd aid about Obama, that she would *"never vote for a nigger,"* and that this comment itself was the end of their troubled romance which never would have even happened had he known what a buffoon she really was. In that instant, his whole life was a bad joke.

Sadique: *"I'm sooooo glad I'm not a lesbian."*

This sent him over the edge. He wanted her away – all of it, right then, forever. The Black Lava erupted like a missile strike in remembering what Miss 3 had said. And like GG Allin freaking out rolling around in his own shit to make the world hate him, Bartek similarly had that anti-social pulse to do or say anything most shocking as to accomplish drastic isolation.

Lacking the power to stop The Black Lava, he reiterated what the mother of his dead child had said, quite loudly, for the entire restaurant to hear: *"I'm so glad I'm not a NIGGER."* And The Black Lava – with it's steely, murderous eyes – looked straight into Sadique's eyes, face to face, with no illusion or adulteration; just raw, savage horribleness, piercing straight through her soul.

The haze of pyromaniac destruction vanished as it always did after manifesting itself in one crazy action, and Bartek was alone. He looked about and the entire restaurant had dropped their utensils, all staring at him in shocked repulsion.

As he turned his vision from their disapproving eyeballs, he looked into the petrified, heart-broken face of Sadique as it gazed back emptily – without love, without understanding, without respect.

Abandoned by Hyde and totally disoriented, Bartek tried to clear up what just happened. *"I didn't... I didn't mean, like, literally. I'm not racist. You know, the Nazis despise me – they want to kick the shit out of me. Where I'm from, Detroit – people use it to mean any piece of shit person. It's not a racist thing, it's just general slang... Most my friends there were black, arab or hispanic... You know I'm not like that."*

Sadique stared blankly, hollow eyes like extinguished lanterns. Bartek sighed, grumbled something incoherent, then looked back: *"Fuck this."* He stood up, slipped on his coat, then walked out of the restaurant into the pouring rain, just leaving her sitting there shocked & bombarded. And that was that.

The next day was Monday; at the end of his shift, he was laid off from the kitchen staff. The work dried up with the season and especially the erosion of the crashed stock market. He too was now one of 10 million people that had now lost their jobs in a month.

With gears turning in his head, Henry Miller's logic had drenched him – he was halfway through *Tropic of Cancer* & it reaffirmed his street urchin roots. But never had he come to embrace his separation in the luminescent sense that Miller did. For once, a positive influence! No other persona helped deflate his convolution.

As every print magazine now withered into nothingness like the extinction of dinosaurs, Bartek realized *Metal Maniacs* time was short. His days as world-famous metal journalist would soon end.

2009 would be pure movement – he'd tour with as many bands as would have him as a reporter/merch guy. Alongside the publication of *The Big Shiny Prison*, his journalism would be pushed hard. He wanted to go out at the top of his game, then people could write about *his* band for once. He'd saved nearly $2000.

Clownbaby was still a touchy subject, and he wanted to see her one last time. She'd been texting him now that phony Manson broke her heart. It wasn't an open call of romance, but they were communicating. He felt it important to see his family members, or at least sit through an awkward meet.

In a flash, he realized he had to finally confront his father. He'd not seen the man since 1993. At some point, he just dropped off. Things were still cloudy to him... This black hole of memory – it was the essential as to why he was always running from himself. His father was a shadow embedded in its central compass.

Anticlimax Leviathan

Bartek never quite understood why he was the way he was. Animated and manic, fast talking & slithery, he was shifty as a used car salesman. Like an Italian, he spoke with his hands.

His thought process was child-like in its directness, wrapped up with projects & activities. When he'd ask women to make art with him, or do "things & stuff," they often assumed this was a ploy to get 'em alone. In reality he really was armed with Crayola products.

His aloofness was legendary. Many assumed it was callousness, if not willing disregard – there was just no way any man could be that out of touch. Such as when he'd go on dates with women thinking in his self-deprecating way that they just wanted to hang out and in no possible way could be looking at him like that – he'd skirt their advances.

Even when he'd bring them home, he'd make no attempt for the bedroom, 'cause he had to show them all the neat stuff he owned. Then they'd get fed up with his weird collections & strange toys & leave frustrated & dejected in the nice dresses they were wore to their encounter. He'd be left scratching his head as to why.

He was a Peter Pan of extended adolescence – a kid-like blur of forward motion counteracted by depressed analysis and photographic memory. The excessive eruption of endless agitation was foreign to his mother, who hated it. She would scold her son and berate him for these qualities.

She would punish him for talking that Mediterranean semi-sign language, yell at him to sit still, curse his abatement of authority: "*Stop making this up/quit talking like that/knock your act off/what did you do with my son?*" Since he was a child, she'd chastened and guilt-tripped him. In his teens, she threatened boot camp or the nuthouse.

His father was a painful shadow, and even when he did try to come around Bartek never wanted anything to do with him. His mother had programmed him to hate the man as if he were the Antichrist. She would spare the man no quarter –he was a liar, a cheater, a no good drunk. That he would rather whiskey hole then see his son.

She taught him to despise his new stepmother, as his dad had left her for the woman and had been cheating on her when they were married. His mother would curse the grandparents, saying they threw nephews like old pairs of shoes. How none of them wanted him, and that to never be anything like his poppa. It was best to stay away.

In response to this, the young Bartek would now and again see his dad at the usual holiday functions. Even if he lived in Indiana with a new family, he would still come to visit his folks in Westland, a suburb of Detroit.

The young boy would often cry before his scary father arrived, because he was such a tyrant. More often the not, he was forced to leave with this strange man. And while shaken up for the first few hours, he would soon stabilize. The more he was around him, the more he recognized his dad wasn't such a bad guy after all – just a grown man totally separated from his son.

And what could this man know? How could he remotely decode what was going on his deranged son's mind, when the kid barely spoke? When the boy did speak up, he just talked about video games or cartoons or child things he thought were cool.

And the father would kind of sort of listen, or pretend to be interested, because he was, after all, an adult. He would leave the real communication for later in life, when he could rap it up about women, action movies, bar-crawling.

For now it was the early 90's, and he would take the kid bowling, or to the movies, or to Coney Island for gyros and check out the waitresses' ass while half-listening to his boy ramble on about whatever *Tiny Toons* was.

By the time the young Bartek was 12, his father had been divorced again and moved back to his parents home in Westland. He was clearly picking up the pieces and trying to reboot his life. It wasn't long before he picked his son up, spending the day making amends. He was determined to be a real presence from then on.

They went to see *Jurassic Park* at the movies, and before dropping his son off the child broke down crying and hugged the father. That all the kids were mean to him, his mother was crazy, all he did was fight people. Things were bad, very bad, and it all needed to change. And his father, in totally empathy, promised that he would be there from then on. They were going to be a team.

That was the last time he ever saw him. Soon after, he just vanished. And it was perhaps that betrayal more then anything else which launched Bartek into his dark, delusional land where reality mutated into a sick hallucination. At the age of 13, Bartek had a schizophrenic break – he was lost in a nightmare, locked in a position of mental checkmate in which he could travel in no direction but pain.

With the shadow of his father at one end and at the other an an emotionally-castigating mother that took from him anything he found solace in as to punish behavior that was quite literally a product of mental illness, all he was left with were the brutal physical attacks and humiliation of his Middle School classmates.

His mind buckled under, and he was lost to a sickly dream-state that climaxed in a failed suicide attempt. When he survived, the focus of his being hinged on revenge.

Following his dark creation, it was as if he applied a willing amnesia to anything that came before. Finally gelling with a group of likewise demented, deluded and violent loners, they united to destroy all which created them. And this savage madness is what fueled the path of destruction that would define his life until Seattle where again he allowed amnesia.

With anticlimactic 2008 & the awful intensity of his extremist "psychedelic research" – with the heartbreak following 3, Clownbaby & Sadique – it was almost as if he had to force some kind of climax, lest it all have been a waste of mad effort.

Dramatically paying Decembers rent in advance & spending nearly 4 days on a Greyhound to Detroit without any car to hunt down his father was the strongest finale he could muster.

His stepfather was the one who snatched him up from the Greyhound depot and allowed their spare car for his visit. He now got along with him a little better then his mother.

The old man had cooled down. When he first entered his life, he was the worst sort of unhinged, racist cop one could imagine – a caricature of right-wing conservatism from the nasty black hole of Vietnam. Back in the day, he was terrifying. Now he'd retired and worked as security chief for a retirement home.

Bartek's mother had nursed humanity back into him. After all she wasn't evil, just stuck in her ways – and she still had a good sense of humor. Also now that his daughters from his previous marriage had grown up – one of them having a half-black child and the other an unshaven, dready hippie girl with numerous liberal-minded young'uns – his tolerance had increased. The fight had left him, and perhaps he felt remorse for a number of unspoken actions he might've done wearing The Badge. He didn't want to harass black people anymore or attack homeowners for not cutting their lawns.

In any case, Bartek accepted the vehicle. He went to Linda's in Royal Oak where he would stay throughout this final visitation. The next day, he drove down to his hometown of Dearborn to meet with a large group of his high school friends who still had a pre-Thanksgiving feast. It was welcoming just as it was depressing.

He'd traveled so far, gained so much experience but the world from which he sprang had fairly much remained static. The people at this party were a bright bunch, and yes the obviously had grown, but not quite to the extent he had.

He felt a little lost with them, and in many ways it was as if he hadn't left. It felt more like a scene perhaps 3 years after high school, as opposed to 9.

He was also shocked to find another old friend had died in a gruesome way. The party itself was hosted by Lisa's best friend Zoe. Their other best friend was a girl who joined The Navy with Lisa, before Lisa had slipped out of it just after 9/11, and then ended her own life tragically.

The friend that had actually gone into The Navy had finally been discharged after 4 long years. She was driving a car with her fiancée and when they got into a high speed wreck both of them flew through the windshield and died instantly.

No one had bothered to tell Bartek, let alone the other 6 deaths he learned of when returning. What bothered him the most was that of these 7 demises, the one that impacted him was the killing of Bruce Wayne a.k.a. Batman in the comic book series! Fiction was more then fact to him! He felt dirty, negligent, supremely disturbed by this and sought to zealously rectify it...

And so it was of little surprise when the search for his estranged father ended at the exact location of his first hunch – *the bowling alley*. The maxim were true: *like father, like son.*

Deep in his core, this is where he always wanted to be – mindlessly chucking a ball down a slippery lane at a stack of wooden logs. If not there, he sought to knock around billiards, or throw around a Frisbee at the park. And even if he abandoned it in youth – even if it just did not fit in with his punk/metal affiliation – he still wanted to play baseball.

He wasn't quite an athlete, but he loved playing football as a kid – even as the other children beat him, spit in his face or mocked him because he screwed up the games 'cause no one existed in his life to explain the rules. They would laugh at him and say: *"why don't you go ask your dad?"*

Remembering this sad aspect so transparently is what came to him as he patiently waited for his father in the bowling bar. He had showed up to the man's house where his current girlfriend wouldn't open the door, fearing this crazy son may be brandishing a crowbar to beat his old man down.

She pushed his phone number on a piece of paper through the

door, as well as the address to the bowling alley. He asked she not notify him, and she agreed to let this surprise visit be what it was.

When Bartek snuck up on his dad about to throw a ball down his favorite lane, he asked the somewhat startled man if he was first-and-last-name. The old man squinted his eyes, thinking perhaps he was a cop or loan shark – but the purple mohawk obliterated that.

When he finally said *"I'm Ryan – I'm your son,"* the elder Bartek's eyes lit up in a swirl of emotions. He had the air of a man who's wife had just caught him in bed with another woman, ready to spout a litany of phony claims to keep her from detonating.

"Um, uh... shit... I... wow, I can't believe... Um.. Look, I... can I just throw this one ball, just finish this frame real quick, and then I'll meet you at the lounge? Is that cool man? This is, um, a big game for me, it's a league thing. I, uh..." Bartek Jr. told Bartek Sr. it was fine, and he would be at the table over yonder when ready.

And so Bartek sat at the tiny plastic table with a calmness that was striking, ready to confront his Old Man. Just as he did at every Greyhound, he stared up at that big institutional clock on the wall and it's arms click away to the future. He would finally have an answer, and the massive anticlimax of 2008 would amend itself.

The elder Bartek rushed into the room, quick as lightning, almost as if his brain were tugging his sloppy body along and thrusting it like a busted up car into the seat before him. *"Wow, Ryan, Jesus, I, um, I'm really, really happy to see you – I just, um, look, I..."* And then, like Groucho Marx, like Roland T. Flakfizer – *like Heath Ledger's Joker* – with his arms flailing about acrobatically, with his mind grappling at trains of thought somewhere hovering in the air, shifting his eyes back and forth, curling his lip like a pondering Darwin before his gopher-out-of-the-hole neck jerks his vision around the empty space of the upper room trying to solve the conundrum – this animated clown looks at his son with a quick stamp of the foot and open palms of exploding fingers like wacky fireworks like a magician unveiling his great illusion, then curling all but his trigger-fingers so that they point forward to him like a motivational speaker unleashing a gem of marketing wisdom to a board of corporate executives: *"So, you're probably wondering where I've been all these years–"* the Old Man paused, again shifting his shifty eyes to the vacant, upper corner in the room before looking right back at him with a zing and again the exploding firework finger-trick: *"I don't have an answer for you."*

He weaselly looked through the lounge door to the lane, then returned his attention to his long lost son finally returned after years of heartache & speculation: "*Hold on – I gotta bowl this frame.*"

The bizarre clone of R. Bartek stood up – and with that same brain-tugging hypnosis of constant addiction to whatever held him hostage at any given time – the one & only Bobby Bartek zapped up like electricity & zoomed out the room like Groucho Marx incarnate.

Ryan slapped his forehead. In, 5 seconds, he saw it all – *like Father, like Son.* He could never escape his parents, because he was equally their creation. He began laughing subtly – it was his luck that after all that build-up all he gets is: "*I don't have an answer – hold up while I bowl.*"

He wasn't sure if he should high 5 him or sock him in the mouth. But when he saw the messy old guy zoom back into the room, dragging along his bum knee and looking like a months-long lost dog rediscovering his kin, he couldn't help but like the guy.

His dad sat down at the adjacent chair: "*Hey man, you want a pack of Reds?*" Bartek's poppa slid an unopened pack of Marlboro's across the tabletop towards his astray child as if an air hockey puck. Junior looked at them and chuckled.

Pops didn't even know if he smoked – he just had his specific brand right there, just like that. That this is how he probably would handle the situation if the roles were reversed... it was perfect.

The Old Man lit up a tailor-made, continuing onward with 37 years of pure chain-smoking. He babbled on & on nervously, never really coming to any full thoughts, never wanting to say the wrong thing: "*Do you want to get lunch with me on Saturday? I don't care, it's fine, you can say all the mean shit in the world to me, you can yell at me, you can spit in my face, I don't care, I just wanna talk.*"

Ryan smiled, and in return the sad old man gazed at his vanished child in the same dumbfounded, speechless way his own son did when lost in his adoration of Clownbaby. He was just so happy to see his baby boy.

The two met at Daily's in Plymouth, where they often ate in his earliest memories. It's not like he forgot his father – Bartek's memories stretched back to when he was a year and a half old. His mother claimed that at age 2 he was already reading and writing (*in a basic caveman sense*).

So in the jumble, he was left with a slide show of impressions. It took little to fill out the man's character with an adult perception. After all, he was him.

Not long after they'd seen *Jurassic Park*, Bartek's Old Man went back home to live with his parents again, reclaiming his teenage room. They had left his old 1970's posters up for the sake of parental nostalgia.

They weren't going to have any more kids, and they had no use for it.

He had been bankrupted, divorced and pushed away by his new family – *"man, she was fuckin' crazy"* – and looming child support and alimony issues, not to mention the extreme amount he legally owed his first born son's mother. He was financially fucked forever – but had one last ace up his sleeve.

Having quit the electric company, he took with him his 401k and early pension. Despite clear and frequently related instructions to his out of state employer, the $30,000 check was sent to the wrong house. His freshly ex-wife cashed it.

Then his mother died, followed shortly by his father. By proxy he inherited the house which was already paid off – but the new ex-wife was legally entitled to half of it, circumvented him, and began causing all sorts of trouble.

Whatever happened next wasn't clear, because the elder Bartek kept dancing around whatever the next chunk of his life was. He didn't want to alienate his adult son by telling him anything he didn't want to hear, but Ryan Bartek was no fool either. He'd probably crawled into some whiskey hole where time passed too rapidly. The next thing he knew, it was too late.

He really wanted to be a family man, he just was never any good at it. Everything about the early days with Ryan's mother was fuzzy to him. His son began asking about random things she'd said negative about him, he now casually brought up with his father predictably relating perfect Bartekian logic: *"Are you kidding me? I had three jobs!"*

His son remembered vague moments where his father tried to reach out, but at that point he was just too far gone to care or want anything to do with it. He was little more then a target for empty rage; just some festering, painful shadow.

The last thing this psychopathic 15 year old needed was for another laughable adult to play human chess with him. He hated authority, and the very idea of a father was in his derangement the absurd peak of it.

When listening to his father's woeful story of his parents dying barely a month apart, it seemed like it was totally disconnected, as if lending an ear to a stranger at the bar.

It didn't settle until now that these people were family. He wasn't close to his grandmother, but she was nice enough. He was a little standoffish with her because she had this heavy Italian mobster housewife vibe – and always too much uncomfortable perfume.

The grandfather he took to very well – he was a pleasant smiling man kicked back on a lazy boy recliner with a love of Verne Gagne's

AWA wrestling.

It wasn't until driving back to his dad's new home that this information clicked – *his mother never told him that both his grandparents had died*. It was a low blow of human chess. It was clear she not only damningly erased his father, but deprived him of grief. The feeling that as a grown man he did not feel anything from their passing as a result of this manipulation infuriated him.

At the wheel, his dad explained how cool his new girlfriend was, that after a life of crazy broads he found one that hated trouble and just lived her life doing whatever she wanted to do, and more often then not their interests keyed up. *"She's great, really, she is. We both hate the same thing... What's it called, she says it all the time, it's like our thing..."*

His son, being of identical DNA, noted that he couldn't recall what "their thing" was because to spend time on it would take away from activities. Thus, the boy finished his thought – *"Drama?"*

The Old Man lit up: *"Yeah! Drama! We hate fuckin' drama!"*

And then, the front wheel popped. With the van shaking from the blown tire, his dad gripped the wheel like a plummeting astronaut. Just as his son had done over and over throughout the years, the bereft father shouted: *"It's always fuckin' somethin'!"*

They both got out and he watched the man inspect his damaged car. With squinty eyes he stalked about the car like an investigating Sherlock Holmes, stopped as if Groucho Marx flinging up his coat-tails. With fluid, watery movements the human cartoon sped up to the front tire, squinted at it again, then kicked it half-heartedly for no real reason, as if having done too much LSD over the course of his life and he just needed to make sure it was actually deflated and not another hallucination. Bartek just didn't believe this guy's claim in never having touched psychedelics.

At the house they dug through boxes he'd dragged with him through the years that were just filled with pictures and Christmas cards and writings to him from the young Ryan. He kept everything.

Ryan got fairly sad in seeing this, and especially looking at his father sit on the floor as he did, knees first, everything spread in front of him like a slop, just kind of sitting there tinkering through stuff the way a little kid would play with hot wheels or Lego trucks.

The father asked: *"Well, I mean, I don't remember too much with your mom. It' all kinda fuzzy, to be honest. I was real young, like 20. At some point she just hated me and wouldn't talk to me anymore. I mean, what did she tell you?"*

"She basically said you were The Antichrist."

He stopped toying with the memorabilia of his son and seemed confounded. *"Well, shit... I'm not the Antichrist. I might've fucked things up but, come on – the Antichrist?"*

"She said you cheated on her all the time and were like this huge womanizer."

"No, look, at the end I hooked up with your last stepmother but when we were together we were together. She already had kids that were in their late teens and I wanted to do it right, start over, you know. So we had kids. But I was with her almost to the end, you know? It was already over we just didn't file no paperwork."

Then his son confronted his reported alcoholism: *"She said you were like a massive drunk."* The father kind of deflated his shoulders, looking to the empty space in the room, saying with autistic simplicity: *"Well... I like my beer."*

And then he continued digging through the pics, like it was all settled, because it wasn't even a thing. No follow up, no remorse. Just some guy that works full time and like his father wants to kick back at the end of the day with a brew and a football game or action flick. And his son understood it all, perfectly, and began cracking up.

It was the black and white photograph of his young grandmother in the early 60's armed to the teeth and clutching Uzi's while draped with bullet straps over her torso as her brother (*his dead uncle*) brandished a shotgun menacingly in the background which now thickened the plot in a way he never saw coming.

His dead relatives were mobsters, and their family business was moving Cuban cocaine into Florida in the late 50's/early 60's. When Fidel Castro overthrew the dictatorship of Batista it effectively ended the family business. They may very well have assumed fake names and identities in Michigan.

The grandmother was supposedly full-blooded Maltese, but she was most likely Sicilian. She and her brother were involved in other sundry occupations, none of which were revealed but certainly implied. Bartek's father had never gotten into this "family business," although his shadowy uncle was apparently a very bad man. He remembered his mother warning to avoid him.

And thus Bartek's secret history was revealed – the black sheep between two tribes of Catholics; one Opus Dei Irish military-cop neo-cons & the other Vatican-minded (likely) Italian mobsters.

Like two huge birds knocked dead with one stone Bartek left his long-lost fathers home and went to confront Lana, his quasi-ex-wife. She had been out of jail awhile and was not keen on getting involved, but wanted to see her nonetheless.

They met up at a Coney Island with Stanley Pluto and a young girl named Ursula. Bartek was shocked at her deterioration – prison had rendered her an empty vessel, and the hollow hole of smack had devoured her soul. With her hair down over her face, her entire vibe was ghostly. All Bartek could think was the well-drowned girl from The Ring.

Stanley had had enough of Lana's drama and had Ursula – this new strange young girl to drive around doing zany stuff with. Lana was now like a mannequin in the backseat.

Stanley was trying to again push her on him, and kept reiterating she was about to inherit $20,000. Her mind was gone, and their romance was no more – she was the walking talking guilt of an ancient phantom.

He knew he'd made a mistake sleeping with her last year. It just kind of happened, and wasn't quite the plan. During his book travel for *Prison*, he'd returned to Detroit 3 times. Each was like a final, grand confrontation with certain ex's.

The first time Zelda had taken him home and cuddled with him all night. She had a boyfriend, but it didn't matter – she absorbed and loved him silly. He didn't need to get dirty to be affectionate. The third one – well, that was Clownbaby.

But in the middle was Lana. He'd hung with her and Stanley before they all ended up at Pluto's ranch house. Lana was all goofy on psychiatric pills, both were a little drunk. She just kind of jumped on him on the living room mattress at night.

They started going at it, and she was more aggressive and feral then he'd ever remembered. Then in the middle of it, riding him hard, she looked down at his face, almost as if in a dream: "*Ryan... what are you doing here?*" And then her weebly-wobbly eyes rolled around in her head and she timbered upon his body, falling asleep.

She wanted it and he let it happen, but he wasn't sure if she even remembered it. He was also paranoid that he may have impregnated her during it, and it may very well have been his child that she went to prison with. He was never sure though, and didn't really want to know. If prison had miscarried his surprise baby, he might plummet to depths of darkness even he couldn't withstand.

So now, in this final of meetings, Bartek took Lana to see the new Batman movie at the dollar show on Dequindre and 12 Mile. She didn't even seem aware there was one. Really, she didn't seem to much aware of anything.

And so the strange Joker-man took his apparition Harley to the blockbuster movie – which she certainly enjoyed much more then

Clownbaby had. She was just so happy, so speechless in her adoration of him the way he was with the aforementioned.

The old lovers hung out at some random punk rock flophouse house filled with metal dudes and SHARPS. Ursula was there waiting for them, and Bartek gave her a ride home once they dropped off Lana at her parents.

Ursula motor-mouthed his ear – how shed heard so much about him, how she was 19 and going to college to be a journalist. How she wanted to know all about he business and do exactly what he was doing, and maybe he could help edit her work, and maybe someday they could work on something, and how much Detroit sucked and how bad she wanted to travel that coming summer, and how bad she wanted to snap photos at music festivals for big music magazines, especially metal, punk and electronic music.

She was way too young for him, but he was flattered because she was obviously smitten by him. He always liked to have younger, energetic girls around – one's that were very sociable and by their appearance make up for his awkwardness in public.

After he dropped her off, he contemplated if it were possible to take her on one of his road missions. Sure it was possible, if he so wanted it to be. But today he at least made a new friend, and it was always cool to have some pretty young girl think his bullshit glowed.

The next day, he visited his stepfather at his work. It was the first time the two ever really spoke at a direct human level. The guy was all burned out, sick of watching his country be pissed down the drain by thief bankers. With his huge Ronald Reagan poster in his retirement home security office, he didn't quite get the problem, and he hated Obama for both all of the wrong reasons.

But at least he didn't hate darkies anymore or want to kill random people for not being organized enough. He traveled to Vietnam as a tourist to make amends with his past and hung out in bars talking to communists. And he was driven up the wall by tinnitus so badly all he heard was constant screeching. He wanted them to disconnect his ears but it wouldn't stop the screech. It had gotten so bad he was close to throwing himself in front of a train.

So they talked, finally, for once. He admitted meeting his father – which his stepfather swore on his life he would not bring up to his mom. He said he met Bartek Sr. in court, when he had to appear for child support processions.

Under oath – never blinking, never showing and remorse for lying – he told the judge straight to his face that he hung out with Ryan all the time, they were in close contact, all of this fantasy nonsense. He hadn't seen the kid in 17 years. Was he that deluded?

Ryan and his stepfather had as close a reconciliation as either of them could get, and Ryan went to the car he loaned him. Then, before turning on the engine, he began sobbing. That guy back there was the closest thing he had to a father and the man always wanted to fill the role, but Bartek could never let him. All he could think was *"let's call the cops on that nigger"* mixed with the smiling, jovial faces of his parents as if an episode of *Full House*.

He felt dirty & ashamed for pushing this man away, just as he did to his real father. And then once again he was filled with rage when picturing his stepfathers mocking laughter, his joke pounding of a nightstick into his palm when discussing his rousing approval of the beating of Rodney King. He didn't know what to do with it.

The next day, Bartek saw his mother. Beat faced, ashamed beyond words, the shrewd berater of his upbringing was deflated to human proportions. She sat blubbering. His stepfather had lied to him the only time he'd confided trust. She was caught red-handed by the eventual trap of all lies leading to the truth – grown adult perception.

She knew that her son saw right through her, and how pathetic her head-games were. She knew that she deprived him of his father, erased him through forced hatred. She covered up the death of his grandparents. She knew that she punished her child anytime she saw his father in him.

And the reason she detested her child's thinking and viewpoints were because Like Father, Like Son. She was a wreck, slowly sobbing as he ate his garlic chicken slowly. They didn't say much, and he soon left for activities.

Thanksgiving passed, as did 2 weeks of recording. He had a new grind EP with Sasquatch Agnostic, and another acoustic album as The REAL Man In Black.

He wasn't sure which direction he should go when returning Northwest, but his muse surely enjoyed both musical incarnations. Clownbaby was still undoubtedly the one he drew inspiration from – even disconnected, he'd be pondering her reactions.

Real life though, this was always tricky – and the moment had arrived for their confrontation. She'd been beckoning yet non-committal at once, keeping him on a back-burner yet still promoting enthusiasm to meet. For whatever reason, she decided that Monday, December 8th would be their reunion. Within an hour of calling he soon arrived like a faithful, simplistic puppy.

Her home was exactly as he remembered it – gadgets and doo-dads, porcelain dolls and half-smash foreign toys. She greeted him with warmth, holding back the rambunctious dog that she and her new boyfriend shared custody with.

Bartek didn't care that she was with someone – after all, why would the hottest woman on earth spend her time alone? He certainly didn't want her to be lonely, and he knew life had put them on different paths. He was still madly in love with her, but he had to roll of the dice & get over it.

Although a little stiff & cautious, he was more talkative then usual. She recognized the man she'd met over a year ago. He prattled on awhile until she was comfortable, and then he got around to the bigger question.

In a final desperate outcry, he'd sent her a 13 page handwritten powerhouse of a letter as well as a copy of his secret book. He'd been waiting for some kind of response to it ever since.

As per usual with his degrading luck, *Clownbaby's mother had thrown the package away!!* The greatest ace up his sleeve was no match for the controlling, over-bearing woman!! Bartek began to laugh as he always did towards his karmic abuse.

Clownbaby looked sad, then spoke conciliatory. Bartek chortled, then explained the contents of the letter. He began laughing harder, and Clownbaby's face lit up with a blush. Whatever hangover was left of the nervous summer blur instantly dissipated.

As for her depressing physical ailments, she was undergoing a battery of tests. She was paranoid she had cancer again, and not long ago she had endured kidney failure. Clownbaby was most certainly drinking herself to death. But it was more disturbing for Bartek to acknowledge this cherished human of his had endured such a terrible cancer battle.

For an unknown number of years, she was in a suicidal heroin hole. Afterwards, she spent a year in chemotherapy, nearly dying. To picture this loved one bald and frail, on the verge of death, broke his heart. He wasn't there for her during any of it, because he was too attracted to the limelight to realize she existed.

The phony Charles Manson was gone, but she was now dating a shadowy Russian. Her table was clogged with DVD's she'd grabbed from his mother – foreign language programs she could not possibly understand. Like Bartek, she was a Europhile, throwing strange movies on for background noise an odd imagery.

He tried to again explain how they were synced up, but she wasn't quite believing it. There was no way this metal/punk guy was web-streaming Slovenian soap operas or Ukrainian pop music stations to nurse the quiet psychedelic rabbit hole in the back of his head. He again tried to push LAIBACH, but she wasn't listening. The woman was a secret NSK art operative, she just had no idea.

The new boyfriend came over, and it seemed yet another divergent thing she was living. In her flight she was pretending she was an immigrant. She had teamed up with this mob of Cyrillic interpreters and changed her entire wardrobe. In Bartek's absence, the anti-social cat woman had went *Breakfast At Tiffany's*.

Whereas before she was quietly existing in a depressed, misanthropic way, dressing in winter Carhart coat & denim jeans interspersed with the wild costuming of an acid-whacked lipstick lesbian – she was now flamboyantly femme-fatale.

The art scene in Detroit recognized her immediately; once they caught her acrobatics of speech and form of twisted, vibrant logic, the entire bohemian circuit of Detroit fell in love with her just as hard as Bartek had.

She went from an entire life of being labeled ugly & boyish for not looking "generic hot" to instantly becoming a well-paid photogenic exotic model for high-grade painters and such. The entire Detroit scene were crawling after her in a detonation of infatuation.

It was karmically fitting, once again – she was sitting there for years same as he, living the same isolated alienation in an identical personal habitat, hanging around the same people, going the same places. The moment he abandoned being a "darling" of the Detroit scene, she took his place as the new fast-talking hypnotist.

But a handsome man with a smile sharp enough to charm a snake was nothing compared to the control a woman of her caliber with proper confidence. Clownbaby had Detroit under wraps, and she would not be budging anytime soon.

And so, after a pleasant evening of *Tim & Eric's Awesome Show Great Job*, he left her and the Russian BFF to their own world and returned to the lonesome coldness of Linda's front room couch.

With the strange tale of Clownbaby's multiple-reality existence (*at least in his head*), it was adequate that he too become the subject of a similar fascination. When he attended the pre-Thanksgiving feast with his high school chums a few weeks prior, there was a woman he'd remembered from years ago.

He only met her once. Same group of people, same reunion dinner but 5 years earlier; in the crowd was an attractive borderline-goth girl with raven-black hair, a black silk dress, tattooed angel wings on her back plus mesmerizing light blue eyes.

She had a boyfriend with her, so they only had time for a brief conversation. She didn't seem interested in knowing him much, or was rather wrapped up in her own life and kind of stopping in. She was a bit of a curiosity, but he never saw her again.

This year, she was again at the party – single and searching. She was on Bartek fast, and they quickly made plans to hang out before he again left to Seattle. It was the day after Clownbaby when he drove to her apartment in downtown Detroit. They transferred to her vehicle, and she escorted them to Greek Town for dinner.

Claudia gripped the wheel. Not knowing the head-trip of Clownbaby or much about him, in her witchy-woman way the oracle turned to him and sputtered it out like a calm, rabid avalanche: "*You know we've been doing this for a long time now? In a hundred different realities, right? Every time you come through this time loop, I keep telling you not to go, just to stay put, because it will save us all the time and hassle. All I have to do is finish my nursing degree – it'll be wrapped up this summer, and then we can just go to Europe like you want. But you never listen to me, ever, ever, ever. No matter what you do, you end up in Portland. It's important that you end up there, because you have a role to play there.*"

Bartek was not surprised with this weird dialogue. He seemed to know all this instinctively when meeting her. Again, he fought his destiny: "*But I don't care about Portland, I don't even know it – Seattle is where it's at.*"

Claudia continued, just staring right through him: "*Yeah, right – Seattle... Anyway, I end up with you in Portland way, way after you get rid of that stupid girl. It's after I'm already married and go through that whole thing. But I don't have to go through that whole thing. You just need to quit the act right now. I'm so sick of telling you this over and over on repeat.*"

Bartek blankly stared: "*But you don't even know me.*"

Claudia continued: "*Oh I know everything. This is why you — that is why you —*" etc. "*And I know just how 'crowded' you are, how 'busy' you are. I know all about your 'visitors' Ryan. I've never quite seen anything like it. You don't see it in me? I have —*" and she explained her phantom problems.

"*So you see, we are very much the same person – and I'm telling you all this now so I don't have to say it again in 9 years or so, because I'm really sick of just wasting time. We can just proceed right now, all you have to do is stay put. And you will be very, very happy. We will be very, very happy."*

Bartek was quietly dumbfounded. In the way that he lived off the directions of fortune cookies and linked insignificant events into some interconnected, epic, he should easily have taken to this. But he just wasn't that "into" her.

This sort of gothy witchy chemistry was best suited to his teen years – and he didn't quite want to mess with supernatural forces anymore. He wanted that muck-rack removed from his life.

The two predictably ended up together that night, although physically they didn't go far. As they sat in bed she spoke to him as if she was already his wife, already so far into their relationship they might as well have been together a decade. She seemed to know everything about him – all the intricacies and balances.

The next morning she prepared breakfast and reasserted he just stay this time as to avoid the mess of the next decade. When he exited he looked back through the closing door at her eyes and felt exactly as he did leaving Kelly in Seattle. Despite the lunatic precision of her insane dialogue that cut through him like a knife, he closed the door and drove away.

3 days later, Bartek was on a Greyhound approaching Billings, Montana on track to arrive in Seattle for Christmas Eve. He had completed his studio records and split without telling anyone except Linda and his parents.

He was able to see Clownbaby one last time at her work, a fancy clothing store in the Northern Suburbs. She was looking at him differently then, seemingly coaxing him to stay. She was as intoxicating as ever. They parted well, and he purchased his bus ticket. The next day, somewhere outside Chicago, he texted her that he'd left and good luck with the BFF. Her text back seemed angry or hurt, but he wasn't quite sure. It seemed clear that it was all wrapped up with her and she wasn't interested.

Despite Claudia's mind-blowing oracle discourse, he just wasn't that into her. Claudia didn't dig heavy metal or horror movies. She could throw all the love in the world at him, all the witchy-woman nonsense, the safety & security of a career medical worker – but if she couldn't hang with Ash J. Williams, she just wasn't down.

After 30 hours on a Greyhound, Bartek arrived at the Billings station to find everyone going to points further West had been trapped by a blizzard *for 13 days*!

Legions were broke & living off donuts; entire platoons on holiday leave from Afghanistan and Iraq, forced to spend their R&R in that stinking Montana death trap! It was the most miserable Greyhound waiting room he'd ever seen!! With the blizzard projections, he'd have to wait 5 days there before moving on!

The only option he had was to turn back and arrive again in Detroit – spit out two days later, on Christmas morning with no refund for his trip ticket!! They pushed him through knowing well that he would be stuck in Montana and then robbed him of $200 by proxy!! *Bastards!! Old Man Winter's elemental bitch fist!!*

Detroit had bested him! And if he stayed in Montana he'd no doubt get into some unpleasant situation with the numerous ex-cons & cracked Marines now sleeping on the Greyhound floor!!!

Thus, Ryan Bartek spent another 30 hours of backtracking only to arrive once again at the squalid dead-center of his Anticlimax Leviathan! His stepfather picked him up just as before, and once they made his apartment, Bartek called his roomies in Seattle. Despite paying 2 months rent in advance, they gave his room to someone else!! *They stole $400 & left him homeless on Christmas!!!*

They promised to pay him back, but they were broke. He'd never see that money again, and without it he'd be scraping his way back into Seattle by his bare teeth!! Was he really homeless this time, in the dead of winter midst the worst blizzard the Northwest had seen in over a century?!? *Was he really trapped?!*

It was clear to him that 2008 was laughing in his face. It was like an execution by karma, and he had little doubt that the year we beat him to a pulp until its brutal end. Comically, he envisioned himself as a sort of bereft Chevy Chase.

He went outside and looked to the sky, egging on the forces of human woe to bring its final assault. Dish it out, get it done – bring it quick & bring it savage. He wanted to go home.

Stanley Pluto called and invited him to another Coney Island reunion with Lana. When he arrived they were in the same booth, wearing the same clothes, as if stepping into a scene from *Groundhog Day*. Pauly looked defeated.

In the time of his Greyhound to Billings, Ursula died of a drug overdose! Too much kilonopin, the anti-anxiety drug – *stopping her heart in the middle of the night!!* The vibrant warrior journalist in the making which looked up to him so much and wanted to follow as an apprentice that summer was dead!! *At 19!!!*

Lana walked back to the table, weaving in her pill-headed mental patient way. Bartek wouldn't be surprised if they came from her. Bartek was in shock, not quite sure what to do with it.

Pauly changed his crazed depression and again pointed to Lana, who was ready to go & had $20 grand. All Bartek felt like was being dispatched to another asylum as a cabbie & legally obliged to care-take someone. He ate his gyro, then departed.

Our bereft protagonist hid at Linda's avoiding the world until the clock ran out. The blizzard was still pounding the West Coast, and it was simply a waiting game. He had no choice but to drag this our until New Years. In the void he wrote to Sadique, but she wasn't having any of it. Clownbaby was an unresponsive satellite.

Bartek rode the Detroit public bus down 8 Mile, down Greenfield all the way to Warren Ave. The ride was ghetto gnarly as always. He'd been raised in East Dearborn, the Arabic side.

After his Grandma's death, he was whisked to West Dearborn. He always considered East D his home. By middle school, he was back much as possible. After high school, there every day.

Everyone was gone except a handful of friends who no longer communicated. 3 guys still lived with their parents, and the other house the old man just died. Other old friends moved in, and it was a void of pot smoke.

This crew had spun out from the heavy abuses of the rave scene. By 2003, it was always like the long Sunday after that raging party. People trickled away, either positively or nastily.

One just died at 25; he'd joined the army and was to be deployed in Iraq, yet died doing heroin in the barracks. Another old friend of theirs had also joined the US Army – literally to legally kill Arabs. So when Bartek saw him again that day, after 4 years in Iraq, he was happy with everything he did. He was proud, excited – he got to kill "13 TowelHeads," and no one could take that away from him. As a civilian he was bored & just signed another 4 year tour for fun!

Bartek left the gloomy malaise of East D in its cold tomb by riding a public bus down Ford Road to Telegraph, where he hopped another bus to Michigan Ave.

He had lived nearby on Outer Drive an equal distance between Edsel Ford and Dearborn High Schools, so he had a photogenic memory of every business, street, alley. Being a loner with a bicycle, all he did was ride; he knew that area like few others.

He returned to it as the wind howled & snow heaved down. Claudia would be coming to get him and he needed to kill time. He felt like a relic, like a time traveler. He drank coffee at IHOP then wandered the Westborn strip-mall. The number of days he'd spent there as a child was immeasurable.

Claudia – who had never been notified of his previous escape attempt – rang. En route to pick him up her car spun out on the freeway & been totaled! She should've been dead!!

Luckily, she was fine – but Bartek was now stuck. Everyone who would've helped him had moved – he had no buddies to call except one guy, who blew him off for a chick he'd already been dating for months. He didn't even ask to intrude on their time, he was just looking for a couch overnight. *An entire life burned away!*

It grew dark, and Bartek arranged for Linda to get him on 12 Mile. He waited in the snowstorm 45 minutes. When the bus came. its route defied all logic & sent him in the wrong direction! He got off & made it to the right stop at 8:30pm; moments later, the last bus of the night sped past him as he chased it through the blizzard!

The snow kept coming, and his fingers were pained with chills. He was wet from the snowdrift and so very, very tired. It was either $60 for a motel and an affirmation of total rock bottom in his home world or just tap out & call the folks. His stepdad picked him up, and the two drove off. *Dearborn was officially over…*

New Years Eve, approaching 9 o'clock. One final grand-slam party, the entire Northern crew at Stoner Joe's house. Sasquatch Agnostic's drummer put the group on edge, 'cause he'd screwed the wife of some hot-headed, gun-slinging steroid rager. Guy was threatening to kill him, and the party was onlooking for creeping vehicles.

Bartek was beyond horny – 27 now, and he'd had sex maybe 6 times that entire year. It was torture. The whole year he felt like he was gonna explode. At least New Years would ring in right – Claudia's car was fixed & she was comin' to love 'em silly.

It was casual how she spoke – her siren call was that of a nurse telling you to undress. She felt terrible about leaving him stranded in Dearborn. He was goose-bumped.

The clock hit 9pm & Claudia rang – *her period started & she was staying home*. She wouldn't pick him up either. So drink champagne & sleep well. Then she hung up.

Bartek envisioned yet another phantom fist whamming into his skull. He was so goddamn hot & bothered & none of these women would ever make out with "The Mole" & his 56 page propaganda thesis on wiping Christianity off the face of the Earth.

With increasing drunkenness spun the hands of the clock – 10 minutes until the ball dropped. Devious wheels spun in his head. What if he just bolted with Lana & her magic $20,000? What if he just waltzed into an arranged marriage with his living dead girl? That's what she wanted, right – to be the abused henchman of some psychopathic clown? An evil grin came to his face…

…until he realized he'd left his journal at Coney Island which contained all matters on Clownbaby, Claudia & unfinished loves. *Which meant Lana knew everything!! Which meant he had to stay in Detroit until Stanley could drop it off!!*

Bartek texted him – unable to meet for 7 days!!! *Bartek was trapped in Detroit another week!!!!!* The Fist of The Anticlimax Leviathan, straight to the solar plexus... Midnight came, the house cheered, and like a wounded, stumbling boxer, Bartek wobbled to the nearest couch & crashed out like a junk pile of desperation...

Morning, 2009 – had the curse lifted? Stanley dropped off the journal, and Ryan purchased the Greyhound home. He'd arranged a 1 month couch surf in Shoreline, at the edge of Seattle.

On January 2nd, Bartek began a trip that was supposed to last 3½ days yet turned into nearly 7. Fighting the blizzard the entire way home, he stumbled upon the suicidal Dr. Jeremy Sullivan. The two started something on that trip, a mutual agenda of epic intensity...

Before Jeremy left, he asked Bartek if he'd heard anything from Clownbaby. "*I don't know... probably sucking face with her BFF.*" Jeremy winced: "*What, her best friend?*"

Bartek: "*No, her BFF – her boyfriend.*" Jeremy looked at him funny: "*Son, you need to study up on all this digital age slang – BFF isn't boyfriend, it's 'best friend forever.'*"

It instantly dawned on Bartek that he misunderstood what Clownbaby was communicating. Given this correction... it seemed clear that she really was trying to get him to stay.

That guy wasn't her lover. How asshole it must have sounded to her reading: "*good luck with your BFF.*" Had he just walked from the love of his life from ignorance of basic text lingo??

Jeremy walked away a newborn homeless anarchist in deep winter. Bartek's phone rang – "*Hi Clown-bay-beeee.*" He expected to hear that crazy tone of hers prattling off disjointed ideas, mixed with totally insane bursts of laughter.

Instead, an ecstatic male voice: "*Bartek! This is amazing!! Crazy!! I just do not fucking believe this!!!*" He sounded familiar, but couldn't place it. The unknown man continued: "*See, I told you – I so told you but you just didn't listen. Oh my, it's just so amazing…"*

Bartek cut to the chase: *"Who is this?"* The voice said *"Josh!"* Bartek still was a little fuzzy. *"Remember? I lived with you at Stoner Joe's! For 8 months!!"*

And then it hit him – the guy with all the fishies & stacks of *Magic: The Gathering* cards. The guy who for *every day of one year* was trying to put him on a blind date with a girl he constantly explained was his likely future wife. That the universe was out of alignment and nothing would be until they met.

That girl was Clownbaby. She was to be his blind date for the Saturday night *3 days after* he ran away to California and launched *The Big Shiny Prison.* That Saturday Uncle Ron of Downtown Brown was to be his bassist audition, and Clownbaby was to be his blind date for that evening.

And had he just never thrown the natural order out of balance, A.K.A. MABUS would have been all he ever wanted it to be, and he would undoubtedly have romanced the absolute love of his life. Bartek hung up the phone and began laughing, laughing, laughing. *The Anticlimax Leviathan was complete…*

Loose Ends

It was a powerhouse of an opening line, one that poignantly described the distance of his prior life: "*My past now holds the distinction of another man passing by in traffic, face blurred by the whirl of rampant automobiles…*"

It wasn't that he really wanted to begin another book. After all, he'd spent an immeasurable chunk of his early 20's writing an autobiography he'd never dared release.

Back then, it felt life or death – *that he could perish from the earth & take with him the liberation of his human experience…*

With *Zug Island*, his intent was to relate a cautionary tale as such to provide strength and proxy sympathy for lost souls of his ilk. There was, of course, serious guilt attached to his impetus – to make right that which could never be fixed, and to subvert the catastrophic trajectory of others.

Through writing this secret book he healed himself – yet he also knew quite well that it's release would spell the death of his career. Perhaps even a sense of fame (*or rather infamy*) he just did not want. It was a strange checkmate.

Looking back, he should've just been playing music. There was a titanic part of him that wished he'd been a total failure at journalism all along, simply to clear the pathway. He was really only happy when performing on stage and living the life of the obscure, underdog musician. It was a simple life, full of camaraderie.

But he had a gift for writing that was far more important to the wider world then his knack for shredding extreme metal – and it would be negligent not to utilize it.

Furthermore, he knew Detroit had a shelf life. In Michigan he could rarely find musicians who shared his influences, let alone his vision. Even if they came close, he trusted none to live in a van like fanatic traveling minstrels.

So it was less an intentional project and more a helpless, vulnerable reaction to Henry Miller's influence when he began *Anticlimax Leviathan*. Construing his bus company grunt-hood was not a flowery experience by any escalation of imagination – it was a noxious poison demanding expulsion.

Whatever this new book now being pounded out was, the finale was unclear. In these misty, mystic Seattle mornings of January 2009, Ryan Bartek now hammered the keys furiously.

The important thing was to get it going, for future's sake. Abandon it, intentionally, as to remain a pilot light quietly maintaining a flame. Feel incremental guilt as if orphaning one's own child & the ephemeral longing that comes with said action.

Just let it wade in its unfinished void so that one day this subdued pyre could be jolted to max temp with a quick flick. Was this the masterpiece he would undoubtedly finish in prison? For once, it was his hobby...

Left homeless by his former roommates in the U District (*who'd also pocketed his advance rent*) – this only led him to "the magic spot": the home he'd first been welcomed into when arriving in Seattle during *The Big Shiny Prison* adventure.

It was here that the general punk mob he associated with maintained a headquarters of sorts. With a studio in the basement and numerous bands practicing there, at any time random members from the two dozen bands on their collective label could appear at any time. It was a cozy hub where family meant something much more then blood relation.

Bartek had now formally joined the team of Beer Metal Records. It was less a label and more an umbrella organization of friendly bands using the same name, with no financial or business obsession attached to it.

He was at the helm of a great foundation, and his grindcore band Sasquatch Agnostic was now an addition to the collective. The album was complete for release – he just needed to commit to forming the live band. He had no intention of wasting anyone's time, let alone his. The next step was two jobs, Econoline van, new gear, musician seeking, then straight for the kill.

His only real obstacle was, ironically, being a famous metal writer. While this undoubtedly helped him in terms of promotion and scenester politics, his status as traveling journalist for both *Metal Maniacs* and *Hails & Horns* was something not easily surrendered.

This allowed him endless opportunities of manifestation with global implications. He wanted to be a weird gonzo journalist as a teen & despite all odds he made it happen.

With 2 of the biggest metal mags in America solidly behind him – one on the West Coast, the other East, and both run two of the most powerful female editors in their respective field – he'd been given the green light: "*just send it, we'll print it*." Both of which, flatteringly, professed he was among their fave writers in metal.

Both editors were to assist promoting "*The Big Shiny Prison*" and whatever new band he chose – both were going to begin pushing him as a modern heavy metal Hunter S. Thompson.

How could he resist? How could he say no? Would it not be a worse regret to turn this opportunity down in lieu of the Sasquatch Agnostic lock-down?

He burned to be a common metal guy again, just another grunt in the trenches. But here was this offer no man could refuse. He had $1500 stuffed away & living on $2 a day. All he had to do was wait for Spring.

It was looking as if he could stowaway with road crew on some mega tour – anything on Century Media or Nuclear Blast seemed fair game. Just jump from tour to tour working merch and doing road reporting with any worthwhile band that might have him.

After all, he still wanted to see what was left of America he'd never encountered. During this human ping-pong of touring, he also would fling copies of his albums. The touring network would be solid; he would no doubt regain his self-confidence to do spoken word, and fine-tune his acoustic return as the satanic Johnny Cash…

Therefore, it was of a great head-kicking when the plug was pulled on *Metal Maniacs* by their newly appointed corporate overlords. 27 magazine titles were hastily closed after the umbrella company *Maniacs* was part of was acquired by a villainous Corporation.

In response to the moribund economy, they immediately ceased publication of all but 5 of their periodicals. At the very moment the death notice for *Metal Maniacs* was announced, the Manhattan-based editorial board were completing their triumphant, double-sized, 20 year anniversary issue in which Bartek was set to be launched into orbit.

He had something being reprinted as an example to the fine journalism the magazine had produced over two decades, with his ever-present footer describing his travel antics.

The chair was pulled out from under his ass by an innominate vulture in some inscrutable Manhattan office. In one stroke of the pen Bartek's dream was rendered extinct and his wild ride concluded. The impact of *Maniacs* closure was felt throughout the underground – salutation emerged internet-wide; editorial pieces emerged in competitor magazines and even the most ardent anti-commercial, anti-trend, uber-underground elitist zines paid tribute to the fallen giant.

Even the other big magazine Bartek still wrote for ran a 3 page spread on the death of *Maniacs* – something unheard of from mass market competition! There he was, in print, mourning over the death of his beloved career peak – quoted alongside members of Slayer, Megadeth & Black Sabbath!

While Bartek still wrote for *Hails & Horns*, he knew it just wasn't the same. *Maniacs* earned its reputation by stubbornly refusing to cover anything remotely mainstream. No trendy bands – it was non-commercial or nothing at all.

And so, when turning the pages away from this pro-*Maniacs* glorification, all he saw was direct marketing targeted at a new generation he no longer understood, and bands he had no interest in. He came from a background of leather jackets & army boots, not foam trucker hats & neon clothes. This was not the stomping grounds of ABSU, but a melting pot of quaffed-hair screamo. It was high time to bow out gracefully. Bartek sent his formal resignation.

In April, he would be 28. He'd completed *Big Shiny Prison* but he still had no publisher. His first book was out of print and would remain so. He'd made a low-budget movie he was proud of, but the director never put it out. No album he made was ever released in official format, nor did he have them on YouTube. He'd no idea what to do with the acoustic albums, and Sasquatch Agnostic was a blur of crazy noise with few authentic "tunes."

His confidence for spoken word was beat out of him. At the outset of 2008, he was poised to hit Hollywood's comedy circuit and gradually make his mark through amateur nights & open mics. He'd go to open casting calls & forcefully crack his way into bit parts. If he set out to make b-movie crap, how could he possibly fail?

With the calamity of San Diego came great despair, a suffocating sadness. The loneliness had grown so tyrannical he could no longer mask it with comedy. He was a washed up comedian.

In always setting out to make music that rubbed people the wrong way – *in basing his entire career on career suicide* – he never actually made one solid, straight-forward record that gave the punk or metal audience exactly what they wanted to hear.

He'd had his name in print enough that he'd become a known writer attached to this fringe, but his serious work remained unknown. Neither did he have a website outside MySpace profiles – and that platform was rapidly dying.

It was in this quagmire of direction when Neil P. called, offering to work merch on a nearly 7 week Downtown Brown tour.

At this point, it was more then just rolling along with his buddies from back "home" – the band was literally one of his favorite punk bands in American history. The wider world had yet to know it, and they probably would never be accepted by that scene.

They were worshiped by the slap-happy & open minded, their

techniques & structures universally respected by musicians, but they were a bizarre curiosity (*at best*) for the non-musically adept punk rock fan – and loathed by the dirtiest punk extremists.

It was a magic opportunity, and probably the last he'd ever be able to tour with them. They were going to every major city in the USA Bartek had yet to experience – and he could avoid deep winter depression by staying on the go. There was no reason not to accept.

To celebrate his decision, that night he headed off with his roommates to see a punk show at their favorite bar in the U-District.

Miss Monster and her boyfriend Gregory (*the roomies*) had really saved him. She was an animated & hyper character, while Gregory was quiet, perceptive. Like that strange, quiet kid in high school who paints pictures all day and the world does not exist.

Miss Monster had two kids from an ex – the boy was 9 and the girl 7. Both were skittish with adults, but they took to him remarkably. He felt like a bonus addition to their family – a weird Uncle Fester lurking in the basement.

He didn't quite realize it at the time, but the boy didn't speak to any adults really. The girl was also very standoffish with anyone not family. It was this magic charm of his that Monster took to, and also what made Gregory a little uncomfortable with this wacky transient getting a little too close.

At the punk show Gregory hung at the bar while Monster and Bartek went for a walk. She had a tendency to get worked up in a spastic way. And people often thought she was fried on meth because she was so hyper, twitchy and fast-talking. She was tiny and had a big mouth and loved to talk shit to people she didn't respect – especially tough-guy rapper guys and meathead jocks. *And cops*.

Bartek explained to Miss Monster the rough story of Lana. It was something he didn't want to think about or bring up much, but it was on his mind. The terribleness he felt from it was a consistent plague, like an ever scabbed wound.

He described the awful feeling he always had when a squad car passed by. He knew what they really were, and he understood their danger and exploitation. Most Americans had no clue the brutal foundations of exploitation and torture holding society in place. They'd call him "*paranoid*," roll their eyes to his tirades: "*Yeah, and what did the cops ever do to you?!?*"

Miss Monster was shocked by the brutality of his tale. To imagine romantically calling up your long lost love, with your heart open & arms outstretched, ready to tell her one message, like fire on your tongue – that now is the time to escape and come to this new world with you, ready to give her your all, ready to live a real life…

…only to find that she is being driven to prison at that very moment, that she is to be incarcerated while 3 months pregnant – *that it may very well be your baby* –then learning that your wife miscarried on the floor of a Macomb County cell from the extreme stress of the situation.

To learn that the pigs killed your fucking child and destroyed your family over a Vicadin pill and a noise complaint, because even if it wasn't genetically yours (*which it probably was*), you'd still have accepted it, still told her to come – that you'd make it work no matter what, no matter anything – and that this child would've been raised as your own.

And then, in the agonizing torment of state-sanctioned bondage, your wife goes completely insane. Her mind crumbles, the soul devoured. Your family is dead, and there is nothing you can do to change any of it.

He told Miss Monster that anytime he felt protective of someone, the cops would seemingly destroy them. In an attempt to cheer him, she said: "*Don't worry, those pigs'll never get me.*" Bartek smiled. He hit the bowl and passed it; they turned the corner, getting closer to the venue.

Monster started getting worked up, talking how she hated the cops, how they were all scum. The pair walked by a dark alley, and Monster hollered "*Fucking pigs!*" and spit on the cement to symbolically show her detest.

Immediately an arm swung from the darkness of the alley, grabbing Monsters coat. A mugger? A meth crazy? It happened so fast Bartek was useless.

All Monster knew was that a stranger was grabbing her violently, so she swung her arm around in defense and slapped this person: "*Don't fuckin' touch me, I'll fuckin' kill you!!!*"

The female cop whom Monster accidentally assaulted immediately pulled out a tazar and electrocuted Miss Monster with the highest voltage she had.

Bartek caught on quick – they were walking past a hidden police car, and when Monster shouted her hatred of pigs, the cop thought she was directly referencing her.

When she spit on the ground, the cop thought she was spitting on the squad car – an offense that counts the same as physically attacking a cop and carries a 10 year felony.

With this insane horse-stunning voltage coursing through the body of this 5 foot 3, 110 pound mother of two, Monster pulled the tazar chords out of her chest and threw the still sparking weapons to the ground. The cop had done pissed her off.

The psychopath in Miss Monster exploded. With the roar of a demonic grizzly right in the cops face: *"WHAT YOU GUNNA DO NOW CUNT?!?"* The cop freaked & tazered her again – and again Monster pulled them out of her chest and threw them to the ground as if dental floss.

"WHAT ELSE YOU GOT BITCH?!? I'LL KILL YOU!!!" The cop again tazered her, and she finally dropped. The cop pounced, struggling to handcuff the thrashing, uncontrollable Monster.

Bartek – fearing if he did not leave immediately he would lose it and beat this cop to death in the street – ran into the bar where Gregory was. When they came back out Monster was handcuffed and pinned to the ground, screaming bloody murder: *"I'll fucking kill every last one of you pigs – I'll hack you into fuckin' pieces–"*

Gregory & Bartek stood shocked. Within 2 minutes, 24 cop cars & a paddy-wagon clogged the street with flashing lights. There were 8 grown men holding her down, and she just would not shut up. She was frothing at the mouth, threatening to kill them all. They black-bagged her head then hoisted the squirming, struggling loon into the paddy-wagon.

Gregory and Bartek went back to the house empty-eyed, trying to figure out what to do. He would have to dump his life savings on a bail bond, and it wasn't even clear what the charges were. If they wanted, they could put her in prison for up to 20 years.

Bartek paced the backyard – the moon was so bright & powerful it had a perfect ring of light around it, like Saturn.

The next day Gregory left for the police station, and the kid's real dad dropped them off after a weekend excursion. Bartek pulled the guy to the side explaining the intensity of the situation, how he didn't know what to say to the kids or how to handle it. The father kind of shrugged his shoulders at this emergency and simply left like it wasn't his problem.

Bartek lied to the kids and said their mom would be back shortly, but after dragging it out 2 hours, they realized something was fishy. He had to keep inventing lies about going shopping, and the kids were panicking thinking something was wrong with their mother, that there was an accident.

Monster walked in the door and hugged her kids in surprisingly good spirits. Bartek sat on the couch as he listened to them weep and cry in the other room when they found out their beloved mother had been beaten by cops. They knew she was lying about not being in trouble, and they were a wreck.

Monster was smart enough to take pictures of her wounds – she was covered in bruises. They humiliated and strip searched her. Even when explaining she had a broken back and one wrong move could paralyze her, grown men three times her weight and size dug their knees into her back laughing. She was all fucked up.

The family quickly got a lawyer, and the police quickly threatened her with 10 years in prison. Bartek was the only real witness, and the lawyer refused to let him testify claiming he was disreputable, that no jury would believe him.

And so in the hustle of it all – with the cops realizing they were caught red-handed in a brutality case and never having read Miranda rights – they offered her a probation plea deal. So long as she didn't get in trouble for 2 years, the case would be dropped. If she had the faintest altercation with the law they'd throw this loving mother of two children in prison for a decade.

Gregory wasn't so keen on Bartek staying there anymore. It was weird enough that he was getting too close, but that anytime he left those two alone they were bound to get in trouble somehow – especially like this...

It was time for Bartek to hit the road. He finally found somewhere he felt wanted, accepted, needed. He had a sincere emotional investment. And once again the pigs had again taken his family from him. And the only reason it happened was because he dared speak up what they did to his ex-wife.

As Bartek tied up his loose ends before tour, he contacted all bands of Beer Metal Records. He had held back on starting his life to hook them up on one final mission. The tour would be a promotional one – handing out 1000's of burn CDR's, stickers & swag. He'd given all the bands advance warning and all pledged to give him an avalanche of promo.

But as he left the house and this new family behind, the only one that came through was Gregory – handing him a skimpy stack of CD samplers. The writing was again blazing on the wall. It would be another cold, lonely Valentine's on the road...

It was late March when the punk rock garrison drove back into Detroit. Downtown Brown had circled the nation, playing 43 dates. At the tours conclusion they recorded their "comeback album" *Back From The Dead* live at The Shelter.

Returning to Neil's home after tour, Bartek was again a free agent. Luckily his stepfather had an extra car parked nearby available for a week's use. He picked it up and head to a used clothing store to accumulate some new duds. After years of looking the metal/punk part, he wanted to mix it up with some cheap suits like he did as a teenager.

As he drove to the Value Village, he ruminated on his meeting with Clownbaby last winter. She'd met him warmly with a hug, and the two sat down to talk. He felt like a religious zealot confessing to a pastor in calm secrecy. Bartek had asked what she thought of the secret book he sent – *but her mother had thrown it away!* His mad love letter went straight to the garbage landfill!

And so Bartek, whom always found himself paralyzed by Clownbaby's presence, began laughing. She asked why that was funny – she thought he'd be mad or hurt, as is why she never mentioned the packages fate. And finally Bartek found the courage to speak what had tormented him so long and had mutilated his ill-fated Big Date with her in Seattle: *"I totally came out to you."*

Clownbaby blushed, and he saw again that smile he loved so much. *"That's why I got the MDMA – to make it easy. I don't even do those drugs, I just knew I could break through that wall. I just wanted to get you to the park in Capitol Hill, just rant and rant and rant... I'm really sorry about that."*

Clownbaby's tune changed – he'd instantly redeemed himself on the level he'd sought. And then she had a bit of a puzzled look, staring at the man who sat below the gigantic rainbow flag pinned on her wall. Clownbaby said: *"That's why I was confused when you didn't want to go to Capitol Hill."*

"To be honest with you I've never even been at a gay bar. I used to eat at Como's now and again, because it was around the block from my old house and had great pizza. The whole living in Ferndale thing – that was just coincidental. Real Detroit was there... You know, the first time we met, you just spoke to me like I was on that side of the fence. I never mentioned anything and you saw right through me. I remember when you mentioned something about the gay scene – I can't remember what it was, or what I said in return – but I definitely batted it away. You just turned to me and looked through me and cut all the bullshit – you said 'get over it.' It was like you hit me with a hammer."

The two spoke at ease. He made clear that this shift was not possible without her. That while it was true he'd missed her in normal life constantly for 6 years, the big message was that if he'd just been real with himself at an earlier stage, he would have sorted it out and met her long ago. After all, she was always crawling through the many gay bars that surrounded his Ferndale apartment...

As with any uncomfortable subject he did not want known to the outside world, he was quite venomous in safe guarding it. Although he enjoyed being hated for the right reasons, it was another thing to be laughed at for the wrong reasons.

This issue was easily the most strenuous for him, and only reveals why he waited 28 years before admitting it. It was also doubly revealing why his flight from sanity was so sickly in early adolescence. In even the earliest stages of puberty he knew what was up – *and wanted it gone.*

If anything had pushed him to the point of suicide, it was this raging confusion of checkmate between mind, spirit, dream, sexuality – and a parentally enforced extremist loathing to the point of supporting genocide against his own kind.

As a rebellious young man who instinctively fought against tyrannical forces he didn't quite understand but nonetheless felt were deeply wrong, he'd no choice but analysis.

When a child is intelligent enough to know the illusion surrounding him is inherently wrong & unhealthy – yet is surrounded by adults telling him he is insane, incorrect, must be punished for thinking the healthy things he does – the child must fight a never-ending battle into adulthood. In retrospect some laugh it off as trials of adolescence.

Others, like Bartek, were profoundly scarred & unforgiving. At 13 it was hard enough for him to defeat Jesus Christ, let alone the urge for gay sex. If anything, it was the taboo of it & wrongful feeling of committed sin that flicked that switch. He thought it was extremely lame for grown men to hold hands, cuddle, treat each other like girlfriends.

Even as an adult openly admitting this was going on, he still wanted nothing faggy about his discreet interactions. He despised girly men even if they were straight – Black Sabbath & flaming skulls were cool, not cross-dressers & hot pink spandex. There was nothing lamer in the world to him then that forced queeny gay accent lisp. He despised its fakeness.

He knew that he wasn't gay in the true sense – he had zero romantic feelings for men. That ship had sailed, as they say. Deep down, hidden away, *yes*, there were a handful of times where it might've been possible at a younger age.

It was a one in a million thing, and never was he looking or accepting when it became available. It just simply was not on the table. He was emotionally castrated by repression. If he'd had a normal development, things may have been quite different.

He hated almost all males as a matter of reality. And if he maintained a truce with them, it was only because they were into metal or had an agenda he supported. His actual friends were scant, yet his acquaintances manifold.

But what if in admitting these impulses existed in him, it actually led him to something tangible? Was anything here other then freaky taboo? If so, it was rare. It was something quite strong when it existed – but it would also be misleading not to consider his attraction to entities as opposed to bodies, towards vibe & aura.

He had no desire to "be gay" with anyone. He had no interest in holding anyone's hand or talking about feelings. He had no interest in t shopping or wearing matching outfits in faggy ways.

He didn't do that with women, let alone some fruit-ball metro-sexual. He'd rather commit suicide then get a manicure or have his chest waxed or whatever it was that these lame motherfuckers did. And he detested the feel of these people's souls whenever they touched him.

Even in this early stage of acceptance, he knew that he was most likely a degenerate and little more. What was important was that he sort it out. Maybe stereotypes were less plentiful then he'd considered. Perhaps like an outsider looking at punk or metal and not getting all the subcultures inherent within them, Ryan was like most of humanity gazing in at the queer world and seeing one uncomfortable gray area.

In any case, he no longer had to play the role of metal journalist guy or crusty punk living in some roach-infested flophouse. Now, he could just sneak away. This handsome devil could just be whatever he wanted to tell anyone he was. After all, his strongest skill was always willed amnesia.

Bartek quickly changed into the pin-stripe suit he'd acquired for $2, then drove off into the oddly warm day.

It was so bright and sunny for a March afternoon in Michigan that he rolled the windows down and let the air wag around his black tie. He was headed towards his old neighborhood in Ferndale. He thought he'd park his car outside his old apartment symbolically, take a breath, then do the unthinkable – hanging out at all the gay bars on 9 Mile that he once avoided like the plague.

The warmth of the day allowed zero sleep, let alone the racing brain that was now on all cylinders. He still had a few hours to kill before it got dark, and feared if he contacted anyone word would spread. They'd rope him in and ruin this repressed attempt. They'd try to get him to come over and be upset when he refused, and he could not tell them why.

So interested in laying low was he that he didn't even notify Clownbaby he was in town. Under no circumstances would he chicken out on this victorious night.

Thus, he never should have answered his phone – he knew the number but was lost on its source. Foolishly, he picked it up anyway – Stanley Pluto. He knew Bartek was back because of his MySpace bulletins. Lana was convinced he was going to swoop her away now. She wanted out, right now, and had $20,000.

Bartek had never given her an answer, yet during the last visit he made clear he had moved on without ever directly saying it. He hadn't spoken to her in nearly 4 months.

Feeling like he owed it to her to gently end this thing, Ryan agreed to confront this ghost of his past. He looked to the front door of their former apartment – and her *other* former apartment with the junkie boyfriend continuing on another year.

Never did any location seem such a time-warp. 7 years ago, looking through his screen door, he never could've envisioned himself pulled to the side of the road looking back as he was now. Never would he have accepted at the age of 21 that this would be his fate, either with Lana or this new direction...

He arrived at another home in Ferndale, an aunt of Lana's. She motioned to the hallway and Bartek followed its corridor, arriving at a half-cracked door. He pushed it open and Lana was hunched over a wooden desk, knitting dental floss into a small ball wrapped around broken paper clips and sewing needles. She was hard at her work.

Her twitchy head kept sputtering and she wouldn't look at him. Lana's hair was cut like renegade Honey Whitlock. She was so whacked on methadone and psychiatric pills it looked like she was equally detoxing and flying. She was making chirping bird sounds like a meth head.

There was no denying it – Lana was irrevocably insane. Heroin had destroyed her, and the cops destroyed the rest. Staring at her dental floss ball of nervous tension, without looking up, Harley asked: *"Can we go home now?"*

Bartek's heart was breaking. Perhaps he should never have come there. He danced around the serious, ruthlessly asked question of when they would be leaving. He was there 3 minutes & she was gathering her explosion of clothing, as if they were to drive off.

He took her to Como's, the gay restaurant around the block where the best pizza in Detroit is made. He'd taken Lana there a few times – the very day he freaked out when she said she loved him and wanted to go to Christmas to meet his family – which led to him wrongly rejecting her, which led to... *this*.

The little gay waiter sat them at a candlelit table. Ryan explained with assertiveness what had been going on, that he would be slipping away from his past. He did this gracefully as he could, but he saw her slipping.

It was not only what she absolutely did not want to hear, but it was not at all what she expected. It was one of the most difficult things he ever had to do.

He escorted her to the apartment in Royal Oak that Stanley was paying for. In Stanley's loneliness he refused to let go of the girl who just was no more. And he'd been footing the bill for a very expensive studio fit for hipster artists to showcase their galleries.

And so the strange Joker man dealt with his zombie Harley in his delicate, soft-spoken way. She was a broken toy that only he could work but the child which owned it had grown up and moved away. The two spoke for an hour, but after awhile he had nothing much to say. It was over, and he just wanted out.

She sensed it too & knew her money had no sway over him. In her rickety insanity, she questioned: *"But you're The Joker – you can't be gay."* He replied: *"No baby, that's the joke... I'm Harvey."*

Back at the Stanley-leased apartment, she told him to wait cause she needed smokes from the corner market. Stanley had warned never to let her out of sight, but Bartek didn't have much fight in him – and neither was he aware the harsh reality of Lana's extreme addiction.

She vanished, and Bartek realized she was getting dope. When she came back he'd have to physically take it.

It was getting dark when Lana returned. Predictably, she needed to use the toilet. She set her purse down on the table, then went into the bathroom. He opened her fuzzy Hello Kitty satchel and picked up a bag of black. He ripped open the bathroom door catching the spoon-burning off guard.

Bartek snatched the bent silverware and chucked it across the apartment. Forcibly he grabbed the dope from her hand and marched to the kitchen sink, pouring it all down the drain.

When the reality of the situation clicked, she grew fierce and violent; the werewolf no longer required a full moon to rip itself from her body. He'd no time to call Stanley, because she was now unhinged & deprived of her fix.

The first he'd ever seen her snap out of her hazy, zombie-like funk. It was an eruption of the worst addiction. She was a feral beast.

She locked her body in the bathroom and began dialing numbers. She was talking to someone, but it definitely wasn't the cops. She came out screaming, pacing, totally insane. The message was clear: "*I am shooting dope, because you will not take me – I am killing myself because you are gay.*"

Three huge black guys show up at the door – her dope dealers. They don't know who he is, don't know what this apartment is, no idea who Stanley is, no idea about his dead child. No idea about bus world, their apartment, nothing. Just some guy needs to get fucked up, says cray cray.

The only way out was to play casual. He walked up to the biggest, baddest one of all and spoke with the air of gee whiz gee whillikers gosh golly. Just some weird white boy with a mohawk & suit & tie looking too goofy to be real danger. And they were in Royal Oak, with too many cops.

Another of the guys unforgiving eyes and scarred face had Bartek ready for a hurting. Really, what was he supposed to do against these guys? All he could hope for was a moderate beating. Harley burst into the hall, finally seeing her for the demon she was.

Her eyes were Black Lava, face contorted like Ted Bundy in that famed court photo: "*Faggot! Faggot! Fuck you FAGGOT! I hope you get AIDS and you DIE! FAGGOT!!! Fuck you! FUCK YOU!!! Two-Face – TWO-FACE!!*"

Bartek emptily paced away down the hall, her insults echoing. Away from his dead ex-wife and her dope slinging D-town thugs. Away from their dead child and Crazy Wendell's blue ear-muffs. Away from Zombie Harley clawing from the grave... *He didn't feel like going out that night.*

When he left town, there'd be no reason to return. This could very well be the last time he'd see his mother in person; sad on both ends. They went shopping; she bought him a black silk dress shirt & tie.

They stopped at a Mexican restaurant and he changed in the bathroom – he wanted to look spiffy for what could be his last dinner with momma. Instead of arguing, they had a nice conversation. The last he'd seen her, she'd been a blubbering wreck knowing he'd met his real father.

He stayed the night at their condo; tomorrow to Lansing with Downtown Brown. As a defense mechanism towards Michigan life, they all conspired to do one last road gig, like an encore of the tour. Bartek's momma cooked breakfast before dropping him off at Neil's.

As he ate scrambled eggs, he could see something let go inside of her – a kind of acceptance. But it wasn't quite realizing your child is all grown up – there was something ominous about it.

The two drove to Neil's and Bartek hugged her goodbye. She squeezed him abnormally long. He went with it, circumstances what they were. He left the car, and walked up his friends steps. Before he knocked on the door he turned to his smiling mother, who stuck her head out the window.

She smiled, then said: "*It's like I always tell the people at work – he could be a serial killer and I'd still love him, so long as he's not a fag... And then I wouldn't love him anymore.*"

His mother's face dropped its plastic smile position and became stern, snaky. She glared at him grimly, with awfulness. She was so direct, so cut-throat it was unspeakable.

Her eyes exported a deeply dogmatic hellfire which spoke: "*Please just say that you're gay so I can drive off and quit pretending to be your mother you little piece of fag shit.*"

Ryan stared back, shocked at its vileness. The message was loud & clear – and she just kept staring, with a Westboro-like stare of absolute hatred for 2 minutes, just waiting to confirm that yes, he was indeed bisexual, so that she could abandon him without regret.

Bartek was so aghast he wasn't quite sure what to say. He found himself stupefied & unable to respond.

She gave up waiting and with a shoulder-roll, raised-chin & dogmatic sigh – as if a Victorian noblewoman shaking her feathered wig – she bobbed her head into the vehicle & stared emptily out the windshield. She looked... *inconvenienced*. Then, without a word, she drove off – the child leaving her child behind...

Free Therapy

After 4 days on a Greyhound, a transient week in Seattle, and yet another 18 hours on a bus south, our escapist arrived in San Francisco the week preceding Easter.

2 years ago he'd shown up here alone on this same time frame, interviewing bands and personalities for his book. When the comfy arrangement he bartered fell apart, it was the first time he ever really went to the streets. It inevitably led him to Golden Gate, and he was soon absorbed by a mob of street punks that brought him up to speed on crust world.

It's not as if he were totally ignorant, because by proxy he was one of them. Yet in Detroit, he never knew anyone riding rails. Anyone he met in passing were usually dark characters with scars of heavy addiction and alcoholism. Even if they were clean, they were likewise arrogant. *"Punker then thou,"* as they say. Bartek always hated the attitude. He'd bite his lip, as any wise man would. Unlike them, he kept it silent.

Dropped into street world at 26, he felt a prince. It's what he always wanted to do but never had the guts. Not until he was hungry enough, crazy enough. The world of the traveling street crazy permanently riding Greyhounds like a mobile isolation tank – this was his version of reality. Everything outside it was delusion.

By the end of his anticlimactic summer in Seattle, the steam ran out on this glorious vision. He felt that creeping 30's chill – time to get training, time for a real job. It was stumbling onto Henry Miller at the right moment that illuminated him.

The dark void at center of street world was replaced by an envisioned nova not of light or dark but instead a rhythmic pulse in which all aware beings gravitate. Ignoring and disobeying it by living contrary to our nature rooted the amplification of misery. It was a question of ebb and flow.

Jeremy the Vegan fanatic & conspiracy hound had dragged him back into the nexus of Planet Street. Throughout Seattle Bartek sought loose roots; one foot in & out the door. In going back to the grid after his *Prison* tour, he felt like a betrayer of impulse. He'd rendered it impossible to ever be happy sitting in one place again. He needed a reason to get back out there – *Jeremy was the key*.

While J. Sullivan remained homeless in Seattle that winter, he crawled his way through every outreach center, alliance group, anarchist squat, soup kitchen, vegan-linked community center & underground punk venue. He was everywhere, exploring Seattle like the labyrinth Bartek similarly understood.

The two would meet downtown twice a week having strange adventures, like little kids inspecting their vast new neighborhoods inner workings as the adults slagged away at their monotonous jobs.

And so it was with a great mental duality that he stepped off the Greyhound in San Francisco – part grid, half street demon. The sharply dressed 28 year old man in a suit & tie wandered into the blustering streets of the Tenderloin District.

It was noon; the weather had warmed and spring was coming. The population wanted to get on with it so heavily their yearning hung in the air like muffled electricity.

His first order of business was Chinese food, followed by an invasion of a hotel's hot tub. He sauntered right past security as if he were supposed to be there, giving a heavy self-important vibe so they'd think he really was some wealthy man they didn't want to harass for ID. He went up the elevator and caught the door of someone exiting in a towel. 2 hours of bubbling later, he'd head to the nearest tattoo shop to get the green hair filled on his Joker tat.

With growing anxiety that some street punk tribe might catch him off guard & drag him to Golden Gate, there was nothing left but take a local bus to Castro, the Gay Mecca of Western Civilization.

Tax returns had increased his savings to $1500 – he really could slip away, so long as he was strong enough. With nothing stopping him, he boarded MUNI & head into self-willed amnesia...

** ...before... **

"*Yo dawgs – they're harvesting people.*" Jeremy is freaked out, his sponge-like void eyes lit as lanterns. "*This woman, she approached me on the street – I was flying the sign, and then she just broke down, explaining she worked for these corporations, and that she was getting out – she was runnin' – and that I needed to tell everyone to run too, just get the fuck outta there, just get out. All these high rises, all these big empty new – she says they are filling them with healthy young people who carefully are screened. They get these people in these apartments, people with no one who'd be lookin' for 'em, then they harvest them – they just reap n' vanish entire buildings of yuppies n' hipsters!*"

Bartek acted as if he wasn't surprised (*because he probably wouldn't be*), but the reality was Jeremy either hallucinated this encounter or she was an utterly convincing schizoid.

Regardless, he knew what it sounded like. He seemed assured of her sincerity, and felt it was best to keep his hawkish eye on these silent, empty buildings she'd tagged as devious, doom-sowing centers of black market organ trafficking.

Jeremy had only learned of this grotesque plot because of a newly invented form of street theater. In fact, it excelled beyond theatre and into an almost magickal form of manifestation. During Bartek's absence, Jeremy and his freshly acquainted street acolyte (Dr. Bryant) had stumbled onto a secret key – a tool to reshape their futures, as well as anyone else with keen imagination & pizzazz.

It was directly because of this new urban propaganda tactic that the repenting organ harvester spilled the beans, broke down weeping and fled on the next train out.

This new technique of street theater came at the most unsuspecting of moments. Before his trip to Castro, Bartek had left a note to Miss Monster explaining the intent of his vacation. He wasn't sure if he was coming back, but wanted to communicate he'd be openly be living in this new way. He knew she had a loud mouth & would tell the key people – something welcomed due to difficulty.

He left the note with her and headed for Easter Resurrection. He had one block to go before the Greyhound station. After all the build-up & violent repression, he now made a quiet evacuation. Nothing could stand in his way...

And then, turning the corner, dodging crowds of the busy streets, he ran smack-dab into Jeremy, standing right in the middle of the sidewalk. Jeremy, who was just standing there, just staring forward with those cavernous eyes as if he knew Bartek would turn the corner right there, right then: "*Yo dawgs, we need to talk – about Free Therapy.*"

In this odd moment outside of time, Bartek had no choice but to listen to this extraordinary idea that was so simple, so jarring in it's potential, that Bartek felt he had no choice but to wander off to discuss its strategy. He still had two hours before the bus left, and even if it momentarily broke the amnesic trance, he could never say no to Jeremy.

Without each other's influence, they weren't quite sure what to do. All winter Jeremy would roll through the city like an explorer, and Bartek would play equal parts Cheshire Cat & Mickey Goldmill.

The two wandered to a concrete flight of stairs. Once seated, Jeremy detailed the genesis. It just hit him – write FREE THERAPY in bold black on a cardboard sign and sit on a corner in public. There's no hustle or money involved – you just listened to people.

No one in America did this – no one just sat down and offered to talk, for free, to try and solve problems of people they didn't even know.

Its basic nature was startling and highly lethal to the personal bubbles which isolated everyone. Scores of people were utterly lonely & confused, and when given this option of someone actually listening it unlocked tsunamis of synergy.

He and Bryant were acquainted through the homeless shelter. He'd come from Sacramento with hard drug issues and was in Seattle for a life restart, studying metaphysics and taking care of all the homeless people under a bridge.

Until he met Jeremy, he'd been lingering into an abyss; because of Free Therapy, he'd gone Crack Cocaine to Cold Turkey! It saved his life and gave him a zealous cause for sobriety.

The first time they tested this technique, a dozen strangers swarmed a street corner ranting one another, methodically solving their problems. Some of them went on dates afterward – some wept or vowed to quit their jobs. Even more offered a night on the town, free booze, a lavish dinner – or money itself, which they refused.

Bartek, Bryant & Dr. J hashed out the code of Free Therapy. If anyone used it as a money scam then they were Sith Therapists; the Free meant <u>FREE</u>.

Secondly, the street patient must write down what they are trying to materialize on the back of the cardboard sign, and this becomes the focus point of the conversation.

Whenever the dialogue ends, that person signs the cardboard; the goal session was 10 signatures. Ten chosen for Jeremy's obsession with dimes. Everywhere he went, he followed the dimes. They would appear randomly, all over – signs of the universe.

Jeremy asked that Bartek hang out one more night. Despite all the build up to this moment, Bartek couldn't say no to him. He also couldn't give a straight answer of why he was going to San Francisco; he *"just felt like it."* Which was true to his nature, and was questioned no more.

After all, Bartek didn't want to alienate him. Jeremy was a straight guy from New York City, and was yet to be comfortable with LGBT world. His immersion into radical politics eventually softened him up.

And so the flight from his old life was diverted by Jeremy's similar flight. The ghost men met with Dr. Bryant and posted on Pike & Broadway. After a first conversation with a random bystander, Bartek pulled the cardboard sign from Bryant's grip and handed it to that "patient."

"Ok, now that you've been properly therapized, it's your turn to give Free Therapy to the next guy walking down the street. Congratulations, you're a new born baby doctor. Your PHD, like us, is a

Pleasant, Happy Disposition."

Bartek turned to Jeremy and Bryant, both whose eyes were bugging out. They hadn't thought of it, simply handing the sign to a patient and making them perform the next session. It was brilliant! Once "treatment" had been given, they'd become another Doctor of Free Therapy, stopping the next interested person on the street!!

With this new strategy, they had 30 people standing around talking within an hour. Bartek had never seen a group of strangers erupt on the street like that. He looked to the direction of Cal Anderson. With a zang of mushroom flashback he united the ideas of Park World & Free Therapy as inseparable. Free Therapy was the key; the question was *how*.

Bartek spent the night at Jeremy's new ladyfriend's home, the feisty Bianca that would one day nearly kill Bartek and Mistress Maam on the freeway. She was Jeremy's ideal of the dreaddy punk rock vegan girl; her smiling, blue-eyed, doll-like appearance masked the worst red flags.

She was bad news, but Jeremy was convinced of her magickal properties, with his dime-like fascination on the numerical order of 222. She was on his mind coming to the Northwest, and sought the image of this woman out time thinking it was connected. Then they met on February 22nd.

The ultimate goal of Free Therapy would now be free-range germination; to export it among travelers so it became an incremental worldwide zeitgeist. One day the Free Therapy sign would be as universal as the peace symbol or common SMILE. Bartek was inspired to personally export it to The Bay.

Bartek head off for San Francisco the next morning. And, after several days exploring Castro as a chameleon drifter, he'd slipped through all the major bars and businesses. He head up to Berkeley for a time-out.

People's Park was very much a symbol of "Park World," as was Golden Gate. The street punks he knew from SF never came out to this neck of the woods, and was at dead center of The Bay's college town. He wanted to lay low and get some rest; every vagrant got away with sleeping there.

It was at 4am when the cop woke him up, politely notifying him to leave. The chilly morning had him shaking, and he immediately cycled through his SF experience. What could be said of his trip? The first night was absolutely comedic and anticlimactic, though a tale best left unsaid.

The second day was on his feet 4am until 2am the next night. He'd met a friendly party that gave him shelter – one of the only times a gay man helped him and didn't expect something in return. It was strange; the kid was gay but never had sex – he didn't like gay sex. He only wanted to cuddle with his chosen mate.

Bartek crashed on the couch and the next day walked untold miles. 14 hours on the scene, and most of it spent eavesdropping hoping to run into the right people.

That night was again short of luck, and he slept at the bottom of a staircase leading to the Muni subway, pressed against the iron gate & kept warm by an air duct. A gay mute home-bum woke him up, giving him a SF baseball cap & blanket. He tried to talk with sign language but Bartek was lost.

Then he raised his finger as if illuminated – he'd just show him what he meant. The homeless man pulled out a crack pipe and offered he join. Bartek instead went back to sleep, and his mute admirer puffed away a few rocks before leaving. *Was there actual sign language for "crack rock?"*

Bartek was feeling low. It was clear that all the terrible stereotypes existed for a reason. Try as he may to feel otherwise, he hated their guts. Gay men were about vanity & decadence – inseparable qualities he hated voraciously. They were cowardly, back-stabbing, materialistic men living in fear.

These gay men of San Francisco 2009 also hated smelly homeless people, they didn't like heavy metal. Rob Halford was not a gay icon, but Ricky Martin was. If they dressed punk it was for fashion fetish; all were in the Hillary Clinton fan club.

Apart from vanity & decadence, the things Bartek hated most in life were money, religion, and domination of any kind. These pussy boys worshiped $$$.

Anytime he walked into a bar they swarmed him. He knew he was a decent looking guy, but he'd never been treated like an Adonis. It was flattering but equally disturbing that in all his attempts with women this never, ever happened.

He was ignored at every straight bar, or maybe it was just that women weren't so pathetically shameless. He would catch eyes... *but then he'd talk*. They had no idea what to do with him.

Every gay bar was like entrapment in an elevator – except instead of descending to a floor they were all just hovering about him, breathing heavy. He was victimized by horrendous pick-up lines and reprehensible flirtation to the point where it grew so heavy every time he had to evacuate.

Every one of these guys spit flirtatious dialogues that mimicked all the lame ways his teenage friends had pathetically tried to pick up women. It was so terrible being on the other side of the coin. His heart leapt out to the women of the world. If he had a vagina, he'd long ago been in prison.

Quixxxote head back towards People's Park and passed a row of dumpsters. A homeless person was digging through one of them – an obese woman that reeked like feces and tuna. She sensed him and flipped around, locking eyes.

She was so sky-high her entire body shook like an earthquake: "*My name is Sunshine Moonbeam – and I'm on crystal METH!!.*" The wobbly woman held up gray stretch pants & tugged them as lumps of caca tumbled off: "*….N' I just shit mah pants!!*"

Bartek bit his lip until he looked down to her legs – her lower torso was naked & smeared with dripping shit. He asked if there was a community breakfast for the homeless at a nearby church. With a feces encrusted finger Sunshine Moonbeam pointed to its location, then went back to her excrement slathered search for new clean pants that somehow may exist in that rotting dumpster.

Among the gutter folk of Berkeley he ate a charming breakfast. Many were fried from LSD while others were cukoo from meth. It was a much welcomed buffet; Berkeley was the easiest place to be filthy home-bum rich. He was given an info sheet to every shelter & outreach in Oakland & Berkeley, then he headed to a quiet avenue to do Free Therapy alone.

Bartek plopped down on the sidewalk in a suit and tie, his FREE THERAPY sign beside him. It was his first attempt at exporting this technique, and his first without Jeremy.

Immediately the most deranged sort of late 40's punk rock hobo train rider gone totally bonkers with meth shows up. He had a leather biker jacket and spider web tattoos on his forehead, nasty prison tats on his hands & fingers; a haphazardly sculpted black goatee, shaved head, and scary violent eyes washed away to some wet-brained plateau.

This amphetamine charged likely GG Allin fan reeked of stale beer as he approached. He asked to see the marker, and Bartek handed it over with a smile. Then the methed-out old punk takes the cap off and starts dragging the sharpie all over his face, deep and hard, squiggling lines all over and breathing hard and heavy and crazy while doing so and humming "*mmmmmm-mmmmm-mmmmm.*"

This is a fat metal Sharpie mind you, the kind from which smelling too much quickly makes the inhaler dizzy and repulsed. This man soaked it up as is a sunflower beneath the Nova.

He handed Bartek a Subway club card: "*Hey bro, thanks for the therapy. It's got 15 cents on it.*" The madman smiled, chirped like a bird, then wandered off to shout obscenities at a nearby tree.

Bartek gave up on Free Therapy and attended a homeless conference in Oakland as if it were a jobs fair pimping minimum wage careers. This was a similar approach, all sorts of outreach groups pooling together to network.

Bartek was one of the only people who actually showed up; there were foundations to stabilize him if he should so choose to stay in SF. But it again dawned him that this was not the point of his mission, and he head back to The City for his big Thursday, Friday and Saturday nights.

He returned to Castro by 7pm, when the sun descended and temperatures dropped with it. It was another long night of bar eavesdropping that left him ever more disgusted. He slept at Delores Park on the sidewalk edge, narrowly missing the sprinklers.

The next day it was gray overcast & chilly. At a laundromat he offered several people $$$ to throw one of his dress shirts in their mix, but all were scowling & rude. He was on vacation, and it would cost $10 if he were to clean it solo. One of them made a lame, faggy tizzy fit and snitched on him to the manager.

He left angrily and went to get Chinese food, stuffing himself with buffet. Should he make a stand in SF? Scramble to Seattle? He missed the kids and wanted to play music – and Seattle already had its own way cooler version of Castro on Capitol Hill. It was the most workable solution possible.

Upon return to the main Castro drag, its scenic charm exploded over the horizon. He realized that its initial charm for the gay community is like a mythical Ellis Island for this different sort of immigrant. The happy contours of San Fran's past however are eroded by this modern mutation which feels like a prison courtyard where the barb wire fence is invisible and built upon the fear of disease, ridicule, hostility.

Everywhere there are victims of AIDS like skeleton people and the younger, rich, healthy-for-the-time-being gay men avoiding the dying ones like the smelly homeless people they despised. No matter where you looked there was The Plague – every telephone pole, billboard, and shop window mentioned treatment or testing. Every "Proud & Queer" propaganda poster with smiling, happy young dudes with disclaimer lines get tested once a month.

And as those less fortunate wasted away in the streets from this withering by lack of immunity, the healthy ones barged right past them without second thought. AIDS was the cancerous rot at the core of this false utopia, and the inhabitants entrapped only herded themselves together uneasily in defense of the wider world which detested them.

Castro was a faux safe-zone where they could forget what existed outside of its proxy protection. It was like some awful Reservation molded from alienation, plague & dogma.

He was stopped by several young men on the sidewalk petitioning a political cause. As always, he took the time to hear them out. These firebrands of democracy were calling for more aggressive hate crime laws – *they wanted minimum sentences of 10 years!*

Ryan calmly explained his position, and that this was wrong. He asked if the 2 years minimum sentence as it was just wasn't enough, which he also explained he was against in principle.

He asked the shocked 20 somethings if any had been terrorized in prison, or forced into solitary confinement, or had cops destroy loved ones.

He asked them what they would say to victims of this law who may have secretly been gay and conditioned to hate? And like robots were acting out forced impulses because what they really despised was their own nature?

And you would now subject them to brutal torture of the system which would in turn create worse hate crimes when let back on the streets? And that people like this often grew up to publicly speak out against attacking people one is brainwashed to hate?

How could they confine a repressed gay man for 10 years minimum over punching someone? Where did this law end? Would a straight guy who politely and constantly reiterated that he was not into it be punished for reacting badly if, say, at a bar a pushy gay guy who would not listen or take a hint still made a move on that straight guy? And he freaked out by their space invasion and punched the guy? Why did they not want to exhibit reverse compassion?

The pro-hate crime advocates scoffed at his rhetorical points. They said he was a shame of a fag, that his ideas were bullocks. And even if someone acted out of their violent repression like a robot, then they damn well deserved 10 years.

Bartek bit his lip again, remembering that one of these guys tried pathetically to hit on him the other night at the bar. If he stood there much longer, he'd only end up showing them what a hate crime really meant.

He walked away rather then continue the argument and tried to mix it back up on the bar scene. But whenever he would get overwhelmed by the awful pick up lines of the horrendously lame men that came at him like sharks he'd ditch out & hit the streets.

Whenever he saw the hate crime activists gathering signatures he noticed they were pointing at him, as if to warn the gay community against his scary ideas, that he was a sell out and to not accept him as a friend or to allow him into their homes.

Ryan slept on the street that night after deflecting the sexual advances of nearly 400 men. He was so unbelievably horny it was mythical in its lust, but he just could not stoop to their level.

He willingly slept on the cold, dicey streets of the Mission District that night, littered with trash and meth-wrecked home-bums rather then withstand another second.

The next day he head to Height-Ashbury. At this point even if the alcoholic GG Allin street punks did find him he'd be courageous enough to tell them the truth. He would just stick his hands in the air as if surrendering and say what's up.

After all, GG was the Antichrist of fags. And he'd be straightforward that he was on vacation.

He slipped by a few clusters of street punks but none recognized him. At Amoeba Music he listened to MUTANTS to help jog his memory of music that was actually cool and not the electronic pop princess teeny girl bullshit they lamely jammed at these gay clubs.

He returned to the street and the sun was shining again – warm like summer. He went to Golden Gate and climbed to his favorite spot on Hippy Hill, an elevated mound more rejuvenating then Cal Anderson.

He took a nap and woke up refreshed. The first thing he noticed was a "caveman" homeless man wandering about the base of the hill. He was filthy to the maximum, bearded, stinking bad even from his distance.

A somber traveler kid walked up to him, locked in a rough acid trip. He sat beside him as a cold wind blew. He looked vacant, as if wandering the surface of Mars. Bartek asked what was wrong. The spaced, grim hippy spoke slowly, explaining his tale in constrained word bursts. About how he wanted someone to be his friend, and they didn't want it. And now he was lost. The lackadaisical quality of his speech was hypnotic in its emptiness.

Quixxxote again looked to the caveman picking the sores on his arm, like a Morgellon's victim tugging out fibers of delusional parasitosis. The gloominess of raw San Fran brought him to his feet. He again slipped past the gaggles of street punks drinking 40's in circles like spottily placed land mines. He ran for the Greyhound and was off before sundown.

The Ballad of Don Juan Quixxxote

As he slept in the doorway of a shoe repair shop, the sky having poured a week straight, Quixxxote wondered how it'd come to this.

As with everywhere he'd gone since launching this travel life, he'd let a sense of magic direct him. He always *"followed the signs"* even though he did not really believe that they existed – the important part was to pretend, because it made things fun.

He sculpted his destiny through ebb & flow, and buckling down for some paycheck-to-paycheck existence was a death sentence. While it was true that he could throw himself at "The Grid" and march alongside drones, his memory was sharp from years of cyborg life. To foolishly bankrupt himself with overpriced rental in this economic climate was absurd.

But as his back ached from lumpy cement mattresses & his sleeping bag grew sodden from incessant downpour, he asked himself if he really was thrown to the street by hostile homophobes, or likewise disowned by family should this revelation be confirmed? Did he actually want to live out such an experience, as if a strange notion to survive the plot of some wild, self-tailored tragedy?

With the gruesome anticlimax of 2008, he was now enthused to make 2009 count. He didn't want to atrophy, let alone waste his 28th year. There was no heaven or hell in his thoughts – only the here & now. Despite his 'Grid Education," to be on the streets of Seattle was The Ritz compared to how most were living in the Third World. It was barely an issue, save for the rain – and the only thing to fear was The Police.

This was about finding himself, and more importantly, urban camping education. Since the economy was tanked, it wouldn't be the first time he'd be homeless in the years to come. He had to toughen up. Seattle was the ultimate training ground, and it worked for his double lives, seeing as that he could retreat at any time.

When he returned to visit Monster, there was a strange air. She was very accepting of him, but Gregory was standoffish. The other guy who lived in the basement was definitely more rednecky, always listening to Metallica, using the insult "gay" to describe things he thought were lame. You know, the *"stop being a fag about shit"* line. The dice were cast against him, and Ryan made no attempt to stay. He waved the children goodbye and sadly left.

He turned to the street and began contacting friends. Word got around about his change, and no one was calling him back. Like all uncomfortable straight men, they probably had a notion that he was wanting to hang out with them in a way, with a new agenda. He wanted to chill and listen to music, go to shows. They thought maybe he was trying to get them alone. After two weeks of being avoided, the message seemed clear. And he felt alone.

And so began the long period of symbiotically grafting his essence to that of the streets. Like Tyler Durden going to cancer survivor groups, he began navigating himself through anonymous discussion crowds that were plentiful in gay culture. He'd just show up and stay mute, listening to the challenges others had faced.

He'd attend maybe 3 such functions a day – talking circles to promote comfortableness, sometimes sex addicts anonymous just to hear the stories. He ventured to all queer community centers he could find, anywhere existing without judgment. These places he could talk openly, even if writing *Planet of The Apes* characters on his "My Name Is" stickers…

Kelly finally called, his ex who 2 years ago urged him to stay. Even though he'd voluntarily left her, when he moved to Seattle March 2008 she began calling him with sultry tones. Perhaps she thought they'd have their day, but when he explained both he & Miss 3 were practically engaged, she stopped calling.

For years she'd enticed him to move to Seattle, and now that he had he never returned calls or email. She was one of his best friends in youth, and her absence was a punishing streak.

Kelly invited him out on the town. He went to the club which didn't want to let him in 'cause his bummy duffelbag. They sat at a candle-lit table while her gay friends danced.

She apologized that she hadn't been around. She described the death of her mother & its impact. She had definitely hit the booze hard for awhile, but she'd regained control. She wanted him to be a part of this restart, and tonight was an amending olive branch.

Bartek realized that she was quietly participating on what she assumed was a date. He explained he was sleeping under a store awning because he'd been disowned for his queer admissions. He was very direct – that this was the scariest thing he'd ever had to do.

Kelly's eyes grew wide as she looked off into space. She stood up and walked away to the other end of the club to talk to other people at the bar, just leaving him there sitting alone. He looked to the burning candle near the end of its wick, grabbed his duffel & walked past the bouncer who despised his vagrancy. It was nearing 2am, and he needed to find an alley to sleep.

A few days later he stopped by her cozy new home. Maybe she just had to process what he'd told her. Kelly was friendly enough at first, though approaching him with a rickety communication.

He was so burned out and tired, so grimy from lack of a shower that he asked to clean himself up and take a brief nap on the couch. Soon as he woke up she pushed him out the door to go out with her new boyfriend – a disc golfer that seemed a teenager in a grown mans body.

The next day he got an email tirade – that he only called when he wanted something, , that he was a "*U-District hood-rat*" like the rest of the scummy punk street dwellers. She no longer wanted anything to do with him and was told never to contact her. After Lana, after his mother – Kelly's ultimate rejection was little more then the dull ache of a minor sliver…

Tonight would be yet another installment in the queer film series – *The Killing*

Of Sister George. It was a welcome escape, seeing as that the unseasonable cold was profound.

With the wintry chill thudding his bones he could only think again of Clownbaby. He wanted to see her again that year, to present the new man he was. Yet he had to embrace this new reality and set things aright –something he had to do alone.

And so it was with the impulse of escape from Clownbaby's memory that he went to the movies that night. For about 15 minutes it worked… *until Clownbaby appeared in the film.* Susannah York's character, "Childie' – it was Clownbaby incarnate – the dolls, the stubbornness, the light blue eyes, the bizarrely gay human porcelain doll. He couldn't help but grin…

Childie and Sister George attended a lezzie club dressed as Laurel and Hardy; he recalled a similar photo Clownbaby had of her ex-lover dressed the same.

He returned to his bum nest he'd nestled at a foreclosed home. He woke up in the dead of night as two meth head creeps were blowing each other near him. Beneath his blanket, he heard moans & dropped pants – one guy fucked the other moaning "*mommy, mommy*" as the other made chirping bird meth noises.

Ryan awoke with a renewed zeal to get out of there. He spent that day on Craigslist putting emergency ads, pushing that he was disowned for being queer. There were quite a few responses, all wanting sex in exchange for shelter. Just horrible people representing the worst of predatory gay society.

He went back to the foreclosed spot but someone had stolen his sleeping bag. He slept in a park 3 hours before the cold had him on his feet again – stalked by a cop car doing circles around the block as he drank hot chocolate from a gas station.

He met with a couch offer the next day – an older lesbian who wrote soap operas. She took to him nicely then dropped a pound of shake weed on the table asking for help in digging out any nugs. She would teach him how to master the screenplay and had free weed & sanctuary so long as he minded his P's and Q's.

He found a job delivering liquor to all the gay bars on Capitol Hill. Soon the writer lady began trying to get him in bed. He wasn't into it and she became aggro, and started lying she was moving. Again to the street – but now he knew how to work a screenplay.

Back onto Broadway midst the sweltering summer, nothing bothered him about living thread-bare or dumpster diving. But when it hit him that in all of this time, with all this money made and spent, that he still did not have an acoustic guitar – it seemed not only unacceptable, but tragic.

Recording the Real Man In Black acoustic records were highly cathartic. Those anti-folk tunes spoke to the flurry of the road and he was able to give voice to his "Classic Americana." It was an act he wanted to push for live performance.

And so once again Quixxxote turned to the sky, asking the universe for assistance. Feeling silly about it, he decided a Pay Day candy bar was cause for a graceful time-out. He went into a gas station and on the ground he spotted a $10 bill. He stepped his foot over it so no one noticed then quietly slid it in his pocket.

Down the street he examined the crisp bill – $100!!! He had asked for a guitar, thinking it may cost at least $100. 5 minutes later fate stuck it right in his palm like a karmic hassle gratuity. He hopped a bus, went right to Guitar Center, and then found the exact guitar he'd envisioned with a carrying case for exactly $100! The REAL Man In Black was back on life support post-defibrillator.

Quixxxote began an oddly juxtaposed existence of working full time while being homeless off the clock. He soon began hopping the fence where the delivery van was parked over night. He'd slip inside when no one was watching and sleep on the floor.

The boss expected them all to be early anyway– he just assumed he was a great employee! With his finances stabilized, so what if he slept in the work van? He had no bills. It was summer now, and the weather was glorious – Not a drop of rain for months! Capitol Hill burst to life, as did Cal Anderson Park.

He began reading voraciously using the library as a constant time-out zone, soaking up excessive amounts of staggering information: *Don Quixote*, *Don Juan*, *Death In Venice*, *Ulysses*, *The Colossus of Maroussi*, *Hunger*, writing from Lawrence Durrell, D.H. Lawrence, Marcel Proust; biographies on Bret Hart, Rick Flair & Ralph Bakshi + the unexpurgated diaries of Anais Nin…

All of this literature not only helped to define his evolving views on the nature of the human soul but aided his process of Free Therapy. On that end, business was booming. Ever since he'd met Jeremy, the two men had galvanized a growing army of comrades. It was hard to imagine life before this essential quest.

After his rough interactions with the shallower sides of music scenesters – and his current and total avoidance of the metal scene at large – he knew that his prospects of doing the band he really wanted was not going to be happening any time soon.

The extreme metal scene was generally homophobic, but he also knew it wasn't completely founded on the idea of two men having sex – it was that they only saw the exact qualities in gay culture that he himself despised. He thought girly glitter men flopping around in pink attire was just as lame as they did.

Apart from Free Therapy, his best interest lay in the safe-zone of anarcho community. When all else fails, seek out the anarchists. That fringe was more punk rock aestheticised and incontrovertibly tied to the radical queer world. Maybe his ideas would be taken to more enthusiastically, seeing as that the Seattle gay community were darker & more cynical then the folk of Castro.

He found a lucky entrance when stumbling onto a protest against the Westboro Baptist Church. Fred Phelps and his crew of hellfire Christians were in Capitol Hill one Sunday shouting at people with their "God Hates Fags" signs. One girly, fake-lisp worker was throwing around his hands like a stereotype valley girl telling the loopy Westboro member that God loved him and Jesus never said "*blah, blah, blah.*'

Bartek interrupted: "*No, he's totally right – God really does hates fags – and that's what makes gay sex is hot.*" He pointed to the stunned twink: "*Unlike him, jacking off to Satan is what turned me onto men – nd I'm gonna ride his goat-shaped cock all over your Messiah's corpse.*" Their eyes Nagasaki, neither knew what to say.

He walked away from them, past the drag queens sprinkling glitter at the anti-gay fanatics, up to the activist types disseminating fliers. They were seeking recruits for L.O.O.N. – LGBT Organization of Non-Compliance. He liked the idea of being a LOONatic and was given meet-up info.

As he left the bizarre protest of angry straight people shouting threats of damnation, Bartek looked back and gave Fred Phelps a raised fist with goat horns: "*Hail Satan.*" Phelps angry eyes moved from Bartek's ass to Bartek's eyes – knowing he'd been caught checking out our plagued Anti-Hero's keester...

As Bartek waited for his first meeting with L.O.O.N., he returned to his efforts with Food Not Bombs alongside Jeremy. Both had gotten heavily involved with FNB, the anarchist group providing free food to the homeless or to protesters at actions.

FNB was like anarchist equivalent of Christian outreaches having mobile soup kitchens and free picnics for the homeless. However, since it was an openly radical organization and handed out fliers against war and capitalism – and was created specifically to feed protesters as a priority – the authorities abhorred it.

In their internal documents the Federal Government and Homeland Security branded anyone giving out free food via Food Not Bombs "Domestic Terrorists." *A terrorist for feeding the homeless, sea to shining sea!!* The man who originated FNB had over 200+ arrests. He was always in a courtroom or feeding mentally ill people that were dumped onto the streets by governmental cuts.

So while these young people would give free food, the cops would arrest, harass, fine or beat them while leaving the Christians alone across the street doing the exact same thing. As a pretext for harassment, the cops used the modernly pushed "neo-liberal laws" of forcing over-the-top food safety rules onto a population.

Apparently after 5000 years of human development it just wasn't safe giving away free food in the public square anymore. One had to be properly certified (*$25 test through The State of Washington*), wear sterile latex gloves, and heavily pay The State to grant a short permit – $100 a day for a negotiated 3 hour period. If not, they'd be find upped to $10,000 or go to prison.

Their group would go to Pike Market and get truckloads of free old veggies cart vendors were tossing, as well as oodles of other products from participating supermarkets. They would bring heaving loads of food to their cooking spot where they had up to 2 dozen people helping at any given time. And they would proceed to rip up the kitchen that was miraculously housed in Bruce Lee's old dojo!

Bartek re-birthed his kitchen experience, becoming a minor chef with a dozen anarchist apprentices! FNB in a general sense was notorious for poorly made vegan stir fry & stews due to untrained amateurs creating their offerings with dumpster scraps.

Since it was vegan, there was little chance anyone would get sick. But too often FNB wouldn't show enough courtesy to food prep & throw gross things in the stew – always bland with a hint of trash.

With his bleach bucket beside him and plentiful knife skills, Bartek gave them a standardized training course in the restaurant industry. The entrées their FNB group were soon producing became "the talk" of bum town!

The homeless were lining up double the amount every Sunday to devour his culinary mastery. At Occidental Park, both he and Jeremy felt they were in the right place at the right time.

Since Greyhound they'd been helping the stranded & unfortunate – and it was as if they were still en route to their destination over 200 days in!

One particular night after the potluck, things grew dark and chilly. Bartek was hanging around Occidental late, not quite sure where to go. Jeremy was nearby doing the same, and randomly they crossed paths in the dark. And then Dr. Bryant of Free Therapy appeared, randomly, like a man in a trance.

The three glanced at each other strangely, the night having circumvented them by chance. All popped their tension at once while examining the teetering zealousness of their larger mission.

All of them knew they could never go back to The Grid and felt as if they leaped into a bottomless pit in Seattle. They were all plummeting down the rabbit hole with no idea of trajectory.

How long could this purgatory last? They felt like men locked into the solitary confinement of a totalitarian freedom. Jeremy needed income, Bryant wasn't sure what he was even doing anymore. Bartek was clam happy, even if just as burned out – it was the freest, happiest, most healing year of his life. He was a creature of the city, and his lust for the concrete utopia was infinite. He begged them to continue.

Bartek woke up early that morning, shivering on the sidewalk & wet from the misty, drizzling rain. If renting a hotel room was $50-$100 a night, his logic was why not mentally rent the street corner for $2 of a thrift store blanket he could give away the next morning?

Part of his huge success as a transient was his ability to avoid carrying a travel pack. He had zero possessions which he physically carted along save for the space of his quaint backpack. If he couldn't carry it, he didn't need it. The point of his life was to write books and music – his life's wealth was gauged in weightless electronic files.

Still, he awoke pining for a warm body to be next to him. Someone, anyone. He reviewed his past loves, grimly thinking of what he'd say to them if explaining this moment. That this unseasonably bone-chilling, drizzling morning would be his fate no matter how hard he attempted to avoid it.

Because he loved it more then he did their memories, no matter how alone he felt. Still, there should be someone there who got it and was not a street junkie or meth head or drunk.

While he did will this wacky street life upon himself and lived it with a thorough lust – enough to make any "normal" woman run screaming – he didn't understand why his life-long, white-hot romantic efforts ended the way they had. Here in the streets they were mere phantoms. There were so many he would've given himself to forever, and all had rejected him. He was cursed – and when not cursed, a fool…

Earlier in the year, he and Jeremy went to the Chamber of Commerce, fronting as if they were travel journalists writing elaborate stories. They'd waltzed in together and laid down the charm like pros. They were handed free passes for attractions around the city – zoo tickets, aquarium tickets, boat & tour rides, museum passes, dinner discounts…

Gripping a handful of unused passes, Bartek ventured to another odd spot he'd never stumbled – the long dock south of Pike Place Market. Sleepy and quiet, it housed a number of tourist attractions that were nearly a ghost town.

He visited the Aquarium, and then found an abstraction of Ripley's "*Believe It Or Not.*" It was a museum of curious oddities – like a hidden treasure trove of the Theatre Bizarre and the circus freak equivalent of Clownbaby's living room.

The day warmed up, and with another freebie ticket he took a boat cruise of The Puget. Afterwards he hit Westlake Park, grooving to a street drummer's bucket rig before a commotion. A huge march started heading down 4th Avenue.

At first, Bartek squinted then rubbed his eyes, but what he saw was true, as if the feared Kracken trouncing from the dark of a sewer main – *thousands of rednecks marching against free health care!! All shouting about communist plots & the execution of freedom!! And their demographic exemplifying the most exploited segment of the population!! Obama with a Hitler mustache!!*

At his food stamp hearing, he told them he was unemployed, homeless & bankrupt. She asked if he'd anyone to contact. He did not. She grilled him if he had friends. He said he did – until he came out of the closet. They disowned him, reason why he was homeless.

The thinly-veiled bible-thumper of a crotchety old woman scoffed at him. He was told it was not a legitimate reason and that The State, for whatever reason, would be denying him $130 worth of benefits per month, instead giving him a minimal $70 a month to live off while admittedly doomed to the street. He lied, of course. But he wanted to know the reality of the rock bottom extreme, and he saw its true ugly face. $70 was what the liberal progressive government of Washington State thought of him…

He passed the Greyhound station and struck up a conversation with a poor soul who'd been trapped in its purgatory 5 days. He was an African kid from Ghana trying to visit his aunt in Canada. He rode all the way from Baltimore and was plagued by delays & bus malfunctions.

When he finally reached the Canadian border he was sent back because he did not have the proper visa. He had to wait a week! His clothes were filthy and he hadn't taken a shower in a week.

Bartek liked his vibe, and especially his nickname was "Endo." He offered to show where the homeless showers were, but unfortunately they were closed. In his usual miraculous way Jeremy walked up out of nowhere. Dr. Endo looked oddly at the strange raggedly mohawked man who was looking more like Blackbeard the train-hopping pyrate every day.

The 3 soon met with Bryant on Broadway to do Free Therapy. Endo was the first subject; he was rambling tiger attacks on sleeping villagers, how where he came from thieves would be chased into the street and stoned to death on hearsay.

People knew never to accuse a thief unless caught red handed, because framing someone for burglary in their culture was cause for violent reprisal.

Dr. Endo became the next doctor, followed by a steady stream of newcomers. Soon there were 30 standing around gabbing at each other. And then a Rastafarian looking black man with graying dreads & cane fit for a pimp sauntered up. He asked what we were doing, and he was so illuminated by it that he jumped into our group with titanic fervor.

He revealed his story about being locked up in a mental asylum for bogus reasons and having his son taken from him. He was a little cracked and totally eccentric – definitely intimidating to white people – but a danger he was not. He wept as he told his tale, 20 people looking on. And then he came out of it with a righteous, mighty roar saying Free Therapy was a new era for mankind.

He, "King Sly," would invest $10,000 in marketing it. Immediately Bartek and Jeremy shut him down – they could never take his money, because it was about the message and had to remain unfunded, spontaneous, and without "selling pizzazz." This just made King Sly light on fire. He was ecstatic, dancing around like a cartoon singing: "*we gunna walk on fire, we gunna walk on fire, we gun-nuh walk on fye-yuuuuuur...*"

King Sly took them back to his apartment. He was so hooked on ways to spread Free Therapy around the world that he summoned his friends over. They were all black gangster types and they busted out a huge bag of coke; neither he or Jeremy touched it.

Sly was adamant they all spend the night – he wouldn't take no for an answer. They had changed his life with Free Therapy and now he wanted to repay them – as their host for an evening of the hip hop clubbing, free booze & blow.

Bartek opted to sleep. He could get little shut eye on the carpet of this muggy, ratty, state-sanctioned apartment. The humidity was thick and painful even with open windows. No fans, no air conditioning – just beaded sweat in a coke snorting room with the stale rank of chain-smoking in the air.

He woke up two hours later – King Sly had brought a cornrow dreaded prostitute back; she was a Nubian goddess. She went into the darkness of the bedroom and waited for the men, one by one, to take turns with her. King Sly looked to Bartek: *"Go ahead – therapize her."* He politely declined.

The rest of the house went whole hog on some freaky gang-bang going on behind that closed door. He woke up hours later, the coked out men still hammering away at the high-priced hooker, and snuck out with Endo.

Dr. Endo couldn't stop laughing, vowing to export Free Therapy to West Africa. Bartek led him to the Greyhound. His aunt had managed to get the paperwork processed as to enter Canada. His bus was due to leave in 10 minutes – *but they wouldn't let him on 'cause he smelled so bad!* They said to come back after a shower! *No way to wash & no choice but wait another 12 hours!*

He was angry, demanding to know what he was supposed to do. He had no money, how would he shower? She ignored him for the next customer and when he got flustered she threatened to not let him on the bus at all, stranding him permanently in bus purgatory! He led Endo to the houseless resource center & slipped off...

Bartek returned for the third meeting of L.O.O.N., the radical queer group. They were friendly enough, but one made snide comments towards him when he introduced himself the way he would at one of his many anonymous support groups.

They discussed direction. Bartek thought to himself the frivolousness of this organization. He imagined going door to door gathering signatures to legalize sodomy. It just seemed silly to him. It was more appealing when the world despised it.

Sandwiched between a hormone-rendered male and a woman with three breasts, he scribbled notes of the organization he really wanted to unleash. As the overly socialist 20-somethings talked about Union rights, marriage inequality and arranging a shared community space, Bartek drew sketches of the black skull he wanted to represent something far more adequate for his punk aesthetics.

Order Of The G.A.G. (*a.k.a. Gays Against Gods*). It worked perfectly as a joke, as an acronym, and GAG as a reminder of the 12 foot snake of a cock they wanted to slide down every homophobe throat. They would be the unrelenting queer equivalent of The Westboro Baptists Church created to promote degeneracy.

The message of G.A.G. was simple – God really does hate fags, and that's why fags should hate God. Their Order would promote intolerance of ideas which were intolerant of them, and glorify the fact that they were condemned to burn in hell and this is what made gay sex hot.

They would be LGBT's Sith force against Castro's limp-wristed Jediness, calling out all that was false while triumphing their banished damnation. The logo was an upside down rainbow flag with a black skull and pirate swords as bones underneath. The skull would have an X scrawled in the middle of its forehead, Xing themselves out of society.

Bartek left the meeting for his magic mound at Cal Anderson. He began to feel ill, even in the pulsating summer. It was sunny now, everything a ripe 90 degrees. He began sweating bullets – within an hour the dreaded Swine Flu. This vicious strain of illness was circulating heavily – people laid out with devastating illness for weeks, with 102 degree body temps. Individuals were dying. When it hit, it hit hard – and Bartek was spared no quarter.

Throughout the next week he was miserable – lucid, hallucinating, sleeping 12 to 14 hours a day. He'd come out his delirium to read Knut Hamsun's *Hunger*, which he basically was living. He felt trapped in some incrementally deteriorating, parallel version of *Death In Venice*. He lagged his way through work and would immediately sleep at the park. *It was brutal…*

That following weekend he had regained his health, and with a lingering, drippy nose he found himself at the start of Gay Pride. Starting Thursday June 25th, Seattle would host the largest pride parade in the Northwest.

The first day started with the death of Michael Jackson. Word came around 5pm; everywhere cars blared the deceased King of Pop or honking in remembrance. People were pulling out boom-boxes and dancing like MJ all over the place – *in every direction an impromptu moon-walker!!*

The first night was a dance-until-you-drop Jackson tribute no matter where you went. For once, Seattle picked up steam. He'd never seen its drabness lifted so thoroughly – nothing but smiles everywhere. He danced until 2am then slipped away to Cal Anderson. He woke up in the field wet from sprinklers with 50 open air yoga practitioners laughing as one in an exercise that seemed purely *Road To Wellville*.

After a filling his belly with blueberry pancakes, he head to the march rallying point to link up with his fellow L.O.O.N.atics. And so Ryan Bartek, the extreme metal extremist, the former child fascist – the long-time hater of all queeny men did what once seemed impossible – marched in a gay pride parade of massive proportions.

Marking the 40th anniversary of the Stonewall Riots, waves of every queer fringe took downtown like an invading army. All the straight people had already split – it was as if downtown had been evacuated! The faggot legions had overrun the machine!

The L.O.O.N.atics held their cardboard signs high and like a paramilitary troop: *"we're-here/we're-queer/get-used-to-us/don't-fuck-with-us…"* The militant fags shouted their anarchist slogans until 10,000 had combined at Seattle Center.

At the water fountain a growing number were stripping naked & dancing in the spraying water – hundreds within minutes, swirled by a battalion of mousy little Clownbabies on bicycles as their own mini swarm, peddling topless with gold & blue boy-scout hats & yellow ascots, all joyfully plowing through the titanic spurts of water jutting like a typhoon on the crowd of queer resistance.

KlownFührer

Not since his nasty last mushroom trip had R. Bartek touched psychedelics. He'd gone so far into the black space he no longer desired return. It was Jeremy that egged him on.

Apart from a few crazy nights of Free Therapy, I hadn't seen him much. Jeremy had been living with Bianca, both working a sandwich shop to fund their coming travel – Oregon Country Fair, a camp out/LSD freak-out through all August. The hippies hi-jacked it in the early 70's; ever since, 10,000+ Deadheads & Rainbows.

Jeremy had never done acid, let alone 'shrooms. He was always sold bunk 'cid – or maybe he was immune. In any case he'd picked up cubensis; both he & Bianca wanted Bartek for the mission.

And so the conspirators meditated on materializing free bus passes. Like always, Jeremy would use "The Force" to make it appear. He was always mythologizing the Jedi.

The two concentrated their duel energy sources, and a random street kid walked up: *"Interested in some year-long bus passes?"* He'd pirated high-quality replicas of the $1200 passes that promised endless free rides on every bus, tram & street car in Seattle through 2009 – *$10 each!!* And Jeremy talked him down to $5!!

The fraudulent passes worked so adeptly that only once was Bartek denied by a cynical bus driver. When called out on packed rush hour, he spoke like a Shakespearian actor doing an Errol Flynn-like Robin Hood: *"Why you"ll never catch me – a-moo-hoo-hoo-ha-ha..."* Then like a man in tights alongside a ballet troupe he did a pirouette out the air-pressured door. Everyone was laughing, driver angry: *"Get back here con-artist!!!"*

By noon they'd munched the bag of shrooms & were on a bus headed for sweltering downtown. Bartek found himself in an odd bubble with pulsating crowds underneath a burning sun.

Jeremy laughed mad – what if their Food Not Bombs crew started dressing like Gestapo officers while dishing out free food? But instead of a swastika the armband will be a fist gripping a carrot. *Totalitarian free food!!* And that would protect us against cops – 'cause with our fancy SS uniforms, they'd never harass their own!

Bartek saw all of Seattle as one huge ashtray. His bad habit was snipes – walking around picking cigarette butts off the sidewalk and rolling them with Zig-Zags. He saw himself as some poor meth-like casualty street crazy, slugging through a disgusting plate of ash like volcanic residue, sniping one by one the gradual carcinogens towards his death. It was high time to start living healthy.

The 3 marched to Cap Hill. As the trip wound down they discovered a tea store with tiny jars of every herb on earth like specimens among the shelves. With a frosty green tea smoothie, they made Volunteer Park & stretched out in the sun. Then, walking just a tad further, they decided to materialize a couch to chill on. And around the next turn? A swanky davenport beside a curb, perfect in every way. Only the rich would toss such glorious comfort...

That weekend, their combined forces gelled at the Food Not Bombs benefit show. With bands all day and a giant potluck, they'd brought in nearly $500! Bartek performed as The REAL Man In Black, at first delighting the crowd with his crooning before shocking them with his politically incorrect lyrics. He was cut off early – *success!!*

Among the crowd was little Fran Simpson. They caught each other's eye, and she invited him to an acoustic open mic. She was going through a rough period, near of abandoning Seattle.

The next night he went with her; they showed up late and the sign-up sheet was clogged – they'd have to wait 3 hours. Bartek tried to bribe the door man $20 to let her cut line, but he was incensed. He wanted to kick them out, and Bartek just laughed.

They left & walked along the Ballard neighborhood where Fran had been living happily 2 years before ending up at her now dying apartment. They strolled along the dock of harbored boats and she looked upon the floating ghostly ships as if surreal ruins.

She brought him home that night, despite being the sort of girl that doesn't quite do that. Might as well go out with a fling, 'cause she couldn't find a job, owed too much, and her landlord gave 2 weeks. She'd just arranged a flight to Germany as to visit her brother at a US Army base.

Fran was from Georgia & had no family here, just acquaintances that previously were her bedrock but in economic straits became what they always were – background characters & fair-weather friends. She was a hair stylist and could not work because Washington demanded extremely expensive courses for re-certification. Like all degrees, nothing from anywhere else was legit.

Midst the collapse of her Seattle existence, she'd adopted him. He lived with her the next week in a dreamy moment outside of time. They dropped all walls & were like a totally functional, honest couple enjoying a crumbling vacation.

Towards the end, she asked where he'd go. He didn't really have an answer. He was packing the duffel bag he usually left inside the work van which he still slept in secretly at night. She saw him look at his little zip-lock bag of toothpaste in a grim, lost way, and she silently snuck up on him & embraced him. He scooped her up into his arms romantically – she melted into him.

As if weightless they spilled onto the bed, and a great storm brewed outside. The smell of rain & wild weather & electricity was bewitching. They had left the windows & balcony door open, and the more intense they physically grew the more savage the storm outside became. They went at it like champs, and fell asleep on each other naked, storm receding into the ocean horizon.

Fran was gone 3 days later, as was Jeremy. Another main guy from Food Not Bombs bolted, and Dr. Bryant returned to Sacramento. For friends, Bartek again had the streets; for companions, the books at the library. He thrust himself at the nexus of his street glorification.

He made another go at the gay scene crawling night clubs only to be disgusted by everyone he met. There was no shortage of people who offered to do the deed, but again there was no one likable enough even for empty sex.

Beleaguered by stereotypes, he kept going on impromptu dates with women he'd met wandering the streets. One girl had a Detroit D tattooed on her arm, and it felt so removed from him. She yearned for aspects of home; his quest was self-incineration of them.

There was another woman, a writer. They had a decent conversation at the park and he took her out for Thai food. He walked her home and then she asked where he was going. He explained he was couch surfing and occasionally sleeping in the park to save money. She was weirded out, never calling back.

After watching street performers do an "Apocalypse Roadshow" – with one guy hammering nails into his face & another eating handfuls of glass – he met a girl collecting fliers off polls; she was like old Lana. She brought him home, sat him on the couch, then quietly went into the other room to smoke crystal meth. She re-emerged, sky-high, nonchalantly: "*oh yeah, I'm dying of cancer.*"

It was time to rent something. He still had around $1000, because his extremely minimal lifestyle maintained it. His only real expenses were bus transfers, rolling papers & coffee – and the cheapest draft on tap. Bartek deposited another $500 in the bank, then went to trash pick chicken nuggets warm from the unrelenting sun.

He took a trip up to Miss Monster's, the first he'd seen the kids in months. He hoped things had cooled down, but playing Texas Hold 'Em poker with some of them was awkward. He went back downtown and texted many of the punk guys from that crew, just to say hi, to see what was up that weekend – *nothin' but crickets*.

He got black coffee and sat down to write a letter to one of these folks. He caught himself, the tone of it – it was almost apologizing. He recalled marching alongside L.O.O.N. in the parade. *What was he doing here?* This was an insult. He crumbled up the sheet and threw it in the trash, then went upon his night.

As Bartek headed towards his meeting for a room rental, The Labyrinth was again weighing heavy, and he was physically in a strange, unknown corridor of it. He followed a huge set of concrete stairs up a hill – on the ground atop an open issue of the *Seattle Stranger* (*their version of a Real Detroit*). A full page advertisement looked back up at him – Detroit's Black Dahlia Murder touring with Slayer on a national sports arena campaign!

Like a stranded islander finding a ghostly message in a bottle, he dusted the dirt off & stared at it strangely, this window to his past. He remembered all the 20 something metal kids at the Novi rec center – how strange, this mad juxtaposition. He wanted to rejoice, but he felt again the dagger Trevor shoved in his back in trying to get him fired from his job because he called his supposed friend's house, as if an annoying fanboy or scummy journalist.

He thought of the Detroit metal scene, the personalities which composed his glory days – that they too would likely disown him for his queer streak. One band, Parasitosis, had a vocalist he dealt with quite often. He was friendly guy, with a wide grin & slight buck teeth. He wondered if that same grin would mock him.

Even though the guy from Parasitosis was a cool person and wouldn't care, for some reason his goofy grin was what came to mind when realizing the hatred & humiliation he might receive. His background was just somehow manifested in that goofy smile.

He picked up the newspaper and the lead article was about the death of the print industry due to the Neo-Depression. There was an illustration of books stacked up as if the Empire State building – moldy, dusty and covered in cobwebs. The quest to put out his road book seemed doomed. Wall Street had stomped his dreams.

The woman offering couch rental was a very nice, albeit depressed person. She was close to his age & had wracked up the bills. She ran her own house cleaning & dog walking business that Bartek joined part time. She was only asking $200 for the front room.

He went to the U-District pondering what he would do for friends and stumbled onto a panhandler. He was definitely not a traveler – everyone knew they'd be written a ticket if caught here. The kid had just escaped Southern California to make a new life. Something had gone down, and he was keeping his mouth shut.

But he seemed friendly enough and knew his metal. He was just living in his car and offered Ryan crash in the back seat. Even though he was no longer homeless, he decided to stay homeless with the poor kid a few days, just to keep him company!

The kid broke the ice – he'd just been released from a mental institution, and his town now threatened him everywhere. *Even the police stalked him!* See, the kid had been walking down the street listening to Deicide on headphones. His metal rebellion got wound up in his hatred of the church, then he stopped in front of a baptist one. He stripped naked in the street, climbed to the apex of the steeple, and hung out with the cross as if a nude gargoyle.

Dozens of cops & firemen, hundreds of bystanders thought he was a suicide jumper. They pulled out the net and were calmly speaking over the bullhorn. The kid squatted down and took a gigantic shit at the base of the cross. Then he grabbed his own turds and rubbed them all over his chest, all over the cross.

He started screaming *"Fuck Christ!"* & throwing excrement at the crowd below – live on TV for all Southern California!! Once down, they threatened him with 25 years in prison as a hate crime! Until the bishop himself stepped in – pleading to release him!!

One month of shock therapy later, homeboy was released – and now a certified YouTube superstar! Guy was an international celebrity to a growing army of GG Allin fans & Satanists! But all he wanted was a job at an organic food store! He lasted one week...

Friendless-feeling, Bartek's direction grew aimless. Nothing about this existence seemed happy anymore. He had ground himself to a brutal anticlimax with the gay scene. After drunkenly making out with someone who afterwards said they had AIDS, Bartek ditched out. He was so close to getting laid, finally, and still The Plague. No matter where he went, everything always crawling with AIDS...

Fran returned, screwed out of 2 months pay and with 24 hours before returning to Georgia. She told Bartek that unless he miraculously found her a job and a place to live she'd be leaving the next morning.

He called his new roommate and offered to trade his job & couch to this forlorn woman and go back to the street. She accepted, and Bartek produced the impossible with one call.

With this self-sacrificing move, she very well fell in love – and cried, cried, cried when he went back to the streets that night. The next 2 weeks were a conflicted romance. She knew his mangled confusion and wasn't comfortable with it. She again reiterated her belief that Seattle would fall by earthquake. The entire city was built on stilts, and she'd dreams of crumbling same as he.

"We talk and she speaks in this language of clown, a mosaic of tendrils from a velvety cocoon of mania. It consumes as siren, this vortex of severed doll heads; this neon lair of schematics & accordion notes. She wails on the Casio a collision of phaser, gondola, harpsichord & beyond. She stops abruptly, speaking in different pitches, voices, tremolos. With 3 voices in her throat she cracks an electric gong, gurgle-crooning 'bout Lucifer like a Viennese choir-girl. She zaps an 80's drum machine then roars with gravel laughter. On this lucid night, I am the caged gorilla which beats itself senseless. She is hurting, and I must reach her..."

The nearby dance academy was blaring swing music as Bartek again found himself brooding at Cal Anderson Park after dark. Clownbaby had called – she'd gotten busted drunk driving and would be incarcerated at the same jail that housed Lana. Her looming trial cut through him like a sword. They began speaking again every day, only now he could talk freely without hesitation.

The two began talking of spending time together. He'd been flirting with a quick visit to Detroit – he still had friends & family. 9 months away seemed legitimate enough for a second appearance.

Fran caught wind just as he returned from buying a stash of those special Amazon chocolates to bring to all his friends back home like belated Anti-Christmas gifts. Fran knew the only way to keep him there was to dive into the world of psychedelics. She never had and wanted to know "The Labyrinth" he spoke of Seattle as.

Bartek was not keen on the idea – he felt he'd go some place bad. She was a nice girl, and it was best he didn't warp her. Still, she demanded to eat them. They went to the park: *"Look, let's just chill and see if it feels right in a bit."* But as they sat there, he knew all he had to do was eat these things with her and they'd be a locked unit.

Bartek's phone vibrated. He looked to Fran, ready to give herself to him in ways he barely understood. He looked at the text – Clownbaby: *"I want to get married in the Church of Satan."*

His heart exploded. He looked again to the girl beside him, eager to jump off the crazy ledge... And said NO. He was going home to Clownbaby, and they spent the night sober on the couch.

The next day, Fran threw herself at him. *"Don't go, please don't go–"* He swooped her up as lightly as when the storm clouds raged, and they slung into his roommates bed. She wrapped her arms around him, her essence fitting him like a glove.

He told Fran that he just needed to visit to get it out of his system, and then they could proceed. Fran knew it was a lie, and she kissed him passionately. He left her with teary eyes, and headed to the Greyhound. He left a voice-mail for the boss of his liquor gig saying he was through.

The bus left that night – another 3 days until Michigan. As he looked back from the window Seattle was luminous in the darkness, its little lights blinking. He knew it was the last he'd see it the way he remembered. Even then, convincing himself nothing could go wrong, he knew that was the end. *Because he could never just stop.*

And so The Labyrinth drifted away as he chugged onward – away from Fran, away from Cap Hill, away from the hopes & dreams of his arrival. And like the embers of a dying fire, his shining street paradise descended into the blackness of night, and slowly faded away with the horizon...

All but 2 days in he wanted to escape. He made a visit to his mother and saw a drab local rock show. While people were happy to see him, they still treated him as if he lived there. They didn't understand that he was an entirely different person. Ryan left them and drove to some well known gay bars in Detroit just to see them – all ugly, in violent neighborhoods. What "could've been" was not appealing.

It was several days in before Clownbaby. When he pulled up, she was hula-hooping in her friend's yard – bright & happy, yet cautious. He drove her across town; she was her old self, cutting through bullshit with cold logic. She left him speechless as ever, even though he had all the room to talk. He couldn't summon it.

As a rule of his nature, he was usually whoever came to the door at any given time. He had so many modes & masks that unless someone was around him for great periods of time they may only assume he was but one. She knew this was how he operated, but she still hadn't seen much anything.

After awhile, he asked what the whole getting married at the Church of Satan thing was about. She was caught off guard, then quickly did the math. *"You thought I was talking about you – that I wanted to marry you?*" Bartek looked emptied and said stagnantly: "*No... I just thought it was affectionate.*" It was just some random gibberish she felt like texting, because she did that all day. She'd transmit strange phrases annotating any acid-headed impulse.

She made it clear she didn't give two shits about gay culture. That she tried to live it in another city but that all she really was was a degenerate. She knew what she wanted – *men*. She thought gay men were gross, vanity-filled scum. Every insult and degradation she hurled at that world in her distaste of it recalled every experience he had that year, and again they were more alike then ever.

She also said she had a new boyfriend, and things were going well. "*Jake,*" he knows you – "*the singer from Parasitosis.*" Bartek looked to the floor, imagining those goofy big teeth smiling back at him, laughing with all the old death metal people of his past and the Neo-Nazi skinheads that wanted to beat him up.

He felt a knife twist deep. As with the fake Charles Manson she'd mated with another symbolic figure. The woman who inspired him to get real with himself and who he loved more then anyone was now lock-step to the painful smile that made him unable to live in his home world again.

She cooled down, and then they cat-napped on her bed. He woke up at some point and just gazed at her. He was hoping she was never as amazing as he thought, that maybe he'd idolized her as wrongly... *but she was The One.*

They hung out on the porch and listened to her rant until she was out of steam, It was his turn. He had waited for the opportunity to do this through the mad darkness of a year. But he just couldn't bring it; her immense power had rendered him a dull, staring robot. He got up to leave, both of them knowing that it was done. She hugged him goodbye and he walked up to the side door of his car...

...and then as he was putting his keys in the side door lock, he stopped. Led by a lost power, he walked up and looked her straight in the eyes: "*I love you.*"

Finally, she saw what was in him, right to the foundation. He held eye contact. "*I'm sorry I couldn't show you. I'm sorry this went down like this., I really believe we knew each other in a thousand incarnations. You may not understand why, you may not think it possible, but I truly do understand you completely. I have to go, that's just what happened. But I love you.*"

She smiled a have curved bit lip smile, the kind where something big is going inside but the clenched lip is only the hard-pressed grip of a mask. Bartek turned, walked to the car, and drove away feeling as close to closure as ever.

He returned to Linda's where in thinking about the encounter only made him fall deeper into her. He had to at least write one last letter. 3 days he spent in a trance writing & editing, just so he could phrase the perfect admission of everything. If it failed it failed.

He emailed it & went to Theatre Bizarre, where he hadn't been since A.K.A. MABUS played the clandestine 6.6.06 show. His friends were throwing an underground wrestling event that was like surrealistic art using live professional wrestlers. The fighters would move to the live bands playing circus music, bouncing around like cartoons, acting out the ring announcer. Everywhere, weird clowns.

Flannigan had put this thing together so everyone could stare at weird shit on acid, and had somehow talked pro wrestlers from the WWE to perform. So many people were there he hadn't seen since his local journalist days – bands that detested him were all relaxed and conciliatory. The feuds of the past had blown over.

As the circus wrestling act ended, the grounds lit up into a wacky adult playground. DJ's came out and a thumping rave erupted. Bartek split the amazon chocolates so that 10 could trip with him, and all launched into their mad night. Bartek ate 3 whole ones – something not advised. He was at the bottom of the rabbit hole.

Before he'd gobble them up, he'd had one of the strange accordion playing faerie girls paint him like a clown; his own rendition suited just for him. With his blue mohawk slicked back, he resembled the clown on *The Silent Burning*.

Claudia came, prettied up in a silk dress. Looking at her tripping, he wasn't sure what to do. She looked like she showed up for a date, and he was flying high. She appeared bummed out, and they spoke in trip logic a bit. She asked him if he was still pretending that he was gay. He started laughing. *"Ok then – I'll see you in Portland."* And she vanished into the night.

By 3am, he was bouncing around the wrestling ring climbing all over those thick blue bouncy ropes. He'd wanted to do that since a kid watching Ricky Steamboat.

Unlike the park scene where he'd stared into the blackness of Meridian Park and saw the evil clown of his future, this time he embraced it. He was that maniac clown at the end of the rainbow, wanting to pull everyone into his disassembling.

As he bounced around the ring, he looked to the giant skull head of Zombo the Clown which loomed over the stage. *It was his new god.* He begged for the mushrooms to kill him, so that his soul may leave to the realm of Zombo and he be a djinn of its bidding – real thought, real demands.

Bounce, bounce – *was he The ClowniChrist?* Bounce, bounce – *was he a Horsemen of the Clownocalypse?* Bounce, bounce – NO – *he was The KlownFührer.* And he would rule the clown masses as the greatest joke of all, the ultimate insult against himself, against his past. He was the dictator of fools, and he wanted to bring everyone over the edge with him...

The trip wore down by dawn. The hot girl with the dreads convinced she was Catwoman gave him her number. He wandered into the garage where main architect John Dunivant painted all his works. It was quiet & empty; freakish new prints were drying.

Bartek looked at himself in the mirror between the two ghoulish new paintings and saw his face. Makeup half smeared off, pupils dilated, he was a dead ringer for the captured Joker in the interrogation room. He stared at his own acute monstrosity.

The next day Bartek was loved so thoroughly by Catwoman he never bothered to check for a response from Clownbaby. She'd shot him down & he knew it. This girl with him now like Clownbaby was a present thrown in at the end of Detroit.

This time, he was AOK walking. Theatre Bizarre wouldn't last forever and when gone there'd be no reason to stay. He was asked if he wanted to work on the upcoming Halloween party, and considered it. It would be the last before the city shut them down.

Bartek left on a Greyhound & returned to Seattle. Fran had been writing this entire time & very much wanted to continue seeing him. He was so happy to see her at the Greyhound – his own private welcoming committee, for once. Things woulds finally be normal.

She drove him back to her new apartment, brought him inside, then told him to lay down on the bed. One year to the day of his buying Clownbaby's bus ticket, he was home at last.

Fran came in and sat down next to Bartek, who was hungry for love & affection. It was going to be one beautiful afternoon – he was going to walk her romantically to every sacred, secret spot in the city and show her the marvelous diamond that Seattle really was, as only a man of the streets could. Fran says: *"So this is my boyfriend's bed. He's out of town these next 2 days. I just wanted to make sure you have somewhere to sleep before you go back to the street."*

Bartek stared at her with a squinty hurt. He exhaled and then started packing his stuff. He snapped at her – why would she egg him on for weeks? Why? He was really real, he was there for once. She looked at him angrily: "*Because he's normal*." Bartek quietly left the apartment and went back to homelessness on Capitol Hill.

It was cold, dark night and surprisingly bright morning. He had $800 left; if he were to stop, it had to be then... but Downtown Brown called: "*Hey Coach... we fired our merch guy. Can you be in Oklahoma in 3 days for another 6 week tour? We need you buddy.*"

Bartek arrived to Oklahoma to stay at Fortress Andromeda. Athena picked him up, and both knew it was the only time they'd have. So they acted as if a newly wed couple for 2 days.

After the gig, he saw the pizza shop was hiring. He knew he could have it – be like Billy Jack raising horses on a farm with her, fighting for Native American rights. But Downtown Brown honked: "*Time to go Coach!*" He kissed Athena on the cheek, and walked...

The tour kept rolling – away from someone or something each stop. Away from Tank Girl in Arizona, away from his Hollywood ex now dating a PG-13 clone of him, away from Bianca & Jeremy whacked on acid at a nudist colony for months, scampering around with leaves on their genitals like Adam & Eve.

Away from Billy Milano & his banana pancakes & Rambo pajama party, away from Wax & Herbal T the two best twin white rappers on the planet, away from Brandon and Onyx & skirting the reconciliation with Skinner; away from Phil Thomas Kat and UZ-TV, away from Rufio from *Hook* and his Sublime cover band...

And eventually, finally, back in Detroit at tour's end to work the final Theatre Bizarre Halloween party. At its end a man walked up: "*I hear you need to go to Portland.*"

Bartek said: "*That's where the signs are pointing me.*"

Dude replied: "*Well I'm leaving in 3 days. I don't know anyone there either and I don't have much money. I'm just going to drive and if I die on the streets so be it.*"

He offered Bartek come along, yet our slaughtered Anti-Hero turned down the offer last moment. He didn't know anyone there – what was he supposed to do homeless in rainy November?

Instead, he began a new book. He wanted Clownbaby to know who he was. He knew she would probably never read it, but what else was there to do?

And so R. Bartek typed away at his little desk – MC Hammer's desk – in the cold back room of the empty 3 level house filled with scary paranormal dolls in-between the walls.

And night after night he would type, type, type. But with every burned out raging impulse of screaming text he would exhale, ingress, then look to the inanimate cell phone on his chilly metal desk. Just waiting, waiting, and waiting. Waiting for Clownbaby.

New Years Eve was hours away. Quixxxote had drifted through the gay scene of both Raleigh and Coastal Florida in a last-ditch attempt to be something he could never be. He lived near one of the largest gay resorts in America, and it was always packed. He was offered a possible job, led in with a friendly smile. But he could never carry a conversation, and felt further lost with every visitation.

It was New Years Eve, and the tropical fag resort would be off the hook. It was as close to a slamming rave as that scene gets. He shaved his head & face, and put on a suit.

Before leaving to catch the bus, his phone erupted with text messages from Clownbaby – *cutting off his head.* After not communicating for months, he'd wished her a happy New Years via text. She said he was a minor chapter of a book she threw away.

Ryan wandered outside, plopping into the flimsy plastic chair in the front yard, and was encircled by a murmuration of crows – a massive flock weaving together in aesthetic patterns and perching on the house, the lawn, surrounding him like an invading army.

As they blackened the foggy gray atmosphere, he at last let her go. The crows dissipated, continuing to migrate. He stood back up, burned yet triumphant. He wandered the subdivision towards the white sand coast, sky charcoal gray as far as the eye could see.

He lingered at the bus stop waiting for the next coach to the big gay party. It didn't matter how society viewed him or what anyone thought – at least he knew who he was.

We Are All Anonymous Now

One by one they came, in plain faces or grinning masks of white. Unshackling their traumatic hermitage, the cockroach people scattered from their places of hiding.

    Like a hidden army plagued by amnesia, the soldiers now recalled their purpose. The great hordes arose from their sarcophagus lives, marching into city centres & town squares worldwide, encamping themselves in ever-increasing fanatic waves.

    From the exodus of youth they'd returned, grasping an empowerment that had long been deemed mythology. In one unprecedented shift, the chessboard pawns of both black & white monarchs united to encircle both their respective kings.

    The Arab Spring had evolved into the Age of Occupy, and as the wave traversed the globe no soil was unaffected. Even as the ranks of protesters swelled, many were unaware how this all began. They did not comprehend the global context of Occupy. For them, Wall Street was enough a vile target to get them into the streets.

    MABUS had already come and gone as foretold, dead before the world knew his story. Occupy was a shock-wave of his rage, an echo of injustice. Bartek had used the idea of MABUS as his artistic platform and never considered Nostradamus valid. Yet now the puzzle pieces fused effortlessly, if one suspends disbelief.

    To Nostradamus, the third and final Antichrist was a conjoining of two vague things – MABUS was the beginning, and ALUS the end result. MABUS would set the precedent of an ideology, and this ideology would quickly sweep the globe.

    It was said that this ideology would go horribly awry and thus be vastly more disastrous to humankind then any ideological system before it. Because of it, something called ALUS would emerge in the Iraq/Syria region, dragging all nations into WW3.

    During a time of conflict between Russia and the New World over an area our maps now call Ukraine, this ALUS thing would somehow balloon and swallow Iraq. ALUS would be something of a state fused with fanatic religion, backed by the worst Islamic extremism on a bloodthirsty crusade.

    Once ignited, ALUS would have juggernaut momentum. It would overrun the borders of the Pan-Arab world, perpetrating barbarism & cruelty unlike the world has seen. The genocidal ALUS would spill into Turkey – and the march of war would head into the heart of Europe, ending with a siege on The Vatican. And although its leader is a madman "chosen by god," he is not ALUS but simply of it. And he is certainly not MABUS, whom sets the tone.

The World Revolution began with Wikileaks, the whistle-blowing website. Having been smuggled a stockpile of classified info by Army Private Bradley Manning, in July 2010 W.Leaks released 92,000 docs related to the Afghanistan

War. This was followed by another 400,000 classified docs – the fintel of the Iraq war – proving systematic war crimes, massacres, rape prisons, assassinations.

Then, on November 28th 2010, they released the US Ambassador Cables from Nixon to Obama – revealing the hidden motivations & criminal conspiracies of the USA in world relations.

The world learned that every US Ambassador was covertly a spy with CIA backing sent with wires to record their meetings with all foreign dignitaries. Global racketeered criminality was also vaulted dead center into public sphere.

In response, the government threatened anyone caught downloading/possessing this info would be classified a "domestic terrorist" and threatened treason. Wikileaks soon dumped the intelligence files of Afghanistan War, again filled with war crimes. The US government expressed the same threats – any US civilian caught possessing any of this was now an enemy combatant...

Within the ambassador cables was a reference to Ben Zine Ali, the dictator of Tunisia. He'd stolen billions from the country and lined his own pockets – the USA knew this fully well, as did Ali's government. The story traveled quickly through the tiny Northern African country, fermenting a nationwide uproar.

This is the tinderbox from which MABUS emerged. Despite all the phony decoders of Nostradamus' writings, not a single one of them could have foresaw that MABUS was a _nobody_.

MABUS was Mohamed Bouazizi, better known by his local nickname Mo Basboosa (_or Mo Bas, for short_). He had no army, no followers, no fanaticism to seduce the masses – he sold mangoes & bananas, scraping by on $140 a month. Harassed and degraded by corrupt authorities who kept stealing his produce unless he bribed them, they made it impossible for him to eat or pay rent. Local cops had mistreated him for years, regularly confiscating his small wheelbarrow of fruit. MABUS had no other way to make a living, so he continued as a street vendor through years of harassment.

Around 10 pm on December 16th, 2010, he'd borrowed $200 to buy the fruit he was to sell. The next morning the police harassed him again because he did not have a vendor's permit – even though the law stated no permit was necessary.

The police were extortionists, and wanted their bribes. MABUS was in debt from the small assortment of goods he was now selling. He refused to comply. The female cop slapped him, spit on him, and made a slur against his dead father. They confiscated his scales, his cart & fruit. They beat & kicked him on the ground.

MABUS, having been robbed by the police and publicly humiliated, erupted in anger. He ran to the governor's office to demand his property back. The governor refused to see him, then when Mo Bas confronted him he still refused: "_If you don't see me, I'll burn myself!!_" The Governor ignored him.

MABUS ran to a nearby petrol station and filled a can of gasoline. Out front, while standing in the middle of traffic, he shouted to the governor, "_How *do you expect me to make a living?!?"* He then burned himself alive – lasting 18 more days in coma before the flesh expired. A parade of 5000 celebrated his sacrifice in his hometown. But the police would not let the angry crowds go anywhere near the spot he'd burned.

Strangely enough, Tunisia's dictator of 23 years visited MABUS in the hospital, in an attempt to stem the growing discontent. Mo had already become a symbol in the newspapers, and Ben Ali promised to send him to France for medical treatment. No such transfer was arranged, and Bouazizi died on Jan 4th, 2011.

Outraged by the events that led to his self-immolation, protests immediately began in Sidi Bouzid. Within hours thousands were encamped in the main square with a slow build-up that coursed through the nation over two weeks. As the police fought against the tide, their attempts to quiet the unrest only served to fuel what was quickly becoming a violent and deadly movement.

The protests became widespread, moving into the more affluent areas and eventually into the capital. MABUS self-immolation created an instant popular revolt nationwide, and the violent momentum it sparked became so intense that the dictator fled the country. It was an 18 day revolution. 6 months after MABUS death, 107 Tunisians copycatted his self-immolation in protest.

It was a strange place for this revolution to begin. Tunisia was the smallest country in North Africa, with no oil to export and barely an army. It was a cozy beach resort for tourists, and strategically irrelevant in every way. But it had unleashed the passion of The Arab World, and millions of people that had for years been oppressed by their dictators and the worst sort of colonialist exploitation simultaneously awoken.

Nearby Egypt, the biggest and most important of the Northern African countries, had for 30+ years been ruled by dictator Hosni Mubarak. In solidarity with MABUS, a 49-year-old restaurant owner named Abdou Abdel-Moneim Jaafar doused himself in gas and self-immolated in front of the Egyptian Parliament.

His act of protest quickly inspired a middle-aged woman to post a YouTube video where she held a hammer. She declared that she would go to Cairo's Main Square armed with nothing more then that bludgeon for defense, and that she would not be moved until Mubarak was overthrown. Within days millions had poured into the streets. The country became a war-zone of protesters battling government forces. And by February 11th, the dictator was overthrown in an army coup welcomed by the people of Egypt.

Protests of similar nature erupted through The Arab World, and the phrase "Arab Spring" was coined. Within 8 months the dictatorships of Libya had Yemen had been overthrown, and both Syria and Bahrain were engaged in bloody civil war. Major ongoing protests continued in Iraq, Jordan, Algeria, Kuwait, Morocco, Israel, Turkey, Sudan – and solidarity protests exploded worldwide.

What started as Take The Square movement in 2010 through Europe and Latin America had echoed around the world like a booming gunshot. By January 2011 it fused incontrovertibly with The Arab Spring, and by the time the global wave landed in the United States it was called Occupy Wall Street.

On September 17th, 2011 it began in Zucotti Park. Push came to shove, and the cops went out of control. With wild footage of police brutality streaking the internet, the bandwagon moved like lighting. Within a week 1500 Occupy encampments had entrenched themselves worldwide in solidarity, many of which now surrounded the parliaments of every major country. The comatose power of the 1960's reawakened as all the former Vietnam protesters returned to the streets alongside the new youth.

To add further legitimacy, every major progressive and mainstream democrat organization jumped on the bandwagon. Occupy was roaring on unlimited engines, but no one knew quite where it would lead or how it would end.

The Americans reacted in many different ways to this uprising. In classic fashion, the wider public had no clue as to why this was happening. With a media blackout and yellow journalism attack they villainized the protesters by framing them unintelligible fools without coherent purpose.

Repulsed by the microcosm of societal ills that materialized inside each of these camps on the front doorsteps of city after city, most the ant people just wanted the smelly, scary people to go away.

Without a singular demand to base the protest around, they felt there was no point. To incense an uprising based on the repudiation of everything that stands was not sensible. But the cockroach people knew better. The great mass of insect humans had been driven to a point of collapse from the utter desperation of hopelessness that was America and it's rampant police state, its horrid economic vulture reality.

In the sporadic evolution of Occupy the well-meaning college-educated "young white professional" protest leaders who upstarted these bastions were overrun by the very problems of society they set out to fix. The homeless, the mad, the impoverished flooded their college-minded protest camps and showed the true ugly face of American society.

The police and those of normal society couldn't stand to look at it, let alone the mayors. While the protest leaders cajoled themselves into believing they could make some kind of unified protest state, the reality was they were a social network based on a freak-out of desperation. There was no ideology except each man become his own leader – *his own dictator, per se* – and to re-imagine his own body as the territory of a state.

And just as the dictators of the Arab world that moved so swiftly to crush the uprising, so did Barack Obama, Homeland Security, and The FBI. With mayors enacting emergency laws, they sent battalions of riot police armed like paramilitaries. The cities privatized parks, made illegal the action of sitting on the ground, criminalizing feeding the homeless. Snipers from Homeland Security positioned themselves around the free speech camps. Courts took custody of children from parents because they were involved.

Thousands of Americans exercising their freedom of speech were classified as domestic terrorists and put on watch lists. Undercover cops and FBI agents penetrated every encampment, DHS planting snitches & actors to destroy it from the inside out.

The Pan-Tribal Conspiracy was solidly in action. Quite literally everything Bartek had stated in his manifesto was here and now, globally. What began as a luminous prank tied to a band no one understood had somehow engulfed the world by proxy.

Ironically Bartek had been promoting Occupy and working under its aegis for years. In 2006 he literally was calling his mission "*The Occupied States of Mabusvania.*" Furthermore, he'd ascribed the Pan-Tribal Manifesto's authorship under the pen name "The Propagandist" which was his way of signing it "Anonymous."

What Occupy achieved was what he sought from a "fan club" in A.K.A. MABUS. Even the cover of their album was eerily coincidental, as it showed the statue of liberty removing a white mask that looked strikingly like Guy Fawkes but revealing a skull underneath – partially in inspiration to the film *V For Vendetta.*

Until Occupy began, Bartek hadn't even heard the name Anonymous. He wasn't a hacker, had no knowledge of 4Chan, and wasn't aware of 2008's Scientology war. But the inherent premise of their prank turned movement was inherently same as his.

Utterly disconnected from Anon and a nocturnal loner, Bartek built his ideas in solitude. For years he planted seeds by spreading information, disseminating propaganda, pushing tribal anarchist and dystopian/utopian messages through art.

In that blur of activity which reflected no pragmatic life or vocation in American society, slaving away like a little Hitler in his bipolar madness, he had solidified all the theoretical foundations of his crazy person's government-in-exile.

Occupy was the moment that he – just like so many other unknown Anons in waiting – simply wandered into the fray. Shaking off the leech-like drain from 10 years of hopeless politics, those of the Pre-911 world re-established that glimmer of grassroots change.

After Bush's Orwellian reign, and after Obama's miserable fail, "people power" exploded as a zeitgeist, a force of magickal magnetism. Every passion of the street crazy and the brilliant loner erupted in frantic acceleration. The more perceptive the individual, the more the fever pitch. Change had come to the world.

Alternative media dominated the language of the internet, and the Government's control of the script eviscerated. No one believed anything major news said anymore, and the collective conscious of the internet was moving in lock step with Facebook, Twitter, YouTube, LinkedIn, Ustream, LiveLeak...

As a torpedo of bipolar mania, Bartek lunged into Occupy, just as any obsession that gripped him this time of year. American society was drastically polarized, so depending on who you ask, his impassioned actions could be considered either.

Yet Bartek knew this was the most startlingly healthy thing that could ever have happened to him, or to anyone affiliated. That he sauntered into the largest and most sophisticated of the Occupy camps in America only fueled his rampage.

No historian on the life of Ryan Patrick Bartek will deny that 2011 had been his comeback year. With his New Years resolution of learning yoga techniques & seriously returning to music, he was determined to embark on a travel of Europe to complete *The Big Shiny Prison (Volume II)*.

He wanted to sever his path from Mistress Maam. Their relationship had formed in a dark moment, emboldened by even darker supernatural forces. It was an awful basis of interconnection, and he'd made a grave mistake taking her to the Northwest. In his weakness he let it continue until its foregone conclusion. It should never have gone as far as it did, but she truly loved him. If anything, they were friends of a rocky synergy.

Mistress Maam made him feel like a castrated, hen-pecked husband. Somehow he'd been brave enough to annihilate his lifelong repression, though he fell back into the malaise which so many men do. What begins as the glorious upheaval of a destitute life settles back into the freakish reality of it. To be open is to become a target of violence & hatred, and the estrangement of it only ferments the bricks of a new wall. Somehow the man crumbles & falls back into the old way. In a secretive solitude he finds himself living in fear, unable to reach out that he may cling to this new way of life.

Imagining that Greyhound ride down to San Francisco he could barely juxtapose his consciousness between the moments of then and now. He had lost himself in failure. He was again a manipulated little boy in fear.

In early December she'd gone to Michigan. Actually, it was more truthful that he sent her there. After a year of explosive fights between the two – which were always followed by her traveling and in the meantime he'd search for another partner – she'd returned to The Acropolis. She wanted to stop. The struggle was done, and they could just be people. She very directly wanted answers and to be the real thing. If they were to continue onward he would have to change his Facebook relationship status.

He sent her away on a Greyhound. It was her idea, but half-hearted. She wanted to confront her mother about anonymous dark issues. She was gone two weeks and had written him an email that he'd avoided reading. She soon called, wondering his answer. Not being strong enough to stop it, he told her to come back.

Soon after they were fighting again. After Christmas he made clear that this was over – he wanted out. She was wrecked: *"How can you say any of this to me after reading my letter?"* When he admitted deleting it accidentally, she burst in tears. Even though she refused to tell him, he knew the score – she probably only said she'd come back if he was serious, that he intended to marry her perhaps.

Until New Years, he avoided her. In denial she convinced herself that nothing was wrong, and it was heartbreaking when he had to spell it out plainly. She cried profusely, and then – hell having no fury like this woman scorned – Mistress Maam instigated a ruthless war for the apartment.

She hadn't paid rent in 8 months, as he forbid it so she could save. She had no financial discipline & was near penniless. But still she was on the lease & legally he could not make her go. She then *literally began living under the kitchen table* like a child in a fort of cardboard, annoying him into evacuation as if Ghandi vs British.

It went on like this for 2 months! Both of them avoiding each other as much as possible yet half the time sleeping in the same bed anyway. They would both be out on the town trying to find new partners and always it would be a disastrous enterprise, ending with both of them sleeping in the same bed every night after striking out.

The worst moment was Valentine's Day, when they went out as a pretend couple. It was the saddest, sleepiest, most unromantic dinner both had ever had. They were ridiculous.

How they made it to March like this your humble Narrator cannot fathom. Perhaps it was the frantic booking of his upcoming European journalism run, working full time that kept him together. For 3 months now he'd been on Craigslist posting for an emergency couch; MM was still living in a cardboard fort beneath the table.

It was at 3am on March 11th when she woke him by pokes. *"Wake up, wake up – we need to drive, FAST. Up up up – or we're fuckin' dead."* Bartek emerged from rocky slumber and looked at the computer screen streaming live aerial footage of northern Japan being wiped out by a mammoth tsunami. The wave looked CGI.

The West Coast was panicking, because the 9.1 magnitude earthquake was sending waves across the Pacific that could very well do the same. They began packing their bags, ready to hail a taxi and blindly drive to Eastern Oregon.

The official warnings dissipated, and a sigh of relief was to be breathed... until 4 nuclear power plants began melting down. The worst they could have imagined barely touched the reality...

Bartek finally discovered a room to rent in SE Portland for $200 a month and left Mistress Maam to the cardboard fort. She didn't think he was serious – they were meant to be and she was hopelessly in love. She nervously helped him move, even as he tried to dissuade her. He just did not want her to know where he was going.

Still, she had her way. Once they dropped off the belongings, she rode with him on the bus to work, where he'd get off and saunter down the street in the pouring rain. She held back tears as he exited, and he looked at her through the bus window.

Through the foggy window she gave him one last look – the taut face of a mask's sorrowful repression. Her burning chameleon eyes changed their color to an indistinguishable hue, and her face a blur as the bus carried her away. Bartek opened his umbrella to avoid the nuclear rain, and sauntered off to the gay bar where he now worked & was socially building a new life.

R. Bartek purchased his airplane ticket to London for June 1st. Blabbermouth had picked up the press release for his new book *Fortress Europe* – the biggest metal news service in the world. His was again a Metal Illuminati "Made Man."

His 30th birthday was triumphant. Holly Doom came down from Seattle to eat mushrooms with his new roommates, and all parties found themselves up to speed in their current lives.

Even if it was a consolation prize, he was able to have his Portland experience with Holly. He was depressed through 2010 that he was with MM and not her. She wanted to move to PDX and live with him. They could have that lost summer... *Europe was calling*.

Bartek visited Mistress Maam one last time. As always, no matter how positive he exits the situation horrible things happen. One of her great fears was abortion, because it once destroyed her as a consequence. Part of Bartek's major appeal was his vasectomy. Yet the second he walked, she got knocked up by the first guy she took home – and he threw her away the second he found out.

It was the day of her abortion that he had to give her the keys to the apartment and sign off on the lease. Outside The Acropolis she stormed up, sky high on pain-pills, spiritually traumatized in tears. Weeping, she screamed at him in the street that he'd ruined her life.

She had just learned that the man she really wanted to marry (and had been speaking of engagement with from Florida) – *the very man she'd turned down to likely marry Bartek instead* – he'd just died from a heroin overdose. She was destroyed. With a shaky hand he gave her the keys and wandered off to thundering echoes: "*DESTROYER... MONSTER... LIAR... I HATE YOU...*"

Bartek left for Europe on June 1st and stayed on the road until August 16th, making it through London, Paris, Amsterdam, Berlin, Prague, Copenhagen, Stockholm, Helsinki, Milan, Venice, Bolgona, Ljubljana, Bruxelles...

The spirit of rebirth that had encapsulated his Greyhound travels in America had again taken root. Experiencing labyrinths beyond his imagination, having traversed the great anarchist squats of Europe, he became a dyed-in-the-wool radical anarchist in result. He was again propelled by his love of music.

Just as when he took that Greyhound to California the first time, he returned preaching that the grass truly was greener on the other side (*which it was*). San Diego was a massive elevation from Detroit, just as Europe was an unspeakable triumph over Portland (*which was still the best America had to offer*)...

...yet the best America had to offer was no longer enough. Portland was just another movie set, plagued by the same forces of fear & control like everywhere else. With knowledge comes distance, and he saw the exploitation of USA life as never before. This time, he felt compelled to try and alter it. Even as he decided upon running away to Europe again in 2012, his heart bled for the people of his origin.

Funny enough, his first thought back onto US soil was that he needed a tent. He didn't know why, he just needed one. After all, he'd made it through Europe with a plastic tarp, rolling himself up like a burrito. It worked like a charm, and a tent seemed like dead weight, but for whatever reason, he felt he needed one.

Bartek returned to his dirt cheap southeast PDX room and resumed his job at the queer kitchen. He had to confront the reality that he was getting older. When the Europe manuscript was done, he wasn't sure which direction to take.

He hoped to marry a European for citizenship, but this too was a likely fantasy. No European woman will romance an American man who think citizens should own guns – this is the ever-present Catch 22. He was adamant about living the rest of his days in Berlin, or starting a grindcore band and touring the anarcho-crust circuit of Europe until he dropped dead.

And there was, of course, a European dream girl that he'd met – someone vastly better then him, stronger then him, with unshakable morals. Within an hour of knowing her, she had blasted to bits any notion that he could ever love an American woman again.

He wanted to impress in the most profound, sincere way – to be more like her, to be free & powerful as she was. And he was quite adamant in returning to her the following summer as to stab his anarchist sword in the ground like a bowing knight, offering to follow her like a soldier to the edge of the world. She knew guns were important.

As always, it would begin another isolated period where he would ignore the immediate and concentrate on the dream. Once he set his sights on someone, he was all or nothing. And no woman but another European could shake his extremist crush. He was damned to Euro crushes for eternity, and would likely be forever miserable...

He had always thought if he never "made it" in a larger sense with his music or writing by the age of 30 then he'd just enroll in a tech trade school. Just become an electrician or a plumber, and live out his days doing his art on the side with better funding. But the time had come to choose an option for The Grid, and he was angry.

Bartek felt his only option was to go back to Seattle for a visit and retrace his steps. He'd wanted for two years to visit Miss Monster and the kids, and it was the boy's birthday party. He had delusions that he'd walk in, and the kids would run up and hug him like family. They would all eat at the dinner table and would enthusiastically listen to the tales of his adventures like he was a Pyrate Lord returning from the high seas.

When he finally did get there, the kids barely looked at him. The girl didn't even lift her head, and the boy was too busy playing video games to say much else then *"oh, hey."* He stayed the night and woke up to the gloomy day. He bid them farewell and jumped on a bus for downtown Seattle, realizing the bitter end of an illusion.

With the gray overcast & cold air giving Seattle the clenched, gritty quality that made it a perpetual downer, he walked the streets aimlessly. Jeremy was long gone, as was the spirit of renewal that Seattle held for him 2 years before.

After Wall Street collapsed, Seattle took a new character – ugly new buildings had sprung up everywhere, the bus fares had increased as well as consumer goods. Packs of cigarettes were going for $10, as if this were now an unwelcoming, wretched version of New York City with vacant streets & cold blowing winds.

The homeless were pushed off the street under bridges and newly constructed banker skyscrapers dotted the landscapes. There wasn't even a water fountain bubbling in public. Every inch of it seemed a horrible perversion of the glorious city he'd once known.

Bartek again thought of the Arab Spring which he'd been so diligently following; watching Mubarak overthrown in Egypt had brought him to tears. The world was on fire everywhere but America, and he felt destitute that he should be walking this grim, lost symbol of 90's freedom. Kurt Cobain had been dead for 17 years, and the freak kingdom had degenerated into an abominable corporate mausoleum.

Then, in his gloom, Bartek turned a corner and found a throbbing mass of protesters in front of the shopping mall. They filled the concrete park out front, and numerous people were shouting impassioned rhetoric through bullhorns at the ever-increasing crowds.

With eyes ablaze and soul malnourished, Bartek walked right into the birth of Occupy Seattle. Three days of inspired revolt followed, and within a week, he was one of thousands that had clogged the park squares of Occupy Portland.

10 days had passed since the initial throng of protesters had entrenched themselves, and a groundswell of concerned citizens from every facet of American society had morphed into a massive social network. Locally they were comprised of untold thousands – and untold millions worldwide.

By Saturday, October 15th Occupy had peaked. It was still something of a novelty, and still so fresh it attracted old ladies with Stop The War signs &

tough-talking college kids & families bringing their children to hold peace signs and get their faces painted like kittens so mommy can pretend she gives a fuck.

The novelty of living some Hallmark Card 1960's protest fantasy had waned with the increasing amount of police pressure, social stigma and yellow journalism. This traditional liberal crowd was also wary of the scary, smelly, crazy people who were eerily & systematically building some freakish Pan-Tribal Anti-Empire.

In those 10 days two distinct divisions were created – those who went home at night, and those that lived on the front lines. The core of Occupy was The Action itself, and it was thoroughly anarchist in every respect. In fact it was one of the largest anarchist mass actions in USA history, simply because it was smart enough not to not even use the term. It brought anarchist theory to the masses, all from wise sloganeering.

Most didn't even know what Anonymous was, or that Occupy was basically another Anon prank. What they knew was Egypt, and that they were in desperate times. The term Occupy brought the Iraq war home again, the 99% vs 1% was classic class warfare, and Wall Street was a fierce focal point of rage midst a Great Depression. All the winning concepts were there, and anarchism was dumped on the front door step of America – yet it was being taken seriously because never mentioned by its name.

The drones were now steering each other in mobs to overthrow the queen, yet many of the worker bees remained loyal to their pre-programmed ways. Even as they were enticed by Occupy, they found themselves cornered against a social wall, be it their place of employment, church, even shopping for groceries – the topic was hot, and it was pariah.

In lieu of social pressure and romantic train-wrecking, many realized they didn't support this thing. They didn't quite understand it either. But what was right for the Pan-Tribal Conspirator isn't right for everyone else, and it does not need to be either.

Occupy was pure reality thrown onto the doorstep of every city centre; a freak-out decrying the need for a unified demand except the impossible demand that they totally overthrow reality.

And as the ant people climbed onto the pedestal one by one, speaking for the first time to the public – with a communication that was strikingly clear and honest – they actually paid heed to the other insect humans before them, in a way they'd never assumed possible until that very moment.

With newfound voices the cockroach bipeds expressed they did not want to be Tyler Durden, but sought through their own peaceful cooperative vision their own self-styled Project Mayhem's expressly created to destroy the tyrants of the world. Their Pan-Tribal conspiracy was aimed at convincing every man to recognize his own physical body as the territory of an anti-fascist state, and for every such man to become his own revolution. In tandem, the DNA sequence of interactivity would accelerate and bloom.

Occupy was a powerhouse of manufacturing charismatic people who very well could have spellbound nations like Pied Pipers in jackboots, but wanted exactly the opposite – for those spellbound victims to instead over-run the theoretical Nuremberg stage in a stampede, trampling and killing Hitler in the process. With the entire crowd now populating the stage, and not a soul left in the audience, each of the former spectator puppets would rip off their clothes and approach the microphone naked & exposed to the elements.

Having disowned the flags of every nation – and replacing the need of nationalism with a patriotism of the soul – these newly crowned emperors of will-power and self-determination would begin, one by one, to recite the text of their own personal anti-fascist *Mein Kampf* expertly crafted to destroy all negative control. Shouting their fanatic designs to an empty stadium, the reverberations would bounce off emptied concrete, because no one would be left to hear it.

One by one, the Anti-Mussolini's would froth at the mouth with impassioned rhetoric, passionately screaming towards invisible crowds the central message that no man should ever convert to their frenzied and fanatic message, because what is right for them is not right for everyone else, and that every man should be free to think for himself, to follow his hearts desires, and that through mutual understanding and compassion they be united in their quest of peaceful individuality, open communication, and respectful intercommunalism.

And then, in glorious unison, they would march until every fabric of the social construct had changed. From the bottom up, teach one by one the empowerment to make good on this promise. Like propaganda missionaries they would spread their fanatic messages. At every opportunity they'd whistle-blow in the most dramatic way all the evidence of criminality they could muster...

Eviction Night – Saturday, November 12th, 2011: In an illegal move, Obama instructed his Department of Justice, FBI and Homeland Security to dismantle the uprising.

The powers that be hosted a multi-mayor conference call where it was determined they'd rather pay off court reparations then endure the cluster-fuck of free speech. All of the Occupy camps were surrounded by riot police and given a deadline to vacate.

Occupy had now evolved into fully functional international tribe that belonged to no nation, that triumphed no state, and existed in a territory that was a pure manifestation of intellect which transcended time and space. If an authority were to demand to see the man in charge everyone would drop what they were doing to hand him a mirror.

The police could smash them, remove them, but it mattered not, because the foundations of this new reality existed totally in the mind. The ground they stood upon had no relevance, though they were prepared to defend it to the last man. There was no leader and no flag, only a fanatic tribe built of men and women that had become fanatics of their own self-styled creeds. Collectively and individually, they were The Hydra.

Knowing that few of these camps could resist the onslaught, the world of Occupy looked to the last remaining major shakers – Portland, Oakland, Philly, Phoenix, St Louis, SLC, Seattle, Denver, San Fran & Wall Street.

From behind laptop screens the Anons honed in on live feed as the showdowns unfurled. International media huddled around the encampments, unsure if it would lead to violence. Dozens of camps were dismantled on Friday, alongside St. Louis. PDX was gearing up for the showdown.

As the midnight deadline approached the inevitable storming of Darth Vader riot cops only served to electrify them. The consensus at Occupy Portland was to go down swinging, hell or high water. In those 43 days of existence, hundreds of desperate people had discovered their home and family *"Come on, just try and take it from us"* while others proclaimed *"You'll never take us alive!!"*

30 minutes until the stroke of midnight, it was the sort of night that breeds pneumonia. The chilly air was filled with rain that came down like a heavy sprinkling mist, and every voice accompanied by thick steam. Many were bailing, dismantling their own tents, ready to take the next train out like Frenchman abandoning Paris hours before the Nazi arrival.

When the time came, at least 30% of these Occu-Warriors who lived in the camps over a month were no longer willing to fight. Like fleas hopping off a wet dog, they evacuated the moment police shouted over their bullhorns.

15 minutes to deadline, the minor army of peace-niks ran about the squares of Lonsdale and Chapman in a scene of chaos. Word had spread that both Denver & SLC had been defeated, and it was inevitable that their home would be taken.

The muddy ground was collecting pools of water, and a shimmering light flooded from the hastily erected stadium lights. It looked like *M*A*S*H** filming set about to be overrun by Viet Cong. As the ship-jumpers evacuated they trampled over the remains of ripped & tattered tents, slipping and falling in the mud.

The legion of Pan-Tribal fanatics prepared themselves for their Alamo. Perhaps 500 were left, vowing to stay the course. With 10 minutes to go, the stage that had been built for participants to say their final peace before laving went dim. The stadium lights went unplugged and the cold, wet night resumed its blackness.

Hundreds of riot police now encircled them from every direction awaiting the order to invade. Pure adrenaline coursed through the tribal crazy men, spurned by memories of an entire life of lies. From the moose statue where they birthed their consensus-based Senate, an earth-conscious radical anarchist suited for battle & dripping with downpour shouted: *"COME N' TAKE IT PIGS – COME N' TRY YOU MOTHERFUCKERS!!!!!!!!!!!!!!!!!!!!!!!!!!!!!!!!!!"*

The ceaseless mist-rain fluttered down from the heavens with the grace of snow. The rain dripped down his mask, rolling off the contours of its skeleton features. Breathing heavy inside the plastic wall between his face and the night, Bartek stared calmly through tiny slits at the madness consuming his "Park World" dream.

His steel toe army boots did little to prevent the rain from soaking his socks, and his green army coat was just as sopping wet & muddy as his SWAT pants. The hooded sweatshirt underneath his bulky, too-large army coat clung to his scalp like a wet blanket.

The hood resembled the shroud of The Grim Reaper, and the mask he now wore which made him appear just that – a hard-plastic skull spray-painted black with dark mesh over the eye slits. All he lacked was a scythe.

Since the early days of Occupy he'd worn this mask – occasionally at camp, but always during actions. It was important to remain anonymous among Anonymous, especially with all the FBI snitches & police informants & recording equipment the FEDS had wired throughout the camp.

Most regarded it as a symbol against war, or just another bohemian weirdo playing dress-up. Bartek also knew it helped to deflect police from singling him out, because for some reason they avoid attacking cartoony costumes and clown paint.

They immediately assume you're one of the joke protesters with no more menacing a threat then a cardboard sign with slogans in sharpie. In aggressively rigging himself as the center of focal attention, he 'd somehow become invisible.

There was something far deeper here in the meaning of this mask. Even after a lifetime of leaving clues as to his secret supervillain identity, none had discovered the trail to his secret master plan. Infantile & ludicrous as it was, he loved his little game.

It was one of the few things left from his childhood that he simply refused to let go of, and not even the most brilliant psychologist could decode the Rubik's Cube that was his internal dreamscape, except the nonexistent one he foolishly had a crush on.

As the steam drifted through his black skeleton nostrils, Bartek siphoned through his memories of all the great villains who'd inspired him. Just as he had put on the mask to channel a persona, he tried on the masks of his lengthy rogue gallery. He thought of himself as General Kael, somehow displaced from *Willow* and thrown into a futuristic, ironic battlefield that's combat objective was world peace. *Nope, not him.*

He thought of himself as The Red Hood – the tragic comedian who is double-crossed by the mob and falls into a vat of chemicals only to be spit out a sewer main with his skin burned white and his hair morphed green. *But that was Jack.*

He conjured memories of the Halloween costume his mother had crafted when he was 7 years old, and how he was paraded on an auditorium stage with the other children his age to showcase to the school their October 31st get-ups.

With a plastic scythe in hand and his skull mask underneath the hood, he stood as The Grim Reaper before the other children. They had all hated the young Bartek, but did not know his. He heard the awe of the crowd as he bowed his skeletal head. He would wear that costume as much as he could in the lead up to All Hallows Eve, because he felt centered wrapped in its shroud. He wanted to wear it during normal life.

He would still slip the mask in his backpack, sticking it on his face to meditate calmly upon his cold breath when the adults and other children weren't watching. He would even walk at nights alone wearing it through his neighborhood, floating through dark alleys and dim corridors, like a specter heralding the four horsemen.

As time progressed, when slinking into his alienation and coldness, he was able to imagine that skull mask on his face even when his skin showed plainly. It was his eyes in this state that perhaps unnerved the other children the most, as if his burning retinas were still beaming through those tiny plastic slits. *Yet he was not the Grim Reaper either.*

7 minutes. Bartek recalled how this self-willed Reaper child would come home to watch Paul Dini's animated *Batman* series, always through those imagined plastic slits. And here he would observe like an administrator his supervillain friends that would be rounded up & locked in Arkham Asylum.

And like many comic geeks, he would obsess over his first crush & plot to steal her from The Joker. Even if he admired the antics of the psychotic clown, he never really assumed him as his secret identity. Sure, he wore that grinning invisible mask sometimes – same as all the Asylum inmates. And if he so felt like being Mr. Freeze or Zsasz or Two Face or whoever, nothing was to stop him.

But he wasn't after Harley in her painted-up clown form, because that would be too simple. No, the man with the skull face was after *Dr. Quinzel* herself. That was the joke – that he would steal her away, deprogram her obsession, and then they as a duo would run the asylum as King & Queen.

And so Dr. Bartek, in his infantile fantasies, played his little game. What was the use of having friends that didn't obsessively scheme for the overthrow of The Bat (*whoever or whatever that meant at any given time*)?

What was the point of relationship, unless they too were a Mogwai fed after midnight? That he had a tattoo of The Joker was only a false flag. After all, none of the crazies would work for him otherwise. It was a joke in itself, and a rallying symbol to accumulate maniacs who played his childish game.

And if there ever were a Batman-esque symbol to target, nothing screamed it louder then the mascot of "The 1%'s" eerie camp at Bohemian Grove. With a 40 foot stone owl & mock sacrifices & secret GOP drag dancing & having gay orgies while still doing everything in their power to criminalize homosexuality, all it would take was the united world of Occupy to shine a raging spotlight on the Cremation of Care to ruin it for their mob forever.

In America it is scandal that ends careers and launches revolutions – and nothing was more damaging for these fake conservative moral majority types then the Bohemian Club. Bartek had them with their pants around their ankles.

As Occupy progressed, he returned to the mask. Spray-painted black, he'd haunt the camp just as he did the children of his elementary. Few realized this was him; local papers would take snapshots & stick him in their stories. Somehow, he became a bizarre mascot whose message was unknown.

But Bartek had his message, and an agenda that had lain in wait. Everything that Occupy had become was destined to reflect Pan-Tribalism – and Bartek remorselessly spammed his manifesto to every Occur-intelligentsia circle, site, forum, zine & blog.

In 5 years of promoting it, he'd received 55 downloads. After 2 months at Occupy, it was 10,000+. The Pan-Tribal Manifesto was appearing on Occupy websites, and its methods were being taught, used & adopted by General Assemblies all over the world.

Yet no one knew its origin or anything about its anonymous author. It was one of many such searing manifestos that circulated quickly throughout this world uprising. It seemed as if every camp had some shadowy Bartek. All the Cockroach Lords unleashed their masterplans at once.

Few of his fellow protesters were aware of his secret activities. For two months now he'd been running international PR campaigns, networking globally, piecing together actions his Narrator best not relate lest he condemn the man to a FEMA Camp. Even in Portland he was on dozens of committees without those committees even knowing it.

He had spies & henchmen allocated deep. And without anyone so much as fingering him he quietly watched from the shadows as a secret ringleader. After years of roaring through America, he now had an operative in nearly every major Occupy camp in USA & Europe, with direct contacts to all the "Big Dogs." He could with one email rig an internationally coordinated effort, and had over 3000 lawyers in Portland.

And thus Dr. Bartek knew that even if the authorities stomped Occupy out of existence, the seeds he so feverishly worked to plant would very well be sown. The ant people were communicating with instant technology, and the Propaganda Manifesto had found its way into their feelers.

Bartek's legacy was the literal ideology of MABUS he had artistically created as a Discordian cartoon religion where at its core lay the idea of Occupy and it's infusion with propaganda – that propaganda is itself the strongest form of magick attack & defense to alter reality, and here he'd decoded & offered the ultimate grimoire.

It was 2011, and MABUS was real. And partially as a prank but altogether serious (*and anonymously*), Bartek may have unleashed upon the world the very ideology Nostradamus warned against by ironic proxy.

It could very well become it, if stripped of its peaceful content and warped to justify violence in the hands of some looming Islamo-Fascist crusade like the prophesied terror army ALUS of Syria and Iraq (*but hey, nothing like that could ever happen, right?*)

So with Jeremy "Two-Face" Sullivan infecting camp after camp with viral vision, and with The Joker as his cameraman – plus a thousand maniac Harley Quinn's spread across protest world & unlimited lunatics fanatically overthrowing reality – there Bartek stood, sopping wet, like Colonel Kurtz midst the absolute chaos of a Riot Cop D-Day.

The hot steam drifted out the nostrils of his black skeleton mask as his true identity was finally revealed: _Dr. Jeremiah Arkham_ a.k.a. _THE BLACK MASK_ – _Kingpin of Arkham Asylum & Terror Tyrant of Gotham City._

And the world would have no choice but to confront the onslaught of his wonderful specimens who in classic Batman fashion stylistically reflected his costume. The Ultimate Anon, the blackened face of death, flanked by his armada of white faced grinning Fawkes's. _Operation: Arkham_ was a success, and the party was just getting started – _Moo-HaHaHaHa…_

Bartek removed the mask and discarded it into a mud puddle – a terrible thing to get arrested with & possible 10 year conviction for shielding one's face in a riot. He no longer needed it anyway – he needed to make room for the cider vinegar bandanna to cover his nose & mouth as to prevent the burning asphyxiation of tear gas.

3 minutes to midnight, and he could taste the metallic zang of the rain. It was probably just another droplet of Plutonium or Cesium 137 from Fukushima. The time to run would have been in the first 3 days before the initial hydrogen explosion drifted to Oregon.

But where was there to run? With 4 nuclear meltdowns turned melt-throughs pumping out roughly 100,000 atomic bombs in the first few months, across the Pacific they burned away and would continue to for the next 6 billion years. Humanity was in the early stages of nuclear winter – it would be years before the accumulation of it would rapidly start mutating cells, animals and plant life.

Bartek remembered how in that first week the falling rains gave him that metallic taste in the mouth. How his gums swelled up and began bleeding, how his thoughts became more convoluted. How his knuckles, knees and elbows now flashed to different colors like oddly timed Christmas lights, at turns orange or dark purple.

He thought about how the government stopped testing the rain water, and how they'd raised Federal guidelines of how much a dosage of radiation was needed to kill you to 10 times what it was. He thought of how in those months from March to May, everyone had a lengthy drawn out sickness nicknamed "The Portland Flu." About how locals would complain of their hair falling out, their teeth bleeding. How everyone they knew was somehow had cancer.

Bartek thought about Grimmson's, how he had to convince management to go back to selling neuro-toxic, brain-bleeding COREXIT 9500 gulf seafood because it was safer then selling them plutonium fish of the Fukushima Pacific.

And he thought about how the entire gay scene abandoned him because of Occupy. About how he was too extreme for even the most persecuted fringe in the world. How he was a black sheep of every stripe, and the only people he wanted to associate with were those now fighting Homeland Security. Just like the majority of exploited citizens, the gay scene howled for the destruction of Occupy. Rid society of all the crazy, smelly people; let them continue shopping in fragrance convenience.

2 minutes to go, and The Batmen in riot gear readied their assault. As Bartek ran to the front-lines and his tribe rushed in a frenzy through the park squares, a wave of light erupted in the street. At the last minute, the citizens of PDX had arrived to support their dramatic last stand. 10,000 ordinary people had arrived holding lit candles, and encircled the camps as a barrier of peaceful protection.

Everyone knew the cops would win, but no one wanted to see Occupy get hurt in the process. Even if they derailed the methods the protesters were using, they still agreed with the premise of their grievances. Portland was a community, not a business.

And no one respected this ruthless P.D. that had executed 13 unarmed homeless people over the last 2 years without anyone getting a disciplinary action. The same police which had dozens of swastika-wearing, "off duty" white power organizers.

The clock struck 12:01, and they moved in – yet the human shield of 10,000 proved too strong. In their full body armor, the cops looked pitifully helpless. The human wall stared them in the eyes, then in unison took one step forward. The police, like a receding wave, went back one step.

The citizens again stepped forward again, and again the police retread. Step by step it continued, live on international TV. Bartek's phone was blowing up with concerned texts as the nation watched the spectacle on CNN, NBC, ABC, FOX.

Expecting the tear gas mortar attack to come any time, Bartek instructed people to grab all the plastic buckets they could as to trap the smoking canisters. They rounded up dozens and soon began beating on them like war drums.

Like a man possessed, Bartek grabbed an emptied drum and ran up to the line of Darth Vader cops alone. He stared them down like a savage, suicidal lunatic. He beat on the drum, like explosions of thunder. THUNK *"kill me"* he thought. THUNK *"do it, I fucking dare you"* THUNK *"come on come on come on"* THUNK. The maniac kept beating away, enticing the riot squadrons to crush him.

And then from behind came a tap-tap-tap on his shoulder. Bartek again went THUNK THUNK THUNK and the tiny finger went tap-tap-tap. He turned around and there Mistress Maam stood, her face concealed behind a white Anonymous mask. It was her last attempt to break through his wall, but it was much, much too late. He returned to his suicidal THUNK THUNK THUNK over and over until eventually the taps stopped coming, and Mistress Maam vanished away into the fog of chaos.

THUNK his vengeance erupted THUNK his hatred assailed THUNK he assassinated an entire way of life THUNK he erased all memories of the past and lunged headfirst into the belly of the beast. Soon dozens of other protesters came behind him and began beating their war-drums same as him. For 20 minutes they pounded, until Bartek dropped his percussion and walked to the center of camps.

The hours passed with wretched standoff. By 4am, most townspeople had left, and there were maybe 400 protesters left with an exhausted police line standing across the street gripping billy clubs & tazers, ready to go wild. Yet for some reason they began pulling out – retreating to the front of the Injustice Center.

The Swarm of 150 bicyclists took their final lap around the park. With the last contingent of riot cops blocking the unopened street, The Swarm zoomed in a game of chicken. A bullhorn thundered: "*You are unlawfully blocking traffic!!*" The Swarm came at them, and the cops parted as if the Red Sea. The tribe cheered from inside the wrecked camps…

And with the light of day softening the blackness to a melancholy overcast, the helicopters that plagued the sky like mechanized demons all but vanished. From any view, the police disappeared; somehow, it just ended. Bartek looked about the smashed tent city, bodies strewn about sleeping in exhaustion as if a war scene.

The police had spent $3 million dollars that night, and still they'd been beaten. Ryan Bartek and his unruly mob were the only Occupy Camp in America to survive this federally coordinated eviction – the only rag-tag contingent of cockroach people to victoriously deflect the armies of Barack Obama.

Bartek looked about the muddy devastation, and wasn't quite sure what to do. The cops would come the next night to end it, but for now they were victorious. He'd expected to be in a jail cell, but was free to do as he pleased. Thus, he simply walked away. As he made distance by a few blocks, the surreal event seemed like it never happened. And all he wanted were blueberry pancakes.

Ryan Bartek made the Roxy Cafe & ordered his breakfast with black coffee. Within minutes some friends arrived, just as weirdly euphoric. They sat down together like the end of a *Seinfeld* episode, cracked jokes & deciphered moral lessons. They filtered out, and Bartek left a monster tip for the waitress. She was, after all, the 99%.

He took the bus to his home he'd barely occupied since Occupy began; it was like a museum exhibit of a bygone era. He removed his soaked clothes & climbed underneath soft bed sheets. Before sleeping like a baby for the first time in decades, he fished his composition notebook off the floor.

He turned to an open page untouched by chicken scrawl notations. Then, in black ink, and with his favorite pen, scribbled the following phrase which in its simplicity gave all the turgid struggles of the past three decades a righteous, vindicating & luminous air:

"We Won."

Ryan Bartek is a writer & musician from Detroit (MI) now living in Portland (OR). He is author of 6 books: "*Anticlimax Leviathan,*" "*The Big Shiny Prison (Volume One),*" "*Fortress Europe (The Big Shiny Prison Vol. II),*" "*Return To Fortress Europe (BSP Vol. III),*" "*The Silent Burning,*" and "*To Live & Die On Zug Island*"

Bartek is guitarist/vocalist of the savage grindcore band VULTURE LOCUST, as well as the extreme metal act SKULLMASTER. He also performs acoustic/antifolk as "The Real Man In Black" and spoken word performances as his regular old self. LURKING STRANGERS, his new multi-styled punk rock band, will be debuting 2018.

Known for his journalism in the metal/punk undergrounds due to his counterculture travel books and long-term output for mass-market magazines, high-traffic webzines & respected print fanzines, R. Bartek is also the shadowy figure behind the press relations firm Anomie PR, servicing thousands of media outlets globally.

All albums & books have been released under Anomie INC / Anomie Press, as FREE digital downloads.

* * *

R. Bartek's book collection & music discography 100% FREE

www.BigShinyPrison.com

…also by Ryan Bartek…

:: Books ::

"Anticlimax Leviathan"
"The Big Shiny Prison (Volume One)"
"Fortress Europe (BSP Vol. II)"
"Return To Fortress Europe (BSP Vol III)"
*"To Live & Die On Zug Island" (*Unreleased)*
"The Silent Burning" (2005; Out of Print)

:: Records ::

Vulture Locust *"Command Presence"*
A.K.A. MABUS *"Lord of The Black Sheep"*
Sasquatch Agnostic *"Complete Mammalography"*
The REAL Man In Black *"GhostNomad Lives"*

Ryan Bartek – best known for counterculture road books *"The Big Shiny Prison"* & *"Fortress Europe"*– again returns with his finest offering to date: *"Anticlimax Leviathan."*

"Anticlimax Leviathan" is a massive departure from Bartek's previous works & purely autobiographical, shining a spotlight on the alienation & confusion that defines America.

It is the story of a strange young man reaching adulthood in Detroit. A blue collar worker for the auto industry, our young Anti-Hero has big dreams. Breaking into journalism, Bartek soon becomes a member of the press, a taxi driver, extreme metal critic, political writer, music promoter & underground filmmaker before hitting the road as a traveling counterculture journalist.

Brimming with adventures alongside the misfit characters of his writings – as well as cameos by a staggering list of celebrities, politicians, metal gods & punk legends – eventually he falls through the cracks entirely, swallowed by traumatic romance.

Ending up on the West Coast as a sort of drifter, he lives off Craigslist, odd jobs & ever-collapsing living arrangements. Finally ending up homeless in Seattle he lustfully embraces it, mentally re-creating himself as the lead character in his own bizarre punk rock romance novel.

Along the way he meets a legion of 'Street Crazies' that have fallen through the cracks as well, uniting to form a Street Theatre movement called "FREE THERAPY." Step by step they build a new world from the ashes of their lives, all which leads to a massive road saga through America & Europe, climaxing with the Occupy encampments of 2011.